D0139034

Debating Social Problems

Debating Social Problems emphasizes the process of debate as a means of addressing social problems and helps students engage in active learning. The debate format covers sensitive material in a way that encourages students to talk about this material openly in class. This succinct text includes activities that promote critical thinking and includes examples from current events.

Leonard A. Steverson, Ph.D., is associate professor emeritus of sociology at South Georgia State College and currently an adjunct professor of sociology at Flagler College, where he teaches contemporary social problems, sociological theory, social movements, and public sociology. He is the author of *Policing in America: A Reference Handbook* (2008), co-author of *Giants of Sociology: A Little Guide to the Big Names in Sociological Theory* (2006/2010), an upcoming work on the sociology of mental health entitled *Madness Reimagined: Envisioning a Better System of Mental Health in America*, and several chapters in edited works.

Jennifer E. Melvin, Ph.D., is assistant professor of sociology at Flagler College. She teaches contemporary social problems, social stratification, and the sociology of health inequalities. She co-authored the textbook *Introductory Sociology* (2009) and is the co-author of several journal articles and book chapters that look broadly at intersections of disadvantage for the physical health of Latino Americans (2014/2016). Her newest project takes an unconventional approach to how intersections of race, ethnicity, social class, and gender expectations shape women's health.

Debating Social Problems

Leonard A. Steverson and
Jennifer E. Melvin

Routledge
Taylor & Francis Group

NEW YORK AND LONDON

First published 2019
by Routledge
711 Third Avenue, New York, NY 10017

and by Routledge
2 Park Square, Milton Park, Abingdon, Oxon, OX14 4RN

Routledge is an imprint of the Taylor & Francis Group, an informa business

Library of Congress Cataloging-in-Publication Data

Names: Steverson, Leonard A., author. | Melvin, Jennifer E., author.
Title: Debating social problems / Leonard A. Steverson & Jennifer E. Melvin.
Description: 1 Edition. | New York : Routledge, 2018. |
 Includes bibliographical references and index. |
Identifiers: LCCN 2018013443 (print) | LCCN 2018015773 (ebook) |
 ISBN 9781315143446 (Master Ebook) | ISBN 9781351388665 (Web pdf) |
 ISBN 9781351388658 (ePub) | ISBN 9781351388641 (Mobipocket) |
 ISBN 9781138309609 (hardback) | ISBN 9781138309616 (pbk.) | ISBN 9781315143446 (ebk)
Subjects: LCSH: Social problems. | Critical thinking.
Classification: LCC HN18.3 (ebook) | LCC HN18.3 .S84 2018 (print) | DDC 306—dc23
LC record available at https://lccn.loc.gov/2018013443

ISBN: 978-1-138-30960-9 (hbk)
ISBN: 978-1-138-30961-6 (pbk)
ISBN: 978-1-315-14344-6 (ebk)

Typeset in Bembo
by Apex CoVantage, LLC

CONTENTS

PREFACE

Debating Social Problems is a sociology text that seeks to develop students' critical thinking skills about social problems by using debate. The authors have attempted to select appropriate problems, including current ones, to be discussed, analyzed, and debated. New social problems are coming to public attention at an almost unbelievable pace and will present other possibilities for debate. It is hoped that the text will provide opportunities for student engagement through lively and spirited discussions that promote greater knowledge about social problems. Many students have gained insight on current issues in this format and hopefully many will continue to do so in the future.

The text provides a consistent format throughout its chapters: basic information about specific social problems are found in chapter sections labeled "About the Problem"; perspectives that seek to give some additional insight from sociology's primary theoretical positions—structural functionalism, conflict theory, and symbolic interactionism—are located in "Theoretical Perspectives"; responses to the problems that seek to provide remedy are addressed in "Searching for Solutions"; and an overview of the problems' particular conceptions are found in "Key Terms". Some possible debate questions are provided in sections called "Now Debate!", though these can certainly be modified or substituted with others. Each chapter ends with a digest of that chapter's information in "Chapter Summary".

Debating social problems can help expand knowledge of our social environment and increase skills in argumentation. It can be a challenging but also an exhilarating exercise for both students and professors. We hope all who use the book will benefit from it and open, engaged dialogue.

ACKNOWLEDGMENTS

We would like to acknowledge all the people who assisted us in this endeavor, including the help-ful staff at Flagler College who supported the project, especially the tolerant employees of Proctor library. We would also like to thank the students in our sociology courses, past and present, who continue to inspire and motivate our pedagogy. We especially wish to thank Meghan Durrance for assistance in the preparation of the manuscript; without her watchful eye this text would lack its cohesion and acuity. And of course, we wish to offer our heartfelt appreciation to our families for the support and comfort they provided during the preparation of the text.

CHAPTER 1

Understanding Social Problems through Debate

THE DISCIPLINE OF SOCIOLOGY

Suppose we are concerned about one of the myriad social problems—or some or several of them—that exist in the world today (and hopefully we are). We would first need some understanding of human activities, human interactions, and human motivation. We would need to look at the internal forces (originating in the individual), and external forces (originating in the social environment), that are the causes or contributors to the social problems under study. The discipline of sociology is primarily concerned with the latter—the external or environmental aspects of the problem—however, if we use our sociological imaginations (to be discussed soon), we also seek to understand the relationship between these two forces. Before we begin with our discussion on some of the various social problems, we need to gain a better understanding of the social science discipline known as sociology. Since many people do not take sociology in high school, many students do not really understand this field of study.

Sociology is "the scientific study of social behavior and human groups" (Schaefer 2014:2). The main concern of this discipline is with understanding social life and the complex interactions that occur between the smallest social ordering of people (called a dyad) to entire cultures. Therefore, sociology covers a wide expanse of human relationships. As a social science discipline, it has as its siblings: anthropology (the study of cultures past and present), psychology (the study of individual mental processes), political science (the study of power and governmental systems), economics (the

> **Sociology** the scientific study of social behavior and human groups from micro to macro levels of analysis.

study of the management of production, distribution, and consumption of goods and services) and even history (the study of key human events and people of the past), along with other relatives such as social work, criminal justice, and others.

Although the study of social life began long before, in the nineteenth century early social philosophers such as St. Simon, Herbert Spencer, and Auguste Comte sought to make their observations more scientific. It was Comte who gave sociology its name, a strange mix of the Latin socio (from *socius* or "companion") and the Greek *logos* ("the study of"). These social philosophers and theorists, including Alexis de Tocqueville and Karl Marx, studied the major issues of society, primarily resulting from the problems associated with industrialization. The principal perspective taken by these thinkers involved an understanding of the cohesive elements that maintain social order on one hand, and the forces that push society to developmentally evolve on the other (Rubington and Weinburg 1989)—in other words, the great social thinkers were concerned with the issues of *order* versus *progress*.

From its beginnings in Europe, sociology has sought to explain social life, especially in times of trouble, turmoil, and of course, revolution. In America, sociology got its intellectual start in Chicago, a city that experienced an amazing population swell in the nineteenth and early twentieth centuries. Many of these people were immigrants of other countries who brought with them their languages and other cultural traditions which created some major communication problems. Mixed with the advent of rapidly advancing industrialization, Chicago became a unique city which was of much concern to people whose job it is to study, understand, and act for social change where needed.

As it can easily be seen, periods of social change or unrest create conditions in which some trained analysts of society attempt to organize their observations in meaningful ways to better understand social phenomena. These people are sociologists. Wars, economic depressions, social movements involving race and gender, and a host of social changes has caused sociology to grow and change (for a discussion of the stages of changes in American sociology, see Rubington and Weinburg 1989).

In his very early text on social problems, a definition of sociology was offered by Ellwood (1935:3): "the science which deals with human association, its origin, development, forms and functions". A more recent definition is "the scientific study of social behavior and human groups. It focuses primarily on the influence of social relationships on people's attitudes and behavior and on how societies are established and change" (Schaefer 2014:3). This latter definition, the one preferred by the authors of this text, reflects the discipline's wide focus: from the personal relationships of a two-person group (a dyad) to the cultural practices of whole societies. It is this variance that makes sociology both interesting and sometimes hard to grasp.

Sociologist Kai Erikson (1997) notes the difficulties in providing a definition for the discipline, a problem that others such as philosophy, history, psychology, and others do not seem to have, at least to the same degree. A reason for this, according to Erikson, is that sociologists view our own discipline not as much as a body of knowledge of social life but as a perspective of viewing social life. In other words, sociologists' training, which has encouraged us to look critically at aspects of society, has also created a rather ambiguous way of defining our own discipline. Despite this unease, the study of sociology is fascinating and it allows us to grasp the complex world in which we live.

Sociologist Peter Berger (1963:23) declared that "the sociologist travels at home—sometimes with surprising results", suggesting that we can learn a great deal about one's current social surroundings by simply observing them from the perspective of a stranger, eliminating (as much as is possible) the constrictive lens that illuminate our preconceptions of the world. By looking beneath the "facades", we can begin to better understand the inner workings of social life.

A contemporary sociologist, George Ritzer, sees his role as that of a "social geologist", a scientist that drills beneath the surface to uncover nuggets of understanding that provide some insight into the hidden aspects of social life that are often not fully analyzed. He also notes the usefulness of approaching sociology as a "social archaeologist" that uses "historical perspectives" to better understand the field (Ritzer 1994:1–5).

Simply put then, the goal of sociology is to better understand social life with the hope that this understanding will lead to methods to improve it. Achieving this goal requires uncovering hidden aspects of society, aspects that are difficult to observe due to our own experiences and understandings of the social world. Certain tools are needed in this endeavor such as intellectual drills that dig beneath the surface, devices to see through walls, surveillance equipment, and vivid imaginations.

It was C. Wright Mills (Mills 1959) who coined the term **sociological imagination** to refer to a way of seeing how personal problems can be viewed from a broader social perspective. To understand the concept of marital problems, for example, one must understand how gender and economic inequality on a much broader social scale might contribute to an individual couple who are experiencing personal difficulties. According to Mills, an understanding between personal troubles (at the micro level) and social issues (at the macro level) must be attained for any real knowledge of a subject to occur.

> **Sociological Imagination** a tool to understand society by analyzing how personal problems can be viewed from a broader social perspective.

THEORY, RESEARCH, AND APPLICATION THE BUILDING BLOCKS OF SOCIOLOGICAL KNOWLEDGE

Sociology is still concerned with all the aspects of social life that intrigued, and in many cases, confounded, the early theorists. In their attempts to understand society, the social philosophers and early social theorists developed different perspectives, or theories, in their analyses of social phenomena. The three major approaches to **sociological theory** that emerged were structural functionalism, conflict theory, and symbolic interactionism.

> **Sociological Theory** a complex framework of ideas based on explaining social phenomena. The three major sociological theories are structural functionalism, conflict theory, and symbolic interactionism.

SOCIOLOGICAL THEORY

Structural Functionalism

Structural functionalism, referred to by some sociologists as simply functionalism, is founded on the observation that society is in many ways analogous to an organism or machine, which has various internal and interdependent parts that make up the whole. Another analogy is the human body; the human body is comprised of separate but mutually dependent parts, i.e., the heart, liver, lungs, and skin. Society is considered "healthy" if the parts are providing their various purposes, or "functions". Functional parts of society that have prescribed purposes are the social institutions—the economy, the government, education, families, and religion. Some proponents of structural functionalism include August Comte, considered by many to be the "father of sociology"; Herbert Spencer, originator of the concept of survival of the fittest; Emile Durkheim, and Talcott Parsons.

An important component of structural functionalist theory was created by Robert K. Merton who distinguished between functions—those aspects of society that contribute to maintaining cohesion and order and dysfunctions—the aspects that undermine social stability. Merton noted how functions and dysfunctions have both manifest and latent properties: manifest refers to those properties of functions and dysfunctions that are easy to observe and are usually intended, and latent refers to the properties that are harder to observe and that are often unintended. Therefore, as an example, a manifest function of the internet would be the ease in getting information very rapidly while a manifest dysfunction would be incorrect or inappropriate material that could be received; a latent function of the internet would be the jobs that are created in the high-tech industry (which one day will be considered low-tech) and a latent function would be that as hardware changes, the old, outdated products will frequently end up in a landfill. Virtually all aspects of society can be viewed from this matrix and it can be a valuable tool in the development of a sociological imagination in studying social problems. This model is especially useful in our approach which uses a dialectic perspective that helps us to argue the sides of a debate; therefore, it is a key component of this text.

Conflict Theory

Conflict theory, sometimes called social conflict theory, is another sociological perspective, and is rooted in the idea that some people in society create and perpetuate a social system in which they obtain and maintain power. Society is then split into the "haves" who have the power through greater access to social, economic, and political resources, and the "have nots" who lack this access. The haves try to maintain control and advantage and the have nots seek to attain equality. Therefore, class, racial, and gender distinctions (among others), create an unequal society—a veritable ball of conflict.

Along with its offshoot *critical theory*, conflict theory is important in understanding social phenomena from the perspective that power struggles are inherent as different groupings of people attempt to coexist. Conflict theorists point out that inequities must be rectified to promote a just society, therefore they maintain a vigilant focus on the issue of power differentials. Conflict theorists often have an element of activism in their approach as social change toward equality is a priority in their theorizing. Conflict theorists such as Karl Marx, Charlotte Perkins Gilman, W.E.B. Du Bois, and C. Wright Mills focused on the inequalities of society and promote measures to rectify them.

Symbolic Interactionism

Symbolic interactionism, sometimes referred to as simply interactionism and the last of the "Big Three" sociological theories, is a theoretical position that uses a micro level of analysis (as opposed to the macro level approach of the structural/functionalists and conflict theorists) to understand society. Proponents of this perspective pay close attention to how the individual person is affected by the larger social systems. For example, social class distinctions often create labels for individuals that become hard to remove. A "self-fulfilling prophecy" often occurs when the individual then begins to accept the label and play out the role that has been predicted for people of that class distinction.

Understanding that macro levels of analysis are sometimes incomplete in understanding human behavior, this microsociology examines the interplay that exists between people and groups and seeks to understand the symbols, including language and gestures that promote this interaction. Researchers who advocate an interactionist perspective often use ethnographies (or field studies) for, as we will see in the next section, this research methodology tends to better capture the lived experiences of the people and groups under study. Symbolic interactionists include George Herbert Mead, Herbert Blumer, the Chicago School of Sociology theorists, Erving Goffman, and Arlie Hochschild.

SOCIOLOGICAL RESEARCH

Sociological research is a key component of all scientific disciplines and, of course, sociology is no exception. Sociology relies on the scientific method which requires strong empirical verification of any claims about social life and doesn't accept common sense explanations. The process of understanding social problems, with the assistance of the scientific method helps reveal these answers—most sociologists find social problems fascinating, like putting together pieces of a complex puzzle (Dentler 1968:11).

> **Sociological Research** a systematic process of exploring phenomena using various methodologies to better understand the social world.

The sociologist studying social problems believes one must determine the "social facts" before launching into a study of specific problems (Dentler 1968). Durkheim ([1892] 2014) states we need to observe social facts as things, meaning we need to study a social phenomenon objectively, delving into it deeply and perceiving it as an external object. That is often easier said than done (suppose you want to study the sexual abuse of children) but being objective and "value free" in our research can help us tremendously. Max Weber believed instead that we should take an empathetic position in understanding the point of view of subjects we are observing—he referred to this subjective position as *verstehen* (Weber [1922] 2013).

Sociologists use a variety of methods to assist in this endeavor such as surveys, field studies (also called observational or ethnographic studies), experiments, analysis of existing data, and program evaluation. Sometimes a theoretical perspective drives the research process (called the deductive approach) and sometimes, the theoretical perspective arises in the course of the research (termed the inductive approach). Theory and research are both needed to promote scientific analysis. Social science research can be seen as progressing through a series of stages—although there are many stage models of this process, Schaefer (2014) proposes this formulation:

1. Identifying the problem under study

2. Conducting a literature review of other research studies in the area

3. Formulating an idea of the relationship between the variables under study (the hypothesis)

4. Gathering the data
   - Surveys
   - Field studies (also called observational studies or ethnographies)

- Experiments
- Use of existing sources

5. Analyzing the data (using statistical methods) and developing a conclusion

6. Preparing the study for examination by others (such as publication in peer reviewed journals or other media)

After the research is published, other social scientists interested in the topic will often complete their own studies, noting the strengths and weaknesses of previous ones to guide their own projects, moving us closer to a clearer understanding of the social problems under study, and hopefully provide some ideas on how to deal with them.

Social scientists use a specific approach for investigating answers to their research questions. These approaches are referred to as research methods since they are tools used to explore and explain phenomenon in the social world. The two main approaches or methodologies are qualitative methods and quantitative methods. Qualitative methods collect data in such a way that it can be converted to numbers, however the raw data itself may take the form of open-ended or semi-structured interviews, field notes taken while conducting observations or field research, or using archival records. These are methods of data collection that take social scientists out into the world as they "do sociology". The data collected is contextually rich and contains a great deal of information that must be coded carefully by the researcher.

In contrast, quantitative methods seek to answer research questions about the social world with information that is either already in numeric form or can be easily converted to numeric form for statistical analysis. Examples of quantitative research methods include using data that is collected through a survey in-person, online, or via the phone. Another approach is for a researcher to design a survey that is employed by field technicians in the respondents' home or place of business. This is more common when researchers want to measure concepts very precisely and a respondent may not know the answer (example, weight, memory tests). The data is then converted to numbers and imported into statistical software to find connections and look for causal relationships. The most common type of quantitative method is using secondary data, such as the U.S. Census data, to explore answers to a research question. In this case, the researcher does not collect data, they employ statistical software to analyze data already collected.

While quantitative approaches aim to state that one condition influences another through tests run in statistical analysis, qualitative approaches are more likely to describe social processes in rich detail. Increasingly, researchers utilize both quantitative and qualitative methods to investigate social life. This approach is called mixed methods. Quantitative methods are often used to provide demographic information and answers to close ended questions while qualitative methods are employed to elicit contextually rich details that tell a story. Through the use of both methods social scientists can stitch together various aspects of social life that take place across diverse platforms and domains. As social life grows increasingly complex and is experienced virtually through social media as well as through face-to-face interactions, the combination of these two methodologies will become increasingly useful for social scientists to unpack the multitude of ways social forces impact and are related to our individual lives.

Social science research is published in peer-reviewed academic journals. Peer-reviewed means that a published study has been thoroughly reviewed for correct methods, ethics, theory, etc. by other social scientists practicing in the field. The most prestigious peer-reviewed sociological journals are published by the American Sociological Association (ASA), the national organization for sociologists. It is home to 14 scholarly journals, all of which can be accessed electronically for free for students through library database search engines. Other reliable sociological research can be accessed online in the form of research briefs from organizations such as the Pew Research Center, The U.S. Census Bureau, The Stanford Center on Poverty and Inequality, and other organizations affiliated with universities, academic think tanks, and the U.S. government. These are all valuable sources for the debates you will engage in during this course. Substantiating your argument with reliable data is the foundation of any debate in the social science issues.

APPLICATION/PRACTICE

Another key element in this trichotomy is the **application of sociological knowledge**. Being able to take the knowledge obtained from theory and research is hopefully transferred to actual practice, or application, to better the lives of people. Practitioners who work with homeless populations, in child advocacy programs, or are employed with women's shelters are examples of specialists who apply sociology in their work lives. While the focus on social theory and research is often referred to as "pure sociology", the focus on application is generally called "applied sociology" or, in a more specialized form such as family therapy, "clinical sociology". Another growing area of the discipline focuses on providing sociological knowledge to a general audience to promote social change, an area called "public sociology". Sociologists such as Jane Addams, Robert Park, and Louis Wirth, worked diligently to improve the lives of people by applying sociological principles to their work with the homeless, victims of crime, recent immigrants, children, and others.

> **Application of Sociological Knowledge** the practical use of the findings from sociological theory and research to assist in solving human problems.

Majoring in Sociology

College students and graduate students who major in sociology are trained to research and synthesize information as well as to analyze statistical data to find patterns and trends. This breadth of skills can translate to career opportunities in research and analysis. Research analysts use quantitative methodology to analyze data from surveys and studies. For example, the U.S. Census Bureau survey data must be analyzed and sociologists are often employed to analyze raw data and turn it into the charts and graphs you see in your textbooks on various social issues such as average household income, poverty statistics, etc. Private companies also collect data for their own use and employ trained sociologists to analyze their data as well. Sociologists are also employed at research think tanks and government agencies such as the Centers for Disease Control, the Brookings Institution, the Human Rights Watch and many other large national organizations. These agencies employ sociologists to analyze data and to conduct research and communicate findings in data briefs or reports.

Sociology majors have excellent communication, research and analytic skills coupled with an understanding of demographics. This makes them attractive to marketing, advertising and public relations firms where they are employed to assist companies in understanding their target audience and working in marketing and advertising.

Community organizations such as non-profits often hire sociologists since they are trained to understand and work with marginalized and diverse sub-populations. These types of careers range from working in the community to heighten awareness about social issues, to working as social media managers, or training and recruiting employees. Sociologists are also well represented in education, as high school teachers or with advanced degrees, as college professors.

According to research by the American Sociological Association's Research and Development department, nearly two-thirds of individuals with sociology degrees reported holding jobs closely related to what they learned as sociology majors and these respondents also indicated they were very satisfied with their current jobs (Spalter-Roth and Vooren, 2008).

SOCIAL PROBLEMS AS A SUBFIELD OF SOCIOLOGY

Sociology, as we have seen, is a very broad science discipline. The study of human social life obviously encompasses many aspects such as the sociology of deviance, race, ethnicity, gender, stratification, and the social institutions of government, economy, family, religion, and education. Sociology has even stretched its tentacles into the study of sports, urban legends, modern technology, and pop culture. A glance through the sociology offerings in colleges and universities will show the rich variation in topics of study in the discipline. Among the various subfields is the scientific study of social problems, which is the focus of this text.

Social Problems the subfield of sociology that deals specifically with understanding the problems that confront society.

When one mentions the term **social problems**, many things often come to mind. Certainly, in our current epoch, terrorism would be considered a salient social problem, as would poverty and unemployment, crime, drug abuse, violence, school dropout, and discrimination in its various forms. Many academic disciplines are concerned with social problems, some with special problems as their focal point relevant to those areas of study. For example, the discipline of political science might be concerned with political terrorism and illegal immigration, economics might be primarily concerned with poverty and unemployment, and education might be concerned with school dropout rates and childhood obesity in the school system. Sociology is especially equipped to deal with the wide array of social problems, including those mentioned above, primarily due to its broad focus. To better understand the discipline of sociology, it is perhaps beneficial to look at some definitions.

The reader of this book should be aware that there is no single, standardized, commonly accepted definition of social problems. In fact, sociologists and other social scientists and theorists have attempted for a very long time to define and analyze the term. Some questions arise:

- What constitutes a social problem?

- Who determines when something is a social problem?

- Can a social problem exist if people are unaware of it?

- Can it (or should it) be eliminated in full or part?

- What is the origin of the problem?

- What is the scope of the problem?

- What will happen if it is eliminated (i.e., will other problems be created)?

Writing very early about this subfield, Case (1924) offers some insight into the terminology of the term "social problems" by explaining that a *problem* is anything "thrown upon", or pushed into someone's field of attention; a social problem, then, is a current condition that "attracts the attention of a considerable number of competent observers within a society, and appeals to them as calling for readjustment or remedy by social, i.e. collective action, or some kind or another" (p. 627). This early interpretation closely resembles the more modern definition of social problems by Kornblum and Julian (2009) as "when enough people in a society agree that a condition exists that threatens the quality of their lives and their most cherished values, and they also agree that something should be done to remedy that condition" (p. 4).

Dentler (1968) provides us with this insight about social problems:

A social problem is not a thing but an event located in the changing network of relations between social groups, the environment, and technology. The magnitude of any one social problem is a product of the scale of the network in question. A vast social problem like war is, for the most part, located in the relations between whole societies. Poverty tends to be rooted in relations between a national economy, the political structure, and the family system.

(Dentler 1968:7)

Therefore, social problems are intricately connected with various social institutions and vary in interest and intensity due to the conditions of different time periods.

Social problems then, as a subfield of sociology, studies and addresses the concerns of social life: problems in the social institutions, problems in social structure, and problems of inequality and seeks to offer reform strategies for those problems. We will now turn to an examination of the essential elements that comprise a social problem.

ELEMENTS OF A SOCIAL PROBLEM

Jamrozik and Nocella (1998:2) give some additional insight into the definition of a social problem by considering its essential elements. They claim that to be considered a social problem the situation in question must:

- Have a clearly identifiable origin

- Contain a real or perceived threat to a society's values and beliefs

- Possess the potential for remediation, resolution, or alleviation of the problem

Without an understanding of the origin of an individual level problem, it is difficult to analyze, much less develop ways to deal with it; the same is, of course true with a social problem. For example, attempting to understand and alleviate poverty is an area that would be difficult without an understanding of the factors that lead to the condition (called the "etiology" of the problem). Social scientists rely on theoretical perspectives, as addressed earlier, to assist in this endeavor; for example, those sociologists who adopt the structural/functionalism theoretical position might consider how the role of social disorganization might be the primary contributor to poverty; proponents of the conflict model might note how greed in a capitalist society is a prime contributor; and symbolic interactionists might observe how the labeling of individuals creates situations that make it difficult to better their living conditions, leading to poverty.

The issue under consideration as a social problem must also carry a real or perceived threat to a group's cherished cultural values. Real threats are an obvious concern—a terrorist attack is a tangible danger to human life and basic beliefs (i.e., in a free society, people should be protected from unprovoked attacks). Perceived, as opposed to actual threats, are also a concern because, as the Thomas Theorem states, if people perceive situations as real, even though they are not based on fact, the situations can be very real in their consequences (Thomas and Thomas 1928). For example, if it is believed by the populace that an elected governmental official is going to push for measures to take away certain citizen rights, even if these claims are simply a matter of negative campaigning by the opponent, it could cost the candidate votes, even if the politician has no intention of doing so.

The potential for a remedy for, or at the least alleviation of, the problem is also a major condition for designation as a social problem. There is no social problem for which there is no possible means for at least alleviation of the effect to some degree. Structural functionalists would normally agree that the social institution whose function it is to help correct the problem needs to enhance their abilities to do so or to receive assistance from other institutions that have a lesser role regarding the problem, at least in the short run. Conflict theorists would ascertain that intervention efforts be implemented that will create equality in society. Symbolic interactionists would seek remedy on a more micro level, such as in the family or community. We will now look at various ways in which social problem formulation has been conceptualized as a process.

THE PROCESS OF SOCIAL PROBLEM FORMATION

It is useful to use a stage model to better understand the process that many social problems go through. Although, there have been many process models to explain how social problems develop, Best's model (2013) provides a highly beneficial way to understand this process. He adopts a natural history model that posits a universal series of stages in the process. These stages include:

- Claimsmaking, in which people assert that a certain social problem exists and needs remedy

- Coverage by the media that report the alleged social problem to a wider audience

- Public awareness and a resulting call for action

- The development of policies by lawmakers and other agents

- Social problems work, whereby the policies are put into place

- Evaluation of the outcomes or responses that were enacted to address the problems

In these models of social problem development, it is noted there must be an observation of a suspected problem followed at some point by actions promulgated to remedy the problem. But at what point is there a consensus that the situation is indeed a problem for society to address? And what method is used to analyze the problem (analysis of the second part of our definition of social problems, if you remember). And lastly, what process allows open discussion about facets of the problem and possible solutions? Crone (2007) asks an important question in this regard: which social problem should we (as a society) attempt to solve first? Should we look at the perceived degree of seriousness of the various problems? Or perhaps attempt to determine how many people are negatively affected by the problem? These should be questions we address in our college classrooms debates.

Although there are experts in all areas considered social problems, they are often not the voices that are heard or endowed to have the final word on remediation. For example, if research studies result in data that are not acceptable to politicians, it can simply be suppressed or denied. In democratic societies, there must be a consensus that the thing is indeed a problem and there is a preferred way to fix it. This is where the activity called debate comes in to the picture.

USING DEBATE IN ADDRESSING SOCIAL PROBLEMS

A good question a student of social problems might ask is: why debate? Why not just read about social problems or even discuss them informally? Debate in an academic format offers many benefits to students. Freeley (1990) lists seventeen such benefits but for purposes of this persuasive argument, We have merged them into fewer categories:

- Debate develops critical thinking through focused inquiry, investigation, and careful analysis of contemporary social problems

- Debate develops other skills such as critical listening, note-taking, and enhanced speaking ability

- Debate is great preparation for future participation in a democratic society

- Debate promotes mature judgment, courage, discipline, and self-esteem

- Debate encourages student participation in discussion, competition, and scholarship by better understanding all sides of an argument

- Debate promotes ethical decision-making, rapid and logical responses, and argumentation skills in general

- Debate helps promote quality instruction by creating a focused and meaningful mentor/protégé relationship between teacher and student

- Debate develops specific skills that can be useful in fields such as law, politics, business, government or any other discipline requiring human discourse

- Debate's interdisciplinary approach provides a more comprehensive student education experience by introducing or enhancing student knowledge of sociology, philosophy, political science, economics, psychology, and others.

In addition, Pfau, Thomas, and Ulrich (1987) add this one:

- Debate develops proficiencies that can be useful later in professional training such as law school (p. 14). Also, graduate training in many areas of social science will certainly also benefit from a knowledge and history of debating. Anyone who has ever defended a graduate level thesis or dissertation can vouch for this.

Debate has had a long history in attempting to deal with the various social problems throughout the ages. Debating these issues has helped to illuminate them, and to expose them for greater analysis, and hopefully to ascertain which policies might better alleviate these policies. If the primary reasons to study social problems are to gain greater understanding of them and to promote policy efforts to eliminate them or to reduce their deleterious effects, debate can be a very useful tool in addressing the goals of social problems. We will now observe how history has, and can be, useful in studying social problems, especially in college classrooms.

| **Debate** a rational process of arguing both sides of an issue with the hope of developing critical thinking skills. |

Debate is defined by Pfau, Thomas, and Ulrich as "a process in which people argue for opposing sides of a conflict, using rational rules and methods in preference to force or emotions, to obtain a decision for one side or the other by an objective third party" (1987:4). It is closely related to argumentation, which is "an evidence based process by which one person may convince another of the rightness of his or her point of view" (Joshi 2016:279). Successful classroom debate, then, involves a comprehensive understanding of a subject, derived through the process of producing evidence and convincing someone to accept a perspective as valid. Through this process, critical thinking on important matters can occur.

In its various forms, the practice of debating has been used differently across the world with a common purpose—to persuade others on a point. Ancient Romans and Greeks used debate to influence major policy decisions. Greek philosopher Socrates, his follower Plato, and later Plato's heir apparent Aristotle, saw debate to better understand the human condition and to develop ways to enhance social life, in contrast to the sophists (itinerant instructors) who thought the goal of debating issues should be to develop competitive skills. Throughout the world, debaters have argued points to combat social conditions deemed harmful to society. Since debate is an intellectual exercise, it is no wonder it has been used in university settings around the globe.

In mid-eighteenth century America, students at Harvard and Yale universities debated theological issues in college classrooms, though the subjects of debate eventually changed to discussions of secular concerns; these debates were delivered in the vernacular, rather than Latin. Along with literary societies, debating societies formed in the universities and such great minds as Alexander Hamilton, James Madison, Daniel Webster, William Jennings Bryan, and Thomas Jefferson were developed in the art of debate. Therefore, students who are actively involved in the debate process are following in the path of some of the great minds who worked to alleviate the country's social problems.

Debating in America's colleges and universities has changed since the early days but the purpose of analyzing social problems through the dialectic process of weighing two sides of an issue is the same process by which laws and policies are made on a larger stage. Careful deliberation and logical reasoning on various concerns assist citizens (or students in a college classroom) in creating a clearer picture of the issue. Each chapter in this text is oriented to giving the student information about the specific problem under review and promoting critical thinking through debates. As we become better educated about social problems and obtain skills in debating these issues in the classroom, we should be better equipped to deal with them in the real world.

GUIDELINES FOR DEBATES

There are many ways to structure debates for the use in classroom debates. Some of these are formal such as the Lincoln-Douglas style, in which two participants (one-on-one) take turns at a podium or other central location to debate issues. This style is normally used for those issues which have strong moral or ethical foundations. This type of debate focuses on logic and the communication of ideas.

There are also the parliamentary styles which have American and British formats and consist of two teams which address issues with little preparation for the topic—the topic is announced just prior to the debate. This format has four construction speeches and two rebuttals which are timed. This style of debate focuses on prior logical reasoning and persuasion more than the understanding of the content under debate.

Spontaneous argumentation is an informal style of debate in which two debaters are given a topic with little advance preparation. While this type of debate develops skills in persuasion and communication, it also does not require a full understanding of the topic under study.

While any of these styles can be used in classroom debates, the goal in this course is to introduce students to pressing social issues which require remedy, rather than just promoting argumentation skills, as with the parliamentary and spontaneous formats. And since the one-on-one format of the Lincoln-Douglas and spontaneous debates fails to have the benefits of group engagement, it is recommended that students work in two groups—one for and one against a certain issue; two to four people per group seems to work well. The group works together and individually in researching a topic and together create a strategy in presenting their side's argument.

The professor will provide a list of ground rules for the debaters (e.g., to be respectful, to respond directly to the responses of the other team) and for the audience (e.g., to remain quiet during the debate, to respectfully comment on issues after the debate). As moderator, the professor will then identify who goes first (by coin flip or some other means), and that group provides an opening statement of their position which will be followed by an opening statement of the opposing side. Then follows a point/counterpoint volley until the moderator decides it is time to end the debate, at which time both sides provide a summation of their arguments. When the debate is over (and normally after an applause from the audience—the other students in the class), discussion continues as the audience makes comments about observations and/or their points of view. The audience participation is an important part of the debate as other perspectives are discussed and shared, augmenting the information received from the debate itself. A rubric for debating will be provided and your professor will share how the debates will be graded in your class syllabus. It should be remembered the goal of debating social issues in the classroom should always be the acquisition of critical learning skills rather than focusing solely on competition, therefore "winning" a debate is not a focal point. It is recommended that students use as many sociological concepts as possible in their debates. It is also recommended that students use Merton's concept of manifest/

latent functions and dysfunctions to create a more sociologically focused debate and to explore not only the obvious aspects of a particular side but also those hidden beneath the surface. We should always remember that the person we learn from is the person who offers an alternative perspective.

CHAPTER SUMMARY

- The discipline of sociology is concerned with understanding social life. One means of pursuing this end is using the sociological imagination, a device that helps understand individual troubles as larger social issues.

- The sociological enterprise has its foundations in theory, research and application. The "Big Three" theoretical perspectives are structural functionalism, conflict theory, and symbolic interactionism; these act as guides in understanding the complexities of social life. Structural functionalism sees the world as an interactive system of parts (social institutions) that are interdependent and function to create a healthy society. Conflict theory notes the inequalities that exist in society between those that have access to resources and those who do not. Symbolic interactionism is a micro level theory that focuses on small group interactions and how information is communicated to other groups and these interactions produce social norms.

- With its various methodologies, research involves a systematic process of understanding the science of society. The research process, involving quantitative, qualitative, and mixed methods, seeks to discover the meanings, often hidden, in social life.

- The application of sociological knowledge, the product of this enterprise, uses what we learn from theory and research to benefit society. This is especially important in social problems, as applied sociologists seek to find remedies for these problems.

- Social Problems is a subfield of sociology and seeks to understand those dysfunctions that exist in society and seeks to remedy, or at least alleviate, those dysfunctions. There are a variety of models that assist sociologists in this aim.

- Debate can be an effective way to develop the critical skills needed to fully grasp the complexities of social problems and the possible interventions that could assist in correcting these problems. By examining the latent as well as the manifest functions and dysfunctions of the interventions, we can hopefully come to a better understanding of social problems.

REFERENCES

Berger, Peter. 1963. *An Invitation to Sociology: A Humanistic Approach.* Woodstock, New York: Overlook Press.

Best, Joel. 2013. *Social Problems*, 2nd ed. New York: W. W. Norton and Company.

Case, Clarence Marsh. 1924. *Outlines of Introduction of Sociology: A Textbook of Readings in Social Sciences.* New York: Harcourt, Brace, and Company, Inc.

Crone, James. 2007. *How Can We Solve Our Social Problems?* Thousand Oaks, CA: Sage.

Dentler, Robert A. 1968. *American Community Problems.* New York: McGraw-Hill.

Durkheim, Emile. [1892] 2014. *The Rules of Sociological Method and Selected Texts on Sociology and its Method.* Steven Lukes, ed., translated by W.D. Halls. New York: Free Press. (Original work published 1892.)

Ellwood, Charles A. 1935. *Social Problems and Sociology.* New York: American Book Company.

Erikson, Kai. 1997. *Sociological Visions.* Lanham, MD: Rowman and Littlefield.

Freeley, Austin J. 1990. *Argumentation and Debate: Critical Thinking for Reasoned Decision Making,* 7th ed. Belmont, CA: Wadsworth Publishing Company.

Jamrozik, Adam and Luisa Nocella. 1998. *The Sociology of Social Problems: Theoretical Perspectives and Methods of Intervention.* Cambridge: Cambridge University Press.

Joshi, Parag. 2016. "Argumentation in Democratic Education: The Crucial Role of Values." *Theory into Practice.* 55: 279–286.

Kornblum, William and Joseph Julian. 2009. *Social Problems.* 13th ed. Upper Saddle River, NJ: Pearson Education, Inc.

Mills, C. Wright. 1959. *The Sociological Imagination.* New York: Oxford University Press.

Pfau, Michael F., David A. Thomas, and Walter Ulrich. 1987. *Debate and Argument: A Systems Approach to Advocacy.* Glenview, IL: Scott Foresman & Co.

Potter, David. 1963. The Debate Tradition. In James H. McBath, *Argumentation and Debate: Principles and Practice* (rev. ed.). New York: Holt, Rinehart, and Winston, Inc.

Ritzer, George. 1994. *Social Beginnings: On the Origins of Key Ideas in Sociology.* New York: McGraw-Hill, Inc.

Rubington, Earl and Martin S. Weinburg. 1989. "Social Problems and Sociology." Pp. 3–12 in *The Study of Social Problems, Six Perspectives*, 4th ed, edited by E. Rubington and M.S. Weinburg. New York: Oxford University Press.

Schaefer, Richard T. 2014. *Sociology Matters*, 6th ed. Boston: McGraw-Hill.

Spalter-Roth, Roberta and Nicole Van Vooren. 2008. "What are they Doing with a Bachelor's Degree in Sociology?" Data Brief on Current Jobs. *American Sociological Association.* Retrieved May 3, 2017 (www.asanet.org/sites/default/files/savvy/research/BachelorsinSociology.pdf).

Thomas, William I. and Dorothy S. Thomas. 1928. *The Child in America: Behavior Problems and Programs.* New York: Knopf.

Weber, Max. [1922] 2013. *Economy and Society: An Outline of Interpretive Sociology.* Edited by Guenther Roth and Claus Wittich. Berkeley: University of California Press.

C H A P T E R 2

Work and the Economy

KEY TERMS	
Alienation	Mixed Economy
Capitalism	Production
Communism	Socialism
Consumption	Social Mobility
Distribution	Social Stratification
Economy	Socioeconomic Status

ABOUT THE PROBLEM: WORK AND THE ECONOMY

Concepts Associated with Work and Economy

Economy
production, distribution, and consumption of goods and services.

The commonly used definition of the **economy** is "the production, distribution, and consumption of goods and services". We will review the components of this definition in a few minutes but let's first have a good sociological examination of this necessary social institution. The economy is one of several other social institutions along with the family, government, education, and religion. Social institutions are macro level establishments created by human societies to meet some social need. The social institution of the economy is concerned with how goods (tangible creations) and services (activities done for others) are produced, distributed, and consumed, or in the case of services, pro-

Production the process of creating goods for human needs and wants.

vided. **Production** refers to how *goods* are made. For example, factories produce cars, appliances, clothes, and other items. Individuals or small groups are also involved in the production process by making items such as baked goods, leather and other crafts, clothes, etc. *Services* are also created by both large and small organizations and involve such activities provided for others such as clothes dry cleaning, haircuts, private investigation, car repair, ride sharing, and others.

Distribution the process in which goods and services are allocated, dispensed, or rendered.

Distribution refers to how goods and services are allocated, dispensed, or rendered to others. The movement of goods and provision of services to people keep the economy running. There is a growing area of business called "logistics" which involves this idea of distribution. Goods must be moved to different areas in a variety of ways (railroad, air, trucking, and perhaps one day, drones) and they must also be stored in a variety of places (storage centers and warehouses, distribution centers) and they must also be protected by security agencies (private or public), using personnel, signage, cameras etc.

Consumption refers to how goods and services are used by people who obtain them. People consume food and other items and often employ such services as a lawn service to maintain their yards. We are obviously all consumers of both goods and services. Consumerism is a very important area of concern in modern society and is obviously a concern of businesses, which operate on a supply and demand model of production based on how people consume goods and services.

So, every society must have some means of dealing with how economies fulfill the functions of production, consumption, and distribution of its goods and services. In fact, even very early human societies had traditional economies which were primarily agrarian and created customs and ritualistic behavior. Now many economies are considered global in scope (not surprisingly, these are called global economies) and many countries and cultures are involved in the transnational trade of goods and services. It is not difficult to see how relationships based on global economies shape the political relations between countries.

Other terms should be noted here: *income* refers to the wages people earn and is distinguishable from *wealth*, which consists of the financial assets of people or corporations. *Assets* are things that people own that have value and that can be used in an exchange if desired. Currently most Americans have few assets and normally their homes and private real estate property constitute their largest asset (Rousseau 2004:121).

> **Consumption** the way in which goods and services are used; the final process in the utilization of goods and services.

FIGURE 2.1 An example of changes in the institution of marriage – specifically the legal marriages of same-sex couples.

Source: Sira Anamwong/Shutterstock.com

Social Stratification a process in which people are located in levels based on their socioeconomic situations.

Socioeconomic Status a certain social status that places a person within the economic system.

Social Mobility the potential for people to move from one social stratum to another.

Closely related to the economic concepts mentioned above are social class, social status, social role, socioeconomic status, social stratification, and social mobility. *Social class* refers to a category of people who have a similar lifestyle or set of life circumstances. *Social status* refers to a position that a person occupies within one of the various groups he or she occupies and the related term *social role* refers to the set of expectations that come with occupying a status. **Social stratification** involves a hierarchal distinction which is often depicted as a ladder, pyramid, or teardrop with gradients; some classes of people are at the top of this structure—the capitalist or upper class, and are followed in descending order by the upper middle, middle, working class, and lower class. A person's **socioeconomic status** (commonly referred to as SES) reflects that person's position in this hierarchy and is generally measured by that person's income, education, and type of occupation.

Social mobility refers to the potential for someone to move from one of these social levels to another; this movement could be upward, downward, or consist of a slight movement within the same strata. Therefore, someone might occupy a status (position) of a working-class employee, and have the expectation (role) of being a hard-working person who strives to move up in the occupation. The status the person occupies is contained within the stratification system and different levels of drive, aptitude, luck, and life circumstances help determine if the person will be able to obtain social mobility, normally desired as upward mobility and within the same generation.

Wealth inequality exists due to the varied levels of access to resources and has significant implications for society. Wealth inequality (including income inequality) can be observed at different levels—inequality that exists among a nation's citizens, inequality as compared between nations, and inequality as observed from a global perspective (see Milanovic 2011). At the national level, the issue of changes in the U.S. economy that have created inequality are especially troubling due to four factors: the decrease in wages results in a corresponding decrease in labor participation by males and lower marriage rates, which are correlated with higher poverty rates; a large wage gap in social mobility and opportunity resulting in greater social distance between social groups; higher unemployment rates due to people believing they are unable to overcome barriers to opportunity; and a lessening of civil engagement (such as voting) which can be detrimental to democratic ideals. Interestingly, American concerns over inequality are more related to economic and social dysfunctions as opposed to European countries where income inequality draws more concerns over ethics and morality (Blank 2011).

It is indeed part of the American Dream to be able to move from a lower class to the higher classes in one generation, a movement termed upward *intrageneration mobility*; however, it is more likely that *horizontal mobility*, moving slightly upward within the same class, is more likely for most people. Examples of the much beloved "rags to riches stories" are admired in our culture as reinforced by the media; however, this idea can be more myth than reality (Rousseau 2004:133). In addition, this ideal can create inspiration for some to work hard to obtain upward mobility; it can also be defeating to those who have numerous barriers to overcome to achieve financial rewards.

Although there are many different variations of economic institutions, there are two basic structures, based on complex economic theories: capitalism and socialism/communism. We will examine both in more detail.

Capitalism

Capitalism an economic system in which the means of production and property are privately owned through the activity of free competition, profit accumulation, and limited governmental regulation.

Capitalism is so imbedded in our understanding of the economy in the U.S., we rarely think about it. We work for someone who pays us for our products or services and we hope to make more income than we must expend on other things we want or need. Hopefully our wages will allow us to pay our rent, tuition, automobile costs, recreation, etc., and hopefully put money in savings. We understand our boss will make more than us, and that people at the higher levels will make more than those below. We also understand that our wages will be taxed. But we rarely consider all the ramifications of this economic system.

Reflecting the economic thought of Adam Smith (amply outlined in his book *An Inquiry into the Nature and Causes of the Wealth of Nations* (1776/1994), normally just shortened to *The Wealth of Nations*), capitalism refers to an economic structure that focuses on a free market system rather than government intervention to set up the structure of providing, distributing, and consuming goods and services. In a capitalistic system, there is a private ownership of the means of production, a profit motive, free competition, and a laissez-faire form approach to government. Private ownership of components of the economic system is therefore a key characteristic in capitalism, removing the government of functions in this area.

The motivations for maintaining these functions are primarily the accumulation of money and financial gain. The profit motive is to obtain a surplus, of money in financial transactions. In other words, a company tries to make a profit by making more than it expends; if a bicycle manufacturer must spend a certain amount of money for parts to create the products (the bicycles) such as tires, chains, and headlights, and labor costs to people to put them together, the manufacturer hopes to sell the bikes for more than expended to produce them. This surplus, or profit, is what drives the capitalistic system. People and businesses work hard to create profits for themselves which will be used to purchase other goods and services from other providers.

Free competition is another important component in capitalism. People are allowed (and, of course, encouraged) to freely compete against each other in attempts to gain more profits for themselves and their business organizations. According to this ideology, unregulated (or loosely regulated) competition ("laissez-faire") results in better products and services since people are constantly trying to, according to an old saying, "build a better mousetrap", or more appropriately today, "build a better smart phone". If a corporation comes up with a great new technological innovation and everyone scrambles to buy this product, competitors will then "up their game" to outdo the competition in attempts to gain the most profit. For this to happen, there must be unfettered access to the competitive field, in other words there must be a "level playing field" for the players in the competition. Obviously, capitalists espouse an absence of regulation of competition; a monopoly, in which one business concern has total access to a market, cannot be allowed in capitalism. For example, if one company has exclusive access to a certain industry, competition cannot occur. The role of government in capitalism should be to simply regulate any possibility for a business concern monopolizing an industry, but not get involved in the production, distribution, or consumption process. A possible inherent problem here is that although companies compete to eliminate the competition (so they can make more profit), they cannot eliminate competition completely, or the system will be prevented from working.

For capitalism to work in its purest form, the government must adopt a laissez-faire (hands off) approach and not get involved in regulation of the economy. The idea is to let the "invisible hand" of supply and demand run the economy as it is believed freedom from government regulation and a reliance on the system itself is more effective. The concept of a "trickle-down" economic model follows this logic—less regulation and additional incentives to the capitalists results in more investments in business, allowing economic opportunity to "trickle down" to the workers, who are then able to experience higher incomes and upward social mobility.

Is "trickle-down economics" an effective economic policy to strengthen the U.S. economy and increase jobs?

Pro: Cutting taxes for high-income tax brackets leaves more money for investors to boost the economy.
Con: High-income tax brackets should pay higher taxes to help the government invest in the economy.

For capitalism to work correctly, businesses (or individuals for that matter) must be motivated by *self*-interest, that is, they must be concerned about creating profits for themselves and not worry about the welfare of competitors. While this may sound self-serving or apathetic about the needs of others, the idea of a self-interest motivation is logical in this framework. If a business is concerned about a competitor and reduces its level of innovation to help the competitor keep up, no one benefits. The business does not create a profit because it is being "pulled down" by a less capable competitor, the competitor gets some of the profits even though they are undeserved, and consumers are negatively affected because they receive an inferior product or service, or one that takes longer to surface. Obviously, there is an element of "survival of the fittest" here—the most capable producers or servicers will stay in business and create wealth while others will reap less of a surplus or simply disappear from the scene.

A common complaint about capitalism centers around the idea that self-interest being a good and desirable thing—some say this is a justification for acting in an egoist, or self-serving way and to treat people who are in financial straits with derision. The "survival of the fittest" idea mentioned earlier also serves as a justification for those with more money to feel superior to those without.

Socialism and Communism

Socialism an economic system in which the means of production are collectively possessed and the motivation is to provide for all citizen's needs.

The intellectual and theoretical position of socialism/communism was best developed by Karl Marx and Friedrich Engels. In their writings, they decried what they saw as the inherent problem with capitalism—the idea that capitalism creates and helps maintain inequality in society. **Socialism** is an economic structure that seeks to thwart social inequality through the public ownership of the means of production, the removal of a profit motive, a reliance on government to control economic activity and equal allocation of resources. **Communism**, in Marxist thought, will follow socialism and will no longer require resource allocation by government officials.

Communism per Marx, the phase after socialism in which the economic conditions create a classless system.

It would be ideal if everyone had an equal playing field (to use the maxim mentioned earlier), but this is not the case. Some people who are equally capable of benefitting society as their wealthy counterparts never get the chance because they did not have the same "connections" or other advantages. For example, many people in the top tiers of business went to the better preparatory schools, Ivy League universities, and rubbed elbows with other well-to-do individuals. Better than anyone, Marx, with his colleague Engels, extrapolated what many see as the evils of capitalism. In direct opposition to Adam Smith, Marx and Engels saw capitalism as not being a case of survival of the fittest but a free ride for those with connections. He wrote extensively on the matter but the most famous is his little pamphlet to workers called *The Communist Manifesto*, written in collaboration with Engels, who was ironically a great beneficiary of capitalism.

In socialism and communism, surplus is viewed as a negative thing. In capitalism, surplus is considered the driving force behind economic success but in socialism and communism, surplus creates the potential for greed and unnecessary competition that harms society. For example, the desire for profit sometimes results in environmental disaster that affects many people in society, all due to some company's focus on profit rather than safety. Another example involves large corporations, in search for great profits, who basically destroy small "mom and pop" businesses that were once the economic foundation of communities. And many people feel that the motivation for work should be the betterment of society, not increasing amounts of personal wealth.

A common complaint of this economic structure is that it discourages economic and social advancement and it allows people who contribute less to society to receive the same rewards. Plus, it is seen by many that the lack of the motivation created by financial gain will contribute to a slowing down of technological evolutionary processes. In addition, it is doubtful if justice is served if those who contribute more gain no social benefits. Another criticism is that nations that have used the communist model have resulted in violent dictatorships that suppress freedom of thought and action; it should be noted the economic systems created by these countries are not based on a true Marxist model—whether socialist and communist structures lend themselves to corrupt authoritarian political structures is up for debate.

We should remember that in their pure forms, capitalism, socialism, and communism do not exist. The United States is certainly considered a capitalistic nation, but we must understand that even though many goods and services are provided by the market, others are still provided by the government. Yes, we have public police forces but we also have private security agencies, we have public schools but also private schools, we have a public postal service but also have private mail delivery services, we have public libraries but also private bookstores, and the list goes on and on. This dual approach to the economy is reflected in a **mixed economy**, which provides services in both public and private sectors.

> **Mixed Economy** an economic system that has characteristics of both capitalism and socialism.

Regulating the Economy

The current state of affairs regarding the political system in America reflects the role of the economy. In the 2016 Presidential campaign, the Republican candidate extolled the virtues of small government and loose regulations on businesses. On the Democratic side, however, the ramifications of an insufficiently regulated capitalism were major concerns; in fact, one candidate who did not win the nomination but had many followers, Bernie Sanders of Vermont, identified ideologically as a democratic socialist—in earlier times, an identification of this type would have precluded a candidate from seriously being considered for President.

After World War II, America experienced great industrial expansion, brought about in part through industrialization and population gain (Chichilnisky 2012). There have been many changes in the U.S. economy in fifty years and many of those are not so encouraging. Wages have been stagnant and unable to keep up with the costs of living for most American families. In addition, housing, costs, transportation, health care, and higher education costs have been out of reach for many citizens while job creation, despite increases since the so-called Great Recession of 2007–2009, has been very slow. These concerns, in conjunction with the increasing power of financial institutions in this period and the fact that the economy has been increasingly service-based, there has been a greater increase in income inequality (Freeley 2016).

The economy, both nationally and globally, has always been subject to both upturns, when the economy is strong, and downturns, when the economy is sour, and many people are affected by these fluctuations in a personal way. Policies have been promulgated by the government when these problems have occurred. In 1929, the Great Depression occurred, the stock market crashed, banks closed, and many people lost the pensions they had counted on for when they were older and unable to work. The social security system was created as a safety net to prevent catastrophes of this type from happening again. Keynesian economics, named after British economist John Maynard Keynes, argued for more governmental regulation of markets to avoid future economic swings; this type of model which integrated regulation into the markets is known as a mixed economy (Sargent 1993). Other efforts to regulate the economy came with President Franklin D. Roosevelt's New Deal policies in which programs were created to assist people negatively affected by the economic downturn. The War on Poverty was waged under the Johnson administration to thwart the growing concern over the plight of the poor, and new programs were created, programs which were continued under the Nixon administration. Johnson's plan had the effect of raising people from poverty through anti-poverty programs such as free school meal programs, the food stamps program, and others and reducing the rates of hunger in the 1960s and 1970s (Braun 1997). It allowed the country to experience its largest drop in poverty in American history and afforded poor minorities at least a limited opportunity to rise to greater upward mobility (Katz 2013).

Many of these programs were discontinued in the 1980s and 1990s as privatization efforts began, removing these social programs from governmental authority to corporate control (Sargent 1993). The debate over the role of government regulation in the capitalist system continues, with libertarians and conservatives arguing against regulation and liberals arguing for it. We will discuss this issue more in the next chapter on government and the political system.

About ten years ago, between 2007–2009, a major economic downturn was created when the real estate bubble burst, causing banks to go out of business, many homeowners to lose their residences, and many workers to be left unemployed or underemployed. This has been termed the Great Recession, and it was triggered by falling home prices, inappropriate lending practices and resulted in foreclosures, large and small business failures, and unemployment (Cushman 2015). This event reinvigorated a social movement designed to call attention to vast inequalities in the U.S. To read more about the movement, see the Searching for Solutions section in this chapter. Some conservative groups disagreed with this assessment of the battle between haves and have-nots and even claimed that "class warfare" existed in which the lower classes were creating conflict against them and the capitalist system.

Income Inequality

The social institution we call the economy so heavily affects our lives and the inevitable social problems that result from depressed economic conditions, the authors decided to put it as the first social problem in this text. Over the past several years, income inequality has become a national and international concern in the political realm. Obviously, this problem affects the poor more negatively than the rich but income inequality also negatively impacts the markets. Attempts to explain the considerable gap between income levels of the "haves and have-nots" must consider the fact that people have differing levels of aptitude, income, skill, interests, inheritance, and many other factors, therefore assessing the issue of inequality becomes difficult. However, income disparities are common throughout the developed world, though none as distinct as in the United States, particularly as it evolved since the 1970s. Some potential causes are increased globalization, which has seen the movement of jobs overseas; a decrease in the influence of labor union activity, particularly as revealed under the Reagan administration; changes in demographics, as older people who tend to have more resources are increasing in number; and the increasing availability of tax breaks for the wealthier strata of the population. And although some argue that a certain amount of inequality is not only inevitable but also beneficial for society as a whole, there are some obvious negative consequences such as a weakening of opportunities, for which the "cream can rise to the top"; a neglect of basic infrastructure issues in favor of income generating investments, and political influence which benefits the wealthy in a host of ways that can negatively affect quality of life issues for the poor, including education and health care (Rezvani and Pirouz 2013).

New Directions: Downsizing, Outsourcing, The Shared Economy, and Moves toward Contingency

Downsizing became a popular occupational practice in the 1990s and refers to when employers reduce the number of employees in the workforce. The term "reduction in force" (or RIF) is often used to refer to what were previously known as "layoffs" in the number of personnel that was previously hired for a job. Automation and technology have created a situation where human labor is not as necessary as it once was in the American (and global) economies. When employers, especially large ones such as large corporations, governmental organizations, and military bases, leave an area, significant social anxiety envelops communities as people are often forced to leave to find work elsewhere, creating instability with individuals, families, and communities.

Outsourcing (a mixing of the terms *outside* and *sourcing*) refers to a situation where jobs are sent to places other than the original workplace, such as when jobs are contracted out to other vendors or to other geographic areas. Employers use outsourcing to cut costs as it is often cheaper to outsource than to provide training, benefits, etc. to permanent staff. Foxconn, a manufacturer of electronics for companies such as Apple, Dell, Motorola, Nokia, and Sony, outsourced manufacturing to China. They make MP3 players, components for cameras, cell phones, and other technology used in the United States. In addition to Foxconn's outsourcing of its factors resulting in thousands of U.S. workers losing their jobs, it had even worse outcomes in the country where it moved its factories. In 2010, 18 Chinese Foxconn employees attempted suicide by jumping from the factory building and 14 died. In 2012, 150 workers threatened to commit suicide to protest their working conditions. Upon an external investigation, it was revealed that economic conditions may have been responsible for these worker suicides. Specifically, low pay, illegal overtime, long working hours, discrimination, and abusive practices including detaining employees who were forced to live in dormitories next to the factories (rent was deducted from their pay), as well as forcing workers to work without days off and in excess of 12 hours a day. Foxconn's response included canceling life insurance for workers and placing netting around the buildings to discourage workers from throwing themselves off the factory buildings.

An example of downsizing is the sweeping layoffs at U.S. automotive manufacturers. General Motors, Ford and Chrysler responded to decreases in sales by laying off employees and this caused serious problems in local economies around these factories. Many of the workers had put in years working for these manufacturing plants and did not have the skills to find other work, or there was no other work in their town as the economy in the area depended on these manufacturing plants for the bulk of the jobs. Many of these manufacturers moved to Mexico or China. Detroit was the hardest hit city and in particular folks in the urban areas who counted on these jobs were not able to follow the jobs or move to new job sites. So, this disproportionately affected working class minority folks who then struggled even more after being unemployed when Detroit's loss of property tax revenues and corporate taxes turned the city into a shell of what it once was. Detroit, once the Motor Metropolis, was in shambles for many years, and now it is being reinvigorated by movements such as "Reclaim Detroit" that are trying to revitalize this once bustling city.

One issue that has recently evolved in the occupational sphere is the use of contingent labor. In the past, temporary employees (or temps) were used by employers to provisionally fill in for another worker who was on leave or who was otherwise unavailable for the job. However, increasingly employers began to use contingency workers in lieu of full-time permanent employees. These are basically contract workers who have in recent years been used for longer periods of time by companies and public organizations, including colleges and universities (in the form of adjunct faculty), and who often receive low pay, lack of benefits, and short term, tenuous work contracts. For employers, who often find themselves in financial situations where they believe this type of model is necessary, contingency labor allows for flexibility and offers companies and organizations considerable savings. For those trapped in what has been termed the "precariat" (referring to the *precarious* working conditions and pay and reflecting the term *proletariat*), the situation is not as attractive. Working in a precariat role creates considerable stress on the worker as the future is always uncertain because the short-term contract can easily be not renewed, which is accomplished at much greater ease than terminating employment.

Should graduate students be paid for their work on college campuses?

Pro: Graduate students provide valuable contributions to the institution through teaching and research and should be financially compensated.

Con: Students in graduate school are learning skills that will assist them in academic and other settings and are compensated through that knowledge and skill set.

The precarious nature of certain jobs is associated with what has been termed the "gig economy". This refers to an economic situation which has occurred over the past several years in which people are forced to take temporary *gigs* (a term often used in the music industry to refer to temporary paid musical engagements) because permanent jobs are unavailable. The related term "shared economy" refers to a situation in which certain individuals rent out (*share*) goods and services that are underutilized to others in need of these goods/services (Cohen and Kietzmann 2014). This is now called a "peer-to-peer" marketplace and can be viewed as an alternative to the traditional capitalistic model where businesses offer these goods and services. Examples include car sharing (Uber and Lyft) as an alternative to taxi services; room sharing (Airbnb) as an alternative to hotels, traditional bed and breakfast establishments, etc.; and small task services (TaskRabbit) in lieu of traditional small job service providers. There are many other forms of these peer-to-peer arrangements currently in operation and these even include the sharing of goods, e.g., tools, furniture, etc. as well as services, for a fee. It is possible the shared economy was created due to rapid industrialization and urbanization and is a measure taken by companies to control costs. Or it can be simply an exploitive activity that increases the gap between the upper and lower classes. In any event, many goods and services are being shared in this new marketplace. It seems the potential for sharing one's property or services is endless—it can be considered "property owners with benefits".

Is the shared economy beneficial or harmful to the current economic system?

Pro: It creates a market for skilled, freelance workers, outside of organizational constraints.
Con: It can drive wages for permanent positions down due to competition.

Consumerism and Credit Card Debt

Many who are concerned with social problems are concerned about the growing aspects of consumerism. Consumerism is the concept that an individual's happiness is contingent on the number of products they purchase and consume. In a consumeristic society such as the United States, marketing and advertising are the vehicles used to create a need to purchase the newest technological gadgets, appliances, software, vehicles, and other objects. Trends such as trading in a vehicle every three years and purchasing an engagement ring worth three months of your salary are created and driven by corporate advertising teams to convince us to buy new products even though the products we have are still working just fine. In a capitalistic economy corporations are under pressure to increase consumption of their products since that is the only way profits are made—by selling goods and services. This ever-constant pressure to upgrade to a bigger home, newer vehicles, and the newest electronics are all created to sustain our economy. Without constant spending, our economy will experience an economic downturn. To prevent this the government also facilitates consumerism with policies that promote spending such as tax write offs and reducing interest rates so borrowing is cheaper. Our latest economic crisis in 2008 was driven in part by people losing their jobs and once unemployed, opting to save their money rather than spend it. This only deepened the recession and prompted the government to promote consumerism as being patriotic as well as to pump money into the economy until people started spending more and saving less.

A classic example of how consumerism affects our society can be observed by looking at trends in credit card debt among U.S. households. Advertising and marketing for increased consumption are not going to promote buying unless people have buying power. Because real wages have declined over the past 30 years, there is less disposable income for families to purchase the newest and best products.

This has given rise to credit card companies aggressively promoting the message that using credit is the path to happiness, freedom, and instant gratification. At the end of 2015 the Federal Reserve reported that American credit card debt had reached a total of 935.6 billion dollars. This amount is staggering, and has grown exponentially over the past five years. In addition, only 35% of households pay off their credit card each month. That means that the other 65% continue to owe money every month as interest builds. An example of why this is problematic is in part how credit cards are marketed. They often come with low introductory interest rates for a short time. However, within months interest rates increase, and generally credit limits increase rapidly as well, allowing for more debt at higher interest rates. In sum, most Americans have some amount of credit card debt that is largely a product of consumerism and not necessarily based on basic needs (Wright and Rogers 2015).

THEORETICAL PERSPECTIVES

Structural Functionalism

In structural functionalist theory, the economy is one of the most fundamental institutions and if the economy is *healthy* (an analogy to conditions of the human body), it benefits (and is benefitted by) the other institutions of family, education, government, and religion. The issue of cohesion, always a concern with functionalists, and with the conservative nature of the perspective, would support conservative and traditional notions of the economy. Capitalism helped make the United States an extremely wealthy and powerful nation and the adage "if it's not broken, don't fix it" would apply with many functionalists. If it is broken, however, society's institutions need to function appropriately, as parts in a machine, for it to return to good working condition. From the perspective of the structural functionalists, cohesion and solidarity through agreed upon cultural values creates a stable and functional society.

In this theoretical perspective, a society with social mobility experiences social stratification from external constraints rather than from internal ones. In other words, in a society such as the United States, there is great opportunity for people to better their stations in life if they so choose. Some people do not have the ability to rise to the higher ranks of society, since they are not seen as benefitting society as much as others. Structural functionalists see this as a natural and inevitable process; in addition, it is more functional for society to have people in all parts of the economy—not everyone can (or should) be bosses, we need line workers as well.

In addition to aptitude, some people simply do not have the desire to be in the higher paying, higher status, and often higher stress occupations. In a democratic society, individuals should be able to make decisions about their occupations freely. People have individual priorities in their lives and they may wish to spend more time with their families or on recreational pursuits than trying to advance in their work lives and earning more money. Freedom to make these decisions benefits our social institutions and our society's stability generally, according to this theoretical perspective.

Conflict theory

Karl Marx (along with his comrade Friedrich Engels) provided some of the earliest work in the field of conflict theory. In observing what they deemed the inequality produced by capitalism during the emerging industrial revolution of the eighteenth century, Marx and Engels sought to expose the harms of capitalism. These thinkers envisioned a radically different economic structure where all people work not for financial profit but for the greater good and where levels of inequality no longer exist.

Marx believed that one day the workers of the world would unite and overthrow the existing capitalistic social structure and replace it with socialism. Since the wealthy in society (called the bourgeoisie) would not surrender their wealth and advantages willingly, it was up to the workers (called the proletariat) to create a revolution that would bring about a new economic and social structure that would entail a more equal society. Marx said that the bourgeoisie used many means of deception to keep the proletariat in their place—these methods created a false consciousness among the workers to keep them ignorant of their subjugation. At some point, however, the proletariat would realize their oppression through a process of class consciousness. Socialism, according to Marx, was the next inevitable step when capitalism was defeated. In a socialistic economy, a group of managers are needed to ensure that factories (the modes of production) produce only what is needed in society, any more than is needed results in the surplus that creates greed, according to this system. Eventually, the next stage, according to Marx is communism, in which the governmental managers will no longer be needed, since society will realize the benefit of working for the good of all rather than pursuing personal wealth and material goods.

Although Marx had a serious disdain for the effects of capitalism, it would be a misconception that he disliked work. Marx believed in the importance of employment but was concerned about how workers became alienated from the product they created in factories. Prior to industrialization, people created products from their own individual efforts and were normally very proud of the result of their labor. Industrialization and factory work became the norm because of the Industrial Revolution and workers were unable to compete against the mass production of factories and were forced to sell their labor power. They then simply became workers on an assembly line doing monotonous labor. They come to feel disconnected from the product, resulting in a concept Marx called **alienation**, meaning the product became "alien" or foreign to the worker.

> **Alienation** in Marxist ideology, a feeling of disconnection from the object a worker produces and from the process of production itself.

Followers of conflict theory observe how economic institutions often promote social inequality through social stratification. Social stratification is acceptable if all people have the same access to social resources, but there is not a level playing field for all players. Many people do not choose to be in the class in which they are located; many people do not choose to be poor (or rich, or in the middle class, for that matter), but circumstances beyond their control (external sources) create their status in society and maintain that status. For example, job loss due to poor economic conditions or failing health are external conditions that can cause one to fall into a lower socioeconomic status. It is not always possible to rise to the level you want in society, even if you have great talent and skill in your field, dedication, and a strong work ethic. Those people born into wealth have social advantages include private preparatory and later Ivy League education which additionally allows them to make personal connections with people who will be occupying the high paying and prestigious jobs. These connections mean that their friends will help obtain high level positions over people who did not have the opportunity to make these connections. To conflict theorists, the extreme variance between high level executives and the people who work beneath them is far too great. Conflict theorists focus on these inequalities.

Symbolic Interactionism

It is often thought that the micro sociological theories known as symbolic interactionism and social exchange theory defers to the two macro sociology perspectives to address a social analysis of the economy. However, symbolic interactionism has long addressed problems of power differentials, especially in the areas of deviant behavior and mental health institutionalization (Dennis and Martin 2005), but issues of power are certainly seen in matters of socio-economic status. Economic conditions create social stratification and those at the upper strata in society often maintain higher echelons of power than those in the lower ranks and that effects the interactions that take place between people. Celebrities receive different types of interactions from outsiders than homeless people.

The larger social institution of the economy also provides the individual lives of people with an identity, or an understanding of themselves. It also provides them with an understanding of others based on the economic institution and on economic situations. In a related manner, it is easy to see how the labeling process affects people in different economic situations. People with higher socio-economic status (SES) might have a higher level of esteem but are sometimes labeled as "blood blues" or "stuck ups" by those who do not have these advantages. Conversely, those with lower SES might have low levels of esteem which is reinforced by pejorative labels applied to them such as "trailer trash" or "welfare moms". According to symbolic interactionists, these terms can result in self-fulfilling prophecies if the people begin to accept these labels as legitimate; self-fulfilling prophecies create expectations which can be easy to simply obey, reinforcing the idea that some people are better or worse than others based on their individual SES. A vicious cycle then is created as stereotypes often are presented as real. Sociologist W.I. Thomas (Thomas and Thomas 1928) stated that if people believe things are real (such as a dichotomy between society's "makers" and the "takers"), even if these things are illusion rather than reality, they become real in their *consequences*—in other words if we see a clear distinction between the good and bad, based on economic conditions, we create and enforce policies and laws that *appear* real, thus keeping the cycle going; as you should recall from Chapter 1, this is an example of what is called the *Thomas Theorem*.

While the field of economics focuses directly on aspects of production, distribution, and consumption, sociology is more concerned with the social aspects of economic behavior. The concepts of social capital, cultural capital, and symbolic capital are a sociological recreation of economic capital. French sociologist Pierre Bourdieu and American sociologist James Coleman each developed their own conceptions of social capital with some variations in their conceptualizations but each formulation contains the basic idea that individuals or families often receive (and work for) social rewards due to their social networks (Portes and Mooney 2002: 304). Whereas economic capital refers to the actual money-driven types of capital, in which efficiency is the goal of capitalism, social and cultural capitalism are both types of symbolic capitalism according to Bourdieu. Social capital refers to the advantages a person has based on the associations and social networks possessed, cultural capital is derived from non-material possessions such as knowledge, educational attainment, and other possessions that can be converted to economic capital. Symbolic capital, as mentioned earlier, is therefore the level of esteem a person receives from others based on these various types of capital (Bourdieu 1998).

SEARCHING FOR SOLUTIONS

The economic institution is closely related to the governmental institution—in fact, economics was originally termed *political economy* but the two were separated to form two distinct fields of study. And as we noted earlier, some political parties believe that the government is necessary to control the economic function while others feel the government should be only tangentially involved. However, most would agree that the government should have some role, whether at the national or local levels, in addressing issues affecting the economy, therefore solutions to problems of the economy have primarily often been sought there.

Unfortunately, there is little consensus on how to solve the problem of poverty in our society. In fact, there is little consensus on what exactly constitutes poverty in our society as well. Our current federal guidelines were set in the 1960s and crudely calculated as three times the cost of food for a family. However, much has changed since the 1960s, including rising housing costs and the costs that arise when women are in paid work force full-time. The current U.S. poverty measure does not include the cost of child care, transportation costs for commuting to and from jobs. These are all costs that have risen significantly since the poverty measure was devised. In addition, currently food costs are now closer to one-eighth of a family's expenses rather than one-third (Iceland 2013). A better poverty threshold would take into consideration geographic differences in the cost of living, the costs of childcare for working parents, and other necessities.

FIGURE 2.2 Protestors hold signs advocating raising the minimum wage at a rally in Los Angeles on April 15, 2015.

Source: Dan Holm/Shutterstock.com

According to the U.S. Labor Department, approximately 30% of all hourly workers earn "near minimum-wage". Over half of these workers are white, female, and do not have more than a high school education and the issue of the minimum wage stems in large part from decades of wage stagnation for the working class while inflation continues and the upper class experience continued gains in their income and wealth. Raising the minimum wage is one way to combat the vast inequality in our society, however, it would not even begin to bridge the gap between the social classes. The federal minimum wage, set at $7.25 per hours, has not changed since 2009. However, according to the Bureau of Labor Statistics it has lost about 10% of its purchasing power to inflation (U.S. Bureau of Labor Statistics 2016). In response, many state, city and county governments have set a higher minimum wage for workers. Support for raising the minimum wage to $15 has been proposed by labor union and anti-poverty groups. The issue is clearly divided along political lines. Conservatives are much less likely to support raising the minimum wage to $15 dollars an hour than liberals (Pew Research Center 2016).

Another viable option for solving the minimum wage issue has been proposed and calls for a *living wage*. A living wage is defined as enough income for an employee to afford basic necessities such as housing, food, utilities, health care and transportation. Cities that have adopted living wage laws include San Francisco, California, Santa Fe, New Mexico and Washington, D.C. These range from $7.50 in New Mexico to $11.50 in Washington, D.C. Proponents of a federal living wage propose $15.00 an hour as the absolute minimum per hourly wage. Those who oppose it argue that the cost of living varies widely by state and city and that it will be too big a burden on small businesses. Most small businesses believe a better solution would be to allow local government to set the minimum wage as appropriate for the cost of living in a particular area. In order to determine the amount of income required to cover necessities by geographic area, a living wage calculator was developed by MIT professor Amy Glasmeier. According to her research, a family of four would need both parents to work 77 hours at minimum wage to earn enough money for basic necessities (Glasmeier 2017). This varies based on geographic region with families in the North and West generally making more money before taxes than in the South and Midwest. And in urban areas that contain the majority of jobs the living wage is higher than the national median. For example, a family of four would need to make $84,206 in Washington, D.C. to cover essential living expenses, while the comparable median federal income for a living wage is $61,336 (Glasmeier 2017).

Should the federal minimum wage be increased to a living wage of $15 for the entire country?

Pro: Raising the minimum wage will help low income workers.
Con: Raising the minimum wage will hurt small businesses.

Another idea that has been proposed is the implementation of the Universal Basic Income (UBI). The UBI is "one of a family of policies designed to ensure that everyone has a small income large enough to meet their basic needs for any reason. It grants this income to every citizen, and then taxes them on their income or their assets or purchases" (Widerquist 2013:569). Since the UBI provides a livable income to all citizens, there is no need for eligibility determination currently used by the U.S. welfare system. If people want to work in addition to this basic income, and it is assumed the clear majority would, they can achieve social mobility; if they do not, they will not have to suffer the indignity of being part of a group that requires state assistance. UBI, however, is seen by some as being akin to socialism and would be an impediment to the free market which will not be acceptable in the U.S.

Is the UBI a viable alternative to the current welfare system?

Pro: The UBI helps the economy and helps maintain the dignity of citizens.
Con: The UBI is an impediment to the free market system and provides disincentives for work.

Sociologist Herbert Gans (2009) provides some insights into those people who suffer from persistent poverty, a group he calls the "excluded poor"; this is a group that is frequently blamed for their own condition, though a wide array of social factors contribute to their poverty. Effective antipoverty programs to assist this group, according to Gans (2009), must move from "blaming to explaining" in that social work practitioners, academics, legislators, the media, and others should seek to understand and explain to the public that external factors such as race, ethnicity, mass imprisonment, substance abuse, and dangerous living conditions have a role to play rather than a simple narrative that attributes poverty to individual failings. These programs should also include several strategies—access to secure employment, subsidies to employers that hire this population, special financial allowances, an expansion of disability options to the persistently poor, assistance in finding and creating family and community supports, early education programs for children, and rehabilitation services for offenders re-entering society and service personnel returning home from military engagements. Acknowledging the barriers associated with such programs, particularly resource allocation, Gans (2009) feels that planning to assist the poor should begin now with the hope that when the political and economic conditions are more accommodating, these policies might be implemented in order to thwart the danger of a growing number of permanently excluded citizens.

Blank (2011) describes four suggestions for eliminating income inequality. The first involves increasing worker skill levels—although workers are more educated than in the past, skill shifts have not been significant and a marked increase in employment skill levels would have a modest effect to help balance out the inequality between lower and higher skilled workers; the increase would have to be at historic levels to have a significant effect, however. A second recommendation is increasing wages to 8% to workers in the lower 80% and 4% to those in the top 20% of the hourly wage distribution over ten years. A third possibility is reversing the number of single parent families by increasing the marriage rate among lower class workers; moves in this direction, however, would have to seriously reverse current marriage trends to thwart income inequality. The last recommendation involves governmental intervention to elevate very low income families at least to the poverty line—measures such as a cash public-assistance initiative, an increase in food, housing, and wage subsidies, and other means; while this might help lower income individuals, it will do little

FIGURE 2.3
Income inequality
is increasing and
potential solutions
are unlikely to
solve this social
problem.

Source: nuvolanevicata/Shutterstock.com

to affect the imbalance in income inequities. Blank (2011) notes that the examples proffered will not have the sweeping changes needed for true income inequality and are intended to illustrate the difficulty in promoting inequality. And any initiative to increase marriage rates among the poor has a dubious chance for success and would create many other questions about governmental intervention into citizens' lives, as well as issues about changing views on family life. However, advancing income equality should be a goal in a democratic society and discussions such as these must be debated for this to come about. Pure income inequality may be an impossibility but fairness and equal opportunity are not.

We can also take a macro level view of problems associated with problems with the economy. Globalization is an extremely powerful force in rapidly moving civilization down a new and different path—one of greater interdependence between formerly autonomous nations (Paul 2015). It is seen by many as a positive solution to inequality since the increased trade between nations promotes a global free market, increasing economic well-being on a much larger scale and, as a latent function, less human right violations by governments. Others argue that economic globalization simply removes the power of states to act for the betterment of their own citizens and that aggressive competition will likely result in lower industrial worker standards and inequality between nations;

FIGURE 2.4 Countries that comprise the Trans-Pacific Partnership; a trade accord promoting lower tariffs.

CANADA
USA
MEXICO
PERU
CHILE

JAPAN
VIETNAM
SINGAPORE
BRUNEI
MALAYSIA
AUSTRALIA
NEW ZELAND

TRANS-PACIFIC PARTNERSHIP

Source: WindVector/Shutterstock.com

due to this inequality, there will be greater political upheaval. The nations with greater economic development will simply exploit those with less development (de Soysa and Vadlamannati 2011). Recently the trade accord called the Trans-Pacific Partnership (shortened to TPP), comprised of the United States and eleven Pacific Rim nations and the largest such trade agreement in history, proposed to lower tariffs and to suppress the rising economic power of China. In addition, the arrangement involves not only labor issues but also environment effects and intellectual property rights (New York Times 2016). The TPP is currently being debated in the U.S. government. Current trends toward economic nationalism under the Trump administration will determine the role of globalization in U.S. trade relationships.

Is globalization helpful or harmful for world economies?

Pro: A strong global economy will help developing nations economically.
Con: Globalization contributes to the exploitation of workers in many nations.

After World War II, America experienced great economic growth, brought about in part by industrialization and population gains. While a focus on present economic growth was the prevalent mode of thinking at that time, currently a new emphasis on sustainable economies arose in order to focus on future ecological concerns resulting from a burgeoning economy, concerns that were officially advocated by a group of nations, the G-20, by endorsing economic sustainability globally. Sustainability, then has become a focal point in both the economy and the environment (Chichilnisky 2012).

Sometimes movements to combat inequality enter the scene quickly. In response to the heightened awareness of vast income inequality that came to the forefront during the Great Recession, in 2011 a group of citizens began occupying parks and other common areas, starting at New York City's Zuccotti Park (in a host of demonstrations known as Occupy Wall Street), followed by other areas around the nation and, indeed, around the globe. At least partly inspired by past protest movements of the late 1960s and early 1970s, and partly by a revolutionary fervor in 2010 resulting from financial concerns in Europe and cities of Arab countries (these protests in the Middle East were labeled the Arab Spring), the American protest groups, dubbed the Occupy Movement, organized around the vast inequality resulting from the events following the Great Recession. Later these progressive movements became known collectively as the "99% Movement" reflecting the idea that they represented the 99% of the population, in opposition to the wealthy 1% who possess most of the money and power in American society.

FIGURE 2.5
PHILADELPHIA, PA
OCTOBER 6, 2011:
Male Occupy Wall Street protester with protest sign.

Source: Nick Tropiano/Shutterstock.com

The 99 percenters protested against the handful of extremely wealthy families and powerful corporate and political figures who were in collusion with them (Calhoun 2013). This movement is now engaged primarily through social media and many Facebook groups are organized around this theme. Individuals can get involved and heighten awareness through social media by aligning themselves with this movement and furthering this agenda on their own social media platforms, such as Instagram, Twitter, Facebook, and other social media directly targeting social injustice.

China can produce goods at a much lower cost than Americans. This allows China to pay their workers lower wages and makes it impossible for American companies to compete with China's much lower costs. This has caused a loss of jobs in the United States, but it also has kept prices low for a vast majority of consumer goods such as clothing, electronics, gadgets, toys, computers, etc. In addition, U.S. exports to China are substantially lower than imports from China. In other words, China is not buying U.S. made products at anywhere near the rate the U.S. is purchasing goods made in China. To complicate matters further, the U.S. debt to China has grown to over a trillion dollars (second only to Japan). As China's economy rapidly expands in large part due to U.S. imports, China can purchase more U.S. Treasury notes and thus maintain a great deal of political and economic power over the U.S. economy. For example, if trade agreements change unfavorably for China with increased duties on Chinese imports, China could stop buying U.S. Treasuries and as a result interest rates in the U.S. will rise. Even more worrisome, China could call in the U.S. debt and this would be devastating to the U.S. economy. However, these measures are not in the best interest for China since they need the U.S. to continue purchasing their products. Many businesses have attempted to solve this problem by outsourcing jobs to China to reduce their costs and remain competitive. However, this solution has caused U.S. manufacturing jobs to decline substantially (U.S. Department of Labor 2016). Increasing U.S. job growth while keeping prices low for consumer goods continues to be a challenge.

> Should workers be given an equal vote in the decision-making process when corporations are deciding whether to close a factory and move production abroad?
>
> **Pro**: Workers have the right to be empowered and participate in decisions that will deeply affect their livelihood, their families, and their communities.
> **Con**: Workers are just employees and as such do own the means of production and are compensated for their labor, not stakeholders in the company.

You may wonder how you can effectively help to eradicate some of these social problems. For example, how can you help workers in China who are mistreated? Individually you can boycott exploitative manufacturers by not purchasing their products, however, because our gadgets and products are not made in one place, but rather assembled from different places, it is hard to know which products to boycott. Therefore, grassroots organizations are forming that can be joined by anyone interested in working against outsourcing jobs by protesting outside companies that outsource, and using social media to heighten awareness about outsourcing and downsizing.

In much the same way, individuals can work to heighten awareness about consumerism and change their own habits to live within their means and not purchase newer vehicles and bigger homes or more products simply because they are available. The Tiny House movement is a social movement among people who want to downsize the space they live in. This translates to owning fewer material possessions since you only need a small amount to fill a tiny house. This movement is in response to the growing size of the American home which is currently around 2,600 square feet. Tiny houses tend to be between 100 and 400 square feet and make for simpler living and more efficient space. Reasons to join this movement range from environmental concerns, financial concerns, and having more leisure time to enjoy life. It also discourages buying larger televisions and other products marketed to home owners because there is simply not space for the newest and greatest technology or appliances. This has been coined "The Tiny Life" and encompasses all aspects of unnecessary materialism and the hyper consumption that takes over so many people's lives. It is also a way to merge your life with nature and have more control over your future and avoid the trap of the "work spend" cycle. Joining in this movement reduces stress, makes a clear statement about consumerism, and drastically changes the amount of money one needs to make to own a home.

You can also work toward social change in consumerism by purchasing used clothing and wasting less clothing by not purchasing trendy pieces that you won't wear for long. This is called "fast fashion"—clothes that are trendy and designed only to be worn more a season. They are mass

FIGURE 2.6 NEW YORK, US - APRIL 13, 2017: Tiny house on display during the 2017 New York International Auto Show held at the Jacob Javits Center.

Source: Ed Aldridge/Shutterstock.com

produced and affordable and attract more sales by getting people into their stores. This disposable clothing is bad for the environment and the economy. By shopping at thrift stores and purchasing gently used clothing as well as buying from brands that recycle and sell used clothing in their stores (i.e. Patagonia) you can greatly reduce your consumption of mass marketed clothing made in Bangladesh, often by child labor. This approach can motivate clothing companies to think more about designing products of higher quality and which are biodegradable. One grassroots movement to bring awareness to the source of our clothing and the waste of consumeristic buying is the Fashion Revolution. Their mission is to promote buying from vintage stores, making new clothes out of old ones, and swapping clothes. They have a strong online presence and ask individuals to make videos of how they avoid consumeristic habits and how to motivate others to join in to reduce waste and fast fashion.

CHAPTER SUMMARY

- The social institution known as the economy addresses how goods and services are produced, distributed, and consumed. The economy's primary function is to ensure that human needs and wants are fulfilled. Because not everyone has access to the same resources, income inequality creates various levels of social stratification, which is a determinant of one's socioeconomic status.

- The major types of economic systems are capitalism, socialism/communism, and mixed economies. Capitalism, as an economic system, depends upon several components: private ownership, profit motive, competition, and the absence of regulations that constrain the "invisible hand" of supply and demand.

- Socialism, as an alternative to capitalism, seeks to provide more individual liberty and creativity to workers in society. It also seeks to correct inequalities by promoting a redistribution of wealth and requires a group of regulators in this effort. Per Marx and Engels, socialism will be followed by communism, a structure that will no longer require the regulators to control the flow of money throughout society.

- New directions in the U.S. economic systems include downsizing, outsourcing, the shared economy, and moves toward contingency. These terms are fairly recent and suggest a decline of traditional, full time stable employment.

- The major sociological theories take different views of the economic system. In structural functionalism, the economy is observed as a social institution necessary to the effective functioning of society and primarily understands social stratification as a natural process. Conflict theory, guided by the work of Marx and Engels, observes the income inequality in society and posits that external conditions are in place that benefit the upper and upper middle classes and disadvantage the middle, working, and lower classes. In symbolic interactionism, a micro level focus is observed; the issue of economics as social behavior, as in social exchange; and of identity, as it relates to one's place in the socioeconomic system, are key concentrations in this perspective.

- Solutions to some of the problems of the economy would include actions that understand the role of increasing globalization such as trade agreements, however, this is a hotly debated item, especially when trends of economic nationalism are a major component of the Trump administration.

- Measures such as increasing the national minimum wage or instituting a living wage or the Uniform Basic Income (UBI) might have the benefit of decreasing economic inequality, however these are hotly debated topics.

- Many policies have been implemented throughout history to deal with poverty and income inequality, some successful and others unsuccessful, and many new ones are currently being attempted. The problems are not easily corrected through government intervention; however, new and innovative policies should continue to be considered in a democratic society to meet this end.

- Consumerism is a product of a capitalist system that is driven by profits and the production and sales of goods and services. The United States is a hyper consumeristic society and the need to own the "latest and greatest" is driven by advertising and marketing. In order for the economy to function well individuals must constantly upgrade and buy new products.

- Solutions that start with the individual include the Tiny House Movement to combat consumerism and materialism. It also greatly reduces the amount of time spent working and allows for more leisure time. Also, getting involved combatting "fast fashion" by buying used clothing, making new clothing from old, and swapping clothing are all ways for individuals to slow down the waste and environmental damage of the clothing industry.

REFERENCES

Blank, Rebecca M. 2011. *Changing Inequality*. Berkeley: University of California Press.

Bourdieu, Pierre. 1998. *Practical Reason*: On the theory of action. Palo Alto, CA: Stanford University Press.

Braun, Denny. 1997. *The Rich Get Richer: The Rise of Income Inequality in the United States and the World*, 2nd ed. Chicago: Nelson-Hall Publishers.

Calhoun, Craig. 2013. "Occupy Wall Street in Perspective." *The British Journal of Sociology*. 62 (1): 26–38.

Chichilnisky, Graciela. 2012. "Economic Theory and the Global Environment." *Economic Theory*. 49 (2): 217–225.

Cohen, Boyd and Jan Kietzmann. 2014. "Ride On! Mobility Business Models for the Sharing Economy." *Organization and Environment*. 27 (3): 279–296.

Cushman, Thomas. 2015. "The Moral Economy of the Great Recession." *Society*. 52 (1): 9–18.

Dennis, Alex and Peter J. Martin. 2005. "Symbolic Interactionism and the Concept of Power." *The British Journal of Sociology*. 56 (2): 191–213.

De Soysa, Indra and Krishna C. Vadlamannati. 2011. "Does Being Bound Together Suffocate, or Liberate? The Effects of Economic, Social, and Political Globalization on Human Rights, 1981–2005." *Kyklos*, 64 (1): 20–53.

Freeley, James F. 2016. "The Troubling Problem of Income Inequality: A Few Thoughts." *UMass Law Review*. 11 U. Mass L. Rev. 6.

Gans, Herbert. 2009. "Antipoverty Policy for the Excluded Poor." *Challenge*. 52 (6): 79–85.

Glasmeier, Amy. 2017. *New 2015 Living Wage Calculator.* Retrieved February 26, 2017 (www.livingwage.mit.edu).

Iceland, John. 2013. *Poverty in America: A Handbook*. Berkeley: University of California Press.

Katz, Michael B. 2013. *The Undeserving Poor: American's Enduring Confrontation with Poverty*. 2nd ed. New York: Oxford University Press.

Lenski, Gerhard E. 1966. *Power and Privilege: A Theory of Social Stratification*. New York: McGraw-Hill Book Co.

Marx, Karl and Friedrich Engels. [1848] 1948. *The Communist Manifesto*, edited and annotated by Friedrich Engels. New York: International Publishers.

Milanovic, Branko. 2011. *The Haves and Have Nots: A Brief and Idiosyncratic History of Global Inequality*. New York: Basic Books.

New York Times. "The Trans-Pacific Partnership Trade Accord Explained." July 27, 2016. GALE Document; GALEIA459271576.

Paul, Joel R. 2015. "The Cost of Free Trade." *Brown Journal of World Affairs*. 22 (1).

Pew Research Center. 2016. "Clinton, Trump Supporters Have Starkly Different Views of a Changing Nation: Voters Remain Skeptical that Either Would Make a Good President." Retrieved April 21, 2018 (http://assets.pewresearch.org/wp-content/uploads/sites/5/2016/08/08–18–2016-August-political-release.pdf).

Portes, Alejandro and Margarita Mooney. 2002. "Social Capital and Community Development." Pp 303–329. In Mauro F. Guillen, Randall Collins, Paula England, and Marshal Meyers (Eds). *The New Economic Sociology: Developments in an Emerging Field*. New York: Russell Sage Foundation.

Rezvani, Farahmand and Kamrouz Pirouz. 2013. "Recent Trends in Income Inequality in the United States." *Journal of Business and Educational Leadership*. 4 (1): 3–11.

Rousseau, Nathan. 2014. *Society Explained: An Introduction to Sociology*. London: Rowman & Littlefield.

Sargent, Lyman Tower. 1993. *Contemporary Political Ideologies: A Comparative Analysis*. 9th ed. Belmont, CA: Wadsworth.

Smith, Adam. [1776] 1994. *An Inquiry into the Nature and Causes of the Wealth of Nations*, edited, with an introduction notes, marginal summary and enlarged by Edwin Cannan. New York: The Modern Library.

Thomas, W.I. and D.S. Thomas. 1928. *The Child in America: Behavior Problems and Programs*. New York: Knopf.

U.S. Department of Labor. Bureau of Labor Statistics. 2016. Labor Force Statistics from the Current Population Survey. Retrieved February 19, 2017 (www.bls.gov/cps/earnings.htm).

Widerquist, Karl. 2013. "Is Universal Basic Income Still Worth Talking About?" In Robert S. Rycroft, *The Economics of Inequality, Poverty, and Discrimination in the 21st Century*. Santa Barbara, CA: Praeger.

Wright, Erik Olin and Joel Rogers. 2015. *American Society: How it Really Works*. New York: Norton.

CHAPTER 3

Government and the Political System

KEY TERMS

Conservativism	Libertarianism	Radical Political Thought
Democracy	Nationalism	Reactionary Thought
Democratic Socialism	Political Ideology	Utilitarianism
Government	Political Parties	
Liberalism	Populism	

ABOUT THE PROBLEM: GOVERNMENT AND THE POLITICAL SYSTEM

The Social Institution of Government

Government (often referred to as *the state*) is the social institution tasked with the protection of citizens and the maintenance of social order. It involves the use of power through a political structure or structures that govern the behavior of its citizens. In the United States, government at the federal level consists of three branches—the executive, legislative, and judicial. At the state and local levels, the structures are often equivalent to the federal level.

> **Government** the social institution that ensures protection of citizens and the maintenance of social order.

Jean-Jacques Rousseau was one of several early political philosophers who envisioned a "social contract," which is basically an unwritten agreement of the relationship between citizens and their government. In Rousseau's vision, the state should provide safety and security along with measures to guard against inequality and in return, the citizens will provide their consent to be governable and to support the state. Because of his influence in this matter, Rousseau's ideas can be considered a forerunner to sociology (Zeitlin 1990). The idea of a social contract is an important one as it emphasizes the role of the individual in society and represents the exchange process in which some level of equality must exist for people to have freedom.

> **Utilitarianism** the political philosophy that states the best policies offer the greatest good for the greatest number of citizens.

Another idea reflected in the relationship of the state and citizen can be found in the concept of **utilitarianism**. Though the concept has gone through various incarnations by different theorists, the basic idea is that government should do what is best for the whole or, as it is often stated, "the greatest good for the greatest number" (Zeitlin 1990). This has many implications for a political sociology in that democracy must meet the demands for the majority but still be cognizant and understanding of the needs of the minority.

Political thought has existed since humans contemplated the role of government in its most rudimentary forms. History provides us with long series of political changes, some of which involved smooth transformations while others were undoubtedly messy. The American Revolution consisted of a difficult transition but produced stable after-effects; however, the French Revolution, whose effects reverberated around the globe, was less stable. The Enlightenment period in Europe that preceded the French Revolution was a period in which many cultural practices and ideas were challenged as freedom of thought and reason became the guiding principles for change. The resulting revolutionary activity that occurred between 1789 and 1795 produced two types of change: distribution of resources that resulted from the violent confiscation of power, and changes that reflected new cultural and philosophical aspects of French society (Dawson 1967). The events of the French Revolution had a significant effect on political philosophy and the early beginnings of what would become known as sociology in that it profoundly affected the ideas of Tocqueville, Comte, Durkheim, and Marx.

American Democracy

Democracy has been the only type of political system in the United States, therefore there has been no direct experience with other forms of government. A very early sociological analysis (originally published in 1835) of this governmental structure was documented by Alexis de Tocqueville in *Democracy in America* (2000). Tocqueville was an aristocrat whose native France was still reeling from the French Revolution and due to this, was interested in the beginnings of democracy as was emerging in America. His observations on the individualistic nature of American democracy was disconcerting to him as he believed that to be effective, government needs to control the level of egoism generated by individualism. The individualism and self-reliance that characterize America was highly valued by other American thinkers (Kivisto 1998).

> **Democracy** a type of government which requires access by citizens to the active participation in their governance.

A democracy requires five components—equal and effective participation in government, equality in voting, an "enlightened understanding" of political issues, the ability to pick items to be deliberated upon, and the inclusion of adult citizens (Dahl 1998). Note here the continued emphasis on equality. Unlike authoritarian and totalitarian forms of government, which have a leader or leaders who regulate many or all aspects of citizen life, democratic structures seek government by the citizens themselves. Dahl (1963) notes four dimensions of involvement in the governmental decision making: interest in the people or issues to be voted on; concern (the importance given to the decision); the amount of information one has in the matter; and the amount of active participation in which one can be engaged. While voter apathy is a deterrent to effective democratic participation, at least that level of disengagement is a personal choice; the issue of voter suppression is of greater concern in that a concerted effort is made by some seeking political power to thwart voting by citizens to increase their chances of winning.

> **Political Ideology** set of political values, preferences, and doctrines.

Political Ideology and Political Parties

A **political ideology** refers to a collection of beliefs based on a certain set of political values, preferences, and doctrines that attract followers of these beliefs.

Different ideologies have long existed in American politics, currently conservativism and liberalism are dominant forms, although other ones exist. **Political parties** follow along ideological

> **Political Parties** collectivities of people that seek to gain or maintain political power and influence.

FIGURE 3.1 Some of the diverse political candidates who have run for office in the United States.

Source: Tetra Images/Getty Images

Conservativism
a political ideology defined by a focus on cherished traditions, a belief in smaller forms of government, and a resistance to social change when it is felt that change represents a loss of control over traditional values and social order.

Liberalism a political ideology defined by a focus on individual freedom, a belief that government is needed to ensure that individual needs are met, and a desire for progressive social change.

lines and its adherents seeks to gain or maintain political power and influence. Although there are two major parties in the United States, other less powerful parties exist and vie for power in the political sphere.

Conservatism is a major political ideology in American politics and can be defined by these characteristics: a focus on maintaining cherished traditions, a belief in smaller forms of government, and a resistance to social change when it is felt that change represents a loss of control over traditional values. There is also more faith in free market forces as the "invisible hand" is seen to better regulate the economy than the government. Currently, conservativism (also called "right wing" ideology) is primarily represented in the United States in the Republican Party, but as we shall see, this ideology is also adopted by other political groupings. The Republican party (also referred to as the Grand Old Party, or GOP) is symbolized by the elephant and when referring to states whose voters are mostly conservative, the term "red states" is used.

Liberalism, the other major ideological force, can be described as having these characteristics: a focus on individual freedom (liberty), a belief that government is needed to ensure individual needs are met, and a desire for social change. Liberals are often referred to as progressives as they favor progressive means to promote social change; in liberalism, there is less faith in the free market and a belief that governmental intervention is needed to ensure fairness and equity for citizens. Liberalism (also referred to as "left wing" ideology) is most often associated with the Democratic Party; this party is symbolized by the donkey and when referring to states with liberal voters, the term "blue states" is used.

Obviously, the two major ideologies do not exist as complete opposites and many people are moderately one or the other. Other voters may fall into the comfortable center, preferring to adopt the doctrine of centrism, often choosing candidates from either party if they align with their general interests and do not fall into either extreme. And other ideologies, such as communitarianism, note the relationship of the citizen to society as ideally being an active one, as increasing political engagement through voluntary associations is perceived as central to effective government; communitarianism is sometimes seen as a bridge between conservativism and liberalism as it seeks smaller government but also rejects the idea of individualism and self-determination (Bronner 1999).

FIGURE 3.2 NEW YORK - SEPT 17: A protester holds a sign with a quote from JFK as she stands in Zuccotti Park on the 1 year anniversary of the Occupy Wall St protests on September 17, 2012 in New York City, NY.

Source: Glynnis Jones/Shutterstock.com

> **Libertarianism** a political ideology that shares with liberalism the belief in the rights of individuals, and with conservativism, it shares a high level of trust in the lightly regulated free market system.

There are other political ideologies that influence American politics such as **libertarianism** which has increased in popularity over the past several years. It shares with liberalism the belief in the rights of individuals, and with conservativism, it shares a high level of trust in the lightly regulated free market system and de-centralization of government. There are other parties such as the green party, which has liberal leanings and a focus on conserving the environment. These two groups, however, have been unable to successfully compete with the two major ideologies in the United States.

> **Radical political Thought** traditionally referred to a far-left ideology, whose proponents, often referred to as the New Left, came to prominence in the 1960s and had a Marxist orientation. Today the term is used often loosely to describe any extreme political perspective.

Other terms associated with political ideology that are associated with right and left ideologies (in the more extreme forms) are reactionary thought and radical political thought. **Reactionary thought** reflects to a desire to not only maintain the status quo but the "status quo ante", a return to the customs in the past that better represents the most favorable way to live; it is often seen as an extreme version of conservativism. The other term is **radical political thought** and, although people now often use the term to refer to extremist political views generally, it has traditionally referred to a far-left ideology, whose proponents, often referred to as the New Left, came to prominence in the 1960s and possess a Marxist orientation.

> **Reactionary Thought** a desire to return to the customs of a time in the past that better represents the most favorable way to live; it is often seen as an extreme version of conservativism.

With the candidacy of Bernie Sanders in the 2016 presidential race, the political ideology of **democratic socialism** became better known to the American public. Sanders, an independent Senator who espoused democratic socialism ideals but who ran as a Democrat, had a strong group of supporters but failed to get the Democratic Party's nomination. Democratic socialism favors public ownership of many industries, increased social services, and governmental regulation of economic activity. Again, this ideology has been mildly effective thus far in challenging the conservative and liberal ideologies in the United States.

> **Democratic Socialism** a political ideology that favors public ownership of many industries, increased social services, and governmental regulation of economic activity.

Current Trends in American Politics

The concept of *American exceptionalism* is one with a long history and one in which the discourse in American politics refers to the idealized uniqueness of the country. The concept very easily augments the American ideals of individuality, pragmatism, and others and is seen in the larger picture of global regulations. Two themes are dominant in the exceptionalism narrative as it relates to international relations: America uses its distinct political system as a model for other nations to emulate and that America has a mission to transfer that perceived exceptional structure (Tomes 2014).

It's easy to see how this concept can create pride and cohesion among Americans. It should also be obvious that it can create nationalist, isolationist, and ethnocentric sentiments by failing to consider the uniqueness and effectiveness of the cultural traits of other countries which are equally valuable. The discussion over the U.S. erecting a wall on the United States–Mexico border and a ban on Muslim immigrants entering the country, which were centerpieces of the candidacy of Donald Trump in the 2016 Presidential election, is an example of nationalistic tendencies potentially engendered by this approach and will be discussed more in the following section.

Is American exceptionalism a beneficial concept for the nation generally?

Pro: American exceptionalism contributes to a sense of cohesion and pride of country.
Con: American exceptionalism contributes to nationalism and ethnocentrism.

Political correctness (also referred to by the initials P.C.) has received much attention in the last several years. Originally a term employed by the political left to mock hard core members willing to follow the orders of a dictator (Brennen and Feldstein 1997), it is now used primarily by conservatives as a derogatory term to suggest that liberals use euphemistic language to advance a liberal agenda and to suppress free speech.

Should professors of social science disciplines openly state their political views in class?

Pro: Students get a better understanding of government by knowing their professor's perspective.
Con: Students could become indoctrinated by charismatic professors.

Populist and Nationalistic Trends

Populism a political movement that makes a concerted effort by certain people or parties that appeal to the needs and the will of the citizens, particularly in the context of opposition to established state power.

Populism is an issue that has recently re-entered the American political vernacular. The concept is not new, however, and has a long history not only in the United States but throughout the world. It also has a host of interpretations and as Youngdale (1975) notes:

Populism was not a static movement, nor can a typical populist be regarded as a static stereotype. People do not experience any social "fact" such as adversity, identically time after time. Rather they learn; they adopt new outlooks and new psychological strategies in response to a repetition of some anxiety-provoking factor.

(p.12)

The term basically refers to a political movement that makes a concerted effort by certain people or parties that appeal to the needs and the will of the citizens, particularly in the context of opposition to established state power. As noted earlier, populism has taken many forms and is associated with different movements. The 2016 Presidential campaigns of both Democratic candidate (who was formerly identified as an Independent) Bernie Sanders and Republican candidate Donald Trump were considered to head populist movements. Certainly, both campaigns made overt appeals to potential voters.

Nationalism involves a sense of pride and unity in one's nation. Minogue (1967) explains that the term *nation* "has had a variety of adventures before arriving at its present eminence. It is perhaps the most successful member of a family of words which all refer to a collection of human beings ... other such words are race, class, people, community, tribe, state, clan, and society" (p. 8). These other terms are important in understanding that nationalism provides feelings other than those involving one's geographic, territorial identity. In areas of nationalism, race has been an especially troubling issue as concerns over racial and ethnic prejudice and discrimination arise as common themes.

> **Nationalism** a sense of pride and unity in one's nation and several dimensions of identity including geography, race, class, people, community, tribe, state, and clan.

Deutsch (1966) notes that nationalism has come to be considered less of an ideology and more of a "state of mind" with the negative characteristics of "unevenness, inequality, relative discontinuity toward persons or things outside the national group ... relative immobility; by preferences or advantages in communication; and by a considerable degree of structure" (p. 16). Hall (1995) notes an important component of nationalism: "the belief in the primacy of a particular nation, real or constructed" (p. 9). Mann (1995) adds that "nationalism is an ideology whereby a nation believes it possesses distinct claims to virtue—claims which may be used to legitimate aggressive actions against other nations" (p. 44). Nationalistic self-determination runs counter to globalization, in which borders are becoming increasingly fluid as people move in and out of different territories, driven by better life chances, consumerism, and other motivations. Although nationalism has several different forms, they all have two common features: an identity that is politically self-conscious and a pursuit of national sovereignty.

Hastings (2000) describes two types of nationalism-*jus soli* ("right of the soil", or citizenship by birthright) nationalism, which has pluralistic underpinnings, accepts groups with national variations, and which will eventually lead to integration. On the other hand, *jus sanguinis* nationalism ("right of blood", or citizenship by parents who are citizens) is exclusive, unaccepting of different groups, and can lead to horrific actions such as ethnic cleansing. Hastings states that categorizing and understanding these different types allows nations to effectively remodel social activity rather than to attempt to abolish nationalism outright, which has historically shown to be ineffective.

In their recent study on American nationalism, Bonikowski and DiMaggio (2016) present a typology of nationalists based on four characteristics: the degree of identity with their country relative to other forms of identity; the criteria of what is considered truly American; the emotional state of pride in being American; and their degree of belief that America is preferable to other countries. The participants of this study were characterized as: *ardent nationalists* who scored high on all dimensions of nationalism; *restrictive nationalists*, who described being American in ways that were exclusive of certain groups but moderate in their levels of pride; *creedal nationalists*, who scored high in national pride but are more inclusive of their ideas of who is truly American; and *the disengaged*, a group that evidenced very few nationalistic beliefs. The array of positions on nationalism reflect the current political divide in America and the study's authors speculate how the certain nationalist ideologies, notably the restrictive and ardent forms, could have possibly contributed to the popular support of Donald Trump of a large part of the electorate, through populist and nativist messaging that appealed to many people who espoused nationalistic tendencies.

With the election of President Trump in 2016, themes of nationalism became more visible in the political landscape. This was in part because President Trump's chief strategist Steve Bannon was a self-proclaimed "economic nationalist"; Bannon was the former chief executive officer of Breitbart News, an outlet that claimed to be the voice of the "alt right" (alternative right). Bannon's ideas are represented by his call for the "deconstruction of the administrative state", in which there is a national control over the economy with less reliance on international trade deals (Fisher 2017). Nationalist leanings were evident in some of the President's policies which were attempted in his first few days in office promised during his campaign— a travel ban which stopped people from primarily Muslim countries from entering the U.S., and the building of a wall or some type of physical structure to thwart people entering the country illegally from south of the border.

Trump's executive order banning people traveling into the United States from primarily Muslim countries was dubbed a "Muslim ban" by opponents and was viewed by these opponents a proof of nationalism based on ethnocentrism, buttressed by the president's determination to build a wall between the U.S. and Mexico. But while many viewed this nationalistic trend negatively, others saw it as positive—a defense against outsiders who would harm American citizens through physical attacks, the loss of jobs, and the general erosion of American ideals and values. Both measures have been highly controversial, sparking strong sentiments and protests on both sides of the issue.

FIGURE 3.3
London, UK. 4th February 2017. Editorial – Stop Trump's Muslim Ban rally – Thousands march through central London, in protest of President Donald Trump's Muslim ban and his state visit to the UK.

Source: John Gomez/Shutterstock.com

The trend in U.S. politics toward nationalism is not exclusive in the world. The departure of Great Britain from the European Union (E.U.) in 2016 was the result of several factors including the "free movement" of people in the member nations and concerns over immigration (Bukhari, Bukhari, and Roofi 2016). This action was given the portmanteau Brexit (for "British Exit"). At this writing, other countries in Europe are currently debating their own "exit" from the E.U.—in part due to fears of immigrants who might be terrorists themselves and commit atrocities on the host country's soil. France, however, opted to elect moderate, pro-E.U. candidate Emmanuel Macron over nationalist Marine Le Pen in 2017.

Globalism could be considered antithetical to nationalism in the sense that in a globalist society, things such as national boundaries, cultural beliefs, and practices begin to meld into one. As Teeple (2000) notes, as aspects of culture begin to become commodified, "all that comprises national identities is increasingly a caricature of previously meaningful historical phenomena" (p. 21). Although individualism might be considered a prized national characteristic (especially involving economic concerns) which values independence, the world has become a complex, interconnected system in which a change in one part affects the others (Elfstrom 1997). Globalism will be examined in more detail in chapter 15.

Government and Political Corruption

Though it comes in many forms, corruption in government is normally thought to consist primarily of bribes and pay-offs by governmental officials. The Watergate scandal of 1974 became the quintessential image of political corruption; this scandal involved the botched burglary of the Democratic national campaign office at Washington D.C.'s Watergate Hotel which led to the eventual resignation of the holder of the country's highest office, President Richard M. Nixon. Many other scandals have plagued American politics at all levels. The types of corruption are varied and the Federal Bureau of Investigation (FBI)'s public corruption force is tasked with investigating these crimes at the federal level. These types of corruption include border control violations, election crimes, prison corruption, international corruption, antitrust violations, and kleptocracy, which refers to political corruption in which governmental leaders benefit illegally financially from citizens (FBI 2016).

Due to a series of leaks coming from the Federal government, the use of the term "deep state" has appeared on the American political landscape in 2017. The term was once used to refer to shadow governments operating within official governments in countries such as Egypt, Turkey, and Pakistan. In the current context, it refers to the conflict that appeared to exist between the administration of newly elected resident President Trump and the various components to the Federal government. The actions prompted the President to condemn those exposing confidential information; the condemnations were particularly severe toward the intelligence community and a tense relationship developed between the administration and this group. The leaks involved not only policy details, such as drafts of executive orders, but information on conversations between the administration and Russian government, amidst accusations that the Russians were potentially involved in hacking activity during the 2016 Presidential elections. The effect was substantial in that newly appointed national security advisor Michael T. Flynn was forced to resign his office due to discovered conversations he held with a Russian ambassador to the United States (Taub and Fisher 2017).

Two Congressional committees were formed to investigate any connections between the Trump administration and the Russian government, one in the House of Representatives and one from the Senate. When President Trump fired FBI director James Comey, whose agency was investigating possible collusion, a special counsel was employed to investigate the matter from a non-partisan perspective. Headed by former FBI director Robert Mueller, the special commission indicted two members of the Trump election committee, Paul Manafort and Robert Gates, for conspiracy, money laundering, and other charges in relation to inappropriate relationships with foreign nations. National security advisor Michael Flynn, who had also been involved in the campaign, and George Papadopoulos, foreign policy advisor for the campaign, both pleaded guilty to lying to the FBI. News reports surfaced in January 2018 of President Trump attempting to remove special counsel Mueller, prompting conflicts between Democrats and Republicans. During this period, there were continued claims of inaccurate news reporting and implications that the FBI was involved in a conspiracy to undermine the President. Supporters of the President believed that the press and the intelligence communities were working against the administration while opponents believed there was an attack by the President on the free press and the intelligence community.

During this period, the role of the media came into the political discussion. While a contentious relationship has often existed between the White House and the press, conflict arose when the media were accused by Trump as depicting him in a negative light and for providing "fake news". The administration went as far as to call the media an "enemy of the people". Another interesting development was the use of the term "alternative facts" by the President's counselor further contributing to the idea that the media misreported factual data, relying instead on sensational headlines from undisclosed sources.

Should the media be penalized by the government for reporting false information as news?

Pro: The media being held criminally liable for false information will deter such misinformation.
Con: Making the media criminally liable will result in a slow response time for obtaining true information.

THEORETICAL PERSPECTIVES

Structural Functionalism

The social institution of the government exists to provide order to an otherwise potentially unruly and ungovernable group of people, if given to their own wishes and ideas of freedom. Government exists to keep citizens safe and secure but there should be a significant amount of order in which to function. The other social institutions—religion, family, the economy, and education—also help to make government more orderly (if they themselves are functioning properly); and the government, if effective, helps them function properly as institutions.

British social philosopher Herbert Spencer saw the role of government as existing primarily for the administration of justice so all its citizens would be able to pursue individual freedom and happiness. Spencer's functionalist view was in keeping with two dominant themes of his work: individualism and social evolution (Wiltshire 1978). Spencer was an original adherent to social Darwinism, coining the term "survival of the fittest", and believed society must have a government that basically stays out of people's lives as much as possible (a laissez-faire arrangement).

The work of Emile Durkheim focused less on political sociology than the other two founding figures, Karl Marx and Max Weber (as we will see), but there is certainly a strong element of the political in his work (Llobera 2002). Durkheim, in fact, envisioned the government as less of a social institution and more as a part of the larger whole—society itself (Lacroix 1981). Like Spencer, Durkheim's approach is evolutionary, seeing societies as evolving from those with mechanical solidarity (cohesion based on sameness) to those with organic solidarity (cohesion based on diversity) (Llobera 2002). Durkheim perceived of anomie, a breakdown of the normative structure resulting in chaos, as something that can be corrected through an enhanced division of labor, which increases the moral order through social solidarity (Durkheim [1897] 2002). Durkheim wrote and lectured on political forms—including socialism and communism—as these were areas of growing interest during his era. However, the conservative strains in his work and his interest in purely scientific evaluation suggests he was interested in these forms as ideas and not functioning alternatives to governments with capitalist economies (Nisbet 1974).

Conflict

If anyone is unable to see the conflict that exists between the political parties, governmental agencies, and other groups associated with the entity known as "the state", they are not looking diligently. As people and groups vie for power, the conflict can become extreme. Conflict theorists observe how these groups compete for power and how people under the state's control must also compete for the betterment of their lives.

The figure most associated with political economy is Karl Marx (Marx and Engels [1848] 2001) who provided us with a well-developed framework with which to understand power relations as they converge with economic inequality. Throughout the history of capitalism, the economic situation has created a division of labor in which certain people, the owners of the means of production (or bourgeoisie), have control over the workers (the proletariat). Economic control also equates to political control as the bourgeoisie create a system (called the dominant ideology) which promotes a society in which the "haves" continue to have and the "have-nots" must continue to struggle for valued resources and, ultimately, political power.

Max Weber is also a key figure in political sociology who has produced many ideas on the role of government in society. Weber ([1947] 1964) saw modern society as evolving with increasing complexity and where informal organizations are progressively being replaced by formal ones, called bureaucracies. While bureaucracies exist to provide an increasingly specialized and efficient society through a process called *rationalization*, it also creates a highly impersonal and disenchanted world, complete with feelings of powerlessness—Weber used the metaphor of *iron cage* to describe this powerlessness. Weber provided us with a greater understanding of the concept of authority—power that has been legitimated and that is seen by the citizenry as appropriately possessed or deserved by the person holding power. Weber identified three types of authority: *traditional*—authority that has been passed down as a matter of convention or tradition, such as the power possessed by kings/queens, tribal leaders, or others granted authority through custom; *rational-legal*—authority that is decreed by a governmental or legal system and that has as its focus the office that maintains the power rather than a specific person, such as the U.S. Presidency; and *charismatic*—authority that comes from personal characteristics (you can see the work *charm* in the term) that a leader possesses.

Symbolic Interactionism

Since the political institution, similarly to the economic institution, is a macro level establishment, it seems somewhat difficult to explore it at a micro level. However, certain sociologists have increased our understanding of the topic at the social psychological level. An understanding of phenomena such as selfhood, political socialization, conformity to dangerous ideologies, and impression management have provided insight into the relationship between individual and government. In addition, this perspective notes the role of symbols such as the national flag or the "I voted" stickers; symbolic gestures such as standing for the national anthem, or soldiers of different rank saluting each other; and the way people are socialized into their culture based on these symbols and gestures.

Should the burning of the American flag in peaceful protest be made illegal?

Pro: Flag burning is a strong representation of anti-patriotism and could contribute to greater national instability.
Con: The American flag represents freedom and liberty and burning is a very visible representation of these basic American values.

George Herbert Mead (1956) posited that a person's sense of self is generated from the responses of others. Extending this idea of a sociological self, Dawson and Prewitt (1969) contend that we also have a political self, which occurs as a person adopts the ideals of a group in which she is engaged. This produces a basic understanding of political processes; feelings of nationalism, patriotism, or other loyalties; and a self-image that reflects the political position that she adopts. This political selfhood grows and changes though the lifespan. And certainly, people possess varying levels of this type of selfhood—from being apolitical to being highly politically engaged. Jaros (1973) notes attempts to indoctrinate young people to a particular political philosophy have occurred since early history, from Plato's *Republic*, Rousseau's *Social Contract*, More's *Utopia*, and the writings of Confucius. Other, more nefarious, forms of indoctrination that promoted nationalistic pride, as that which was used in Nazi Germany, serves as a reminder of the potential effects of political indoctrination.

Although the Frankfurt School of Critical Theory is primarily associated with conflict sociology, some members of this group sought to understand how the role of government could be used to promote an injurious ideology such as fascism. In the preface of *The Authoritarian Personality* (1950), Frankfurt School Director Max Horkheimer claimed the work is an investigation of "social discrimination" and the use of an "anthropological species called the authoritarian type of man" (p. ix). Adorno and his colleagues (1950), who published the study, sought to identify if there is a certain personality type that can identify if some people are more susceptible to mass conformity such as that required for Nazism. A flawed study on many levels (Martin 2001), it is still an important social psychological work in that it attempted to locate the roots of dangerous national social movements in the individual—producing an early form of behavioral profile.

SEARCHING FOR SOLUTIONS

Solutions to the problems and challenges we have in the government and our political system are complex since national level administration-driven changes depend in large part on the presidential administrations' political parties and what is perceived as a solution for one party, is not generally viewed as a solution by the other party. For example, Republicans may view less regulation and lower taxes for the wealthy as a positive change, while Democrats would view these changes as socially irresponsible and not in the best interest of most people. In other words, we have a complex system of checks and balances that make it very difficult for change to occur unless it is sparked by special interest groups or the interests of the political party in power. However, there are ways that you can get involved in social change on the individual level within your community or even to work toward state or national change. The United States does not have a perfect political system by any stretch of the imagination, but we do live in a democracy and individuals can work toward affecting social change through many different avenues including social media campaigns, grassroots advocacy groups, community-based groups, and through the state representatives who do have a great deal of power in Congress to affect large scale change.

The solution to any political issue starts with believing you can affect social change. The most basic way to make your voice count in a democracy is to vote in local, state, and national elections. Unfortunately, millions of people who are eligible to vote choose not to vote and millions are not even registered to vote. This is paradoxical in that most individuals are interested in politics and political topics. However, registration to vote is required in the U.S. and this takes some amount of effort as well as transportation and filling out paperwork. In many countries if you are a citizen you are automatically registered to vote. Our current system requires time, agency, and resources. Researchers estimate that at least 51 million eligible U.S. citizens are unregistered, more than 24% of the eligible population (Pew Research Center, 2012). Voter registration in the U.S. is a tedious process in part because Americans tend to move often and that involves changing your registration to vote in local political elections. Registering to vote must be conducted in person in the U.S. and any change in address, name, or party affiliation must also be made in person.

An area where individuals can make a difference is volunteering with voter advocacy groups and going into neighborhoods with low voter turnout to register individuals there to vote. These are often low income areas where many people do not have cars, who work multiple jobs, and do not have time to figure out how to register to vote. By going to these neighborhoods voter registration can be increased and once registered, there is one less barrier to voting. In addition, voting advocacy groups need volunteers to work on campaigns to improve voter turnout. For example, *Rock The Vote* is the largest nonprofit in the U.S. devoted to increasing the young adult vote by simplifying and demystifying voter registration and elections. They offer internships and volunteer opportunities for pro-voting activists.

Source: Hill Street Studios/Getty Images

FIGURE 3.4
Individuals wait in long lines at voting polls – this is just one barrier to voting for individuals with time constraints..

Federal government-based programs aimed at increasing voting include extending early voting to avoid the long lines on election day and absentee voting for folks who have not changed their voting registration after moving. However, after the 2012 election, many states introduced measures to make it harder to vote for minorities and low income voters. At least 14 states created restrictive voting laws including photo ID mandates, less time for early voting, creating constraints for the working poor who may not be able to vote on election day, and made it more difficult to regain voting rights for individuals with past criminal convictions.

Some cities removed voting precincts from areas that were mainly Latino or African American, eliminated same day registration for voting, and/or refused to allow voters to vote outside their home precinct. These discriminatory practices by conservative states reduce the success of efforts by the federal government to increase voting beyond the 36% of eligible voters who vote in the United States (Brennan Center 2017). Stricter voting laws have been passed to block the vote of African Americans, and more recently Hispanic Americans. These laws are passed under the guise of eliminating voting fraud.

Should there be a national holiday for voting?

Pro: A voting holiday would allow many people who work daily to vote, making the system more democratic.

Con: A voting holiday is not feasible as some people will have to work on that day anyway and it would put a hardship on businesses and government.

You may wonder how you can possibly combat these kinds of strategies to suppress voting on the state level. Individual opportunities include, volunteering in voter advocacy groups focused on eliminating voter suppression and actively working to get more folks registered to vote and to the polls on election day. Every person you empower to believe their vote counts or assist in getting registered to vote is a small victory. Large scale change is started by folks in a community who are willing to work toward a new vision. There are many elderly people who need to mail in ballots but do not receive their ballot in the mail because of a move; there are also folks who need transportation on election day or to register to vote. Lack of information on candidates, election day procedures, and how to vote, are all barriers to voting. Minorities and immigrants may feel intimidated by the voting process and marginalized to the point they don't believe their votes make a difference. Grassroots organizations of individual volunteers working in their community to increase voter registration and assisting in getting underrepresented populations to vote is the best way to address this problem, especially as many states continue to make it harder for these populations to vote.

For example, of the estimated 803 million Latinos who turn 18 each year, very few show up at the polls to vote. It is estimated that 11.9% of all eligible voters are Latino, and this number will continue to rise for the second fastest growing group in the United States (Pew Research Center 2016). Young Latino adults along with immigrant Hispanics who become citizens are the main source of the eligible Hispanic vote. However, they are one of the least likely groups to vote. An organization that is working to change this is *Voto Latino*, an organization started in 2004 as a PSA project to increase voting among Hispanics (Voto Latino 2017). Since then they have grown quickly with a mission to educate and empower Latinos to vote through digital campaigns, grassroots advocacy, and pop culture. They recruit interns for marketing, development, graphic design, digital media, social media, and field campaigns. Though based in Washington, D.C., they offer volunteer positions across the nation and a strong online presence.

A Movement on the Right

The Tea Party started as a grassroots movement that began to receive national attention in 2007 when supporters held a high profile 24-hour fundraising event. The group came to the forefront shortly after the 2008 election of President Barack Obama. The goals of the movement were to lower taxes and encourage deregulation of the federal government. Once the Obama administration took office the party coalesced and launched protests across the country against President Obama, capitalizing on anti-government sentiment driven by the mortgage and banking bailout (Perrin et al. 2014). It is important to note that this group did not have policy development on their agenda; the focus was on defensive measures against President Obama. Media outlets such as Fox News promoted the movement and it became highly publicized with Fox News hosts often speaking at Tea Party events (Perrin et al. 2014). High profile supporters include presidential candidate Sarah Palin and Fox News hosts Glenn Beck and Sean Hannity, as well as the founder of the Tea Party caucus, Michele Bachmann. The Tea Party movement worked to oppose the Affordable Care Act, federal spending increases and gun control. Most members of the Tea Party movement were registered as Republicans although in elections candidates associated with the Tea Party were generally more conservative than other republicans (Perrin et al. 2011). By 2014 the Tea Party had lost many of its leaders and was investigated by the IRS for tax fraud. Although it no longer hosts public events it is speculated that the movement still operates on a smaller scale, continuing to work toward lowering taxes and decreasing government regulation.

A Movement on the Left

After the election of Donald Trump as U.S. President in 2016, a grassroots movement, inspired by the success of the Tea Party started to oppose the newly elected President using the Tea Party's model. Much like the Tea Party this group is focused on the power of local advocacy tactics and locally-led groups, to resist President Trump's agenda. The group is called the Indivisible Project and it is a self-proclaimed progressive grassroots network dedicated to resisting Trump's agenda by empowering local groups to hold their members of Congress accountable (Indivisible 2017). An entire page of their website is dedicated to the strengths and weaknesses of the Tea Party movement as a model of powerful grassroots advocacy. They use Tea Party strategies to fight the Trump agenda by stalling his priorities, influencing state legislators and members of congress to vote in their interests (against Trump), and objecting publicly to the Trump agenda (Indivisible 2017).

In essence, they are harnessing public anger to promote local groups to mobilize and build the movement. Using social media and offering toolkits for organizing groups on college campuses, the movement targets young adults in particular. With a digital approach, they utilize social media, email, online news alerts, and state legislator websites to build advocacy activities. They appeal to the growing Latino population with all literature available in Spanish and a toolkit for immigrant allies. Indivisible recognizes that some opposition may be semi-confrontational and encourages members

FIGURE 3.5 July 4, 2017 Everett Washington parade. Indivisible Marchers for single payer healthcare.

Source: CL Shebley/Shutterstock.com

to film any intimidating behavior by law enforcement. It is a progressive and modern movement that has garnered a great deal of support and continues to gain momentum. Interested citizens are encouraged to join the local group in their community.

In sum, solutions for creating change in the government and political system start at the individual level and as they garner the support of state legislators they come to the forefront of the national agenda. This is a process however, and often it takes years for national level progress to be enacted through policies and laws. Much like the Civil Rights Movement, people must organize, protest, and make their voices heard to heighten awareness around social problems. Leaders of these movements must be chosen to represent the people behind the scenes so that national attention is directed at righting social injustices and opposing state and national agendas that are not in the best interest of most Americans. If you have the time and resources to work toward the solution from within your own community, then you have a certain amount of privilege that can be used to promote social change for less privileged groups that continue to be marginalized by the political structure of the country they call home.

Should all Americans be required to perform some type of civil service?

Pro: Civil service requirements create greater cohesion, a sense of national pride, and personal accomplishment, not to mention the betterment of communities.

Con: Not everyone is physically able to perform such service and even those that are should not be subjected to governmental mandates.

FIGURE 3.6
Immigration activists, including U.S. Rep. Judy Chu (D-CA) and Rep. Luis Gutierrez (D-IL), stage a protest on the steps of the U.S. Capitol December 6, 2017 in Washington, DC. Activists urged Congress to pass a clean Dream Act and protect Temporary Protected Status (TPS) beneficiaries before the end of the year.

Source: Mark Wilson/Getty Images

CHAPTER SUMMARY

- The government is the social institution that is tasked with protecting citizens and maintaining social order through the use of power and political systems. The American political system is a democracy with three branches of government on the federal level: executive, legislative, and judicial. To qualify as a democracy a political system must at least be perceived as having equality across every dimension, since it is a government run by its own citizens. Political parties are composed of representatives for political ideologies held by the citizens, individuals who represent each party are voted into power on local, state, and federal levels. In America individuals generally choose to align with the political party that most closely represents their political ideology. The major political ideologies can be classified as conservatism, liberalism, libertarianism, and democratic socialism.

- Current trends in American politics include exceptionalism, populism, and nationalism. American exceptionalism and nationalism are based on patriotism, pride, and the idea that American values and ideals are superior to those of other countries. Populism regards the needs and well-being of its citizens as more important than state power. All three of these trends were embodied in the 2016 presidential election.

- Structural functionalism regards government as a way to create order in what would otherwise be a chaotic society. According to this perspective, the government relies on other social institutions including the family, religion, the economy, and education function to assist in creating stability and order in society. Conflict perspective focuses on how political parties compete for power and economic control. According to Max Weber, bureaucracies create rationalization that makes society very impersonal and creates a feeling of powerlessness, an iron cage, for those without privilege or power, who end up feeling they have little control over their lives. Symbolic interactionism is a micro-level perspective that focuses more on how individuals adopt the ideology of the group they engage in, and the relationship between the individual and government; only symbolic interactionism looks at the importance of symbols and traditions and how they bring people together to unite around common values and ideals that embody what it means to be an American.

- Voting rights have become an important topic once again as many states have mandated policies that make it difficult for marginalized populations to register and vote. Voter advocacy groups promote social change in this area through social media campaigns, volunteers to assist in registering eligible voters, and heightening awareness about the importance of voting. Minorities, in particular, are underrepresented at the polls, partly because of restive voting laws and a lack of information about elections and how to vote in their community.

- Movements such as the Tea Party and Indivisible have been created to oppose the agenda of presidential administrations. The Tea Party is a conservative movement that worked to oppose President Obama's agenda and Indivisible is a left leaning movement to oppose the agenda of President Trump. These movements are important to understand as they reflect widespread public distrust of the government, which has grown steadily since the Great Recession that started in 2008. They also bring to the forefront the lack of transparency in presidential administrations and empower the American people to become more engaged and active in politics.

REFERENCES

Adorno, Theodor W., Else Frenkel-Brunswik, Daniel L. Levinson, and R. Nevitt Sanford. 1950. *The Authoritarian Personality*. New York: Harper and Brothers.

Bonikowski, Bart and Paul DiMaggio. 2016. "Varieties of American Popular Nationalism." *American Sociological Review*. 81 (5): 949–980. Retrieved March 10, 2016 (http://asr.sagepub.com) doi: 10.1177/00031222416663684.

Brennan Center. 2017. Voter Advocacy. Retrieved May 5, 2017 (www.brennancenter.org/advocacy).

Brennen, Teresa and Richard Feldstein. 1997. *Political Correctness: A Response from the Cultural Left*. Minneapolis, MN: University of Minnesota Press.

Bronner, Stephen E. 1999. *Ideas in Action: Political Tradition in the Twentieth Century*. Lanham, MA: Rowman and Littlefield.

Bukhari, Shahid H., Mussawar H. Bukhari, and Yasmin Roofi. 2016. "Brexit: A Challenge for United Kingdom and European Union." *Pakistan Journal of Social Sciences*, 36(2): 665–674. (Retrieved from www.bzu.edu.pk/PJSS/Vol36No22016/PJSS-Vol36-No2-6.pdf.)

Dahl, Robert A. 1998. *On Democracy*. New Haven, CT: Yale University Press.

Dahl, Robert A. 1963. *Who Governs? Democracy and Power in an American City*. New Haven: Yale University Press.

Dawson, Philip. 1967. "Introduction". Pp. 1–3 in *The French Revolution*, edited by P. Dawson. Englewood Cliffs, NJ: Prentice-Hall.

Dawson, Richard E. and Kenneth Prewitt. 1969. *Political Socialization*. Boston: Little, Brown, and Company.

Deutsch, Karl W. 1966. *Nationalism and Social Communication: An Inquiry into the Foundations of Nationalism*, 2nd ed. Cambridge: Massachusetts Institute of Technology Press.

Durkheim, Emile. [1897] 2002. *Suicide*. Kenneth Thompson. Routledge: London, New York.

Elfstrom, Gerard. 1997. *New Challenges for Political Philosophy*. Houndmills, Basingstoke, Hampshire, UK: Macmillan Press.

Federal Bureau of Investigation. 2016. *What We Investigate: Public Corruption*. Retrieved March 10, 2017 (www.fbi.gov/investigate/public-corruption).

Fisher, Max. 2017. "Bannon's Vision for a 'Deconstruction of the Administrative State'." *New York Times*, February 25, 2017. Retrieved March 10, 2017 from (https://research.flagler.edu:2048/login?url=http://link.galegroup.com/apps/doc/A482573 318/BIC1?u=st36940&xid=cfbe16d8).

Hall, John A. 1995. "Nationalisms, Classified, and Explained." Pp. 8–33 in *Notions of Nationalism*, edited by S. Periwal. Budapest: Central European University Press.

Hastings, Adrian. 2000. "The Nation and Nationalism." Pp. 506–537 in *Nationalism: Critical Concepts in Political Science*, edited by J. Hutchinson and A.D. Smith. London and New York: Routledge.

Horkheimer, Max. 1950. "Preface." Pp. ix–xii in *The Authoritarian Personality,* Adorno, Theodor W., Else Frenkel-Brunswik, Daniel L. Levinson, and R. Nevitt Sanford. New York: Harper and Brothers.

Indivisible. 2017. Retrieved May 6, 2017 (www.indivisible.com).

Jaros, Dean. 1973. *Socialization to Politics.* New York: Praeger Publishers.

Kivisto, Peter. 1998. *Key Ideas in Sociology.* Thousand Oaks, CA: Sage.

Lacroix, Bernard. 1981. *Durkheim et la Politique.* Montréal: Presses de l'Université de Montréal.

Llobera, Joseph R. 2002. "Political Sociology." Pp. 69–79 in *Durkheim Today,* edited by W.S.F. Pinkering. New York: Berghahn Books.

Mann, Michael. 1995. "A Political Theory of Nationalism and Its Excesses." Pp. 44–64 in S. Periwal, Ed. *Notions of Nationalism.* Budapest: Central European University Press.

Martin, John Levi. 2001. "The Authoritarian Personality 50 Years Later: What Lessons are There for Political Psychology." *Political Psychology.* 22(1): 1–26. Retrieved March 10, 2017 (www.jstor.org/ stable/3791902).

Marx, Karl and Frederick Engels. 2001 [1848]. *The Communist Manifesto.* New York: International Publishers.

Mead, George H. 1956. *The Social Psychology of George Herbert Mead,* edited and translated by Anselm Strauss. Chicago: The University of Chicago Press.

Minogue, K.R. 1967. *Nationalism.* New York: Basic Books.

Nisbet, Robert. 1974. *The Sociology of Emile Durkheim.* New York: Oxford University Press.

Pew Hispanic Center. 2016. Hispanic Voter Statistics. Retrieved May 6, 2017 (www.pewhispanic. org/2016/01/19/millennials-make-up-almost-half-of-latino-eligible-voters-in-2016).

Pew Research Center. 2012. Hispanic Voter Registration Statistics and Trends. Retrieved May 6, 2017 (www.pewtrusts.org /2012/pewupgradingvoterregistration.pdf).

Perrin, Andrew J., Stephen J. Tepper, Neal Caren, and Sally Morris. 2011. "Cultures of the Tea Party." *Contexts, 10*(2): 74–75.

Perrin, Andrew J., Stephen J. Tepper, Neal Caren, and Sally Morris. 2014. "Political and Cultural Dimensions of Tea Party Support, 2009–2012." *The Sociological Quarterly, 55*(4), 625–652.

Rock The Vote. 2017. Retrieved May 6, 2017 (www.rockthevote.com/get informed/elections).

Taub, Amanda and Max Fisher. 2017. "As Leaks Multiply, Fears of a 'Deep State' in America." *New York Times.* February 16. Retrieved March 10, 2017.

Teeple, Gary. 2000. *Globalization and the Decline of Social Reform: Into the Twenty-first Century,* 2nd ed. Aurora, ON, Canada: Garamond Books.

Tocqueville, Alexis de. 2000 [1835–1840]. *Democracy in America.* New York: Perennial Classics.

Tomes, Robert R. 2014. "American Exceptionalism in the Twenty-first Century." *Survival.* 56 (1): 27–50. Retrieved March 5, 2017. doi: 10.1080/00396338.2014.882150.

Voto Latino. 2017. Retrieved May 6, 2017 (http://votolatino.org/initiative).

Weber, Max. [1947] 1964. *The Theory of Social and Economic Organization*. New York: Free Press of Glencoe.

Wiltshire, David. 1978. *The Social and Political Thought of Herbert Spencer*. Oxford: Oxford University Press.

Youngdale, James M. 1975. *Populism: A Psycho-historical Perspective*. Port Washington, New York: Kennikat Press.

Zeitlin, Irving M. 1990. *Ideology and the Development of Sociological Theory*, 4th ed. Englewood Cliffs, NJ: Prentice-Hall.

CHAPTER 4

The Educational System

ABOUT THE PROBLEM: THE EDUCATIONAL SYSTEM

Educational System the social institution that promotes the transfer of knowledge from instructors to students.

Pedagogy the area of study that is concerned with the theoretical and practical application of the profession of education.

The **educational system** refers to the social institution that promotes the transfer of knowledge from instructors to students; this system is comprised of many institutional types with varying degrees of bureaucratic complexity from homeschooling to advanced graduate and professional study. A related term, **pedagogy** (the "guidance of children"), refers to the area of study that is concerned with the theoretical and practical application of the teaching profession. The importance of education is understood by most Americans as a vehicle for better job opportunities and for personal growth but strategies to accomplish this end vary greatly.

The sociology of education is the subfield of sociology that focuses directly on this social institution. The early sociological study of education can be found in the work of Durkheim and Weber (Hallinan 2000). Social thinkers before these founders such as Herbert Spencer offered theoretical analyses of education, but more sophisticated examinations came later. It could be stated that more than one sociology of education exists as there are many theoretical orientations, research curricula, and general areas of interest in the field of education itself (Lynch 2000). The sociological perspective is valuable in that it considers many factors of social life including race, ethnicity, gender, class, sexual orientation, institutional functionality, power, social psychology, and social justice, among others.

AMERICAN PRIMARY AND SECONDARY EDUCATION

Traditional Public Education

America's **primary and secondary education** system includes the schooling received from kindergarten through the twelfth grade (often referred to as "K through Twelve"). Some are public schools, which are governed by a local school board and others are private and provided education for a fee and might be religious-based, secular, or have a specialty area. Newer initiatives such as charter and magnet schools have presented themselves as alternatives to traditional methods of schooling. Homeschooling, a reversal to the past, has also seen a revival.

> **Primary and Secondary Education** the schooling, public or private, received from kindergarten through the twelfth grade.

While elementary schools are relatively small and local neighborhood-oriented schools providing undifferentiated education programs in a close-knit supportive environment, secondary schools—especially public high schools—bring together a more diverse body of students from different neighborhoods. Most people did not attend high schools in the United States before the twentieth century and when these schools began, primarily in the urbanizing areas, they offered a curriculum with a diversified set of alternative courses and course areas (Lee 2000).

American primary schools are operated and are provided oversight by a state or other public entity, are located in urban, suburban, and rural areas, and are normally not-for-profit (with some recent exceptions). Private schools are maintained by a non-governmental entity and come in a wide variety of types: religious (with different denominations) nonsectarian, selective, for-profit and nonprofit, with overlapping characteristics. There are different outcomes for public and private schools but there are also many factors which do not allow for definitive findings on one type's superiority (Percell 2000).

> **School Choice** the idea that parents and guardians of children should have choices in the type and location of schools attended by their children.

Alternatives to Public Education—School Choice

School choice has been a major point of discussion in America and alternatives to traditional public and private schools have appeared on the scene over the past few decades. **Magnet schools** were conceived to better racially diversify the student body, to raise the quality of education in certain areas, and to offer a wide range of educational or technical specialty curricula or teaching methodology to students with interests and aptitudes (Goldring and Smrekar 2004). These schools were legislated in 1984 and there are currently less than 3,000 of them in the nation, representing only 3% of public schools. These schools are of two types: traditional magnet schools and destination magnet schools. Traditional magnet schools are often converted from schools in low income areas and target higher performing students from more advantaged neighborhoods. Destination magnet schools begin in higher income areas but attract racial/ethnic minority students from other neighborhoods (Kitmitto et al. 2016).

> **Magnet Schools** traditional magnet schools are often converted from schools in low income areas and target higher performing students from more advantaged neighborhoods. Destination magnet schools begin in higher income areas but attract racial/ethnic minority students from other neighborhoods.

Another alternative is the **charter school** system, which started in Minnesota in 1994 and which grew in enrollment from a few dozen students to over three million, located in approximately 7,000 schools across the nation. Charter schools are a community effort, and rather than being governed by a school board, are governed by local community leaders. Despite a cumbersome application process, these schools have less regulation and oversight than traditional public schools. Because of the demand and lack of available slots, competition is stiff and lotteries are often used to determine which applicants are selected. While charter schools were conceived as laboratories for progressive education, they are now more likely to be seen as alternatives to public education.

> **Charter Schools** schools that are governed by local community leaders and have less regulations and oversight than traditional public schools.

While they allow more autonomy, minority students are underrepresented in these schools and they are subject to suddenly close (Chabrier, Cohodes, and Oreopoulos 2015).

Homeschooling has been another alternative to traditional schools and it is currently the most prominent form of education reform; it has been growing at a remarkable rate—from 10,000–15,000 children in the 1970s, increasing to around two million by 2010, and these are conservative figures. Though research findings are varied on this issue, the growth of this type of schooling says much about cultural issues of choice, the relationship between religious beliefs and education, and the role of conservative political ideology (Murphy 2014).

> **Homeschooling**
> alternative to traditional schools and it is currently the most pronounced form of education reform.

Is homeschooling an effective alternative to classroom schooling?

Pro: Homeschooling provides greater liberty as it involves the family directly in the education of the child.
Con: Traditional schooling involves social interaction and these skills are important in making a well-rounded citizen.

Famed education scholar John Dewey (1959) sees the process of education as possessing two components—the psychological, in which students rely on their own initiatives to learn various aspects that exist in their experiences and observations, and the sociological, in which it is up to trained educators to help students translate these experiences and observations into social understandings of the world, with the past as a guide and the future as an imagined outcome. The educator, then, is an important part of this process by seeing in the "child's babblings the promise and potency of a future social intercourse and conversation which enables one to deal in the proper way with that instinct" (Dewey 1959:21). In other words, teachers are important.

Perhaps education can be extended into learning that helps young people develop a greater connection to politics and government. Chomsky (2000) notes that the best way to tell how well a democracy functions is observe it in practice; schools, however, do it poorly—there is a wide gap between educational theory and education practice. Chomsky (2000) posits that rote memorization rituals that attempt to inculcate patriotism are ineffective; allowing students to participate in and experience democracy in action is a more effective strategy. His comments reflect an important question currently being discussed: should the voting age be lowered to include younger citizens and, if so, what should this age be?

Should the voting age be lowered to age 16 to produce better citizens?

Pro: Lowering the voting age to 16 would promote more engagement in our democracy.
Con: Many students at age 16 lack the maturity, knowledge, or interest enough to vote in important elections.

Current Issues in Primary and Secondary Education

In his insightful work, *Life in Classrooms*, Jackson (1968) brilliantly analyses the educational system, at least from the vantage point of the late 1960s, a time when many traditions were being viewed critically. Jackson describes not only the official curriculum of education—the teaching and learning of specific subjects, but also a **hidden curriculum** in which institutional conformity, reflecting the norms of society, play an important role in determining what students are taught and what they learn. Jackson critically notes that "intellectual mastery calls for the sublimated forms of aggression rather than for submission to constraints" (Jackson 1968:36). The hidden curriculum can be positive as it reinforces standards of the community and society but negative if those standards are harmful.

> **Hidden Curriculum** the unseen practices that reflect the norms of society, play an important role in determining what students are taught and what they learn.

Schools have long had to deal with the education of students that might be in some way different from others; students who are racial or ethnic minorities, students who are LGBTQ, and children with disabilities often do not have the benefits other students in the educational system have. Current approaches in education involving **inclusion** seek to remedy this situation by diversifying classrooms to accommodate students and thwart discrimination. Inclusive education engenders diversity, multiculturalism, cultural sensitivity, and social justice.

> **Inclusion** diversifying classrooms to accommodate students and thwart discrimination.

Many scholars have noted the existence of a *prison-industrial complex* in which the advent of privately-run incarceration facilities is correlated to an increase of the number of people incarcerated. Elaborating upon this idea, educationists have described a **school-to-prison pipeline** in which recent education policies have helped to create a "pipeline" that removes drop-outs and cast-outs of the school system to the juvenile, and eventually, adult prison systems. Education policies, such as the

> **School-to-Prison Pipeline** policies that support the removal of at-risk, underprivileged, and marginalized children from the school system to the correctional system.

FIGURE 4.1
Alajandra Guizar, 10, helps a classmate during a fourth-grade match class at Ralph Bunche Elementary School in Carson. Students at Bunche are meeting achievement standards set by the No Child Left Behind federal law. Photo taken 11/30/06.

Source: Luis Sinco/Los Angeles Times/Getty Images

No Child Left Behind Act, have created a situation in which strict zero tolerance policies for school infractions, the increased surveillance created by school police (school resource officers, or SROs), and formalized punishments which have, in effect, expunged students from school and into prisons.

Since children who drop out of school are eight times as likely as others to become incarcerated, the result is an institutionalized pathway to prison (Schept, Wall, and Brisman 2015).

Another important topic in education today is *bullying*. While bullying probably began during the first formalized schooling (and before), the issue has garnered much attention over the past several years in both face-to-face (and behind-your-back) bullying as well as the more recent cyberbullying. Bullying can be defined as behavior that is aggressive and unwanted in which there is a real or perceived imbalance of power and cyberbullying is harassment involving the use of technology, such as texting, emailing, and posting on social media sites (U.S. Department of Health and Human Services 2017). Though the potential sources and harms are beyond the scope of this text, some facts and figures help to grasp the problem: almost 18% of school children have been victims of taunting and other forms of harassment, 18% have been the subject of rumors, 8% have been physically victimized, 5% have been purposely excluded from social interaction, 5% have been physically threatened, over 3% were forced to do things against their will, almost 3% have had property damaged, and 9% have been cyberbullied. School bullying reaches its peak in middle school and girls generally experience bullying more than boys. Many laws and interventions have been implemented to combat bullying such as anti-bullying programs of different types; research has provided mixed results but overall the programs have been effective (Seeley et al. 2011)

AMERICAN HIGHER EDUCATION

Higher Education
colleges and universities of various types, different sizes, different missions, etc.; academia.

The American system of **higher education** is comprised of colleges and universities of various types, different sizes, different missions, etc. Community colleges primarily offer two-year degrees (with limited four-year degree options) and often have a mission to offer courses for transfer to a four-year college or university and to offer coursework that is more vocational in nature. Four-year colleges offer baccalaureate (four year) degrees and sometimes a limited number of masters' degrees. Universities often have a research focus and offer baccalaureate, masters, and doctoral degrees. Some colleges and universities are public institutions, others are private, some have a special focus, e.g., historically black colleges and universities (HBCUs); others are religious institutions, technological institutes, or online institutions. Some are liberal arts schools while others focus on technical/occupational training. Some have a research program while others have a teaching focus. As you can see, the American higher education system, like the primary education structure, is complex and varied.

The American university historically had these reasons for existing: to preserve religious beliefs, to advance new religious beliefs, to increase worker skills, to increase the proficiency in the professions, to increase knowledge, and to educate young people (Wolff 1969). The university is an educational institution' thus it has a public role—a role in which it serves the society by producing learned people to fulfil many important social obligations, but it also has a private role—a role which promotes individual growth. As Anderson (1993) notes, education should focus on developing the "thoughtways, those habits of mind, that it can show work well in comprehending the world and deciding what to do with it" (Anderson 1993:59). This ideal is akin to the psychological and sociological components as proposed by Dewey (1959) and represents how these two work in tandem in developing critical thinking in individuals, and at the same time benefitting society.

Institutions of higher education have a rich history involving the direction of training. From the earliest times in educational history, societies have grappled with whether the purpose of education should be oriented toward individual intellectual enrichment and a greater understanding of the world, in other words, a **liberal arts education**, or the acquisition of occupational skills, termed a **vocational education**; this is what Horowitz (1975) describes as the distinction between professionalism and vocationalism, or "head versus hand". In sum, the task of providing the former type falls to liberal arts institutions and the latter falls to vocational, technical, and community colleges, although community colleges also provide academic coursework that normally can be transferred to institutions that grant four-year degrees. American colleges and universities often have specialty areas (such as art or engineering programs); have historical designations (such as HBCUs); can be public, private, for profit, or non-profit; have graduate or professional training, and be teaching or research oriented; fall upon a continuum of status and prestige; as well as a host of other distinctions.

A relatively new form of education is found in online learning. Found in both primary/secondary and higher education, it is most prominent in colleges and universities. Online education, which consists of education administered over the internet or other types of technological media, is becoming an increasingly familiar part of the academic landscape. Course offerings provided in an online format have outpaced those of their traditional counterparts and college administrators have had to adjust to this new type of course provision. Administrators tend to respond favorably to online instruction while faculty members and students are less enthusiastic (Seirup, Tirotta, and Blue 2016). While the distance learning option offers greater access to education than any other format in the past, there is less direct correspondence with professors and other students.

> **Liberal Arts Education** comprehensive educational experience that provides individual intellectual enrichment and a greater understanding of the world.
>
> **Vocational Education** practical educational experience that provides occupational skills that can easily be transformed to the workplace.

Is online education a format that should be increased in colleges and universities?

Pro: Online education provides access to people in remote areas or who otherwise could not receive an education.

Con: Less professor face-to-face interaction and supervision makes online education a less quality product than traditional education.

Current Issues in Higher Education

American higher education has changed much since John Dewey was a dominant force in the field. Many issues have surfaced over the decades since that time. After World War II, students entered the nation's colleges and universities in record numbers and many changes have occurred, some positive, some negative, and some still being debated. One of those changes being debated involves college *tenure*, which has been a major part of academia for some time. The work of professors is often called "the life of the mind", which indicates thinking outside the box is a large part of what college professors' work entails; a concern over being protected to do this task resulted in the granting of tenure, which is basically a guarantee of continued employment if certain tasks and proficiencies are met (teaching, scholarship, and service). Many academics feel that tenure preserves their ability to teach and write without constraints on academic freedom that would stunt the acquisition of knowledge. Opponents note that other fields do not grant this privilege and that the granting of tenure has negative outcomes such as rewarding professors who have "checked out" of their responsibilities.

Is professor tenure beneficial to modern higher education?

Pro: Tenure ensures that academic freedom is maintained in college classrooms and aids in critical thinking.
Con: Tenure makes it difficult to remove ineffective professors, thereby lowering the quality of higher education.

Academic Freedom
the freedom tenure allows for professors to question norms and ensure research is free of outside involvement.

Closely related to tenure is the issue of **academic freedom**, a salient issue in higher education. Since sociology is a discipline that closely analyzes social norms and requires research that is free from outside involvement, the freedom to question these norms is needed for accurate analysis, and can contribute to positive social change. One of American sociology's founding figures, E.A. Ross, lost his position at Stanford University due to suggesting some ideas that some interpreted as social-ist and for disagreeing with the use of cheap immigrant labor. This was at the end of the twentieth century and professor Ross was not even a radical! The boundaries of free speech are fluid, however, as represented by the case of University of Colorado professor Ward Churchill who, shortly after the 9/11 attacks, referred to the survivors of this horrible event as "little Eichmanns" (O'Neil 2008); his dismissal, which received much press, tested the limits of free speech in academia.

One particular freedom of speech issue that has surfaced in the past few years in American education involves the use of trigger warnings. This refers to basically an announcement by the instructor or someone giving a presentation that something is about to be mentioned in class that might negatively affect some students. For example, if a student experienced sexual assault, a discus-sion or reading on this topic might trigger a traumatic response. While proponents of these warnings see them as a thoughtful act—an expression of sympathetic concern for students, opponents see them as creating undue restrictions on the freedom of speech and requiring duties that are outside the job responsibilities of faculty.

Are trigger warnings an appropriate practice in the educational system?

Pro: Trigger warnings prevent students from developing traumatic responses in class.
Con: Trigger warnings prevent freedom of speech and can be used to manipulate instruction.

Campus assaults are a concern in higher education and, while this activity has always taken place on college campuses, there is a renewed interest today. Assaults which are the result of sexual

FIGURE 4.2
EUGENE, OR - APRIL 28, 2016: Sexual Assault Awareness Month demonstration and visual display on the lawn in front of the Lillis Business School on University of Oregon campus.

Source: Joshua Rainey Photography/Shutterstock.com

violations or hate activity are not uncommon on campus. Questions arise as to who should handle these cases—the college administration or the local police authorities—is a persistent issue. Colleges and universities are supposed to be safe places; however, this is often not the case. One issue that is related to school safety involves the recent changes in law that allows students in some states to carry firearms on campus; whether or not this will deter or stop assaults or contribute to the problem is currently a hotly debated topic—on campus and off.

Another issue that has become prominent in the last several years is college loan indebtedness. Though Federal student loans have been around since 1958, and many different government programs have been available to students, access to these loans has dramatically increased. To show the impact of mounting debt on a recent graduate—a $30,000 Stafford loan with a 6.8% interest rate and a 10-year repayment schedule would require the graduate to pay $345.00 per month. Major life changes, such as postponing marriage and a family, might have to be considered to pay off their college debts (Cornelius and Frank 2015).

Is free college a better option than the current tuition system?

Pro: Colleges in the past, and in some countries now, have free college education, requiring no large debt to be repaid.

Con: Taxes must be increased or other funding sources would need to be found in order to offset this massive amount of money.

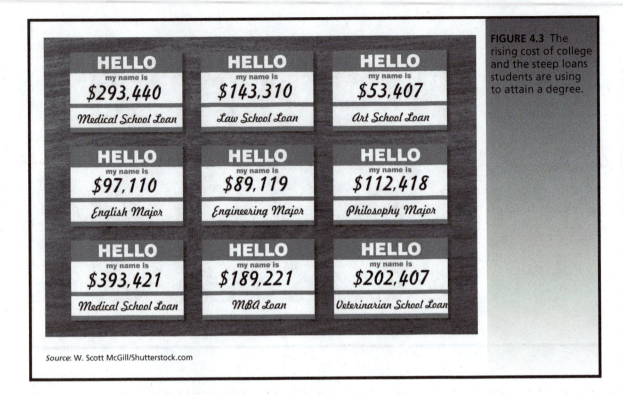

FIGURE 4.3 The rising cost of college and the steep loans students are using to attain a degree.

Source: W. Scott McGill/Shutterstock.com

Food insecurity is a fact of life for many Americans and school students are no exception. Food security exists when people obtain inadequate amounts and types of food for effective functioning. It seems incongruent that people in college experience food insecurity but this is a growing problem among some low-income students, particularly in community colleges. In California, which has the largest community college system in the nation, 12% of students in these schools experience a lack of food. Compounding the problem are the facts that many students also experience inadequate housing needs (some students are even homeless), and the stress that comes from knowing a large college debt awaits them after college (Community College Week 2016).

THEORETICAL PERSPECTIVES

Structural Functionalism

Of all the social institutions—family, education, economy, religion, and government—education is the one most responsible for providing people with social mobility and equal opportunities (Walters 2000). Structural functionalists pay attention to how cohesion and consensus aid in promoting a strong educational system; a social institution is imperative for society to correctly function by appropriately training people in areas that will benefit themselves and others. Functionalists note the close connection between education and the economy, especially education's role in placing the most skilled people in the most skilled occupations and teaching those skills in an increasingly technological world (Walters 2000). An example of this is the current focus on providing STEM (Science, Technology, Engineering, and Math). While structural functionalists tend to believe there is a naturally occurring relationship between the education institution and the job market, many workers presently in the workforce are overqualified for their positions while some occupations are unable to find skilled workers. It has also been noted that the functional model needs outside intervention—ways to make employees and employers connect (Rosenbaum and Jones 2000); as this connection between the education and economic institutions might not be as automatic as some would like to believe.

Parsons (1967) observed the socialization function of education that internalizes the norms that will guide the young in their work and personal lives. This functionalist noted that since the family has its roots in biology, the school is the first non-biological socialization agent. According to Parsons, the educational system will allow the educated to adopt a higher level of status in society, propelling their success as adults. The teacher acts as an agent of the community school board in exercising the task of socialization. Students with high levels of cognitive ability will find a better fit in technologically oriented occupations (although not specified, presumably Parsons was referring to professional jobs in science, medicine, and business among others), while those with high levels of ethical development will fit into jobs requiring "people skills" (apparently jobs in education, social work, and counseling, among others). As students progress through the educational process, their exposure to new people and ideas grows, advancing new understandings of relationships and status. It also creates peer bonds in a stratification process that results in diverse reference groupings. Parsons also saw a gender socialization effect in education as women prepare for their future positions as wives and mothers; he was not against educated women, but he saw their role in passing down the importance of education to the children.

Clark Kerr, a progressive social scientist and educational scholar who was president of the University of California during the turbulent campus protests of the 1960s, is considered here due to his ideas on the functions of education. Kerr (1964) envisioned the ideal modern university as a "multiversity", a community of the many groups that are incorporated into the system of higher education (undergraduate schools, graduate schools, professional schools, the professoriate, administration, and the outside community, among others). As a testament to his academic training in economics, he is famous for his belief that higher education should be responsible for "the production, distribution, and consumption of knowledge" (Kerr 1964:88) for the greater society, in effect connecting the multiversity with other social institutions in a functionalist framework. The theoretical perspective is democratic pluralism, analogized with political theory, and not without its detractors (Wolff 1969).

Conflict

Not all forms of education are equal and the same opportunities do not exist for all students. Education, then, can help perpetuate forms of inequality to new generations. Critically examining the role of government in society has been a primary focus of conflict theorists. As those in power grapple with policy issues about how to make education better, conflict/critical theorists will continue to examine policy and make their voices heard. Reflecting this approach, Jackson (1968) notes "from kindergarten onward, the student begins to learn what life is really like in The Company" (Jackson 1968:36).

W.E.B. Du Bois, in his seminal work *Souls of Black Folk*, gives voice to the issues of inequality in education based on race. He is well remembered in his philosophical debate with another prominent African American thinker, Booker T. Washington. Washington's stance is that black people should pursue vocational forms of training and not antagonize the white power structure. Du Bois' position was the opposite—blacks should pursue academic training, despite white resistance. To Du Bois, African Americans have a duty "stern and delicate" (Du Bois [1903] 1995: 94) to work toward racial equality without submitting to continued conformity to appease the more powerful whites. He would modify this position in later years, promoting a curriculum that included both classical academic training and vocational training for black children. In higher education, Du Bois preferred a separate black college and university system, as it was felt that African Americans would be excluded from full educational attainment in co-racial colleges. His college curriculum has a Marxist understanding of labor and alienation and one that emphasizes black identity, which would later appear in black studies courses in the 1960s (Alridge 2008).

Another key social theorist whose work extended into the field of education, Michel Foucault, was concerned with how power is broadcast throughout society in social institutions such as prisons, mental institutions, and, of course, schools. Foucault believes that to understand any social institution, one must understand how its history developed and how power and control manipulates that institution. Knowledge, the product of education, is directly connected to power to the extent that Foucault used the combined terminology "power/knowledge". The discourses that shape the current educational curriculum to produce knowledge are an effort to exert power and control over not only the student but also to society generally. Foucault, in his desire to find the historical antecedents to the modern educational system, observed the early Paris military schools as a system of hierarchies and surveillance techniques to control students. Educational exams, according to Foucault (and many, many students), are an especially controlling mechanism—they are a ceremonial means of qualifying, stratifying, classifying, judging, and punishing students (Foucault 1977).

One of the most prominent current education theorists is Henry Giroux, who adopts a "critical pedagogy", owing a debt to the Frankfurt School critical theorists and radical educationist Paulo Freire, whose *Pedagogy of the Oppressed* (1970) is a classic work in the education field. Giroux (2012) sees education as linked to the inequalities that exist in society and sees primary public education controlled by elitists who insist on enforcing conformity, rote learning, and "high stakes test taking" and describes these schools as "intellectual dead zones and punishment centers as far removed from teaching civic values and explaining the imaginations of students as one can imagine" (Giroux 2012:117). He also sees charter schools as a money driven "hostile takeover of public education" and claims public higher education is similarly corrupt, focusing less on enriching liberal arts education and more on training students to compete with China and other Asian nations. According to Giroux (2012), society is currently turning education's role from a public good to a private one.

Symbolic Interactionism

Rather than seeing the educational institution as a macro level institution, interactionists observe the micro level dealings that exist in the school systems. Schools do not just help increase academic knowledge, they also contribute to the development of a social identity. Schools, especially primary and secondary schools, comprise different groups—academic students, athletes, members of various

FIGURE 4.4 Parents, schoolchildren and education activists rally during an event supporting public charter schools and protesting New York's racial achievement gap in education, in Prospect Park, September 28, 2016 in the Brooklyn borough of New York City. The #PathToPossible rally and march, organized by the Families for Excellent Schools, is calling for New York City to double its public charter school sector to 200,000 students by 2020. An estimated 25,000 people attended the rally.

Source: Drew Angerer/Getty Images

fringe groups, and a host of others. These groups constitute reference groups who help formulate ideas of selfhood in young people.

Sociologist James Coleman was a theorist who was interested in the norms that shape social activity and social status in the various educational systems. He is perhaps best known for a study he conducted on the relationship between education and race as it related to the recently passed Civil Rights Act of 1964. In his study he found, among other things, that minority students benefitted from attending white schools and, though white students did not experience such benefits from co-racial education, they did not exhibit a decline in school performance. This study, known mostly by the Coleman Report, was met with much criticism in a racially charged era (Schneider 2000; Applerouth and Edles 2011). Coleman's interest in schools as social systems was overshadowed by the fact that this study was a policy study rather than an academic one (Schneider 2000). This report resulted in the increased use of busing in the recently integrated school systems; in 1975 Coleman reversed his position on busing and this new position was met with great consternation within the discipline of sociology (Applerouth and Edles 2011). The report, despite its controversy is a good illustration of how theory and application work together and can influence policy issues.

Another example of a study with education policy implications (in this case social, as opposed to political) on an interactionist level is the famous study by Robert Rosenthal and Lenore Jacobson which resulted in a book entitled *Pygmalion in the Classroom* (1992). The researchers sought to see if increased teacher interaction with students was positively correlated with intellectual academic competence (sometimes referred to as expectancy theory); they arrived at the finding that these two variables are indeed correlated. The study's findings and methodology has been widely disputed, but the correlation between teacher expectations and increased academic performance in school (if not intelligence), illustrates the symbolic interactionist concept of the self-fulfilling prophecy.

SEARCHING FOR SOLUTIONS

As income inequality continues to rise along with the need for higher level skills to compete in a technology based economy, schools in low income areas have continued to experience lower quality education that does not prepare students for jobs that pay middle-class salaries. A study on education by Heather Schwartz of the Rand Corporation compared schools in Montgomery County, Maryland and her findings were summed up in a few very important words that are now well known among education sociologists: "Housing Policy Is School Policy" (Schwartz 2010). In other words, public school districts are segregated along class lines and this equates to de facto racial segregation as well. This is a problem that goes beyond spending more money per pupil, because high poverty schools do not receive the very important benefits of high levels of parent involvement, high quality teachers, low turnover and low absenteeism or high-quality facilities (Gallagher 2013). Any approach to improve the quality of education for students who attend public schools in impoverished districts must include collaboration among parents, community leaders and teachers. Involvement is just as important for the solution as funding is and that gives individuals agency to go into their communities and promote equality in education.

Community-based involvement for individuals includes improving literacy rates by starting a book drive for children living in low-income communities, or volunteering to tutor children who need extra help. Organizations that promote change through individual efforts include www.dosomething.org. Through this organization campaigns range from promoting support for refugees and immigrants to hosting a college advice event at which college students can share their advice on how to navigate applying to and transitioning into college.

One of the most well-known groups working to not only narrow the achievement gap in low-income classrooms, but also to train leaders in all areas of education and social justice promoting equality in education, is TeachForAmerica. This national organization has had a great deal of success recruiting young college graduates to teach in America's most poverty-stricken communities. In addition to receiving training and experience, members are eligible for college loan forbearance and depending on the geographic area, housing assistance and even loan forgiveness. Critics of this program believe it displaces older veteran teachers with young inexperienced teachers who only have a two-year commitment to fulfill. Critics believe that community-driven reform that unites parents and teachers advocating for change in class sizes, more funding allocated to technology in the classroom, and revamping the taxation structure for school funding are better long-term solutions.

There are many national advocacy groups that work to promote awareness around bullying in schools. For example, The Trevor Project is a volunteer based group that works in communities to provide suicide and crisis intervention for LGBTQ young people who have been bullied at school. STOMP out Bullying is the organization that started Blue Shirt Day to help raise awareness about bullying in schools. Also, a volunteer based group, individuals can learn how to start anti-bullying movements in schools in their communities.

FIGURE 4.5
'Hamilton' actor Javier Munoz (center) poses with CEO of STOMP Out Bullying, Ross Ellis (left) and John B. Kessler, (right) president and COO of Empire State Realty Trust, during STOMPOut-Bullying & Blue Shirt Day World Day Of Bullying Prevention at The Empire State Building on October 3, 2016 in New York City.

Source: Astrid Stawiarz/Getty Images

In his second inaugural address, President Barack Obama stated, "We are true to our creed when a little girl born into the bleakest poverty knows that she has the same chance to succeed as anybody else" (Obama 2013). President Obama and his administration started a number of initiatives to provide equality of opportunity to children attending schools in impoverished areas. The approach included education initiatives that ranged from community based to state and federal level initiatives. Community-based programs include resources to educate parents on how to promote equity through family–school partnerships. Family–school partnerships were designed to involve parents in efforts to advance equity in achievement for all students regardless of race or family income level. Connecting parents and teachers in the school district gives parents the opportunity to promote student achievement by partnering with teachers to create community based initiatives for higher quality education. This initiative was encouraged on the state level but utilized community mobilization and support and is intended to get families involved in addressing racial and economic disparities in their communities.

The national Preschool for All proposal was based on research that found the education gap between children in poverty and middle-class children started the first day of kindergarten and only widened as children progressed through school (Barnett and Freed 2010). By providing quality programs for four-year-old children from low income areas, these children will have a better chance of starting out their education on a level playing field with their more advantaged peers.

Supporting teachers is an essential element for effectively increasing the quality of education. The U.S. Department of Education partnered with the National Board for Professional Teaching Standards to create national initiatives such as Teach to Lead, which provides resources and expands opportunities for teachers to become leaders in the process of developing and implementing education policy. This initiative is based on the idea that teachers should be considered the foremost experts on how to improve public education. Although this may sound like common sense, teachers have not historically had any voice in education policy or improvement. Empowering teachers to exercise leadership within their schools and more broadly, to inform education policy at local and state levels, will greatly benefit both educators and students.

The Department of Education has additionally set into place *inclusionary policies* designed to reduce the inequality caused by school zoning laws. These inclusionary policies include setting aside a proportion of homes in higher income areas and using federal subsidized housing to rent to low-income families with children so they can attend local schools. These inclusionary zoning policies increase classroom diversity and provide a way to close the achievement gap between minority children and white children that lead to differences in income, wealth, and health over the life course. Across the nation mandatory schooling zoning laws have been enacted that have given thousands of children living in poverty the opportunity to receive a higher quality education. The policy has had positive outcomes for low-income student's test scores and literacy rates and has introduced diversity to schools that were mainly white and middle or upper class.

As mentioned earlier, problems in higher education that require solutions include college loan debt, campus sexual assault, and the rising cost of college, just to name a few. According to data compiled from the Association of American Universities (AAU), 23.1% of female undergraduate students have experienced rape or sexual assault through physical force, violence, or incapacitation (Cantor et al. 2015). The vast majority of these incidents went unreported to campus officials or law enforcement. National organizations that provide a tool-kit and other resources for college students interested in reducing sexual assault at their college campus include the American Association of University Women (AAUW), The National Alliance to End Sexual Violence, Center for Changing Our Campus Culture, End Rape on Campus, Know your IX and Futures Without Violence, among many others. What all these organizations have in common is the goal to provide resources for campus advocates—not just for college students but they are also geared toward involving faculty and administration. This goal includes educating students on how to organize a group on campus that can utilize the resources of these advocacy groups to heighten awareness, provide strategies, and effectively end the growing social problem of sexual assault on campuses. Armed with resources from these organizations, college students are uniting to combat sexual violence on their campuses.

College based initiatives to reduce sexual assault on campus are more effective if the university administration partners with students to heighten awareness and open a dialogue about rape culture, consent, and dating violence. To assist in a concerted collaboration between administration, students, college security officers and faculty, the U.S. Department of Justice awards grants to colleges and universities to reduce sexual assault, dating violence, and stalking, by training campus security to respond more effectively to these crimes, to educate campus disciplinary boards on the dynamics of these crimes, and to provide culturally specific prevention services for underserved populations such as LGBTQ students, racial/ethnic minorities, and students with disabilities (U.S. Department of Justice 2017).

An issue that has received a great deal of media attention is the burden of college loan debt that many students carry for years and even decades after attaining their college degrees. Spurred by the rising cost of a college education, the proliferation of for-profit colleges and universities that are primarily online, and the Great Recession that began in 2008, students are borrowing more money than ever before to attain a college degree. The media introduced the idea of rising college loan debt as a national "crisis" in 2008 when the recession made private college loans more difficult to obtain. However, when President Obama took office in 2008, he had campaigned on the promise to make college affordable for everyone.

In general, student loan debt does pay off as far as income earned for those college educated students with at least a bachelor's degree. The income of college educated households with student debt is nearly twice as high as that of households without a bachelor's degree. However, the net worth of a college educated household without student debt is much higher than a college educated household with student debt (Fry 2014). And young professionals with student loan debt reported being less happy with their financial situations than those who did not take on debt. So, what exactly is the social problem that needs to be solved? Is it the rising costs of college (while incomes remain stagnant) that appears to be driving higher student debt? Or is it a more complex problem that involves the Obama Administration increasing federal loan amounts and colleges and universities increasing tuition in response to attain as much of this money as possible? And what about the jargon used in student loan applications and the lack of transparency on how much payments will be after graduation and lack of information on how much a student should borrow depending on the income they can expect for their particular career field? This is indeed a complex social problem with no clear immediate solution.

The first and most important task is to provide more education to college students taking out loans. Students sign contracts with no idea how much their monthly payments will be and often borrow more than they need since they do not understand how to calculate how much they truly need. The legalese in the loan documents and lack of transparency by loan officers have made acquiring federal college loans a mysterious process. In addition, students can empower themselves to become more knowledgeable about student loan debt. Organizing groups on campus, in collaboration with the financial aid or career services departments, are a way for students to heighten awareness and provide education that empowers them to make sound decisions about how much they really need to borrow and how it will affect their future. College students are truly their own best advocates for change. If their student loan process is an intentionally confusing process with few concrete details, students can contact the Institute for College Access and Success to find resources on private and federal loan debt. This organization can assist with consumer protections, how to read the fine print, tips on options for repaying loans, and perhaps most importantly, how interest rates are calculated, which loans have the best interest rates, and the fees for these loans. Additionally, it provides publications available on the net price of different colleges, how to navigate the student financial aid system, and how to determine your payment amounts depending on amount borrowed. These resources can empower students to take charge of their debt and educate other students on the realities of student loans.

From a broader policy standpoint one of the biggest hurdles is that students must pay back loans when they are just starting out in their careers. This can lead to stress, falling behind on payments, and ultimately defaulting on loans. One strategy on the national level is to change the

FIGURE 4.6
Teachers often begin their careers with substantial student loans and low salaries.

Source: Monkey Business Images/Shutterstock.com

payback period, which is currently 10 years, and extend it out further so students are not burdened with heavy payments as they start new careers. Another solution along these lines is income based repayment structures where students who have lower incomes can pay lower monthly payments than students who start out in highly lucrative career fields. Since one in five households owed student debt in 2010 and by 2012 more than 30% of student borrowers were delinquent in paying back these loans, the best prevention and thus solution is to heighten awareness and education for students and families (Fry 2014). Transparency and mandating borrowers are given information in a way they can understand is crucial. For example, if a student is up to $30,000 in student loans they should receive an amortization schedule just like mortgages provide to buyers. It should include monthly payments and how these match the median salaries in their field. In other words, more regulation, education, and transparency in the very profitable student loan market.

Should student loans be capped using the median income of the career field the student is planning to enter?

Pro: This method provides an appropriate measure of the field's financial value and thwarts college indebtedness.
Con: This method places more value on certain high-income earning jobs over others that are equally important to society.

CHAPTER SUMMARY

- The American educational system is a social institution that transfers knowledge from teachers to students. It is a complex system that includes homeschooling, public schools, private schools, alternative schools, as well as colleges and universities. It relies on pedagogy that is agreed upon by society as important for attaining a job and becoming a responsible member of society.

- The sub-field of sociology of education is founded on the work of Durkheim and Weber and includes many focuses, including the many different types of social stratification within education by race, gender, sexual orientation, and the like, as well as how power works to set the agenda for schools.

- Primary and secondary education include the basic education of kindergarten through twelfth grade. Schools vary in their curriculum and delivery, depending on whether they are public or private. Alternative schools include magnet and charter schools that began to proliferate as Americans demanded more school choice. In addition, homeschooling has had a rising popularity as an alternative to traditional schooling.

- According to education scholar John Dewey (1959), education has two components: the psychological and the sociological. The latter is the role of education in socializing students to understand the structure and rules of society, while the former refers to the individualistic nature of learning and interpreting social life. A hidden curriculum in the educational system encourages conformity to the norms and values of mainstream society. These are very traditional values and to do not consider the diversity of students. This includes racial/ethnic minorities, immigrants, children with disabilities and LGBTQ students, all of whom will benefit as schools begin to encourage inclusion to support all students and discourage discrimination.

- Problems in our school system include bullying and harassment that often start in elementary school. A growing number of high schools have implemented zero tolerance policies and formalized punishment that have resulted in a large group of students that public high schools have expelled, the composition of which is mainly minority males in impoverished urban neighborhoods. These students have few options and are very likely to end up in prison in short order, hence, the school-to-prison pipeline.

- Higher education has its own set of challenges. Currently there is a concern over the growing number of institutions that do not offer tenure to professors, while academic freedom has slowly begun to disappear for professors as well. Sexual assault on college campuses and rising student loan debt are major problems that many college students must deal with during their college education.

- Functionalist theory focuses on the role of education in creating a solid foundation for developing the economy as well as contributing to the other social institutions. Conflict theory pays attention to the inequities in the educational system that reinforce social stratification. Adopting a micro level approach, interactionism notes the ways in which identity formation occurs in the educational process and how concepts such as the self-fulfilling prophecy are manifest.

- Solutions for these problems start with individual efforts and community based involvement in grassroots organizations that promote equality in education. In addition, organizations such as Teach for America place young high quality teachers in low performing schools as they work to close the education gap. Advocacy groups for LGBTQ students and anti-bullying groups are popping up across the nation to combat exclusionary practices.

- Solutions on the national level include, inclusionary policies put into place to reduce inequality caused by school zoning laws by allotting up to a third of all homes in a middle-class district to be government subsidized for low-income students living in high poverty communities. This not only allows children to attend high performing schools, it also creates racial and ethnic diversity in primarily white schools.

- Colleges and universities are working to reduce sexual assault on their campuses using resources from national advocacy groups to educate and heighten awareness about consent, stalking, and sexual violence. In addition, the U.S. Department of Justice awards grants to universities to reduce sexual assault and provide culturally specific prevention serves for LGBTQ students, racial/ethnic minorities, and students with disabilities.

- Solutions for the growing cost of college that has resulted in higher levels of student debt include: educating and empowering college students to be informed consumers with the capability to calculate future loan payment amounts and the amount of income they can expect to make with their chosen major. Information on private and federal loan debt is confusing and complex, organizing groups on campus in collaboration with financial aid and career services departments, and requiring more transparency from loan officers, can empower students to make better choices.

REFERENCES

Alridge, Derrick P. 2008. *The Educational Thought of W.E.B. Du Bois: An Intellectual History*. New York: Teachers College Press.

Anderson, Charles W. 1993. *Prescribing the Life of the Mind*. Madison, WI: University of Wisconsin Press.

Applerouth, Scott and Laura Desfor Edles. 2011. *Sociological Theory in the Contemporary Era: Text and Readings*, 2nd ed. Los Angeles: Sage.

Barnett, W. Steven, and Ellen Frede. "The Promise of Preschool: Why We Need Early Education for All." American Educator 34.1 (2010): 21.

Cantor, David, Bonnie Fisher, Susan Chibnall, and Reanna Townsend. 2015. Association of American Universities, Report on the AAU Campus Climate Survey on Sexual Assault and Sexual Misconduct. U.S. Department of Justice, Office of Violence against Women. Retrieved April 25, 2017 (www.justice.gov/ovw/protecting-students-sexual-assault).

Chabrier, Julia, Sarah Cohodes, and Philip Oreopoulos. 2015. "What Can We Learn from Charter School Lotteries?" *Journal of Economic Perspectives*. 30 (3): 57–84.

Chomsky, Noam. 2000. *Chomsky on MisEducation*. Lanham, MD: Rowman and Littlefield.

Community College Week. 2016. 28–11–2016. "Colleges Grapple with Rising Food and Housing Insecurity." Retrieved March 22, 2017 (http://eds.a.ebscohost.com/eds/pdfviewer/pdfviewer?vid=1&s id=e1ee1dff-2861-43df-9bd8-2c7ff75ed503%40sessionmgr4009&hid=4113).

Cornelius, Luke M. and Sharon A. Frank. 2015. "Student Load Debt Levels and Their Implications for Borrowers, Society, and the Economy." *Educational Considerations*. 42 (2): 35–38.

Dewey, John. 1959. *Dewey on Education*. New York: Teachers College Press.

Du Bois, W.E.B. [1903] 1995. *The Souls of Black Folk*. New York: Signet.

Foucault, Michel. 1977. *Discipline and Punish*. New York: Pantheon Press.

Freire, Paulo. 1970. *Pedagogy of the Oppressed*. New York: Herder and Herder.

Fry, Richard. 2014. Pew Research Center. "Young Adults, Student Debt and Economic Well-Being." Retrieved April 25, 2017 (www.pewsocialtrends.org/2014/05/14/young-adults student-debt-and-economic-well-being).

Gallagher Megan. 2013. "Why Housing policy really is education policy." The Urban Institute. Retrieved May 1, 2017 (www.urban.org/urban-wire/why-housing-policy-really-education-policy).

Giroux, Henry. 2012. *Education and the Crisis of Public Values: Challenging the Assault on Teachers, Students, and Public Education*. New York: Peter Lang.

Goldring, Ellen and Claire Smrekar. 2004. "Magnet Schools: Reform and Race in Urban Education." *The Clearing House*. 76 (4): 13–15.

Hallinan, Maureen T. 2000. "Sociology of Education at the Threshold of the Twenty-first Century," in *Handbook of the Sociology of Education*, edited by Maureen T. Hallihan. New York: Kluwer Academic. Pp. 65–84.

Horowitz, Irving Louis. 1975. "Head and Hand in Education: Vocationalism versus Professionalism." *The School Review*. 83 (3): 397–414.

Jackson, Philip. 1968. *Life in Classrooms*. New York: Holt, Rinehart, and Winston.

Kerr, Clark. 1964. *The Uses of the University*. Cambridge, MA: Harvard University Press.

Kitmitto, Sami, Jesse Levin, Julian Betts, Johannes Bos, and Marian Eaton. 2016. "What Happens when Schools Become Magnet Schools? A Longitudinal Study of Diversity and Achievement." *Society for Research and Educational Effectiveness*. Pp. 1–23. Retrieved April 20, 2017 (http://files.eric.ed.gov/fulltext/ED567120.pdf).

Lee, Valerie E. 2000. "School Size and the Organization of Secondary Schools." In Hallihan, Maureen T. Ed., *Handbook of the Sociology of Education*. Pp. 327–344. New York: Kluwer.

Lynch, Kathleen. 2000. "Research and Theory on Equality and Education." Pp. 85–105 in *Handbook of the Sociology of Education*, edited by Maureen T. Hallihan. New York: Kluwer Academic.

Murphy, Joseph. 2014. "The Social and Educational Outcomes of Homeschooling." *Sociological Spectrum*. 34 (3): 244–272.

Obama, Barack. 2013. Inaugural Address to America. Retrieved April 27, 2017 (https://obamawhitehouse.archives.gov/the-press-office/2013/01/21/inaugural-address-president-barack-obama).

O'Neil, Robert. 2008. *Academic Freedom in the Wired World: Political Extremism, Corporate Power, and the University*. Cambridge, MA: Harvard University Press.

Parsons, Talcott. 1967. "The School Class as of Social System." Pp. 647–666 in Peter I. Rose. *The Study of Sociology: An Integrated Anthology*. New York: Random Press.

Percell, Caroline Hodges. 2000. "Values, Control, and Outcomes in Public and Private Schools." Pp. 387–407 in *Handbook of the Sociology of Education*, edited by M.T. Hallihan. New York: Kluwer.

Rosenbaum, James E. and Stephanie Alter Jones. 2000. "Intersections Between High Schools and Labor Markets." Pp. 411–436 in *Handbook of the Sociology of Education*, edited by M.T. Hallihan. New York: Kluwer.

Rosenthal, Robert and Lenore Jacobson. 1992. *Pygmalion in the Classroom: Teacher Expectations and Pupil's Intellectual Development*. Norwalk, CT: Crown House Publishing Co.

Schept, Judah, Tyler Wall, and Ari Brisman. 2015. "Building, Staffing, and Insulating: An Architecture of Criminological Complicity in the School-to-Prison Pipeline." *Social Justice* 41(4): 96–115.

Schneider, Barbara. 2000. "Social Systems and Norms: A Coleman Approach." Pp. 362–385 in *Handbook of the Sociology of Education*, edited by M.T. Hallihan. New York: Kluwer.

Schwartz, Heather. 2010. "Housing Policy is School Policy." The Century Foundation, 225. Retrieved April 20, 2017 (https://tcf.org/assets/downloads/tcf-Schwartz.pdf).

Seeley, Ken, Martin L. Tombari, Laurie J. Bennett, and Jason B. Dunkle. 2011. *Bullying in Schools: An Overview*. Office of Juvenile Justice and Delinquency Prevention. NCJ 234205. Washington, DC: U.S. Department of Justice.

Seirup, Holly J., Rose Tirotta, and Elfreda Blue. 2016. "Online Education: Panacea or Plateau." *Journal of Leadership and Instruction*. 15(1): 5–8. Retrieved March 22, 2017 (http://files.eric.ed.gov/fulltext/EJ1097549.pdf).

U.S. Department of Health and Human Services. 2017. *What is Bullying?* Washington, DC. Retrieved March 22, 2017 (www.stopbullying.gov).

U.S. Department of Justice. 2017. Office on Violence Against Women Grant Programs. Retrieved May 2, 2017 (www.justice.gov/ovw/grant-programs).

Walters, Pamela Barnhouse. 2000. "School Expansion and School Reform in Historical Perspective." Pp. 241–261 in *Handbook of the Sociology of Education*, edited by M.T. Hallihan. New York: Kluwer.

Wolff, Robert Paul. 1969. *The Ideal of the University*. Boston: Bacon Press.

CHAPTER 5

The Family

ABOUT THE PROBLEM: THE FAMILY

Arriving at a Definition of Family

The social institution known as **family** is a foundational unit of human existence. As one of the other five institutions, it is prominent in guiding how new people are brought into and socialized into society. Three centuries ago, families performed the functions of all the major social institutions—the economic, educational, political, and religious purposes. Many of these functions have dispensed to other entities, leaving the family primarily concerned with socialization and the provision of support and affection (Mintz and Kellogg 1988). Kephart (1972) calls family the "remarkable institution ... which concerns itself with love, sexual relationships, marriage, reproduction, socialization of the child, and the various status and roles involved in kinship organization" (p. 1). These components of family are some in which we are all familiar, however coming up with a definition of family has proven difficult.

> **Family** an organized unit of individuals who strive to achieve a supportive environment, have created a common culture, and who consider themselves family.

In an early text, originally published in 1949, Murdock (1960) defines the institution of the family as:

> a social group characterized by common residence, economic cooperation, and reproduction. It includes adults of both sexes, at least two of who maintain a socially approved sexual relationship, and one or more children, own or adopted, of the sexually cohabitating adults.
>
> (p. 1)

In this decades-old definition, it should probably be obvious to most students that this description doesn't fit what many people today would call a family. Regarding the common residence, for example, if a daughter in a family is at college in another town, is she still not in the family? Does the two-year-old son contribute to the family income? Is sexual cohabitation necessary? These questions demonstrate that defining exactly what constitutes a family has never been easy and certainly is not today.

Another early definition by Burgess and Locke (1945) describes family is this way:

> a group of persons united by the ties of marriage, blood or adoption; consisting of a single household, interacting and inter-communicating with each other in their respective social roles of husband and wife, mother and father, son and daughter, brother and sister creating a common culture.
>
> (p. 2)

Most people would agree that this definition is outdated as it fails to account for many other accepted structures today. For example, what type of interaction is necessary? Does it have to be face-to-face or does interacting via Facebook count? Would same-sex marriages be represented in this definition? Again, these questions suggest there is not an easy way to define family.

The U.S. census (2012) gives the following definition:

> a family consists of a householder and one or more other people living in the same household who are related to the householder by birth, marriage, or adoption. Biological, adopted, and stepchildren of the householder who are under 18 are the "own children" of the householder. Own children do not include other children present in the household, regardless of the presence or absence of the other children's parents.

FIGURE 5.1 As alternative family forms become increasingly common our ideas about what constitutes family have changed.

Source: Westend61 / Getty Images

Obviously, this definition is a practical one, reflecting the intent to provide quantifiable data on household information. However, it would certainly be inappropriate for understanding the qualifiable aspects of family life.

Noting the changing trends in family structures, Naisbitt states modern families have been extended to "important relationships between people not related by blood or marriage, but by voluntary association: unmarried couples, close friends or roommates with long-standing friendships, group houses where people living together have grown into a community" (1984:261). This definition is certainly inclusive of emerging family forms but seems to suggest families have little more substance than what we consider (and as he mentioned) a community.

In developing a definition, we believe it best to invoke Occam's Razor (the best explanation among a variety of choices is the one with the least assumptions). Therefore, we offer the following definition: an organized unit of individuals who strive to achieve a supportive environment, have created a common culture, and who consider themselves family.

The Nuclear Family as an American Ideal

A graduate school professor of one of us (LAS) told the class "the family doesn't exist". While her comments made the students pause, she explained there are many types of family structures, not just the commonly accepted image of the **nuclear family,** therefore *the* family doesn't exist—*families* do. People often think of this type—consisting of two parents and their biological children—as the model family type. There are many different family structures; extended families, blended families, single parent families, cohabitating couples, same-sex couples, among many others represent families today.

> **Nuclear Family** a family type consisting of two parents and their biological children that is often considered the model family type.

Should the traditional nuclear family be advocated in family policy?

Pro: The traditional nuclear family is the most beneficial to society, therefore policy should be directed toward advocating it.

Con: Family structures are evolving and family policy should reflect modern family life rather than an ideal.

The nuclear family "ideal" was not always the prominent American family structure. The **extended family**, consisting of several relatives, often from different generations, was common and families were much larger in the past due to the growth of single-parent families and lower fertility rates. The use of **fictive kinship** is also an alternative to traditional nuclear families and includes people who are not related by blood, marriage or adoption but still considered family due to the close ties that transcend predominant views of family membership; sometimes these members even have a family title such as uncle or aunt, even though the lack of blood relationship is known and accepted.

Still, when people think of the ideal family image, they think of the 1950s-nuclear family. After World War II, an economic boom resulted in many changes, including reasonable housing rates, movement to the suburbs, infrastructure improvements, and governmental assistance for families; the

> **Extended Family** a family unit that includes family members that extend beyond those of the nuclear family.
>
> **Fictive Kinship** the acceptance of people as family members who do not have blood, marriage, or adoption ties that traditionally denote family membership.

FIGURE 5.2 How families continue to change as we move toward a multi-racial society.

Source: Westend61 / Getty Images

family changed as well in refusing the extended family pattern adopting the nuclear family structure. The nuclear family was perceived as a nurturing environment where individuals could grow and prosper. However, this ideal image, as depicted in television series of the time such as *Leave it to Beaver* and *Father Knows Best*, was not as rosy for poor and minority families as women were forced to adapt to domestic roles or to accept jobs that paid less than men (and less than the jobs available to women during World War II); they often felt trapped. In addition, Cold War concerns created much anxiety for families of this era. Rather than being the "golden era" of family life, a culmination of traditional values and prosperity before the drastic changes that took place in the coming years, it was in fact the product of macro level changes in the country and not great for many families (Coontz 1992).

A few facts clarify the changes in the traditional family structure. In 1960, most families were of the nuclear type; 73% of children were born into families with two parents who were in their first marriage. By 1980, that number had dropped to 61%, and today has dropped to 46%. Increasing divorce rates have created a situation in which children being raised by both parents has declined: children living with both parents accounted for 87% of families in 1960, 73% in 2000, and 69% today. In relation to racial differences, children are most likely to be living with two parents can be broken down as follows: Asian-Americans 87%, white children 78%, Hispanic children 66%, and African-American children 38% (Livingston 2014).

Alternative Family Structures

In the early 1980s, which was already experiencing changes in family structures, Naisbitt described the diverse family arrangements through the imagery of the Rubik's Cube—increasingly complex and, even though those advocating conservative profamily values would like to return it to a former state, is as difficult to return to its original state as is the toy (Naisbitt 1984). In addition to the nuclear family and the extended family structures, there are other types of families. The term **binuclear family** is used to describe a situation in which couples with children are separated or divorced but the children remain connected to both parents, even though they are living in different households. A family with children in which there has been dissolution and remarriage create what is called a **blended family**, or reconstituted family, which must adapt to the changes of merging two families into one. And, of course, not all couples are married; **cohabitating couples** are certainly more socially accepted today than in the past, however, they are less stable than families with married couples (Livingston 2014). In addition, interracial and same-sex marriages are much more prominent than in the past.

PROBLEMS OF MODERN FAMILY LIFE

Violence and other forms of abuse

Family life is not the haven it is often imagined to be. Domestic violence, also commonly referred to today as **interpersonal violence** (or IPV), also known as domestic violence, is unfortunately commonplace in many American homes. Types of behavior that fall into this category are physical, emotional, sexual, and economic abuse along with forced isolation and entrapment, and the control and abuse of children (Almeida 2010). Abusers of IPV use a complex variety of manipulative behaviors to control their victims (NCADV 2016). Many people who study IPV describe a cycle of abuse in which after the abuse happens, the abuser expresses contrition, and after a honeymoon period, the abuse reoccurs. Many are familiar with the **power and control wheel**, a diagram which shows the common progression in relationships in which power and control are used against someone in an interpersonal relationship.

IPV has many victims. Regarding adults in families, 1 in 3 women and 1 in 4 men have been victimized by IPV in their lifetime. When considering serious physical abuse, the number is 1 in 5 women and 1 in 7 men. People in same-sex relationships also experience IPV—almost half of homicide victims are LGBTQ men and most homicide victims are gay or lesbian. Older adults are often victims of family violence as well, as 76.1% of physical abuse of the elderly is committed by family members (National Coalition Against Domestic Violence 2016).

Violence of children in families is also a major concern as 1 in 4 children in America experience violence in the home and in 2014, almost 1,600 children died from the abuse (CDC 2016). In addition, children exposed to domestic violence experience high levels of depression, anxiety, and a host of negative emotions. They also experience problems in school, aggressiveness, delinquency, and later problems in their own families (Cahn 2006). The idea of a family as a haven for its members is often shattered by revelations of extreme forms of abuse. In January 2018, an emaciated 17-year-old girl reported her captivity and that of her 12 siblings by their parents, David and Louise Turpin in California. The children, who at the time of discovery were aged 2–29, were not allowed to leave the home, were not given proper nutrition, and were subjected to torture and abuse. Attempts have been made to find supportive home environments for the children, who suffered trauma, cognitive impairment, and other physical and emotional maladies. Stories such as this disturb our understanding of family.

Binuclear Family a family structure in which couples with children live separately but the children remain connected to both parents.

Blended Family a family that is the result of dissolution of the adult couple, bringing in family members from the previous unions.

Cohabitating Couples couples who live together, and potentially raise children, but are not married.

Interpersonal Violence violence that exists between people in a relationship framework or which existed previously.

Power and Control Wheel an illustration, presented in the form of a wheel that reflects the cyclical nature of interpersonal violence.

Source: Gina Ferazzi/Getty Images

FIGURE 5.3 David Turpin (2nd-R) confers with attorneys Allison Lowe (back of head) and David Macher (R) as Louise Turpin (L) confers with attorney Jeff Moore (2nd-L) during their court arraignment in Riverside, California on January 18, 2018. The California couple who held their 13 malnourished children captive in a suburban home were charged with multiple counts of torture and child abuse as prosecutors said the youngsters had been shackled even to go to the bathroom. David Turpin, 57, and his wife, 49, were hit with 12 counts of torture, 12 of false imprisonment, six of child abuse and six of abuse of a dependent adult at a court hearing in the city of Riverside.

Serious Marital Discord and Divorce

Marital discord, or conflict, defined as interpersonal interaction involving differences of opinion by the adult couple, does not always result in serious problems in the family, in fact, conflict that is appropriately addressed can lead to a remedy for the problems causing the conflict. However, when the discord is severe, it can lead to a host of problems, including the maladjustment of children which involves conduct problems, aggression, delinquency, school problems, physical problems, and social skills deficits (Cummings and Davies 2010).

Interestingly, the divorce rate for couples aged 25–39 has decreased since 1990, for couples 40–49 it has maintained steady, but for couples aged above age 50 it has increased significantly since 1990. The effect of divorce on the older group is less financial stability and emotional support. However, the divorce rate for parents of younger children has decreased, which could be a good sign since the effects of divorce on young children has a host of negative effects. In fact, the "baby boom" generation now experiencing the high levels of divorce also experienced several maladaptive issues of their own growing up such as marital instability as youngsters (Stepler 2017). They also experience other problems in their own marital lives regarding commitment and confidence in marriage—this is especially true with females (Whitton et al. 2008).

Inequality in the Family

In using his concept of the sociological imagination to analyze private troubles as public issues, Mills (2000) stated "In so far as the family turns women into darling little slaves and men into their chief providers and unweaned dependents, the problem of a satisfactory marriage remains incapable of a purely private solution" (p. 10). The structural problems of gender inequality on a macro level affects couples on a micro level—if gender inequality exists in the greater society, it will exist in the family. And gender inequality does exist: women earn 80% of what men earn. The gender wage gap of 20% rose only one percentage point in 2015. At the slow rate the gap is closing, it will not be until 2152 when there is gender pay equity (AAUW 2016). Educational opportunities have increased for women, which is a positive trend, but the cost of higher education is a factor that creates financial burdens for both sexes.

Feminist sociologist Arlie Hochschild explored the issue of two wage earner families in *The Second Shift* (2003). In this work, she observes how the work lives of heterosexual couples were based on a "his and hers" economic system in America (p. 11). Married women have traditionally been tasked with the housekeeping and child rearing duties after the paid workday ends, while their male counterparts were often exempt from this extra responsibility. This "second shift" that women were expected to perform corresponded with ideas of earlier times, leading Hochschild to conclude that a "stalled revolution" (p. 11) has occurred. Economic changes allowed (and forced) women to work outside the home but a true equalitarian system would ensure a couple's equal time at both work and at home.

Poor Socialization and other Parenting Problems

There are many areas of our occupational lives that require licensure or certification to prove that we have mastery over some craft (medicine, law, engineering, even cosmetology and engine repair)—some entity provides oversight to make sure that we are adequately trained in these fields as they are important to the functioning of society. However, parenting—perhaps the most important task many people undertake—requires no oversight at all, unless problems are reported to local family welfare agencies. The successful socialization of children is certainly an important endeavor, however, when children are inappropriately socialized, this creates other problems in their lives, the lives of their families, the community and society generally.

Should any person who assumes the role of parent be required to complete a parenting "certification" or series of parent training sessions?

Pro: The effective parenting of children is essential to the overall functioning of society, therefore it deserves some degree of oversight and training.

Con: An issue is who will provide the training. The government's role should not be to intervene in family issues such as this; if private industry is responsible, poor parents will have difficulty paying for the service.

Mental illness in families can often present many problematic issues. The unpredictability and inconsistency that can occur in families with mentally ill parents puts children at risk for mental problems themselves. Marital stress between the parents or adult members of the family can also be a contributor to this transfer of mental problems. Often, a parent with mental illness will be raising children alone and there is a strong possibility that children will be removed from the home. And due to the stigma of mental illness that continues to pervade our society, the parents will not seek professional help that could assist in breaking the cycle (Nicholson et al. 2001).

Likewise, families that have members that are addicted to alcohol or other drugs can experience problems in socialization. People who are in families with an adult member or members who have substance addiction experience an increase in physical ailments, stress, interpersonal violence, inappropriate levels of functioning and boundary maintenance in and outside the family, and conflict and behavior problems in children. Family members with addicted persons in the home have fewer opportunities for treatment to assist them in dealing with the systemic problems (American Psychological Association nd). Specifically related to the maladaptive parenting patterns in families with drug abuse, Dore (1998) describes three specific effects: the particular effects of the drugs that thwart the competency and consistency of appropriate functioning by parents, the maintenance of the physical environment which often creates conditions for child maltreatment and neglect, and the fact that addicted parents often have a history of childhood trauma which also contributes to the maltreatment of their children.

THEORETICAL PERSPECTIVES

Structural Functionalism

Structural functionalism was an early contributor to knowledge about family life and was influenced by anthropological scholarship, especially in the areas of kinship relationships. We have already discussed the work of George Murdock in the introduction but we will revisit his work as it provides a good foundation for understanding the functionalist perspective, whose definition of family observes the functions provided by families. Talcott Parsons provided this functionalist framework to a large audience at mid-twentieth century.

Murdock (1960), posited these four functions of families: sexual—sexual urges are best kept in check through marriage; reproduction—the introduction of children into the world is best served within the confines of a family unit; socialization—the socialization and nurture of the young should be accomplished within the family structure; and economic—a strong division of labor and cooperation between members helps ensure the family's ability to survive and thrive. These four functions are still commonly considered as the norm in society even though other institutions have recently evolved to incorporate some of these functions in developed societies, such as the educational system as a socializing agent. The functionalist element, mentioned in more detail in the theoretical perspectives section below, is so engrained in American culture that the term "dysfunctional family" is commonly used to describe a family that is not fulfilling its obligations to its members, and society in general.

Talcott Parsons reflected the conservative era in which he was writing as well as a vantage point of the white, middle class, suburban environment of which he was familiar. Regarding family life, Parsons (1954) maintained that young boys and girls have very little gender differentiation as they are growing up. The mother, who is "continually about the house" (p. 90), is a good role model for girls. If a father figure is absent, due to work or other extra-familial obligations, the son is left without "a gradual initiation into the activities of the adult male role" (p. 90), in other words, he is left without an adequate understanding of the male role. Adolescents move into a "youth culture" and boys often become "star athletes", which helps them later as they become businessmen and professionals; girls accentuate their looks to become "glamour girls" (a complementary role to the "star athletes"), and take on the "domestic pattern" of wife and mother. The father, due to his material achievements, is the most important member as he creates the social standing of the family. As the couple ages, males have an especially difficult time since they are "cut off from participation in the most important interests and activities of society" (p. 103). Readers today often have a hard time with Parsons' work due its vision of men and women in family life from a long bygone era, an era in which only people of a certain race, class, ethnicity, sex, etc. reside.

Conflict

Conflict theorists reject the idea of families as primarily being cohesive and harmonious safe havens from a threatening world. They note the power differentials that exist within families and how these differentials, which are generated both internally (with internal family struggles and conflicts) and externally (from violent communities, structural poverty, sexism, and racism), affect family members. The comments by Mills in the "Problems of Modern Family Life" section reflect these two areas and how they are related.

Friedrich Engels (2001), collaborator with Karl Marx, provided us with an early conflict view in *The Origin of the Family, Private Property and the State*. He took a historical view of the evolutionary development of families (a common theme with early sociologists and anthropologists) and documented a change from group marriage arrangements to a nuclear family structure which he called the "pairing family". With this family structure, a division of labor was created in which men performed the hunting and outside labor while the wife took care of the familial duties. Previous customs of maternal inheritance were overthrown to provide men with paternal control. With the advent of industrialization, a new family structure emerged, the monogamous family, which was based on economic rather than familial ties and further reinforced male dominance by ensuring the female was the actual mother of the children and so maintained the new paternal structure. Engels' work has been criticized for historical inaccuracies but his suggestion that gender inequality has its genesis in economic, rather than biological conditions is noteworthy (Edles and Applerouth 2015).

Sprey (1969) challenged the functionalist approach, which he called the "consensus-stable equilibrium approach framework". Sprey posited that conflict is not the problem; in fact, conflict is often beneficial in that it can "reinforce solidarity, aid in the maintenance of a functional division of labor, and generally alleviate the boredom of too much marital consensus" (p. 70). Disharmony is a natural condition of family life. And far from being a safeguard and place of refuge, families are often violent or abusive. To assume that the natural state of family life is harmonious creates an unrealistic image that is unattainable. Sprey's work in this area well represents the basic conflict perspective.

The feminist theories that emerged in the 1960s and 1970s also challenged structural functionalism. Talcott Parsons, mentioned in the previous section, was particularly a target in a society that increasingly questioned the traditional role of men and women and families. Although there are many kinds of feminist theory (this will be discussed in more detail in Chapter 6), it can be noted that feminists oppose any actions that create inequality between the sexes. Nancy Chodorow, a sociologist who also happens to be a psychoanalyst, diverges from many feminist thinkers who reject Freudianism and examines the role of parenting in the development and maintenance of traditional gender roles. Chodorow (1979) posits that children early on identify primarily with the mother as she is the primary caregiver. Boys are socialized up and achieve a masculine identity by separating with the mother while girls are socialized to maintain their identification with the mother. Thus, men have been reinforced into instrumental roles and women into expressive ones (to use Parson's terminology).

Symbolic Interactionism

Symbolic interactionists are concerned with the micro level interactions that comprise the social institution of family. This institution has people, at differing levels of age, status, responsibility, development stage, and power, interacting in very complex patterns. There are alliances, collusions, loyalties, and conflicts that are a salient part of family life. Family members are often given labels (e.g., little angel, black sheep, breadwinner).

George Herbert Mead (1977) focused on the self, which develops in relation to the reaction of others. Mead was concerned with how a person becomes an object into herself—through the socialization process, she will eventually be able to understand herself as a part of society rather than just as subject, seeing the world from her own perspective. Mead proposed a series of stages in the development of the self—the pre-play stage in which a child only observes the roles of others, the play stage where a child "plays" the role he sees, and the "game stage" in which he will, through the understanding of the roles of the other "players" in a social situation, actively become a part of society. When a person has successfully inculcated the norms of society, the generalized other stage is said to occur—at this point the adult is a fully vested member of society and the socialization process is complete. The concept of the generalized other, an important one is sociology, resembles Durkheim's concept of the collective consciousness and Freud's concept of the superego (Collins and Makowsky 1998). Socialization, then, primarily begins in the family.

Exchange theory is listed in this section because, although not normally considered an interactionist perspective in the Chicago School vein, it is a micro level theory that focuses on interactions between people or groups of people and offers a social psychological explanation for the motivations behind the interactions. George Homans (1958) is often credited with the formation of the social exchange theory, which draws from behavioral psychology and classical economics to explain that human behavior is a rational calculation in which rewards are sought for good behavior and punishments are expected for bad behavior. This position is especially relevant for families because family members (as everyone else) act in certain ways in return for an expected reward or to avoid an expected punishment. Peter Blau (1964) augmented exchange theory by integrating power issues into the perspective. Blau proposed that not all exchanges between people are based on equality— someone often has more power than the other and this power differential changes the nature of the exchange. In families, rarely are the relationships between parents (or adults generally) and children egalitarian. Parents are less likely than children to act in a way that will avoid punishment from the other (though many of us have seen situations where children "rule the roost"). We often like to think that we act in certain ways to others "out of the goodness of our hearts" with no personal rewards for that behavior but exchange theory teaches us that we get some reward from what we do, even if it is an intrinsic one.

SEARCHING FOR SOLUTIONS

As the first agent of socialization, and generally the most important stage of socialization for children, the American family is crucial for producing new generations of workers. To that end, it is in society's best interests collectively to offer support and resources for parents and caretakers. Historically, the extended family was the primary informal support system for parents. However, many young adults now relocate away from family for jobs and professional responsibilities. This is a recent occurrence and has left many young parents without informal social support systems in place. Coupled with an economic climate that makes participating in the paid labor force a necessity for most parents, this can cause a great deal of emotional and physical stress on the family.

Affordable Childcare

The most important support families need is affordable high-quality childcare, paid parental leave and job flexibility for working parents. This is especially true for low-income families and yet they are the least likely to work for companies that provide on-site childcare or telecommuting and other flexible work schedules. The U.S. is the only developed country that doesn't guarantee paid maternity or parental leave for employees. The UK, for example, guarantees 39 weeks of paid leave for mothers. Australia provides 18 weeks of paid leave and even Mexico guarantees employed new mothers 12 weeks of reimbursed maternity leave. The U.S. considers paid parental leave to be the responsibility of employers. However, according to the U.S. Bureau of Labor Statistics National Compensation Survey, only 12% of workers reported having paid leave in 2013 (United States Bureau of Labor Statistics 2013). Under the Family and Medical Leave Act of 1993, parents are entitled to 12 weeks of unpaid family leave time when they have a child. However, this policy only applies to companies with at least 50 employees and parents must have worked at the company for at least 12 months. In addition, this is not an option for many American families who simply cannot afford to take off work without pay.

However, many companies are beginning to realize that they cannot retain talented and focused employees without creating a family friendly workplace culture. Helping families balance work and family life is beneficial for families and for employers. This goes beyond offering unpaid maternity or paternity leave that most families cannot afford to utilize. Working mothers need more paid leave and more flexibility around when they take their leave. For example, Google found that when it increased parental leave from 12 to 18 weeks, the number of new mothers who quit their jobs after childbirth declined by 50% (Casserly 2012). In addition, Google allows new mothers to split up their time off however they wish, rather than forcing them to take it all at once. Mothers can take time off before the birth, return in a part-time capacity, and take the rest of the balance of the leave when the baby is older. This policy is atypical for employers in the United States, but it

Source: Kit8.net/Shutterstock.com

FIGURE 5.4 An example of the multitude of responsibilities mothers have in the United States due to a lack of parental leave policies.

illustrates how generous leave for parents is also beneficial for companies. Google reported that these new policies were cost beneficial since recruiting and training new employees is more expensive than paying for parental leave (Casserly 2012).

Should fertility technologies such as IVF be covered by employer sponsored and national health insurance?

Pro: Women are putting off childbearing in part because it takes longer to establish a career and purchase a home than it did a generation ago. These women should not be penalized when they want a child but cannot conceive due to their older age.

Con: Women need to manage their childbearing years better and not rely on science/technology to make pregnancy viable at advanced ages.

Assistance for Low-income Families

Unfortunately, most working parents do not receive any paid leave after having a new child. In a recent report on 'Parents and the High Cost of Child Care', child care was found to be the most significant expense for a family (National Association of Child Care Resources and Referral Agencies 2016). It often exceeded the cost of housing, college, and food. And yet, according to a 2014 report from the Office of the President, high-quality child care increases tax revenues since mothers can return to work, increases readiness for school, reduces likelihood of juvenile arrests and is associated with better health outcomes for children. How can we find a way for all children to experience the equality of opportunity that high-quality childcare offers? Some solutions include a proposal by the Center for American Progress for a Federal Child Care Tax Credit that implements a sliding scale, targets high-quality providers, and incentivizes increases in the supply of high-quality child care offerings (Hamm and Martin, 2015).

Should women who choose not to have children receive the same paid maternity leave their counterparts receive (if they work for a company that offers paid maternity leave)?

Pro: Why should women who choose not to procreate be forced to work harder to compensate for co-workers who receive months off after giving birth?

Con: If a woman chooses not to have children she is forfeiting maternity leave. This is her choice.

Government safety nets for low-income families include: Temporary Assistance for Needy Families (TANF), Supplemental Nutrition Assistance Program (SNAP) and the Earned Income Tax Credit (EITC). The Earned Income Tax Credit reduces the amount of taxes owed for families with low to moderate incomes. As discussed in the chapter on education, Head Start is also a program to help low-income children catch up to their middle-class peers before kindergarten. However, it is only for children who are one year away from entering kindergarten. None of the federal safety-nets effectively offset the cost of high-quality childcare for working parents, nor do they offer work/family balance. In addition, only three states currently offer paid family leave; California, New Jersey, Rhode Island, and New York will add paid leave in 2018 (National Conference of State Legislatures 2017).

In response to this shortage of resources and childcare, community oriented grassroots movements started by and for parents to share resources and offer support are becoming more proliferate. For example, the Child Care Resource and Referral (CC&R) in California works to build social support networks and shared resources for child care, as well as improve the quality of child care and support families who

Should childcare be provided by the government so that all children have the same opportunity to receive quality care?

Pro: Providing high quality childcare for children from low-income families would help these children start kindergarten without an achievement gap and help their parents retain their jobs.

Con: The American public should not have to pay for childcare as it is a choice to have children and to work while they are young.

cannot afford child care. These organizations are not only for parents, they also seek to build relationships with local and state elected officials to advance a better quality, affordable, and accessible child care system for all families. In addition, childcare cooperatives are gaining in popularity and have received more support from states. Parents can combine their efforts and rotate as responsible caregivers and there is no cost since it is run and established by parents (Sustainable Economies Law Center 2017). This arrangement requires that states allow groups to care for children without licensing requirements.

Combating Interpersonal Violence

Exposure to interpersonal violence as a child often results in adverse outcomes across the life course. This includes physical, cognitive, and social effects. These children are more prone to depression, anxiety, poor physical health, and elevated rates of suicide. They are also more likely to become pregnant as teens, engage in risky behaviors, experience substance abuse, as well as display violent behavior as adults (Hamby et al. 2011). Exposure includes abuse, neglect, and witnessing violence between family members. Finding solutions to the problem of interpersonal violence is no small task considering the traditional family structure, and historical views regarding interpersonal violence as just a part of family life. However, many communities have mobilized to reduce this type of violence in the home. Community mobilization initiatives include, The Community Engagement Continuum, The ICP Model, The Spectrum of Violence, The Delta Project, and Men Stopping Violence. These models target change at many levels, including, individual, family, neighborhood, social institutions, and public policy (Shepard 2008). Community initiatives to stop family violence started in the 1970s with the Battered Women's Movement. In the 1990s the focus of these movements shifted to providing direct services to survivors and to offenders (Shepard 2008). More recently community initiatives have shifted to a focus on prevention and building informal and formal social networks within the community. To create social change efforts must start at the community level and involve community organizations and the cultural environment of the community. Community services include emergency shelters, counseling and support groups, help with childcare, employment, and transitional housing for survivors trying to rebuild their lives. More communities are now offering culturally specific services for racial and ethnic minorities, immigrants, LGBTQ members, the disabled, pregnant women, and teens (National Domestic Violence Hotline nd).

National organizations that work to end interpersonal violence are often composed of local chapters in communities. For example, INCITE! Women of Color Against Violence, is a national activist organization that works to end violence against women of color. It is composed of grassroots chapters across the United States. INCITE! works to develop policy and social change within these communities. Other national organizations, such as the National Coalition Against Domestic Violence (NCADV) take a different approach. NCADV is based on the premise that violence results from the abuse of power both within the family and within broader society (sexism, racism, homophobia). They believe that major social change is needed and must start with public education, community coalitions, and supporting shelter programs. There are countless other national organizations that work to eliminate different types of interpersonal family violence with the single focus to promote awareness, provide support to survivors, and work toward equality and social change more broadly in our society.

There are a variety of ways individuals can get involved in their own community to end interpersonal violence and support survivors. These include, being a source of support for survivors,

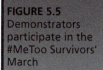

FIGURE 5.5
Demonstrators participate in the #MeToo Survivors' March

Source: David McNew/Getty Images

volunteering at battered women's shelters, and integrating education programs in schools, on college campuses, and community events. The National Domestic Violence Hotline is a national organization based in Austin, Texas, that offers many opportunities for individuals across the United States who are committed to ending domestic violence in their communities. These include internships for peer advocacy, volunteer opportunities to provide support and information via phone, social media, and text messaging, and connecting survivors with community services. They maintain a database of over 4,000 domestic violence programs across the United States and refer individuals to resources available in their community.

Support for Single Parent Households

Divorce is considered a social problem when it affects children negatively by increasing mental stress, and subsequently decreasing quality of life. Women are most likely to act as the custodial parents for children after divorce and are also more likely to experience a sharp decline in their standard of living after a divorce. According to the U.S. Census only 41.2% of custodial parents received the full amount of child support owed to them and 82.2% of custodial parents were mothers (U.S. Census 2010). In addition, 41% of single mother headed households were living below the poverty line. According to research conducted at the University of Texas, single mothers face more financial and caregiving stress and have more difficulty balancing employment and family life than married mothers (Umberson, Pudrovska, and Reczek 2010).

Advocacy groups for single parents are an important resource for support, education, assistance, and networking. Community advocacy groups also help single parents find state and federal support programs. For example, The Single Parent Advocate, a community advocacy group in Dallas, Texas, provides information for state and other resources, recruits volunteers to become single parent advocates, and connects single parents with affordable child care, retraining programs, as well as mental health resources. Parents Without Partners, The Single Parents Alliance of America, and The Mommies Network, just to name a few, are national groups that offer social support to single parents through local community based chapters that meet and form informal social support networks. Through these groups single mothers can find support and friendship from other single parents, share resources, and network to form alliances for car pools, shared child care, and other forms of support traditionally found in extended family and kinship networks (The Single Parent Advocate nd).

Other community based volunteer driven groups include Helping Hands for Single Moms, a group that helps single mothers pursue a college degree, as well as charity organizations such as Catholic Charities, that offers rent and housing help as well as self-sufficiency programs for single mothers and their children. Partnerships between national organizations and community based groups create strong alliances. The Salvation Army works with local food banks and partners with community based charities and non-profits to provide housing assistance, emergency and food assistance, as well as homeownership programs.

As family structures grow more diverse and encompass more than just individuals related by blood or marriage, our society may take a less private and more communal attitude toward parenting. This would likely reduce interpersonal violence, child neglect, food insecurity, and family poverty. Collective social responsibility for children shifts the family from a private sphere of Western individuality to a collective approach that involves partnership and collaboration within a neighborhood or community.

CHAPTER SUMMARY

- The American family has grown more diverse in form and now consists of single-parent families, blended families, binuclear, cohabitating and same-sex families, as well as the traditional nuclear family form. Delayed childbearing, women's increased participation in the labor force, and the increase in births to unmarried single women are all factors driving these changes.

- Social problems within the family include interpersonal violence, marital discord, divorce, and the financial hardship single mothers often experience after a divorce or transition to single parenting. Inequalities in power, emotional work, housework, as well as the gender wage gap contribute to problems in the family.

- Solutions to the problems faced by the contemporary American family include social support networks for single parents, community based groups that help families with child care, housing, and retraining programs, and national organizations with local chapters that aid and support. Survivors of interpersonal violence can find many advocacy groups that offer housing, counseling, and social support. In addition, grassroots organizations dedicated to preventing interpersonal violence have shifted the focus to structural changes that are necessary to reduce violence within the family. These include imbalances of power, working toward gender equality, and addressing sexism and traditional norms about marriage and childrearing roles.

- The American family continues to change as do ideas about what exactly constitutes a family in a society where the strongest support and commitment is not necessarily a role filled by individuals connected by blood or marriage.

REFERENCES

Almeida, Rhea V. 2010. "Domestic Violence in Heterosexual Relationships." In Barbara J. Risman, ed. *Families as They Really Are*. New York: W.W. Norton and Company.

American Academy of Child and Adolescent Psychiatry. 2008. Mental Illness in Families. Retrieved May 24, 2017 (www.aacap.org/AACAP/Families_and_Youth/ Facts_for_Families/FFF-Guide/Children-Of-Parents-With-Mental-Illness-039.aspx).

American Association of University Women (AAUW). 2016. The Simple Truth About the Gender Pay Gap. (www.aauw.org/research/the-simple-truth-about-the-gender-gap).

American Psychological Association (APA). nd. Family Members of Adults with Substance Abuse Problems.

Blau, Peter. 1964. *Exchange and Power in Social Life*. New York: John Wiley and Sons.

Burgess, Ernest W., and Harvey J. Locke. 1945. *The Family: From Institution to Companionship*. New York: American Book Company.

Cahn, Nancy. 2006. "Child Witnessing of Domestic Violence." In Nancy E. Dowd, Dorothy G. Singer and Robin Fretwell, eds. *Handbook of Children, Culture, and Violence*. Pp. 3–19. Thousand Oaks, CA: Sage.

Casserly, Megan. 2012. "Google Employees Family Leave Perks." *Forbes*. Retrieved June 12, 2017 (www.forbes.com).

Centers for Disease Control. 2016. Child Abuse and Neglect Prevention. Retrieved May 5, 2017 (www.cdc.gov/violenceprevention/childmaltreatment/index.html).

Child Care Resource and Referral. 2017. Retrieved June 12, 2017 (www.parentvoice.com).

Chodorow, Nancy. 1979. *The Reproduction of Mothering: Psychoanalysis and the Sociology of Gender*. Berkeley: University of California Press.

Cohen, Philip N. and Danielle MacCarthy. 2004. "Inequality and the Family." In Jacqueline Scott, Judith Treas, and Martin Richards, eds. *The Blackwell Companion to the Sociology of Families*. Pp. 181–192. Malden, MA: Blackwell Publishing Co.

Collins, Randall and Michael Makowsky. 1998. *The Discovery of Society*, 6th ed. Boston: McGraw-Hill.

Coontz, Stephanie. 1992. *The Way We Never Were: American Families and the Nostalgia Trap*. New York: Basic Books.

Cummings, E. Mark and Patrick Davies. 2010. *Marital Conflict and Children: An Emotional Security Perspective*. New York: Guilford Press.

Dore, Martha Morrison. 1998. Impact and Relationship of Substance Abuse and Child Maltreatment: Risk and Resiliency Factors: What Research Tells Us. Paper prepared for presentation at the conference entitled "Protecting Children in Substance Abusing Families," September 28, 1998, sponsored by the Center for Advanced Studies in Child Welfare, University of Minnesota School of Social Work, Minneapolis, MN. Retrieved May 24, 2017 (http://cascw.umn.edu/wp-content/uploads/2014/04/SubstanceAbuse-_Maltreatment.pdf).

Edles, Laura D. and Applerouth, Scott. 2015. *Sociological Theory in the Classical Era: Text and Readings*. Thousand Oaks, CA: Sage Publications.

Engles, Frederick. 2001. *The Origin of the Family, Private Property and the State*. Edited with an Introduction by Eleanor Burke Leacock. New York: International Publishers.

Hamby, Sherry, David Finkelhor, Heather Turner, and Richard Ormrod. 2011. "The overlap of witnessing partner violence with child maltreatment and other victimizations in a nationally representative survey of youth." *Child Abuse and Neglect*. 34 (10) 734–741.

Hamm, Katie and Carmel Martin. 2015. "A New Vision for Child Care in the United States: A Proposed New Tax Credit to Expand High-Quality Child Care. Center for American Progress." Retrieved June 6, 2017 (www.earlychildhoodfinance.org /dev/wp-content/uploads/2016/07/Hamm-Child-care-report1.pdf).

Hochschild, Arlie Russell. 2003. *The Second Shift*. New York: Penguin Books.

Homans, George. 1958. "Social Behavior as Exchange." *American Journal of Sociology*. 63 (6): 597–606.

Kephart, William M. 1972. *The Family, Society, and the Individual*, 3rd ed. Boston: Houghton Mifflin Company.

Livingston, Gretchen. 2014. "Fewer than Half of U.S. Kids Today Live in a 'Traditional' Family." Pew Research Center. Retrieved June 8, 2017 (www.pewresearch.org/fact-tank/2014/12/22/less-than-half-of-u-s-kids-today-live-in-a-traditional-family/).

Mead, George Herbert. 1977. *George Herbert Mead on Social Psychology*. Chicago: University of Chicago Press.

Mills, C. Wright. 2000. *The Sociological Imagination*, 40th anniversary edition. New York: Oxford.

Mintz, Steven and Susan Kellogg. 1988. *Domestic Revolutions: A Social History of American Family Life*. New York: Free Press.

Murdock, George Peter. 1960. *Social Structure*. New York: The Macmillan Company.

Naisbitt, John. 1984. *Megatrends: Ten New Directions Transforming our Lives*. New York: Warner Books.

National Association of Child Care Resource and Referral Agencies. 2016. *Parents and the High Cost of Child Care*. Retrieved June 8, 2017 (www.ccrcca.org/resources/family-resource-directory/item/national-association-of-child-care-resource-and-referral-agencies).

National Coalition Against Domestic Violence. 2016. Who is Doing What to Whom? Determining the Core Aggressor in Relation to Where Domestic Violence Exists. Retrieved May 24, 2017 (www.ncadv.org/files/Who%20is%20 Doing%20What%20to%20Whom.pdf).

National Conference of State Legislatures. 2017. Washington D.C. Domestic Violence Hotline. Retrieved June 1, 2017 (www.thehotline.org/).

National Domestic Violence Hotline. nd. Retrieved June 4, 2017 (thehotline.org).

Nicholson, Joanne, Kathleen Beibel, Betsy Hinden, Henry Alexis, and Lawrence Stier. 2001. *Critical Issues for Parents with Mental Illness*. Center for Mental Health Services, Substance Abuse, and Mental Health Services. Retrieved May 24, 2017 (www.uwgb.edu/bhtp/tools/critical_issues.pdf).

Parsons, Talcott. 1954. *Essays in Sociological Theory*, revised edition. New York: Free Press.

Potuchek, Jean L. 1997. *Who Supports the Family? Gender and Breadwinning in Dual-Earner Marriages*. Stanford, CA: Stanford University Press.

Shepard, Melanie. 2008. Mobilizing Communities to Prevent Domestic Violence. National Online Resource Center on Violence Against Women. Retrieved June 2, 2017 (http://vawnet.org/sites/default/files/materials/files/2016-09/AR_MobComm.pdf).

Sprey, Jetse. 1969. "The Family as a System in Conflict." *Journal of Marriage and the Family*. 31 (4): 699–706 (www.jstor.org/stable/349311).

Stepler, Renee. 2017. "Led by Baby Boomers, divorce rates climb for America's 50+ Population." Pew Research Center. Retrieved May 15, 2017 (www.pewresearch.org/fact-tank/2017/03/09/led-by-baby-boomers-divorce-rates-climb-for-americas-50-population/).

Sustainable Economies Law Center. 2017. Retrieved June 20, 2017 (www.co-oplaw.org/co-op-basics/types/childcare-cooperatives/).

The Single Parent Advocate. nd. Retrieved June 4, 2017 (www.singleparentadvocate.org).

Umberson, Debra, Tetyana Pudrovska, and Corinne Reczek. 2010. "Parenthood, childlessness, and well-being: A life course perspective." *Journal of Marriage and Family*. 72 (3): 612–629.

United States Bureau of Labor Statistics. 2013. *National Compensation Survey*. Retrieved June 4, 2017 (www.bls.gov/ncs/).

United States Census Bureau. 2010. Custodial Mothers and Fathers and Their Child Support. 2010. Retrieved June 12, 2017 (www.census.gov/hhes/www/childsupport/source09.pdf).

United States Census Bureau. Household and Families 2012. 2010 Census Briefs. Child (Lofquist, Daphne; Terry Lugaila, Martin O'Connell; and Sarah Feliz).

Whitton, Sarah W., Galena K. Rhoades, Scott M. Stanley, and Howard J. Markman. 2008. "Effects of Parental Divorce on Marital Commitment and Confidence." *Journal of Family Psychology*. (22) 5: 789–793.

CHAPTER 6

Sex and Gender

ABOUT THE PROBLEM: SEX AND GENDER

Definitions

Sex the biological distinctions of male and female.

Gender the social expectations that exist for males and females.

Gender Roles cultural norms that create the differential expectations for both sexes.

Gender Identity how people perceive themselves based on the culturally-imposed understandings of gender.

Sex and gender are two terms that are often used interchangeably, however these concepts are very different. **Sex** refers to the biological distinctions of male and female, while **gender** refers to the cultural expectations that exist for males and females; these specific expectations are dictated by norms that express differences and are referred to as **gender roles**. "Sugar and spice and everything nice, that's what little girls are made of" while "snips and snails and puppy dog tails, that's what little boys are made of", to quote a very old ditty, expresses these distinctions. Differences do exist between the two sexes, but what drives these differences is an important question and one that is often considered by sociologists.

The terms sex and gender reflect the age-old nature and nurture debate: do people think and act based on the forces of biology (nature) or socialization (nurture)? The question does not, of course, pose a binary choice; few sociologists would take the position that nature plays no part in human activity, however, most would challenge some commonly held beliefs about its dominance in human life. Children develop a deeply ingrained **gender identity,** how they perceive themselves based on gender, due to responses from parents, school, peers, communities, and later, employers, as children envision jobs that might be appropriate for their gender. The terms *gender scripts* or *gender schemas* are sometimes used to explain the ways that people understand their roles based on gender and gives children a guide on how the society expects them to act and behave as males and females. Some people do not feel their sexual identity fits with the gender roles they have been assigned; the experiences of transgendered people have come out in the open within the last few years and have created a reconsideration of sex and gender (this will be addressed in the next chapter).

The Ties that Separate

Not only do males and females receive differential treatment, people are differentiated in many areas such as our actions (including speech patterns), our interests (recreational pursuits and others), and certain ritualistic behavior (think of males retiring to the "man cave" or females spending a "girl's night out"), and even the choice to buy and wear certain clothes. Around the turn of the twentieth century, early feminist sociologist Charlotte Perkins Gilman, noting that clothing reinforces notions of gender, stated that "cloth is a social tissue" (Gilman, Hill, and Deegan 2002:3). The clothing issue was addressed many decades later by Brownmiller (1984), who asserts that activists of all three waves of feminism (to be discussed soon) have struggled with the appropriateness of women's dress, defined as the "chief outward expression of the feminine difference" which offers a "continuing reassurance to men and themselves that a male is a male because a female dresses, looks, and acts like another sort of creature" (p. 79).

A question about gender roles deserves investigation: what happens when differences between males and females are exaggerated? Do the exaggerations reflect quaint traditions, promote a harmless social deception, or does it lead to other problems such as gender inequality? The last possibility in that list is included in the recent focus in the sociological literature on "social space". Spain (1992), for example, notes this importance of space in gender relationships, in this case how society has used spatial constructions to thwart women's access to knowledge, which in turn results in less access to power and privilege and, correspondingly, less access to social status. These "gendered

FIGURE 6.1
Differences in gender role expectations make it difficult for women to have both a career and a family.

Source: nuvolanevicata/Shutterstock.com

spaces", in the form of segregated homes, educational institutions, and workplaces, create barriers that further discern and separate based on gender.

There are certain behavioral traits that are predominately linked to males and others to females, e.g., men are rational, detached, in charge, and dominant; women are nurturing, emotional, placating, and submissive. While these traits are descriptive for *some* males and females, they are not descriptive for *all* males and females in *all* situations. They are persistent generalizations based on gender, often called **gender stereotypes**, rather than exact observations. In this case, the "opposite sex" designation is actually in itself a stereotype (Lips 2005).

> **Gender Stereotypes** persistent generalizations about people based on perceived gender characteristics.

A Social Construction?

Gender is considered by some to be a social construct because society has prescribed the thoughts, actions, and roles that people are expected to fulfill based on whether they are born into the categories of male or female. These roles are not inherent, they are culturally generated. As Koss et al. (1994) note, the cultural variations that formulate gender roles are complex and traverse other categories such as ethnicity and sexual orientation. If we remember from the first chapter of this text, Mills (1959) encouraged the use of the *sociological imagination* to understand the connection between social forces and the individual concerns—this can easily be seen in the social construction of gender, as larger forces create the gender role norms we follow so stringently at a more localized level. The reason these roles are so engrained and rigidly adhered to is a major area of study for sociologists.

Not all people, of course, accept the premise that gender is a social construction. Opponents state that differences between males and females are primarily biologically imprinted rather than socially influenced and that biology is important in defining one's involvement in employment, sports, and other areas of life (Rhoades 2004). The differences in gender, using this line of thought, should be accepted and attempts should not be made to integrate the two sexes into areas in which they are not biologically suited, lest society will become dysfunctional and disordered.

In chapter 3, we explored the idea of the social contract that binds humans with their government. In *The Sexual Contract* (1988), Pateman explains that the social contract theory of Rousseau, as well as those of Locke and Kant, emphasizes the social responsibilities of men, as citizens to their governments, while at the same time emphasizing the "natural" qualities of females, with responsibilities to the home. The freedom which social control theory is supposed to offer citizens often do not include female citizens. Early political theories, therefore, failed to account for the subordination of women embodied in these theories.

> **Sexism** prejudice and discrimination based on sex and gender.
>
> **Institutionalized Sexism** when sexism is built into the social structure.
>
> **Glass Ceiling** a situation in which women can enter the workplace but are unable to get promoted due to sexism.

The basis of gender inequality is sexism. **Sexism** refers to both prejudice and discrimination that exists because of ideas about sex and gender. Sexism is **institutionalized** when discrimination is built into the structure of society, for example, when women are employed into lower level positions but are unable to rise in the organization (a term called the **glass ceiling**).

The Violent Consequences of Gender Inequality

As Koss et al. (1994) note, male violence against women is "a manifestation of gender inequality and as a mechanism for the subordination of women" (p. 4). Rape is especially prominent among

FIGURE 6.2
Jerusalem, Israel-May 13, 2016: The 5th 'SlutWalk' march in Jerusalem. The Slut Walk rallies across the world started after a Toronto cop said in 2011 'Don't Dress Like Sluts' To Avoid Sexual Assault.

Source: Avivi Aharon/Shutterstock.com

women as nearly 1 in 5 reported experiencing rape as opposed to 1 in 71 men; this figure shows the disparity between males and females in this criminal activity. Regarding coercion, 13% of women and 6% of men report being coerced into some type of unwanted sexual conduct (Centers for Disease Control 2012). Rape and its brutality is a universal trait that is linked to power, control, domination and feelings of privilege to violate others and requires that society take a close look at the patterns of patriarchy that allow this abuse (Madhubti 1993). A look at how rape is used in times of war and political unrest globally amplifies this use of power and control. We will provide more attention to this issue in chapter 12.

Estrich (1987) describes two types of rape: "real" and "simple"; real rape refers to sexual assaults that, due to the circumstances involved, are uncontested by those in authority and simple rape refers to those situations where people normally know each other and where consent is questioned (we often call this date or acquaintance rape today). Both, as Estrich notes, are really cases of rape, however. The use of the term "simple rape" is obviously problematic and could be referred to by some other name—suggestions, students?

College campuses are places where sexual victimization is widespread due to several factors, including the fact that people of dating age are together in a constricted social space, are normally away from home, and social settings are available where alcohol and other drugs are omnipresent. The age factor is significant: among female rape victims, 37.4% were first raped between 18–24 years of age. A recent study found that 19% of undergraduate women experienced some type of sexual assault while in college. However, non-college women are more at risk for rape than their college counterparts and they experienced rape and other forms of sexual assault at a rate 1.2 times higher. A very bothersome figure which colleges must address is that non-reported rapes and other forms of sexual assault are very high (80%); this non-reporting behavior is lower for non-students (67%) (Sinozich 2014).

The issue of "consent" for college students and teens is an area of ongoing controversy. There is no single definitive definition of consent. In general, it means agreement that is voluntary and the person can make an informed decision in the context of the situation. However, a person's capacity to consent is based on factors such as age, disability, intoxication, and power differentials. States have different laws and on college campuses Title IX committees must sort out whether consent was given. Some of the questions that arise focus on how accurate a person's memory is if the person was intoxicated. What if both parties were intoxicated and one party claims it was rape? Other questions that arise are how to determine consent. Should it be verbal? And does non-verbal consent include when a person stops saying "no"? Many of these questions are based on the concern that women will falsely report a sexual assault either because they don't remember giving consent or because they regret their decision afterward. However, according to current data, between 2% to 8% of sexual assault reports are considered false (Lisak et al. 2010). And the meaning of false in this context is that the sexual assault report could not be proven for any number of reasons, including not enough evidence, etc. Issues of consent continue to be debated both on and off college campuses.

One of the difficulties facing many survivors of sexual assault is the long tradition of "blaming the victim" especially in situations where abuser and victim are or were in intimate relationships. In the 1960s, a study of "wife beaters" (to use an older term) suggested that the pathology resided in the battered female who failed to meet the batterer's "masochistic needs". Attempts were made in the 1980s to diagnose female interpersonal violence victims with "masochistic personality disorder" in the Diagnostic and Statistical Manual of Mental Disorders (DSM); this diagnosis implies that the battered person remains in relationships with the abuser despite the interpersonal violence. This resulted in several feminist groups intervening. The predominantly male psychiatrist establishment that oversees the DSM initially balked at changing this diagnosis but eventually offered a compromise—the new diagnosis (for the victim, remember) was called "self-defeating personality disorder", which was placed in the appendix of the manual (Herman 1997). Problems with this diagnostic label should be obvious.

Prostitution, a form of sex work, has long been considered to continue to exist due to patriarchy and sexism, and feminists and sex workers challenged the laws that end up prosecuting the sex workers (normally female) rather than the customers (normally male) and pushed for protection from worker violence and other forms of exploitation. Sex trafficking results when people, often women and girls, are forced into prostitution and other forms of sex work and labor, and is a global concern due not only for being a civil rights violation but also for the transport of humans across national borders. Sex trafficking victims are overwhelmingly female (94%) and the trafficking suspects are overwhelmingly male (81%). The victims of sex trafficking are controlled through physical and sexual violence, threats, isolation, shaming, debt servitude, and false promises of protection and a better future (Bureau of Justice Statistics 2011). As Cobble, Gordon, and Henry (2014) argue, sex work that is performed because this is the most available employment that pays a living wage is in itself coercion, and a reflection of greater gender inequality in society.

Is sex work a legitimate occupation that should be protected by law?

Pro: Sex work can be a legitimate way to make a living and the government should not be allowed to regulate how an adult chooses to use their body for compensation.
Con: Sex work is demeaning to women and rarely a choice a person would make if they had other options, thus it is coercive and a product of gender inequality that should remain illegal.

Sexual harassment is "another problem without a name" (Rosen 2006:23). Sexual harassment can be defined as unwelcome physical or verbal sexual behavior which interferes with a person's work performance or that creates an offensive or hostile work environment (EEOC nd). Sexual harassment was only given a name in 1975 when a group of activists exposed the unwelcome sexual activities of a male professor; before that, this phenomenon was once just considered by females entering the workplace to be an occupational hazard they sometimes had to endure. The very public case involving United States Supreme Court Justice Clarence Thomas and former aide Anita Hill during Thomas' confirmation, followed by a number of other high-profile instances, made the matter public and produced debates about this and other sexual behaviors that have been long hidden (Rosen 2006).

THEORETICAL PERSPECTIVES

Structural Functionalism

Structural functionalists view the role of males and females in a functional society as requiring some degree of complementarity to produce a balanced system. The views seem a bit old fashioned today but many people see the need to distinguish gender roles to maintain traditional values that are deemed favorable. The role of biology seems to find its place in functionalist views, though one could argue that regardless of biology, socialization processes still need cohesion, balance, and complementarity to keep society functioning correctly. If America is indeed a melting pot, or patchwork quilt (or other similar metaphor), pluralism must be maintained, allowing all groups to maintain their own unique heritage, without the existence of dominance and submissiveness. This interdependence is important to society, according to the functionalist perspective.

Parsons (1954) observes the complementary and functional roles of males and females and posits two types—*instrumental*, the practical role which deals with the task orientation normally associated with masculinity, and *expressive*, the nurturing, familial orientation normally associated with femininity. As mentioned in chapter 5, Parson's ideas reflect his own "standpoint" (a concept which will be discussed in more detail shortly) from a subjective perspective based on personal experience. And while this perspective might seem outdated today, it should be noted that many people in America, and around the world, still adopt this viewpoint.

Goldberg presented a theory that is summed up in the title of his book *The Inevitability of Patriarchy: Why the Biological Difference Between Men and Women Always Produces Male Dominance* (1974). Goldberg states the role of biology explains that males have always been and will always be in leadership positions due to the naturally aggressive tendencies in men. His strict emphasis on biological determinism refutes feminist explanations of patriarchy, for which he claims there are four fallacies: feminist "nurture" explanations fail to account for anthropological and biological evidence to the contrary; they assume that since there are some common sexual aspects, all are "functionally identical"; they cannot face the inevitability of innate sex differences, therefore they reject or rationalize scientific findings; and most importantly, there is a confusion over "cause and function", in that feminists, particularly those of the socialist or Marxist types, believe capitalism created sex differentiations—a historical perspective tells us that patriarchy existed well before then. As he notes, "because the social and economic must conform to the biological, we can change any variable and patriarchy will not be diminished" (p. 167). This perspective assumes a functional society if the two sexes follow their predetermined biological roles.

Conflict

Rejecting the consensus and conformity issues of gender espoused by structural functionalists, conflict theorists note the inequality which exists due to a societal focus on the differentiation of sex and gender. Oppression that is based on such a differentiation, an oppression found in patriarchal societies is a focus of conflict theory. The work of feminist sociologists has been especially instructive in this area. Understanding the standpoints of how different characteristics and social identities (e.g., sex, gender, race, ethnicity, sexual orientation), have been affected by inequalities and oppression have further developed into the field of inquiry area called intersectionality, as will be discussed soon, an area that is getting much recent attention in feminist sociology.

In a work originally released prior to the turn of the last century, Charlotte Perkins Gilman offered some incredibly insightful ideas on how male/female relations were affected by economic conditions. In *Women and Economics* ([1898] 1966), she notes how men use economic power to subjugate women into roles as housekeepers and child raisers. By controlling the family income, the wife/mother is denied independence to have outside employment, therefore the husband/father becomes "her food source" (p. 22). Gilman notes how such an arrangement is unnatural and is not found anywhere else in the animal kingdom, as other females are not reliant on male sustenance. Gilman goes on to ask why women's labor in the home is unpaid labor.

Susan Brownmiller (1975) offers an interesting and controversial thesis on female inequality which involves the consequences of the first sexual assault of a woman by a man. She posited that the first rape of a woman by a man made females keenly aware of the danger that exists for them. Coalescing with other women would not be an acceptable strategy as men, often larger and stronger, would render them unable to protect themselves collectively. The only strategy was for the woman to enter into a personal contract with a male in which he would offer her protection if she agreed to take a subordinate role in the relationship, tending to the children and settling into a lifestyle where the children and the property were his—in effect, the wife, children, and physical property would be controlled by the male. This idea does little for promoting the romantic ideals of marriage and family life but it does have some merit, even if the "female fear" (Gordon and Riger 1989) was a general fear of violence by males, rather than specifically sexual assault.

Symbolic Interactionism

Sex and gender create an idea of how a person sees himself or herself (note the gender specific pronouns?) and how identity is based, to a large degree on these attributes. Gender is basically understood as a social construction and people are expected to follow social norms regarding gender roles, especially as these roles are presented to others. Stereotypes and self-fulfilling prophecies are derived from the compliance or non-compliance with gender roles. These areas are critical to the theory of symbolic interactionism.

The work of feminist sociologist Dorothy Smith and feminist theorist Patricia Hill Collins both encompass many theoretical perspectives, however, they are considered here as their work focuses on identity, a key concern of symbolic interactionists. Smith (1987) uses the concept of "standpoint" to describe how people understand the world based upon their own subjective experiences; for Smith, this concept is necessary in understanding gender differences. Collins (1991) extends the idea of standpoint theory by stating that people must adopt a standpoint to fully understand the experiences of not only gender but also race. She notes that, in an ironic twist, feminist theory has not been beneficial to black feminist thought, as race has been excluded in the overall feminist discussions over the years.

Philosopher Judith Butler is mentioned in this section as some of her ideas on gender performativity reflect and extend the dramaturgical work of sociologist Erving Goffman and others while being based on sex and gender. Butler (1990) presents an intriguing idea—that gender, the socially constructed designation of either male or female, creates a worldview in which people are forced to perform as the sex they were assigned. The idea of performativity reflects the fact that humans perform roles—unconsciously, enduring, and continuous—based on these assignments. This is contrasted with Goffman's ideas of impression management in which people perform roles consciously, often deceptively, and often for a limited period. In both cases, though, the performance contributes to the development of self, and correspondingly, identity.

SEARCHING FOR SOLUTIONS

Addressing Sex and Gender Inequality: Feminist and Masculinist Movements

Feminism has long sought to promote a society that treats males and females equally. Simply put, it is the idea that men and woman should have equality in political, economic, social, and family arenas. The term **egalitarianism** refers to a situation where both males and females receive this equal treatment. This term refers to a more intellectual and philosophical approach that informs feminism but does not necessarily advocate for gender equality. Cobble et al. (2014) advocate that in lieu of the term feminism to describe advocacy of feminist ideology, the term "feminisms" is better used to express the variety of perspectives that have long existed to attend to the issues of women. Tong (2009) notes this diversity in the existence of many types of feminist groups: liberal, radical, Marxist/socialist, psychoanalytic, care-focused, multicultural/global/post-cultural, postmodern/third wave, and ecofeminism.

Feminism an advocacy of equality for both males and females in all areas of social life.

Egalitarianism the equal treatment of both males and females.

FIGURE 6.3 From left to right, female MPs Edith Summerskill, Patricia Ford (MP for County Down), Barbara Castle (1910–2002, MP for Blackburn) and Irene Ward (MP for Tynemouth) make their way to the House of Commons with a petition from the Equal Pay Campaign Committee demanding equal pay for women, 8th March 1954. They have collected 80,000 signatures on the petition.

Source: Terry Fincher/Keystone/Hulton Archive/Getty Images

It is generally agreed that there have been four waves of feminism in American history: the first wave that occurred in the mid-eighteenth and early twentieth centuries was organized around women's suffrage, voting rights, child labor, access to birth control, prohibition, the needs of pregnant mothers, poverty, international relations, civil rights, and war. This first wave was considered a movement by privileged white women who had the resources, time, and support to work toward women's rights. However, it planted the seed that women have as much or more to contribute to the public sphere as men. At the core of the first wave was the focus on legal and political issues (Humm 1992).

The second wave, that developed in the 1960s and 1970s questioned many social concerns of the day; in 1963, Betty Friedan published the bestselling book *The Feminine Mystique* which addressed the "problem that has no name" (p. 15), a growing dissatisfaction with the lack of freedom and choices that suburban wifedom and motherhood offerred women in post-World War II America. Second wave feminists tackled the gender discrimination that continued after World War II in employment and other areas, sexuality, reproductive rights, the Vietnam War, and other oppressions that thwarted "women's liberation". This wave was set against the backdrop of the Civil Rights movement and was very involved in working to pass the Equal Rights Amendment (ERA), a proposed constitutional amendment that would guarantee social equality for women.

Starting out as a grassroots movement in 1966, the National Organization for Women (NOW) has grown to be the largest organization of feminist grassroots advocates in our society (NOW 2017). It is still one of the largest feminist organizations and has local chapters across the United States. The organization is committed to action through grassroots activism aimed at protecting the

FIGURE 6.4 NEW SMYRNA BEACH, FL - 1983: African-American writer, feminist, poet and civil-rights activist Audre Lorde (1934–1992) poses for a photograph during her 1983 residency at the Atlantic Center for the Arts in New Smyrna Beach, Florida.

Source: Robert Alexander/Getty Imagesv

rights of women in all aspects of social, political, and economic life (NOW 2017). Individuals can join and volunteer with their local chapter to work toward social change in their community. Some of the issues they work toward include LGBTQ rights, racial equality, abortion rights, and ending violence against women. The second wave was met with some backlash from minority women who felt that feminism did not represent their experiences and ultimately did not include women who were not white and middle class. This inspired the creation of organizations like the National Black Feminist Organization in 1973 that focused on the issues that were central to the experiences of black women. Unfortunately, this organization only lasted three years. The group's demise was attributed to its inability to reach a consensus regarding what constituted black feminist politics (White 2001).

The third wave of feminism, beginning in the 1990s, produced more young women seeking to overcome the problems left unaccomplished by the second wave, focusing their activism on the newly emerging issue of **intersectionality**—the confluence of gender, race, class, nationality, and sexuality (Cobble, Gordon and Henry 2014). Intersectionality was first introduced to analyze intersections of disadvantage. For example, an African-American woman who is a sexual minority occupies several positions of disadvantage: gender, race, sexual orientation. These intersections create multiple forms of disadvantage for women that shape their experiences—making it impossible to compare the experience of a middle-class heterosexual white woman with the experience of a woman who identifies as a low-income, sexual and racial minority (Collins 1991). To address the different challenges women experience depending on their positions of disadvantage, the third wave

Intersectionality an understanding that there is a convergence of and interconnectedness between sex, race, class, and other social characteristics that result in systematic oppression.

of feminism was much more inclusive of all women. In addition, the third wave questioned heteronormativity and conventional standards of beauty. They refused to think in terms of "us-them", and felt that identifying as a "feminist" was limiting and exclusionary. They viewed feminism as a limiting and heteronormative category much like gender and sexuality, and pushed for a post-modern view of feminism that focused more on the performative aspects and less on the power dynamics and structural aspects (Mills and Mullany 2011).

As Rosen (2006) notes, "each generation of women activists leaves an unfinished agenda for the next generation" (p. 344). Each new wave represents the growing concerns of that era, for example, third wave feminism had to deal with the backlash from the second wave. Schacht and Ewing (2004) note that if feminism seems to project an anti-male line of thought, men will not seriously consider adopting the approach and recommend that feminism be viewed as a perspective that seeks to improve the lives of both sexes and questions if "the term feminism has too much baggage, too long a tradition of exclusiveness, to be a banner under which all people can unite" (p. 55). If this is so, an interesting intellectual exercise would consist of claiming a new name to address this issue.

Feminism should change its name to something that better identifies its focus on equality.

Pro: Because of anti-feminist propaganda, feminism has become equated with male-hating; a new name would reduce the stigma of feminist thought.

Con: Changing the name would take it from its early roots and a name change could be confusing, slowing the evolution of feminist thought.

A more inclusive definition of feminism is being adopted as simply "gender equality", and promotes a less polarizing view of feminism as a "women's issue". According to gender studies scholar, Michael Kimmel, gender equality has advantages for men, women, families, and society. Countries with high gender equality are healthier and rate higher on happiness for both men and women (Kimmel 2015). Kimmel further points out that when men share equally in housework and childcare, their children and wives are happier and healthier, and men themselves are less likely to be depressed, smoke or engage in risky behaviors, and more likely to receive preventative health care and thus experience fewer illnesses. From this perspective, embracing gender equality is good for everyone in society. Companies that have high gender equality are more profitable and their employees are happier and more productive. Countries that rank high on gender equality also rank higher on overall rates of happiness (Kimmel 2015).

With the rise of the fourth wave of feminism, there are already signs that the millennial generation does not identify as the feminists their mothers and grandmothers labeled themselves (Baumgardner 2011). This wave started around 2008, is still coalescing, and has strong ties to social media as its main platform. Rather than meeting in a physical location, this wave is more likely to use Twitter, blogs, and online media to organize. This wave is founded on rejecting gender and sexual binaries, taking on trans-issues, and sex positivity (the idea that all sex, as long as it is consensual, is positive). It calls for men and women to utilize their power, skills, and knowledge to advocate for a world where all people are accepted regardless of sex, race, sexuality, class, or national identity.

In addition, the concept of **masculinities** has been used to describe a gender focus on men's experiences—the plural form is used due to the number of different forms of masculine perspectives (Morgan 1992); this can be compared with the use of the term "feminisms" in the previous section. The so-called "men's movement" began in the late 1970s and bifurcated into camps: a pro-feminist movement which asserts that sexism is deleterious to both sexes *equally*, and a counter-feminist movement which sees modern society as providing more power and privilege to women and more degradation to men, often called "male bashing" (Clatterbaugh 1997). Two key authors were instrumental in bringing the men's movement to the forefront. Robert Bly's *Iron John* (1991) creates a narrative about "the grief of men" and describes a world in which male power is slipping away, leaving it up to the Wild Man, an archetypal shamanic teacher, to guide young males in this unfamiliar new world. In a similar vein, Sam Keen's *Fire in the Belly: On Being a Man* (1991) takes readers on a journey which allows men to "concentrate on recollecting and savoring their uniqueness" (p. 10). Both authors, primarily from the pro-feminist camp, gave voice to the new men's movement.

> **Masculinities** a form of gender exploration that emphasizes male experiences.

In contrast, The Promise Keepers is another men's movement that is comprised of evangelical Christian men. Started in 1992 in Colorado, although its genesis can be found at least a decade earlier, this movement has grown very rapidly since its inception. The group sees current society in a moral crisis that needs leadership by men who practice virtue to women; men are asked to keep their promises to women by providing respect, protection, and a good living to their spouses (Clatterbaugh 1997). Related to this movement is the purity ball phenomenon which began in the late 1990s, also in Colorado; purity balls are elaborate events that often resemble weddings in which daughters give a pledge to their fathers of sexual abstinence until they marry—it should be noted that in this group there is not an equivalent ceremony for sons (Ehrlich 2014). While some find this movement respectful and admirable, others see it as fostering patriarchal relationships.

Masculinist movements are beneficial to the study of gender inequality.

Pro: Gender studies would not be complete without an understanding of male experiences.
Con: Masculinist movements suggest that male experiences with gender oppression are equivalent to female experiences.

As discussed earlier in the chapter, sexual assault is an issue of critical importance and disproportionately affects young women. Specifically, high incidence of date rape has given rise to the concept of a larger **rape culture** that is based on the unequal balance of power between men and women. When a society normalizes sexual violence, and blames the victims it creates a rape culture (Buchwald et al. 2005). The normalization occurs through social institutions, such as media portrayals of women as sex objects, high school, and college campuses where cases of sexual assault are often ignored or blamed on the victim, and law enforcement attitudes that are apathetic and slow to move against the dominant patriarchal culture. Fortunately, rape culture has slowly become part of the discourse on college campuses nationwide as students organize to heighten awareness about and combat sexual violence. Student led advocacy programs include: Students Active for Ending

> **Rape Culture** when a society normalizes a climate of sexual violence and blames the victims for the violence perpetuated against them.

Rape (SAFER), End Rape on Campus, and Know Your IX. These groups formed through grass-roots activism in response to inadequate support from colleges in their handling of sexual assault complaints.

Initiatives to Prevent Gender-based Assault

As student activists mobilize and heighten awareness about specific cases of sexual assault on their college campuses, the media has responded with increased coverage of high profile cases, and university officials have started to recognize that sexual assault occurs more often than it is reported. Student activism has led to unique approaches for protest. For example, a student and survivor of sexual assault at Columbia University used performance art to protest that her attacker was still on campus by carrying a mattress everywhere she went on campus, including her graduation ceremony. Two female students who filed complaints against the University of North Carolina for mishandling their sexual assault cases co-founded the student advocacy group, End Rape on Campus. Their experiences along with the similar experiences of many college students were highlighted in *The Hunting Ground*, a documentary that exposes the epidemic of campus rape culture and the prevalence of sexual assault as well as the attempts made by college campuses and university officials to cover up these crimes (Hunting Ground 2015). This documentary has been a catalyst for student groups, intervention strategies and local legislation inspired the campaign *It's On Us*. This movement focuses on creating a culture of consent, bystander intervention and survivor support (It's On Us 2017).

Should it be illegal for consent to be granted for sexual intimacy if the person who must grant consent has ingested any alcoholic beverages or mind-altering substances?

Pro: A person who is drinking or taking drugs does not have the mental capacity or reasoning skills to give informed consent for sexual intimacy.
Con: If a person has a drink they are still responsible for their behavior, and they can still give informed consent for sexual intimacy.

Another initiative that takes a unique approach to reducing sexual and interpersonal violence is Green Dot. This grassroots community organization focuses on bystander intervention to reduce sexual and interpersonal violence. Volunteers as well as front-line professionals are trained to implement the program in their community, including in schools and universities. The training is based on interdisciplinary theories regarding sexual violence and unequal power relations and focuses on the belief that the community has a social responsibility to keep their members safe (Green Dot Etc. 2017). This shifts the responsibility from the victims and perpetrators and onto bystanders. Engaged and pro-active bystanders can heighten awareness, intervene, and advocate for a safer community through individual actions. For example, putting up posters about sexual violence awareness and responding when friends are in high-risk situations are actions by individuals making choices to be involved and aware of interpersonal violence through their behavior, attitudes, and voices.

FIGURE 6.5 A woman holding a banner saying "don't get raped" during a rally to remember the gang raped victim from New Delhi in the year 2012 – on December 16, 2014 in Kolkata, India.

Source: arindambanerjee/Shutterstock.com

More broadly, national advocacy groups that work to eliminate rape culture and sexual violence in our society include, the National Network to End Domestic Violence (NNEDV), The National Alliance to End Sexual Violence, the Rape, Abuse, and Incest National Network (RAINN), and the Victim Rights Law Center. These groups have local chapters and train volunteers as well as work with various community organizations to provide resources and support for victims. The Victim Rights Law Center provides free legal services for sexual assault victims and trains attorneys, medical professionals, law enforcement, military personnel, and other professionals across the nation to work to end sexual and interpersonal violence (Victim Rights 2017).

In 2013, the Campus Sexual Violence Elimination Act was passed by Congress as an addition to the Violence against Women Act (VAWA). This was the first federal legislation that required colleges and universities to publicly report the number of dating and sexual violence claims filed in their annual crime reports. It also required colleges to put into place specific policies, protocols, and training programs for sexual violence on campus (Bishop, 2015). Although this legislation was considered a major step forward, many colleges and universities have found legal ways to under-report. According to the American Association of University Women (AAUW), in 2014, 91% of college campuses reported zero incidences of rape. These numbers suggest that students do not feel comfortable reporting sexual violence, and colleges are quite likely not reporting accurate data. If students feel their college has a hostile climate for reporting they are less likely to report their experiences. Clearly, there is much work to be done and federal policy is not the solution to such a complex problem.

CHAPTER SUMMARY

- Sex refers to the biological categories of male and female while gender refers to the social expectations that come with being male or female. Gender roles specifically define those sex-based expectations. Gender identity is formed early in life and children are socialized from a young age to conform to societal gender roles that align with their biological sex.

- Ultimately gender is a social construct and what is considered masculine of feminine in any given society is dynamic and shifts as women gain more equality. In fact, it is gender inequality that is a driving factor behind male violence against women, high rates of sexual assault, sex trafficking, and wage inequality. Women not only make less money than men for the same jobs, they are more likely to suffer from sexual harassment in the workplace as well.

- Structural functionalism views gender roles as natural and biological, with females caring for and males providing for the next generation. Conflict theorists focus on the oppression inherent in a patriarchal society and power differentials between men and women. In contrast, symbolic interactionism focuses on how we perform gender and use social constructs to form our gender identity.

- Equalitarianism between men and women is the focus of feminism. Feminism is dynamic and changes as the norms and values in society change. The United States has experienced several waves of feminism, with one wave building on the progress of the prior wave. Masculinities research has found that men are happier and healthier when they embrace gender equality in their personal lives and nations with high gender equality have higher rates of happiness.

- Unfortunately, in our society there is still a deeply rooted patriarchy that is illustrated in the high prevalence of interpersonal violence and a larger rape culture that normalizes violence against women. Grassroots community groups formed by college students have mobilized to reduce sexual violence and policy initiatives have made reporting of sexual assault mandatory for colleges that receive federal funding. However, the fight for gender equality in the workplace, on college campuses, and in the home, continues and gender equality will not be achieved as long as we have a patriarchal power structure in society.

REFERENCES

American Association of University Women. www.aauw.org.

Baumgardner, Jennifer. 2011. *F'em! Goo, Gaga, and some Thoughts on Balls*. Berkeley, CA: Seal Press.

Bishop, Tyler. 2015. "The Laws Targeting Campus Rape Culture." *The Atlantic Monthly* (www.theatlantic.com/education/archive/2015/09/the-laws-targeting-campus-rape-culture/404824).

Bly, Robert. 1991. *Iron John: A Book About Men*. New York: Vintage Books.

Brownmiller, Susan. 1975. *Against our Will: Men, Women, and Rape*. New York: Simon and Schuster.

Brownmiller, Susan. 1984. *Femininity*. New York: Ballentine Books.

Buchwald, Emilie, Pamela R. Fletcher, and Martha Roth, eds. 2005. *Transforming a Rape Culture*. Minneapolis, MN: Milkweed Editions.

Bureau of Justice Statistics. 2011. "Most Suspected Incidents of Human Trafficking involved Allegations of Prostitution of an Adult or Child." Retrieved March 21, 2017 (www.bjs.gov/content/pub/press/cshti0810pr.cfm).

Butler, Judith. 1990. *Gender Trouble: Feminism and the Subversion of Identity*. New York: Routledge.

Centers for Disease Control. 2012. "Sexual Violence: Facts at a Glance." Retrieved March 20, 2017 (https://www.cdc.gov/ViolencePrevention/pdf/SV-DataSheet-a.pdf).

Clatterbaugh, Kenneth. 1997. *Contemporary Perspectives on Masculinity: Men, Women, and Politics in Modern Society*, 2nd ed. Boulder, CO: Westview Press.

Cobble, Dorothy Sue, Linda Gordon, and Astrid Henry. 2014. *Feminism Unfinished: A Short, Surprising History of American Women's Movements*. New York: Liveright Publishing Corporation.

Collins, Patricia Hill. 1991. *Black Feminist Thought: Knowledge, Consciousness, and the Politics of Empowerment*. New York: Routledge.

Ehrlich, J. Shoshanna. 2014. *Regulating Desire: From the Virtuous Maiden to the Purity Princess*. Albany, New York: State University of New York Press.

Equal Employment Opportunity Commission (EEOC). nd. https://www.eeoc.gov/facts/fs-sex.html.

Estrich, Susan. 1987. *Real Rape: How the Legal System Victimizes People Who Say No*. Cambridge, MA: Harvard University Press.

Freidan, Betty. 1963. *The Feminine Mystique*. New York: W.W. Norton and Company.

Gilman, Charlotte Perkins. ([1898] 1966). *Women and Economics: A Study of the Economic Relations between Men and Women as a Factor in Social Evolution*. Edited by Carl Degler. New York: Harper Torchbooks.

Gilman, Charlotte Perkins, Michael R. Hill, and Mary Jo Deegan. 2002. *The Dress of Women: A Critical Introduction to the Symbolism and Sociology of Clothing*. Westport, CN: Greenwood Publishing Group.

Goldberg, Steven. 1974. *The Inevitability of Patriarchy: Why the Biological Difference Between Men and Women Always Produces Male Dominance*. New York: Morrow.

Gordon, Margaret T. and Stephanie Riger. 1989. *The Female Fear*. New York: Free Press.

Green Dot Etc. 2017. https://www.livethegreendot.com/index.html.

Herman, Judith. 1997. *Trauma and Recovery: The Aftermath of Violence—From Domestic Abuse to Political Terror*. New York: Basic Books.

Humm, Maggie. 1992. *Modern Feminisms: Political, Literary, Cultural*. New York: Columbia University Press.

Hunting Ground. 2015. http://thehuntinggroundfilm.com/.

It's On Us. 2017. http://www.itsonus.org/.

Keen, Sam. 1991. *Fire in the Belly: On Being a Man*. New York: Bantam Books.

Kimmel, Michael. 2015. *Gender Inequality is Probably the Best Thing that has ever Happened for Men*. Social Trends Institute. http://socialtrendsinstitute.org/.

Koss, Mary, Lisa A. Goodman, Angela Browne, Louise F. Fitzgerald, Gwendolyn Puryear Keita, and Nancy Felipe Russo. 1994. *No Safe Haven: Male Violence Against Women at Home, at Work, and in the Community*. Washington, DC: American Psychological Association.

Lips, Hilary M. 2005. *Sex and Gender: An Introduction*, 5th ed. New York: McGraw-Hill.

Lisak, David, Lori Gardinier, Sarah C. Nicksa, and Ashley M. Cote. 2010 "False Allegations of Sexual Assault: An Analysis of Ten Years of Reported Cases." *Violence Against Women* 16(12): 1318–1334.

Madhubti, Haki R. 1993. "On Becoming Anti-Racist." In Emilie Buchwald, Pamela Fletcher, and Martha Roth, Eds. *Transforming a Rape Culture*. Minneapolis, MN: Milkweed Editions.

Mills, C. Wright. 1959. *The Sociological Imagination*. New York: Oxford University Press.

Mills, Sara, and Louise Mullany. 2011. *Language, Gender and Feminism Theory, Methodology and Practice*. London and New York: Taylor and Francis.

Morgan, David. 1992. *Discovering Men*. New York: Routledge.

National Organization for Women. 2017. http://now.org/.

Parsons, Talcott. 1954. *Essays in Sociological Theory*. New York: Free Press.

Pateman, Carole. 1988. *The Sexual Contract*. Palo Alto, CA: Stanford University Press.

Rhoades, Stephen. 2004. *Taking Sex Differences Seriously*. New York: Encounter Books.

Rosen, Ruth. 2006. *The World Split Open: How the Modern Women's Movement Changed America*. New York: Penguin Books.

Schacht, Steven and Doris Ewing. 2004. *Feminism with Men: Bridging the Gender Gap*. Lanham, MD: Rowman and Littlefield.

Sinozich, Sofi. 2014. "Rape and Sexual Assault Among College-Age Females, 1995–2013." Center for Disease Control.

Smith, Dorothy E. 1987. *The Everyday World as Problematic: A Feminist Sociology*. Boston: Northeastern University Press.

Spain, Daphne. 1992. *Gendered Spaces*. Chapel Hill: The University of North Caroline Press.

Tong, Rosemarie. 2009. *Feminist Thought*, 3rd ed. Boulder, CO: Westview Press.

Victim Rights Law Center. 2017. www.victimrights.org.

White, Frances E. 2001. *Dark Continent of Our Bodies: Black Feminism and the Politics of Respectability*. Philadelphia, PA: Temple University Press.

Sexuality

ABOUT THE PROBLEM: SEXUALITY

In the last chapter, we discussed sex and gender. Now we turn to sexuality, an area that encompasses both gender identity and the many facets of sexuality. **Sexuality** is a broadly descriptive term which encompasses the sexual identity, sexual behavior, and sexual attraction that may or may not align with the sex and gender we are assigned at birth. As we learned in Chapter 6, sex is based on the biological reproductive anatomy we are born with, and gender is a social construct assigned to us based on our biological sex characteristics. In this chapter, we will explore various aspects of sexuality, including the differences between sexual attraction, sexual behavior, and sexual orientation. We will also delve into the sociological theories that explain societal reasons for regulating sexuality. This chapter approaches sexuality as a social construct that is always evolving and changing based on the culture of a society.

In the previous chapter, we discussed the social construction of gender. Relating social constructionism to sexual relationships, Freeman, and Rupp (2014) state the general belief about sexuality by "queer theorists" (scholars who study nonnormative sexuality) in this comment: "societies shape the way sexual desires are understood, the sexual practices in which people engage, the meanings people attach to their sexual desires and behaviors, and the identities people embrace" (p. 11). This line of thought challenges the nature/biology argument by interjecting the influence of society into the very personal lives of individuals—another example of the sociological imagination in action.

> **Sexuality** the sexual identity, sexual behavior, and sexual attraction that may or may not align with the sex and gender we are assigned at birth.

A Brief History of Sexuality

Sexual culture refers to the values, beliefs, and norms a society has about sexuality. These are always in flux and vary widely based on historical context. Societies have long sought to control

> **Sexual Culture** the values, beliefs, and norms a society has about sexuality.

117

the sexuality of their citizens. In ancient Rome sexuality was an important part of the culture and appeared in art, literature, artifacts, and even architecture (Langlands 2006). As a patriarchal society, women were held to a strict sexual code, however, for men prostitution was legal, homosexuality was practiced without a label or stigma. Older well-positioned men who engaged in same-sex relations were expected to penetrate younger men of lower status as it was considered demeaning for an older man to be penetrated (Langlands 2006). Because the concept "homosexuality" did not exist there was not a name for this type of sexual behavior and it was considered acceptable if respected men initiated it. These men had sexual relations with male slaves, younger men of lower social class, and male prostitutes, without any loss of their masculine status.

> **Nonnormative Sexuality** sexuality (including identity, orientation, behaviors, and attraction) that does not conform to traditional heterosexual norms in our society.

Historical examples of **nonnormative sexuality** in the United States date back to European settlers who observed some Native American males engaging in sexual behaviors with other men. "One group displayed what is often called effeminate characteristics" (Rupp 2014); this group has been referred to as "two-spirit people" and were considered a third gender (Gilley 2006). Though the idea of same-sex activity existed in Europe as well (special places called molly houses were areas where gay men met in European cities), homosexual activity was generally scorned by the settlers in the new world. The first Puritans that migrated to America in the 1600s brought with them their religious belief that sex should occur only within the confines of marriage and should be limited to intercourse. As the Puritans settled and colonized they created policies that outlawed pre-marital sex, extra-marital sex, homosexual sex, masturbation, and even oral or anal sex, regardless of marital status (D'Emilio and Freedman 1997). Sodomy laws were created to discourage male homosexuality although female homosexuality existed in the colonies as well (Foster 2014). Those who violated these laws were publicly punished or shamed, ostracized, and sometimes even put to death. They were operating from the logic that their responsibility was to populate New England as quickly and efficiently as possible and to do that they needed babies—both to increase the population and as a labor supply. Their strict laws about sexual activity stemmed from both religious beliefs and practical concerns. Sexual intercourse was the only acceptable sexual behavior since it produced the next generation. Children were needed as free labor sources at a young age in an agricultural society. And since both infant mortality rates and mortality rates in general were high, they needed to quickly replenish the individuals who died in childbirth or from a host of diseases, malnutrition, and illness.

The Victorian era (1837–1901) began during Queen Victoria's (and her husband Prince Albert's) reign over Great Britain and Ireland. It was an era of outward morality, sexual restraint, and a strict sense of moral standards regarding sexuality (Merriman 2004). Sexual desire was perceived as primitive, crude, and the domain of the lower classes. Writing about or verbalizing sexual feelings was prohibited, as was masturbation. However, it has been suggested that sex was not censored as much as it was used as a means of social control and patriarchy (Foucault 1990). To control sexual urges, norms that curbed sexual behavior were introduced. Men were instructed that their mental and physical health depended on avoiding masturbation as it was thought to cause insanity, physical illness, and other disorders (Furneaux 2014).

In the United States, the Industrial Revolution ushered in societal changes as the economy shifted from primarily agricultural with the advent of factories and industrial jobs that in turn necessitated in urbanization as jobs moved to urban areas, and people began to reside in densely populated areas. As industrialization progressed, cultural values changed as well with technological advances such as vehicles, radios, and movies. This new social landscape led to modern dating rituals

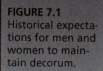

FIGURE 7.1
Historical expectations for men and women to maintain decorum.

LADIES   GENTS

Source: alex74 / Shutterstock.com

as the mass media transformed sex from a private experience in the home to public venues where young people could watch romantic movies at drive-in theaters and the freedom that comes with having a car and a less religious and restrictive society.

Many decades followed in which gay and lesbian activity had to be kept underground. It was not until the 1960s that people began to participate in movements that brought their issues to the public in "coming out" activities (Lekus 2014). The AIDS epidemic of the 1980s created progressive levels of activism and called global attention to the plight of gays and lesbians during a very serious time (Brier 2014). When same-sex marriages were legalized in 2013 by the federal government, many began to believe in the promise of sexual equality, however, the individual state governments have not all been in accord with the federal government, rendering same-sex marriages legal in some states but not in others.

The Sexual Revolution

The sexual revolution began earlier than the 1960s. It started in the 1920s when women gained the right to vote and began to enter the paid labor force. In the 1940s, World War II provided women the opportunity to work outside the home and work in jobs that had traditionally been held by men. Although there was a push toward traditional gender roles after the war, many women remained in the workforce and by 1960 there were twice as many women working as there were

FIGURE 7.2 July 24, 2005 License Bella Abzug (1920–1998) is running for Congress and is one of the chief organizers of the Women's Liberation Day parade in New York, on the 50th anniversary of women winning the vote in the United States. She is carrying an anti-motherhood sign reading 'Free the female body from pain and inequality. Put motherhood in a test-tube'.

Source: Keystone/Getty Images

during World War II (Dunphy 2000). In the 1960s the sexual revolution took on more public exposure and momentum as it intersected with the second wave of the feminist movement and centered around women challenging existing political and economic roles in society. This encompassed traditional gender roles and the prevailing belief that men had a biological need to engage in sexual activity while women passively complied. Feminists challenged this notion and argued that society, not genetics, determined gender and sexuality (Millett 1970; Dunphy 2000).

The idea that the birth control pill started the sexual revolution has been debated widely and most scholars believe that the pill was not the great liberator it was depicted as (Dunphy 2000). Women were still expected to procreate within marriage, and traditional cultural notions about women's sexuality did not accompany this technological advance. Women were still considered the gatekeepers of sexual activity, responsible for fertility and reproduction and were not suddenly free agents who could engage in sex for recreational purposes without stigma or being labeled promiscuous. Doctors generally refused to grant prescriptions for the birth control pill to unmarried women and even married women often needed permission from their husbands. Thus, the pill, without a transformation in cultural beliefs, did not liberate women and grant them sexual freedom, but rather added to the tools they could use as they worked toward social and political equality.

Sexual Orientation Identities

Historically, sexual orientation has been categorized as heterosexual, bisexual, or gay/lesbian. These mutually-exclusive labels present a very limited view of sexuality. For example, what about individuals who are currently having a heterosexual relationship but have had a bisexual relationship in the past? Or individuals who identify as asexual? Many people now feel that the three-category system is limiting and propose adding two additional categories: mostly heterosexual and mostly gay/lesbian. Others propose abandoning the labeling system altogether for a sexuality continuum with opposite-sex identity at one end and same-sex identity at the other end (Vranglova and Savin-Williams 2012; Morgan 2013). In a recent study that focused on three dimensions of sexuality, including self-reported sexual orientation identity, sexual attraction, and sexual partners, the authors found that patterns of sexual attraction and choice of sexual partners often did not always align with respondents' sexual orientation identity (Vranglova and Savin-Williams 2012). In other words, an individual who reported identifying as heterosexual may still report same-sex attraction and/ or partners. Importantly, these three dimensions of sexuality may or may not overlap and thus sexuality must be considered multidimensional and not simply an ascribed status based on one aspect or characteristic. By categorizing sexuality so narrowly the nuances of the multiple dimensions of sexual identity are ignored and we assume that sexuality is clear-cut even though early studies on sexual behavior dating back over sixty years ago by Alfred Kinsey and his colleagues (1948), found that sexuality is not a category, but rather a continuum and most people fall somewhere between exclusively heterosexual or non-heterosexual.

Beyond the Binary

Adding another layer of complexity to sexuality, gender is woven into this continuum since sexual identity is based on the gender one is assigned at birth. As discussed in the previous chapter, gender is a social construction and our society has begun to abandon the outdated notion that gender is a binary system consisting of male or female. Gender scholars agree that additional gender identities exist outside our binary system. For example, when a person's biological sex does not align with their gender identity, and/or when an individual is born with ambiguous biological sexual characteristics, known as intersex. These sexual characteristics may include genitalia, reproductive organs, and/or chromosomes that do not align with male or female sex. Additional non-binary identities include gender-fluid, gender non-conforming, genderqueer, and transgender, among others. What these identities have in common is that they reject the traditional dichotomy of male/female and instead identify as existing outside or even beyond this binary. This can vary from feeling you are more male some days and more female on other days, to feeling like a mix of both genders, or feeling as if you exist completely outside of any socially constructed category. Many individuals who are non-binary prefer pronouns that are not gender specific, such as they/them instead of he/him or she/her. A recent study conducted by GLAAD, a national media monitoring organization, found that the Millennial generation is much more likely to openly identify as LGBTQ than older generations. It is estimated that 12% of Millennials identify as transgender or gender nonconforming and 63% of those who identify as transgender or non-conforming also report they do not identify as heterosexual (GLAAD 2017).

Transgender and nonbinary identifying people have historically been marginalized within the LGBTQ community. Although the U.S. Census still doesn't collect data on gender identity, according to state and federal data, in 2014 an estimated 1.4 million adults, or 0.6% of the population identified as transgender (Flores et al. 2016). Transgender is an umbrella term that is used to refer to people who were assigned a male or female gender identity at birth and do not identify with the category they were assigned. Some transgender folks undergo a transition, a complex process that is a metamorphosis of living as a member of one gender to living as another gender. This does not necessarily mean they have undergone gender reassignment surgery. This could be a social transition intended to align more clearly with the gender with which they identify—for example, using a different name, changing pronouns, changing physical appearance such as clothing, makeup, non-verbal body language, and/or using the bathroom that aligns with their gender identity. It can also include undergoing a legal transition to the gender they identify with by changing their sex on their birth certificate, license, passport, etc. Depending on the state, a legal transition is often restricted to people who have proof of an "irreversible sex change surgery" or is not allowed at all. Other types of transitioning include hormone replacement therapy to change estrogen or testosterone levels, and surgical procedures that change physical characteristics to align with perceived gender identity. For example, transwomen may undergo surgery for breast augmentation, vaginoplasty (creation of a vagina), labiaplasty (creation of a labia and usually a clitoral hood), vocal cord alterations, and facial feminization procedures (National Center for Transgender Equality 2017). These are very expensive surgeries, rarely covered by health insurance, and only a small percentage of transwomen and transmen have the resources to undergo all or some of these surgeries. Regardless of the level of transitioning transgender people elect to undergo, they should always be treated and addressed as the gender with which they identify. For example, a transwoman did not "used to be a man". She lived in a man's social role, and her sex and gender were classified as male, but that does not equate to being a man.

Should transgender and gender non-conforming individuals have the right to change their gender and sex on official documents such as birth certificates, passports, driver's license, etc. to match their gender identity without having to undergo complete gender reassignment surgery?

Pro: It is discriminatory to prevent individuals who do not have the resources for complete gender reassignment surgery from legally changing their identity. This should not be a choice only privileged individuals are able to make.

Con: Gender is linked to our biological sex characteristics and it would be confusing for law enforcement and others if people who appear to be one gender could legally change their gender on important identifying documents regardless of their biology.

In addition, occupying the status of transgender does not denote your sexual orientation or behavior. A transwoman may identify as a lesbian—her gender transition is independent of her sexual orientation, sexual attraction, and/or sexual behavior. It is common for those who are cisgender (their gender identity aligns with their biological characteristics) to try to "figure out" a person's "true gender" or sexual orientation based on gender assigned at birth. However, keeping in mind that these are social constructs, there is not anything concrete or real to *figure out*. Individuals are complex and sexual and gender identity are highly nuanced, while in contrast our society has very rigid and narrow categories for what is deemed acceptable. Just keep in mind that all of these concepts were invented to establish a sense of order in our society, thus none of them exist outside of our agreed upon social construction of reality.

From a medical standpoint, gender identity conflicts that last for a long period of time and cause mental distress and anxiety are considered a disorder called **gender dysphoria** (APA 2013). Gender dysphoria can affect choice of sexual partners, mannerisms, choice of clothing, as well as self-concept. Symptoms can manifest in different ways. Both children and adults have similar symptoms—cross-dressing, habits typical of and wanting to live as the opposite gender, and high levels of anxiety and/or depression, and withdrawal from social interaction. Imagine walking around in a society where everyone sees you one way and you don't see yourself that way. For example, think of how stressful it would feel if you identify as a if female but everyone thinks you are male and treats you like a traditional man and when you look in the mirror you see what people consider "male". Clearly, this could cause ongoing stress and mental distress and you will most likely not want to interact in public or even with family and friends who do not understand that you identify as a woman.

> **Gender Dysphoria** gender identity conflicts that last for a long period of time and cause mental distress and anxiety.

Children and adolescents who identify as gay, lesbian, bisexual, or gender non-conforming are at risk for a host of mental health problems that are correlated to the stigma and prejudice they face in society (Russell and Fish 2016). Multiple studies have found that the depression, mood disorders, posttraumatic stress disorder, suicide ideation and attempts in LGBTQ adults started for LGBTQ youth prior to adulthood (Russell and Fish 2016). These rates vary across sexual and gender identities, race and ethnicity, culture, and social class. Thus, future studies of mental health for LGBTQ youth and adults should be situated within an intersectionality framework (Russell and Fish 2016).

Prejudice and Discrimination Against Sexual Minorities

In our society, heteronormative views on sexuality are predominant in our social discourse, beliefs, values, and social institutions. **Heteronormative** refers to the idea that heterosexuality is the normal or "natural" sexual orientation and thus needs no explanation or justification, unlike non-heterosexual sexual orientation, where there is an expectation of "coming out" or identifying and justifying your sexuality. Heteronormativity then is the belief system that heterosexuality is the only acceptable sexual orientation and monogamy is the normal sexual arrangement. Society uses heteronormativity to regulate individuals who conform and fall within its boundaries and marginalize those who do not conform and operate outside these boundaries (Jackson 2006). This creates an "othering" that rejects all sexual orientations and gender identities that do not conform to this norm. We include gender identity in heteronormativity since heteronormative sexuality depends in large part on men and women identifying with and conforming to traditional gender roles (Seidman 2005). Thus, heteronormativity is aligned with patriarchy and both depends on and necessitates gender stratification, which in turn justifies the traditional power structure that privileges heterosexual men and oppresses non-heteronormative men and all women regardless of their sexual orientation (Jackson 2006).

> **Heteronormative Sexuality** the belief that heterosexuality is the normal or "natural" sexual orientation and thus needs no explanation or justification, unlike non-heterosexual sexual orientation, where there is an expectation of "coming out" or identifying and justifying your sexuality.

The term **homophobia** literally refers to the fear of non-heterosexual sexual behavior—it does not refer to the fear of individuals but of a differing form of sexuality that creates anxiety in a heteronormative society. Noting the importance of "political or collective homophobia", which acknowledges how political power is used in various governments to control sexual behavior, newer terms such as

> **Homophobia** the fear of non-heterosexual behavior by a heteronormative society.

biphobia and transphobia, will expose the political consequences that result from these "fears" (Altman and Symons 2016). The fear of non-heterosexual (lesbian, bisexual, gay, transgender, and questioning, or LGBTQ) behaviors is certainly a part of the political discourse in America and around the globe.

Social Control and Sexuality

We now turn to how heteronormativity is produced and reinforced in our society from a very young age. Emerging research has found that the public education system promotes a **hidden sexuality curriculum** in which heteronormative sexuality is promoted and enforced by schools (Epstein 1994; Miceli 2006). Heteronormativity is the only visible sexual orientation in most schools, both in and outside the classroom. This includes school organizations, sports, and other extracurricular activities such as school dances and proms. This dominance of heterosexuality and the expectation that prom and school dances will be attended by male/female couples, reinforces a "hetero-romantic" norm that sets up an expectation for boys to be openly and clearly masculine and for girls to perform femininity in a traditional, passive way (Best 2005). This norm structures interactions between students, and between teachers and students. For example, teachers are generally not comfortable revealing a non-normative sexual orientation or non-conforming gender identity. In fact, teachers who do not conform are generally thought of as sexual deviants who should not be educators. In addition, very few schools (with the exception of public schools in California) include an LGBTQ curriculum that is taught in history and social science classes. And the current political climate is hostile to students who are not heterosexual or gender conforming. For example, almost immediately after being elected into office, the Trump administration revoked protections for transgender students in public schools (Human Rights Campaign 2017). This includes the bathroom directives put into place by the Obama administration as well as other protections for transgender students.

> **Hidden Sexuality Curriculum** the process of heteronormative beliefs about sexuality being promoted and enforced by schools.

Students who do not conform to heteronormative roles are often bullied, harassed, and left to exist on the fringes without any support from school administrators or formal social support systems. The National School Climate Survey is a large-scale survey of high school students that is conducted bi-annually. According to data from 2013, nearly 60% of LGBTQ students reported having been sexually harassed at school and nearly 80% had experienced mean rumors or lies told about them at school. About half of LGBTQ students had experienced cyberbullying in the past year and a majority (85%) experienced verbal harassment at school based on their sexual orientation or gender identity. Verbal harassment included being called derogatory names or threatened. Among those who experienced this type of harassment over a quarter (27%) reported that it occurred on a regular basis. Even more troubling, in just the past year 40% of LGBTQ students reported being physically harassed (i.e. shoved or pushed) and nearly 1 in 5 (19%) had been physically assaulted at school (this includes being punched, kicked, and/or injured with a weapon) (Kosciw et al. 2014). Altogether, 56% of students felt unsafe at school because of their sexual orientation and over a third avoid the bathrooms and locker rooms because of this unsafe feeling and constant harassment.

These negative and traumatic experiences that students experience in school start early in life and last until emerging adulthood. The hostility and bullying along with the lack of support from school administrators clearly affects the life opportunities and experiences of LGBTQ students. They leave high school with higher levels of depression, lower levels of self-esteem, and lower GPAs than their heterosexual peers (Kosciw et al. 2014). This translates to poor educational outcomes and poor psychological well-being that makes entering college less likely. The constant psychological and physical stress of a hostile school environment leads to higher rates of attempted suicide, substance abuse, and cigarette smoking. According to a 2013 national study of transgender and gender non-conforming adults by the Williams Institute, 46% of transmen and 42% of transwomen had attempted suicide at least once. Rates were highest for young adults and those who were publicly "out" as transgender or gender non-conforming (Haas, Rodgers, and Herman 2014).

The Family

Currently adoption by single LGBTQ individuals and same-sex couples is legal in all 50 states (Montero 2014). However, in many states only one same-sex parent can be the legal parent. This presents potential challenges if the legal parent dies or if the couple were to divorce or separate. However, the current conservative political climate may prove to be challenging for LGBTQ parents. For example, in June of 2017, Texas Governor, Greg Abbott signed into law a bill that allows adoption and foster care agencies in the state of Texas to turn away qualified potential parents based on sexual orientation and religious beliefs (Human Rights Campaign 2017). The bill also allows agencies caring for LGBTQ youth to force them to submit to "conversion therapy" or "faith based" treatments that shun science in favor of religious prayer, biblical teachings, and religious counseling that tries to force young people who identify as LGBTQ to change their sexual orientation to heterosexual.

Violence and Hate Crimes

Anti-LGBTQ hate crimes are crimes committed against individuals that are based on their perceived sexual orientation or gender identity. These crimes range from verbal threats to rape, physical assault,

FIGURE 7.3 Hate crimes still occur against same-sex couples for their perceived sexual orientation.

Source: Diego Cervo/Shutterstock.com

and murder. The U.S. Department of Justice crime statistics (2015), reported that in 2014 18.6% of all hate crimes were based on sexual orientation and 1.8% were based on gender identity. Transgender individuals of color are disproportionately targeted. Transgender women of color comprised 54% of homicide victims. Hate crimes are often intended to send a message to the LGBTQ population that they are legitimate and deserving targets of abuse and violence. In 2016, a mass shooting at a LGBTQ nightclub in Orlando, Florida, killed 49 people, wounding 53 others. Most of the victims were LGBTQ and the attack was the country's largest mass shooting specifically targeting LGBTQ people.

Transgender people of color, particularly women are more likely to be victims of violent hate crimes. In 2016, at least 21 transgender people were murdered and the clear majority were trans-women of color (Human Rights Campaign 2017). This number most likely underreports the number of deaths since there is no way of knowing in many cases whether the individual was targeted for their transgender status. Unfortunately, the factors driving this violence are found within our society. The transphobic climate in our society normalizes discrimination and violence against the LGBTQ community. Over half of transgender people report being uncomfortable reporting violence or harassment to the police (Human Rights Campaign 2017). Institutional discrimination in the workforce leads to the inability for transgender people to access basic needs like housing, employment, and healthcare. In 2011 national survey data collected by the Human Rights Council (HRC) and Transpeople of Color Collation (TPOCC) found that 90% of transgender people reported harassment at work and 25% reported losing their job based on their non-conforming gender identity. This at least partially explains why transgender people are more than four times as likely to live in extreme poverty than the general population and have double the unemployment rate (trans-women of color have up to four times higher rates of unemployment). High unemployment leads to the economic strains of housing insecurity, food insecurity, lack of healthcare, and often leads to underground, illegal, sex work that is often called "survival sex" since it is a last resort for income.

Lack of healthcare for most of the transgender population is problematic not just for individuals, but also from a public health standpoint. Nearly one in four transgender women have HIV, the same demographic that is most likely to turn to survival sex to afford the essentials and the least likely to have health insurance or adequate medical care. With homeless shelters denying access to transgender people and few job opportunities in sight, survival sex work is prevalent among transgender adults, and has increased for transgender youth as more of these young people are homeless and live on the streets (Bay 2006).

Masculine Sexuality in the Black Community

In the early 2000s researchers began to document a social construction of black sexuality that was coined "the Down Low" (DL). This is a subculture of mainly African American men who outwardly lived as heterosexuals, often with wives and children, while secretly engaging in same-sex relations with other African American men (Nero 2016). This secret sexual behavior has a specific vocabulary, an underground culture, and agreed upon customs (Denizet-Lewis 2003). This includes the use of private DL internet chat rooms, private parties, and specific locations that are known as meeting places for anonymous sex. It is driven by a culture that equates open same-sex behavior to effeminate white men and expects black men to be traditionally masculine, heterosexual, and focused on marriage and family. Religion, hyper-masculine values within the black community, and distrust of mainstream gay society are all driving factors behind this sub-culture as well. We will discuss how this same-sex sexual behavior by men who identify as DL relates to HIV rates in detail in the Health chapter.

THEORETICAL PERSPECTIVES

Structural Functionalism

A structural functionalist approach to sexuality would consider the sexual norms that are deemed most beneficial to proper functioning of society. Sexuality has the potential to promote both cohesion and disorder in society, therefore those sexual norms considered most order-inducing are the ones supported. Early on, sociologists of sexuality adopted a functionalist approach which drew from Sigmund Freud's drive theory, which posits that sexual urges are primal and determine the course of society (Stein 1989). Norms are formed to keep in check sexual behavior to ensure order and predictability. Relaxing those norms would result in, as Durkheim would say, anomic conditions that threaten society.

Functionalists such as Talcott Parsons, Kingsley Davis, and several other early American sociologists linked the drive of human sexuality directly to the family since this institution primarily places restrictions on sexual behavior (Stein 1989). Although the family is the earliest agent of socialization, religion also plays a role in enforcing sexuality; in societies throughout history, these have also been affected by, and have attempted to regulate, the sexuality of the citizenry. According to functionalist theory, these regulations are attempts to ensure the continued adequate functioning of society.

Conflict

It is certainly easy to ascertain the importance of sexuality in social life due to the ways in which institutions and other social arrangements have tried to control it (as reflected in the functionalist approach above). However, this regulation has not always been applied evenly across society. Michel Foucault's seminal work *The History of Sexuality* (1990) explored how sexuality has been used to promote conformity, thus subordination to those in power. As mentioned earlier, Foucault was ever concerned with how people have historically been controlled by social institutions—institutions maintained by social elites. Those who engage in nonnormative sexual behaviors have been subjected to various sanctions. As one anthropologist noted "if Foucault taught us anything, it is that knowledge about sexuality is an exercise in power" (Kulick 2014).

Following this line of thought, feminist poet Adrienne Rich, in her essay on the "lesbian experience" (1980), describes a "compulsory heterosexuality" that sees heterosexuality as the natural state of sexuality and all other forms as being deviant. Like theorists with a conflict perspective, Rich stresses the problems of dichotomous ways of viewing sexuality. Conflict theorists are always aware of social factors (such as heteronormality) that create separations between those that have power and those who do not (which, ironically is also a dichotomy).

Symbolic Interactionism

Human sexuality is more than just physical contact between people. It represents ideas of selfhood and is related to some very fundamental aspects of personal identity. In America, the interactionist perspective directly challenged the functionalist approach, with its emphasis on drive theory, and posited that social behavior is not totally shaped by social norms—perhaps sexuality is a learned response that is developed through interaction. Rather than seek universal laws about innate sex drives (which certainly do not explain the variances of sexual behavior), interactionists began to focus more on "nurture" than "nature" and seek to understand not only how people learn sexual behavior, but how it becomes a part of one's personal identity (Stein 1989).

The idea of a **sexual script** has become recently explored in sociology, sexology, and psychology; it refers to "cognitive schema that instructs people how to understand and act in sexual situations" (Masters, Casey, Wells, and Morrison 2013:409). Moving away from biological explanations of sexual behavior, the developers of the term sexual script posit that their scripting theory understands sexuality not as "an intrinsically significant aspect of human behavior; rather it views the sexual as becoming significant either when it is defined as significant by collective life…or when individual experiences or development assign it a special significance" (Simon and Gagnon 1986:104). In this approach, culture is a better explanation of sexuality than biology.

> **Sexual Script**
> cognitive schema that instructs people how to understand and act in sexual situations.

Interactionism also notes how symbols are important in understandings of sexuality. One example is the famous sculpture of David by Michelangelo. A fig leaf was placed over the genitalia of the statue, which is an interesting dichotomy in that the leaf acts as both a censor of and a focal point to this region of the body. This act of censorship lasted for 400 years before the symbol was removed, reflecting Foucault's ideas on how certain groups can impose power over other people's lives (Colburn 1987). The example of the censorship of David's "junk" is one of countless others that illustrate a convergence of symbolic interactionism and conflict theory.

SEARCHING FOR SOLUTIONS

Advocating for Change

Acceptance of LGBTQ people and homosexuality has risen over the past few years (Fingerhut 2016). Many of the changes in attitudes, policies, and acceptance of non-heterosexual and non-gender conforming individuals can be attributed to the work of advocacy organizations such as the Human Rights Council (HRC), GLSEN (formerly known as the Gay, Lesbian, and Straight Education Network), the National Gay and Lesbian Taskforce (NGLT), and the Gay and Lesbian Alliance Against Defamation (GLAAD). These national advocacy groups focus on community based mobilization and action that include young people, heterosexuals, schools, and community organizations, to work toward building communities that unite to protect the civil rights of LGBTQ individuals.

Advocacy groups that bring people of diverse backgrounds together are able to employ a psychological concept known as the *contact hypothesis*. According to the contact hypothesis, the more personal contact individuals have with members of an out-group the more accepting they become (Pettigrew and Tropp 2005). And research has shown that personal contact with gay and lesbian

FIGURE 7.4 An example of changes in the institution of marriage – specifically the legal marriages of same-sex couples.

Source: Anton Havelaar/Shutterstock.com

individuals is predictive of same-sex marriage support (Merino 2013). It makes sense, therefore, that personal contact with members of the LGBTQ community by heterosexuals will lead to increased support for policies and initiatives that reduce discrimination for this population.

Equality in Schools and Colleges

The formation of gay/straight alliances by students in high schools and middle schools, bring students of different sexual orientations and gender identities together to support each other and provide a sense of community for LGBTQ students and heterosexual "allies". In addition, these alliances can work to educate the larger school community about sexual orientation and gender identity and create an inclusive school climate that promotes tolerance and acceptance. Unfortunately, not all schools permit these alliances, and according to the Gay Straight Alliance Network (GSA 2017), the Department of Education under the Trump presidential administration has removed Federal Title IX protections for transgender youth. However, GSA also reports that only 21 school districts have taken measures to support the rights of transgender and gender nonconforming students. However, many of these school districts have made public statements that they will not rescind guidelines on already existing discrimination policies that prohibit discrimination based on gender identity, gender expression, or sexual orientation.

Many colleges have added dormitories and bathrooms for non-gender conforming and transgender students. And advocacy groups created by and for LGBTQ students have gained acceptance

FIGURE 7.5
London, England. 8th July 2017. - Celebrating Pride In London 2017 as thousands turned out for the colorful, fun-filled parade through the streets of central London.

Source: John Gomez/Shutterstock.com

and many heterosexual students join these groups as allies in support of equal rights for LGBTQ students. Campus Pride, a national organization for LGBTQ and ally college students provides resources and services to nearly 1400 college campuses (Campus Pride). Groups like Campus Pride and GLSEN collaborate with student groups at colleges across the country to create campaigns for hate crime prevention, safe spaces for LGBTQ students, activism, and advocacy, among others. Campus Pride trains college students to hold events on campus that raise awareness rights, address health and safety issues, and combat violence for LGBTQ students.

Is it preferable for colleges and universities to ask students to identify their pronoun preference?

Pro: Everyone has the right to be addressed by the pronoun of the gender with which they identify.
Con: Confusion occurs when addressing people in a non-traditional way.

Transgender Rights

The issue of bathrooms and locker rooms for transgender students gained media attention in 2016 when North Carolina became the first state to legislate policy banning transgender people from using the bathroom that aligns with their gender identity. Media coverage garnered instant support from LGBTQ advocacy groups and thousands of individuals who protested using social media. The outrage over this discriminatory legislation prompted the National Basketball Association (NBA) to pull its All-Star game out of Charlotte, and The National College Athletic Association (NCAA) to move playoff games in several sports out of the state. Private industry followed, and at least one company, PayPal, which would have added an estimated $2.66 billion to North Carolina's economy, canceled plans to open a facility in the state (New York Times 2017). Altogether, it was a financial disaster for the state. In addition, President Obama's administration took legal action against the state with letters sent to all school districts in North Carolina outlining measures that should be taken to ensure transgender students were not discriminated against and the implicit threat that schools that didn't follow the Obama Administrations guidelines could face lawsuits and lose federal funding (New York Times 2017).

To mitigate the negative publicity and appease LGBTQ rights groups, in April 2017, the state passed a new bill that it considered an attempt at compromise. The new bill, however, still gave the state control over multi-stall bathrooms and put a temporary halt on allowing local governments to create non-discrimination policies until 2020. The new bill garnered more negative media attention as LGBTQ groups flooded to social media with pushback, arguing that the compromise was not a compromise at all and was simply an attempt for the state to regain a positive image. Although this was not a win for transgender rights, this controversial bill has opened a public discourse, heightened awareness about an issue many people had not considered, and opened the door to a new activism aimed at protecting the rights of the transgender population.

Should transgender and gender non-conforming individuals have the right to utilize the bathroom that aligns with their gender identity?

Pro: We should not discriminate against people based on their gender-identity by forcing them to use a bathroom with the gender with which they do not identify.

Con: Biological characteristics should take precedent over gender identity since this is how bathrooms have always been divided and changing this norm could make cisgender individuals uncomfortable.

In May of 2017 another important milestone was reached when the first transgender person successfully sued her employer under the American Disabilities Act (National Center for Transgender Equality 2017). Kate Lynn Blatt, a transgender woman in Pennsylvania was harassed by her employer and coworkers during her employment at Cabela's (a national retail chain) for months, called "fag", "ladyboy", "freak" and other expletives, denied use of the women's bathroom, and then fired (Nadig 2016). She sued under two federal laws: Title VII which protects employees from sex discrimination and the American Disabilities Act (ADA) which protects people with a disability. A Pennsylvania court ruled in in her favor when a judge decided that the Americans with Disability Act can cover gender dysphoria as a disability because it is a medical condition. Although the battle is not over, this landmark case is an important step toward protecting transgender people from discrimination in employment, education, and housing and allowing those individuals with gender dysphoria to qualify for public accommodations and government services. In the past transgender people have won wrongful termination based on state disability laws, but they have not had any federal protections or constitutional rights in large part because the ADA act passed by Congress in 1990 included an exclusion that specifically stated "transsexualism" and "gender identity disorders" do not count as disabilities. According to the Department of Justice Civil Rights Division, "although the laws do not explicitly refer to sexual orientation or gender identity, they prohibit sex discrimination, which protects all people (including LGBTI people) from gender-based discrimination, including discrimination based on a person's nonconformity with stereotypes associated with that persons real or perceived gender" (U.S. Department of Justice 2015).

However, this is a somewhat controversial issue since being transgender is no longer classified as a medical disorder by the American Psychiatric Association, however our social construction of disability has shifted to include conditions that are a social disadvantage. All transgender or gender non-conforming people do not have gender dysphoria. Transgender people can be diagnosed with gender dysphoria if they have severe anxiety and distress based on their gender identity. This could potentially lead to stigma for transgender and gender non-conforming populations since it could be perceived by the public as a medical condition, which implies that it can be "treated" and "cured". However, considering the high rates of workplace harassment and lack of employment opportunities for transgender people, this protection is a step toward protecting the rights of transpeople with gender dysphoria so they can live as the gender with which they identify.

Should all people who experience gender dysphoria be protected by the U.S. Constitution in employment, education, and housing and qualify for public accommodations and government services under the Americans with Disabilities Act (ADA)?

Pro: Gender dysphoria is a medical condition that should be classified and treated like any other disability.
Con: Gender dysphoria is a social construct and not a medical condition that should qualify people for special treatment.

Marriage Equality

Public support for same-sex marriage is at an all-time high. As of 2016, 55% of Americans reported support for same-sex marriage, an increase from 35% in 2001 (Pew Research Center 2016). In 2015, the Supreme Court struck down the parts of the Defense of Marriage Act (DOMA) that defined marriage as exclusively being between a man and a woman and allowed states to refuse to acknowledge same-sex marriages. Some of the rights that partners of same-sex marriages had been denied included insurance benefits, social security survivor benefits, filing joint tax returns, estate taxes and inheritance issues, among others. There are more than 1,000 federal rights and benefits of marriage that same-sex couples had been denied until DOMA was repealed. The importance of this federal precedent aimed at providing same-sex couples the same rights and recognition as heterosexual couples cannot be overstated.

Not all Americans support same-sex marriage and there are still areas of discrimination that need to be addressed. For example, there is debate over whether businesses that provide wedding-related services should be allowed to refuse services for same-sex couples for religious reasons. A 2016 survey conducted by the Pew Research Center found that folks who rarely attend religious services are more likely to agree that businesses should be required to serve same-sex couples regardless of their religious objections to homosexuality than those who attend church regularly. The difference in viewpoints is largest between those who attend church once a week or more (63% said should be able to refuse services) and those who are unaffiliated with a religion (64% said should be required to provide services). Interestingly, Catholics who rarely attend church, were more likely to agree that they should be allowed to refuse services to same-sex couples based on their religious beliefs

> Should private businesses that provide wedding services such as venues, catering, flowers, etc. be required to provide their services to same-sex couples regardless of their religious beliefs about sexual orientation?
>
> **Pro**: It is discriminatory to refuse to do business with people based on their sexual orientation.
> **Con**: These are privately owned companies and they should be allowed to uphold their religious values and refuse service to same-sex couples.

(59%) than Catholics who attend church regularly (41%). This survey was limited to white and black individuals and did not include Jewish respondents (Pew Research Center 2016).

Hate Crime Policy

In 2009, Congress passed the Matthew Shepard and James Byrd Jr. Hate Crimes Prevention Act. This law expands the federal definition of hate crimes and includes hate crimes based on actual or perceived gender, disability, gender identity, or sexual orientation (U.S. Department of Justice 2015). It also includes longer sentencing for violence or criminal acts that can be proven to be hate crimes. According to data from the Human Rights Campaign, 17 states and the District of Columbia have hate crime laws that include sexual orientation and gender identity. Another 13 states have hate crime laws that only cover sexual orientation. At this point, there are still 16 states that have hate crime laws that do not include sexual orientation or gender identity and four states (Arkansas, Indiana, South Carolina, and Wyoming) without any hate crime laws in place.

Moving forward, there is still much work to be done to reduce violence against LGBTQ and gender non-conforming individuals. Some of the initiatives that are promoted by the Human Right Council include: more training for local law enforcement agencies so that crimes based on sexual orientation and gender identity are correctly identified and dealt with as hate crimes. This would provide better data on the prevalence of these crimes which in turn could pinpoint social policy initiatives that are critical to addressing this issue.

CHAPTER SUMMARY

- Sexuality is a broad area that encompasses both gender identity, sexual identity, sexual behavior, and sexual attraction. Because sexuality is based on a society's sexual culture and is socially constructed, it is always in flux and varies widely depending on the historical context.

- In our current society, we have recently seen an expansion of gender identity, sexual identity and sexual orientation categories that challenge prevailing notions about sexuality and open new dimensions for thousands of people who did not identify with traditional categories of gender and sexuality. However, with change comes inequalities and protecting the rights of sexual minorities, including transgender and gender non-conforming individuals has become, in many ways, a new Civil Rights area.

- Heteronormative culture still exists in our social institutions and can be very limiting for anyone who does not conform to heterosexual and gender norms. Luckily, we have experienced changes in policy and a proliferation of advocacy groups working toward recognizing and protecting the rights of the LGBTQ community and gender non-conforming individuals. Despite the progress made there is still a great deal of discrimination in this area that continues to need to be addressed.

REFERENCES

Altman, Dennis and Jonathan Symons. 2016. *Queer Wars: The New Global Polarization over Gay Rights*. Cambridge, UK: Polity Press.

American Psychiatric Association Diagnostic and Statistical Manual of Mental Disorders. 2013. VA: American Psychiatric Publishing. 5th ed. Retrieved June 18 (http://medlineplus.gov).

Bay, Nicholas. 2006. "Lesbian, Gay, Bisexual, and Transgender Youth: An Epidemic of Homelessness." New York: National Gay and Lesbian Task Force Policy Institute and the National Coalition for the Homeless. Retrieved June 19, 2017 (www.thetaskforce.org/downloads/homeless youth.pdf).

Best, Amy L. 2005. *Prom Night: Youth Schools and Popular Culture*. New York: Routledge.

Brier, Jennifer. 2014. "How to Teach AIDS in a U.S. History Survey." In *Understanding and Teaching Lesbian, Gay, Bisexual, and Transgender History*, Leila J. Rupp, and Susan K Freeman. Madison: University of Wisconsin Press. Pp. 279–288.

Colburn, Kenneth. 1987. "Desire and Discourse in Foucault: The Sign of the Fig Leaf in Michelangelo's 'David'." *Human Studies*. 10 (1): 61–79. Retrieved June 5, 2017 (http://www.jstor.org/stable/20008988).

D'Emilio, John and Estelle Freedman. 1997. *Intimate Matters: A History of Sexuality in America*. Chicago: University of Chicago Press. Pp 48–59.

Denizet-Lewis, Benoit. 2003. "Double Lives on the Down Low." *New York Times Magazine*. Retrieved June 20, 2017 (www.nytimes.com/2003/08/03/magazine/double-lives-on-the-down-low.html).

Dunphy, Richard. 2000. *Sexual Politics: An Introduction.* Edinburgh: Edinburgh University Press. Pp. 38–56.

Epstein, Debbie. 1994. *Challenging Lesbian and Gay Inequalities in Education. Gender and Education Series.* England: Open University Press. Pp 1–10.

Fingerhut, Hannah. 2016. "Support Steady for Same-Sex Marriage and Acceptance of Homosexuality." Pew Research Center Fact Tank. Retrieved June 20, 2017 (www.pewresearch.org/fact-tank/2016/05/12/support-steady-for-same-sex- marriage-and-acceptance-of-homosexuality).

Flores, Andrew R., Jody L. Herman, Gary J. Gates, and Taylor N.T. Brown. 2016. "How Many Adults Identify as Transgender in the United States?" Los Angeles, CA: The Williams Institute.

Foster, Thomas K. 2014. "Sexual Diversity in Early America." In *Understanding and Teaching Lesbian, Gay, Bisexual, and Transgender History*, Leila J. Rupp, and Susan K. Freeman. Madison: University of Wisconsin Press. Pp. 123–131.

Foucault, Michel. 1990. *The History of Sexuality: An Introduction.* New York: Handom House. Pp. 21–38.

Freeman, Susan K. and Leila J. Rupp. 2014. "The Ins and Outs of U.S. History: Introducing Students to a Queer Past." In *Understanding and Teaching Lesbian, Gay, Bisexual, and Transgender History*, Leila J. Rupp, and Susan K. Freeman. Madison: University of Wisconsin Press. Pp. 3–16.

Furneaux, Holly. 2014. *Victorian Sexualities.* Retrieved June 20, 2017 (https://www.bl.uk/romantics-and-victorians/articles/victorian-sexualities).

Gay Straight Alliance Network. 2017. "These Schools Protect Trans and GNC Students." Retrieved July 21, 2017. (https://gsanetwork.org/These-Schools-Protect-Trans-and-GNC-Students).

Gilley, Brian Joseph. 2006. *Becoming Two-spirit: Gay Identity and Social Acceptance in Indian Country.* Lincoln, NB: University of Nebraska Press.

GLAAD. 2017. *Accelerating Acceptance.* Retrieved June 17, 2017 (http://www.glaad.org/files/aa/2017_GLAAD_Accelerating_Acceptance).

Haas, Ann P., Philip L. Rodgers, and Jody L. Herman. 2014. *Suicide Attempts among Transgender and Gender Non-Conforming Adults – Findings of the National Transgender Discrimination Survey.* The Williams Institute. UCLA School of Law.

Human Rights Campaign. 2017. Retrieved June18, 2017 (www.hrc.org/blog/Texas-Gov-signed-HB-3859-into-law).

Human Rights Campaign. 2017. Retrieved June 20, 2017 (www.hrc.org/blog/Trump-revoked-directives-transsstudents).

Jackson, Stevi. 2006. "Interchanges: Gender, Sexuality and Heterosexuality: The Complexity and Limits of Heteronormativity." *Feminist Theory.* 7 (1): 105–121. DOI:10.1177/1464700106061462.

Kinsey, Alfred, Wardell B. Pomeroy, and Clyde E. Martin. 1948. *Sexual Behavior in the Human Male.* Philadelphia: W.B. Saunders Co.

Kosciw, Joseph G., Emily A. Greytak, Neal A. Palmer, and Madelyn J. Boesen. 2014. *The 2013 National School Climate Survey: The Experiences of Lesbian, Gay, Bisexual, and Transgender Youth in our Nation's Schools.* New York: GLSEN.

Kulick, Don. 2014. "Merely Sociological." Social Anthropology/Anthropologie Sociale. 22 (1): 25–27. DOI: 10.1111/1469–8676.12057.

Ingleheart, Jennifer, ed. 2015. *Ancient Rome and the Construction of Modern Homosexual Identities.* Oxford: Oxford University Press. Pp. 8–31. DOI: 10.101093/acprof:oso/9780199689729.001.0001.

Langlands, Rebecca. 2006. *Sexual Morality in Ancient Rome.* Cambridge: Cambridge University Press.

Lekus, Ian. 2014. "Queers of Hope, Gays of Rage: Reexamining the Sixties." In *Understanding and Teaching Lesbian, Gay, Bisexual, and Transgender History*, Leila J. Rupp, and Susan K. Freeman. Madison: University of Wisconsin Press. Pp. 224–237.

Masters, N. Tatiana, Erin Casey, Elizabeth A. Wells, and Diane M. Morrison. 2013. "Sexual Scripts among Young Heterosexually Active Men and Women: Continuity and Change." *Journal of Sex Research*. 50 (3): 409–420. DOI: 10.1080/00224499.2012.661102.

Merino, Stephen M. 2013. "Contact with gays and lesbians and same-sex marriage support: the moderating role of social context." *Social Science Research*. 42 (4): 1156–1166. DOI 10.1016/2012.02.004.

Merriman, Joan. 2004. *A History of Modern Europe: From the French Revolution to the Present*. New York, London: W.W. Norton and Company.

Miceli, Melinda S. 2006. "Schools and the Social Control of Sexuality." *Introducing the New Sexuality Studies Original Essays and Interviews*. UK: Taylor and Francis.

Millett, Kate. 1970. *Sexual Politics*. Garden City, NY: Doubleday. Pp. 41–44.

Montero, Diane. 2014. "America's Progress in Achieving the Legalization of Same-Gender Adoption: Analysis of Public Opinion, 1994 to 2012." *Social Work*. *59*(4): 321–328.

Morgan, Elizabeth M. 2013. "Contemporary Issues in Sexual Orientation and Identity Development in Emerging Adulthood." *Emerging Adulthood*. 1(1) : 52–66. DOI 10.1177/2167696812469187.

Nadig, Alok K. 2016. "Ably Queer: The ADA as a Tool in LGBT Antidiscrimination Law." *New York University Law Review*. 91(5): 1316–1317. Retrieved June 23, 2017 (www.nyulawreview.org/sites/default/files/pdf/NYULawReview-91-5-Nadig.pdf).

National Center for Transgender Equality. 2017. Washington D.C. Retrieved June 21, 2017 (www.transequality.org).

Nero, Charles I. 2016. "Nobody's Supposed to Know: Black Sexuality on the Down Low." *QED: A Journal in GLBTQ Worldmaking*. (1): 157. doi:10.14321/qed.3.1.0157.

New York Times. 2017. Understanding Transgender Access Laws. Retrieved June 22, 2017 (www.nytimes.com/2017/02/24/us/transgender-bathroom-law.htm).

Pettigrew, Thomas F., and Linda R. Tropp. 2005. "Allport's Intergroup Contact Hypothesis: Its History and Influence." *On the Nature of Prejudice*. Eds John F. Dovidio, Peter Glick, and Laurie Rudman. New York: Wiley. Pp 262–277.

Pew Research Center. 2016. "Where the Public Stands on Religious Liberty vs. Nondiscrimination." Retrieved June 22, 2016 (http://www.pewforum.org/2016/09/28/2-americans-divided-over-whether-wedding-related-businesses-should-be-required-to-serve-same-sex-couples).

Rich, Adrienne. 1980. "Compulsory Heterosexuality and Lesbian Existence." *Signs*. 5 (4): 632–660. Retrieved June 10, 2017 (www.jstor.org/stable/3173834).

Rupp, Leila J. 2014. "Outing the Past: U.S. Queer History in Global Perspective." In *Understanding and Teaching Lesbian, Gay, Bisexual, and Transgender History*, Leila J. Rupp, and Susan K. Freeman, Madison: University of Wisconsin Press. Pp. 17–30.

Russell, Steven T., and Jessica N. Fish, 2016. "Mental Health in Lesbian, Gay, Bisexual, and Transgender (LGBT) Youth." *Annual Review of Clinical Psychology*, *12*: 465–487 Doi.org/10.1146/annurev-clinpsy-021815-093153.

Seidman, Steven. 2005. "From Polluted Homosexual to the Normal Gay: Changing Patterns of Sexual Regulation in America." *Thinking Straight: The Power, The Promise, and the Paradox of Heterosexuality*. New York: Routledge. Pp. 39–61.

Simon, William S. and John H. Gagnon. 1986. "Sexual Scripts: Permanence and Change." *Archives of Sexual Behavior*. 15 (2).

Stearns, Peter N. 2009. *Sexuality in World History*. New York: Routledge.

Stein, Arlene. 1989. "Three Models of Sexuality: Drives, Identities, and Practices." *Sociological Theory*. 7 (1): 1–13. Retrieved June 9, 2017 (www.jstor.org/stable/202059).

United States Department of Justice: Civil Rights Division. 2015. "Protecting the Rights of Lesbian, Gay, Bisexual, Transgender, and Intersex (LGBTI) Individuals." Retrieved June 23, 2017 (www.ada.gov/hiv/lgbti_brochure.html).

United States Department of Justice: Federal Bureau of Investigation. 2015. "2014 Hate Crime Statistics." Retrieved June 20, 2017 (https://ucr.fbi.gov/hate-crime/2014).

U.S. History in Context. Retrieved June 15, 2017. (link.galegroup.com/apps/doc/CX2876200037/UHIC?u=midd46556&xid=9060792f).

Vrangalova, Zhana and Ritch C. Savin-Williams. 2012. "Mostly Heterosexual and Mostly Gay/Lesbian Evidence for New Sexual Orientation Identities." *Archives of Sexual Behavior* 41(1): 85–101. DOI:10.1007/s10508–012–9921–y.

CHAPTER 8

Race and Ethnicity

KEY TERMS

Cultural Pluralism

Cultural Relativism

Discrimination

Ethnicity

Ethnocentrism

Institutionalized Racism

Minority Groups

Multiculturalism

Prejudice

Race

Racialism

Racial Profiling

Racism

Reference Groups

Race a biological distinction that assigns certain physical features, e.g., skin color, skin texture, and facial and other bodily features, with a certain racial category.

Ethnicity the cultural standards that are passed down, e.g., religion, language, dialect, cultural customs that creates separate social groupings.

Prejudice preconceived notions of people based on perceived characteristics of their group.

Discrimination the actual action that someone takes based on their own prejudices of a certain group.

ABOUT THE PROBLEM: RACE AND ETHNICITY

Definitions

Many years ago, sociologist Robert Park stated that "every individual is the inheritor of a double inheritance, physical and moral, racial and cultural" (1950:4); this reflects the race/ethnicity duality. **Race** refers to a biological distinction that assigns certain physical features, e.g., skin color, skin texture, and facial and other bodily features, to a certain racial category. Being Caucasian (European American), African American, Latin American, Asian American, and Native American constitutes one's racial background. **Ethnicity**, which is often confused with race, refers to the cultural standards that are passed down within a group, e.g., religion, language, dialect, cultural customs, that creates separate social groupings. Being Jewish or a member of a group with national ties such as Polish American, Italian American, or Irish American would constitute an ethnic group.

Other terms which have different meanings but are often confused or used interchangeably are prejudice and discrimination. **Prejudice** (to "pre-judge") is a way of perceiving people different from oneself and ascribing certain characteristics to them. For example, to believe people of a certain racial category (or other characteristic) are prone to criminality, is an example of prejudice. **Discrimination** refers to certain actions that are taken (or not taken) due to certain prejudices that exist—using the previous example, if someone is prejudiced against a certain group they feel are born criminals, they might refrain from any contact with them; the term discrimination denotes *action* while prejudice refers to *thought*. Prejudice and discrimination refer to characteristics other than just race and ethnicity, however, it was placed in this chapter due to its relevance here.

The term **racism** refers to prejudice and discrimination based on a person's race or perceived race. Racism becomes **institutionalized** when it becomes part of the social system and forces a racist perspective into the core of society; an example is *red-lining* in which people who live in an area with a certain zip code are automatically prohibited from getting loans due to people in the area having a poor repayment record—many racial and ethnic minorities often live within the same area, therefore making it difficult to receive loans. Essed (1991) uses the term *everyday racism* to describe "a familiar world, a world of practical interest, a world of practices we are socialized with in order to manage in the system" (p. 3). In other words, racism should be perceived as a complex and pervasive process that continually exists in our everyday experiences and is a social rather than an individual process. **Ethnocentrism** refers to the cultural biases that result in a judgment of a person of another culture based on the person's real or perceived ethnic background, primarily because that person has different cultural traditions and beliefs. The term **cultural relativism** refers to a belief that another person's cultural background should be viewed from that person's perspective rather than one's own, thereby refusing to cast judgment—in effect, it is an antidote to ethnocentrism.

Sociologist William Graham Sumner (1940) speaks of a simple dichotomy in which people tend to classify themselves into groups of people with whom they identify (their in-group) and those they do not (their out-group)—often these **reference groups**, that help create their self-identity based on group identity, are based on race and ethnicity. The recent term *othering* represents this idea where people are perceived as different and are treated differently as well. The issue of othering is found throughout the literature in various social types who are perceived as different from the majority and who are often excluded from normal social activities; the term is useful in understanding the treatment of marginalized and excluded people.

Cultural pluralism is a social situation in which people of different racial and cultural backgrounds coexist together but maintain their distinctions. Often the attempted assimilation of different racial and ethnic groups has resulted in tension and strain. Some of these groups have segregated themselves and moved into ethnic enclaves with names such as Little Italy, Little Poland, and Little China Town to maintain some degree of their original culture; therefore, the nation is becoming encompassed by many "polyglot cities", or communities of different cultures with diverse languages (Douglas 1971:254). The positive function of the various racial and ethnic groups should be obvious—they bring together the cultural beliefs and practices that add flavor to the American landscape. To drop the hyphen from hyphen-Americanism means we all become one, but lose the distinct cultural traits that make our society American.

Closely related to the term cultural pluralism is a term that hit its zenith in the 1990s: **multiculturalism**, which is the opposite of the idea of assimilation (the "melting pot"). The term is multifocal (and often used in relation to education) and difficult to explain but Kivisto (2012:4) describes it as ideology having the goal of learning "to live with diversity in ways that promote equality, justice, and expanded levels of societal solidarity, predicated on mutual recognition and respect, intercultural dialogue, and exchange, and a fair distribution of resources". The concept of cultural pluralism has created much vigorous discussion, both agreeable and combative, and both inside and outside academia (Trotter 2002). The idea of multiculturalism echoes a respect and concern for the various groups that inhabit the country that many scholars find appealing. On the other hand, critics such as Schmidt (1997) see it as a "Trojan horse" that seems alluring but in actuality holds some cultural groups in excessive regard, ignoring their flaws, while treating others, such as European Americans as being more blemished—in essence it is believed to encourage "white bashing".

Racism prejudice and discrimination based on a person's race or perceived race.

Institutionalized Racism becomes part of the social system and forces a racist perspective into the core of society

Ethnocentrism the cultural biases that result in a judgment of a person of another culture based on the person's real or perceived ethnic background, primarily because that person has different cultural traditions and beliefs.

Cultural Relativism a belief that another person's cultural background should be viewed from that person's perspective rather than one's own.

Reference Groups groups that help form our own personal attitudes, conduct, and sense of self.

Cultural Pluralism a social situation in which people of different racial and cultural backgrounds are together but maintain their distinctions.

Multiculturalism support for the existence of diverse cultural groups.

Early Understandings of Race—Racialism

The commonly understood markers that signify racial categorization are skin color, hair texture, and other physical features, as well as the color system denoting human beings as white, black, brown, yellow, and red. These characteristics assume "clear cut, discrete, homogenous, and easily distinguishable subgroups or 'races' –that people can be easily categorized into these racial groups" (Mukhopadadhyay, Henze, and Moses 2014:5). The idea that distinct groups have different geographic origins and dissimilar biological characteristics is known as **racialism** and has a long history. Since people of different cultures and nationalities first came into contact with each other, there have been reasons to account for their differences. Philosophers and other social thinkers made sense of the distinctions by assuming non-European, non-white civilizations were inferior to people "like them". These ethnocentric thoughts were soon reinforced by pseudoscientific explanations that claimed to offer "proof" of the superiority of whites and their descendants.

> **Racialism** the idea that distinct groups have different geographic origins and dissimilar biological characteristics.

British social theorist Herbert Spencer, creator of the term "survival of the fittest", made this statement: "society advances where its fittest members can assert their fitness with the least hindrance, and where the less fitted are not artificially prevented from dying out" (Spencer, cited in Wiltshire 1978). The term "social Darwinism" developed in the convergence of Darwin's theory of biological evolution and the developing ideas of social evolution. A byproduct of this thought consisted of explanations of how some groups evolve at a faster rate than others, thereby endorsing racist and ethnocentric lines of thought. Bannister (1979) notes that in the 1880s, the term social Darwinism had been applied to a host of social maladies and movements including racism, imperialism, and militarism. Embryologist Earnest William MacBride even favored the involuntary sterilization of the Irish "race" as it was assumed that the Irish were a derivative that had evolved separately from the Anglo-Saxons of better stock (Bowler 2015). Whereas early social thinkers Spencer and William Graham Sumner embraced social Darwinism, others such as sociologist Lester Frank Ward opposed it as he rejected the "separate origins thesis" and the fear-producing idea (for many people) that interracial mixing would create inferior quality people—ideas that were being advanced under the Neo-Darwinist, Neo-Spencerian "social Darwinism" (Hofstadter 1955).

Current Understandings of Race—The Social Construction of Race

Early understandings of race involved racialism, the idea mentioned earlier, but in the last several decades, ideas about race being socially constructed have entered the mainstream. In 1949, a group of scientists who specialized in race convened at a meeting of the United Nations Education, Scientific, and Cultural Organization (UNESCO) to get a better understanding of the concept.

In 1950, the scientists produced a report with a call to abandon the term race as a scientific reality—in fact, referring to it as a "myth". No surprise, this report was met with both praise and condemnation (Yudell 2014).

This new idea, called the social construction of race approach, is currently the dominant view regarding the issue of race and challenges the traditional racialist concepts which use a classification system of certain physical traits and sees this traditional view as a "pseudo-biological concept that has been used to justify and rationalize the unequal treatment of people by others" (Machery and Faucher 2005:1208). Omi and Winant (1986, 1994) formulated a socially constructed position based on the social meanings assigned to race rather than a simply biologically constructed one. The social constructionist approach suggests that people with any differences beyond those physical categories mentioned above, e.g., height, weight, income, musical ability, technical aptitude, could be considered a race; it would, of course, be silly to speak of the tall race or the guitar wizard race, but that is basically the same as the racial categories currently in use that have no true biological basis.

Due to scientific advancements in evolutionary psychology and evolutionary anthropology, there are currently some challenges to the social construction approach to race (Machery and Faucher 2005). Specifically, Shiao et al. (2012) provide a "genomic challenge", noting that the idea of the biological connection to race is a reality, even if only to a limited degree. The researchers favor the term "clinal groups" over racial groups they claim represent scientific distinction between groups. Whether this approach signals a return to an explanation of race based on biological as opposed to social distinctions remains to be seen. The biological paradigm of the past has resulted in racial inequality and additionally resulted in atrocities such as internment, banishment, lynching and genocide, some of the darkest stains on world history.

Racial Inequality

A very important work on race relations that was originally published in 1944, Swedish Economist Gunnar Myrdal's *An American Dilemma: The Negro Problem and Modern Democracy* (1962/1944), described the so called "Negro problem" as a moral issue for both white and black Americans. He sought to explain the state of race relations at the time from the standpoint of the Thomas Theorem (things are real if people perceive them to be) and used the symbolic interactionist concept of the "definition of the situation" to better understand the point of view of other races (Madge 1967). Myrdal was selected to undertake the mammoth task of the work, which would grow to over 1500 pages, and despite his training in economics, he placed race relations in a sociological frame, particularly regarding social stratification. Myrdal enlisted the assistance of many race scholars to contribute to the project, including a young sociologist named E. Franklin Frazier, who became well known for his African American scholarship (Southern 1987); we will discuss him more in the theory section of this chapter. Racial inequality was the focus of *American Dilemma* and was groundbreaking in its treatment of race relations as a moral issue.

An important concept recently gaining currency is that of *white privilege*, or white skin privilege. The term has become commonplace to denote the fact that Caucasians have inherited "whiteness" which in turn creates certain expectations or rewards granted for that status. A look at U.S. history provides some insight into the concept. In early America, poor whites had basically the same material circumstances of African Americans and Native Americans but a propaganda campaign was promoted by the politicians and moneyed whites to make the lower-class whites feel at least superior to the other two groups. The elites received political and economic gain from this arrangement and it had the additional benefit of not costing them any money. The benefit received by these whites, rather than an economic one, was a "psychological wage" (Buck 2004). Today the idea of white privilege can still be found when people of European descent expect preferential treatment or when non-whites feel they should offer this preferential treatment to whites. Feagin (2013) extends the white privilege concept in his discussion of the "white racial frame" which fosters a pro-white and anti-other perspective; it exudes a dominant, superior, and hegemonic existence and has been used for centuries as a "tool kit" for use in understanding all phenomena and interactions from a Caucasian standpoint. Guess (2006) suggests that discussions on the construction of race concept also require discussions on the social construction of whiteness. By focusing of the race construction of non-Caucasian groups, current investigations fail to understand the political benefits that whites have maintained since the country was founded. This can be closely connected to the terms white privilege and the white frame which will be discussed soon. These benefits have, of course, contributed to white privilege.

Is the idea of white privilege useful in understanding race relationships in America?

Pro: White privilege allows white people to better understand the social benefits they receive for simply being in a racial majority and this understanding could lead to better understanding of race relations.
Con: White privilege is simply a way to promote "white bashing" and promote ideas of racial victimization that causes more conflict in society.

Issues of Racial and Ethnic Minorities

Minority Groups not only members of a group who are fewer in number but also those who have less power, control, and advantage than another group that has these attributes.

From a sociological perspective, the term **minority group** refers not only to members of a group who are fewer in number but also those who have less power, control, and advantage than another group that have these attributes. Therefore, racial and ethnic minorities are those groups that do not have the same levels of status and power as majority groups. We will look at different racial and ethnic minority groups in America and some of the issues they currently face.

African Americans

African Americans have long suffered racial prejudice and discrimination and the history of black people in America reveals a continuing struggle. Achieving racial equality post-slavery has been an arduous task due to Jim Crow policies, segregation in most areas of life, denial of civil rights, and other ways in which black people were perceived as inferior and treated as such. Currently, conflict between black communities and the police has become a national issue and centers around the highly-publicized claims of excessive force, including death of blacks; black men have especially been affected and the use of phone videotaping has given many of these events wide exposure.

Some would like to believe that the quality of life for blacks is now equal to that of whites and that prejudice and discrimination of this group is a thing of the past, especially since the nation nominated its first black President, Barack Obama, in 2008. Recent events such as the shootings of unarmed black men by police in cities large and small around the country have cast some doubt as to the idea of a post-racial America.

Latin Americans

Latin Americans now make up the largest minority group in America. As most people know, before certain portions of county were part of the United States, they were Mexican territories. However, Mexican Americans are only part of a very large group of people considered Latinos/Latinas, or Hispanic. Other groups such as Puerto Rican Americans and Cuban Americans fall under this category as well, therefore, Latin Americans have a host of different cultural practices, beliefs, and customs, and should not be perceived as one monolithic group.

Latin Americans were recently victims of the "papers, please" laws that allowed the police to arrest people if they did not have the required documentation showing they were here legally—this has been perceived by many as a case of **racial profiling** due to people being questioned because of their perceived racial background. The current immigration debate has placed this group in the spotlight in American politics in the early twenty-first century. Since Mexico borders the Southern United States, many people from south of the border enter the country illegally and many of the border crossers are impoverished and seek a better life in the United States. The issue of a 2,000-mile-long wall across the border, highlighted in the 2016 Presidential contest, has been a hotly debated topic and, due to the cost of such a wall, might make it prohibitive, even if Congress agrees to its utility.

> **Racial Profiling**
> singling out certain groups due to their real or perceived racial background.

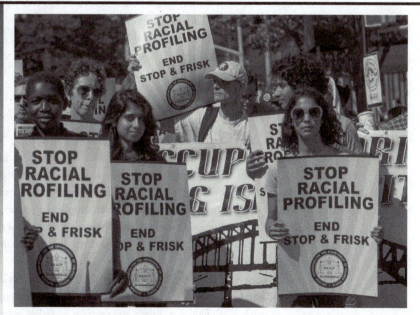

FIGURE 8.1 Stop and Frisk March - Tens of thousands of New Yorkers participated in a silent march to protest NYPD racial profiling, including the Stop and Frisk program which dissproportionally tarkets young men of color as well as the spying on Muslims as was recently reveiled in news reports. Sunday, June 17, 2012.

Source: Tony Savino/Corbis/Getty Images

The immigration issue which has been a major area of contention in America has reached higher levels over the political battle resulting from the Deferred Action for Child Arrivals (DACA), which was instituted in 2012 under the administration of President Barrack Obama. DACA allowed young people brought to the country by undocumented parents to remain in the United States. In 2017, Attorney General Jeff Sessions announced the Trump administration was rescinding the program, paving the way for the recipients to be returned to the lands of their parents, areas they had in many cases never visited and about whose culture they knew very little. Currently a political battle is being played out that puts the DACA recipients (also known as "dreamers") in the middle of the immigration debate between Democrats, who normally support the continued stay dreamers, and Republicans, who favor stronger immigration laws. This debate is not only about illegal immigration but also legal immigration, and lawmakers seek to determine who will be allowed to migrate to America. Latin Americans are at the core of this debate.

Asian Americans

There are also several groups that comprise Asian Americans. This group has also been subjected to prejudice and discrimination and the internment of Japanese Americans after the bombing of Pearl Harbor has been a dark spot in American history. Numerous stereotypes have plagued Asian Americans over the years but one stereotype has been unusual—that of being the so called "model minority", a term that has been used to describe this group as having more promise in achieving the American Dream than other non-whites. The stereotype suggests a racial group with exceptional innate intellectual ability and occupational prowess as well as a strong work ethic, however a host of factors suggest this is an illusion (see, for example, Wu 2002). It is perhaps another factor that Asian Americans are perceived as less of a threat to whites since rarely are Asian Americans associated with gang violence, ghettos, poverty, and "threatening" music as are African Americans, Latin Americans, or even Native Americans. That Asian Americans do not participate in gang activity is also a misconception.

Native Americans

Native Americans, also called American Indians or America's "first people" have a very well-known story that involves genocide, forced removal and relocation, and an elimination of their cultural ways. Like many other racial minority groups, they have been the victims of much stereotyping, however, unlike other minority groups, Native Americans are represented by sports mascots that many non-Natives do not interpret as insulting, even despite derogatory names ("red skins"), or highly caricatured images ("chief Wahoo"). Some schools and professional sports organizations have been moving away from the practice of using Native Americans as mascots but others remain firm in refusing to change.

Although Native people are not the only group to experience what has been termed "historical trauma", indigenous people have especially experienced this in our country. Historical trauma, which refers to the loss of cultural traditions and customs in earlier generations, has been passed down to current generations and is important in understanding the present condition of groups with a past of oppression and subjugation. As Derezotes (2014:5) notes "historical trauma has helped

Should the use of sports mascots that represent Native Americans be discontinued?

Pro: The use of Native Americans as mascots further demeans indigenous customs and traditions, continuing a long history of stereotyping and disrespect.

Con: Native Americans are represented as mascots in an honorable manner, depicting them as admirable brave and noble warriors, and should be seen as a source of pride for them.

design the architecture of human beings. Probably everything we feel, think, or do reflects at least in part the ways our ancestors responded to challenges they faced in the past."

The issue of the Dakota Pipeline Access (DPA) in which an oil transferring pipeline was allowed to pass through sacred Native American land, potentially polluting the water used by the Native Americans, seems to be a continuation of the struggle between American Indian culture that values tradition and the environment and a mainstream culture that values economic development.

Ethnic Groups

Not all European Americans comprise the group known as White Anglo-Saxon Protestants (WASPs), a group that has been the dominant and most powerful racial grouping in America. Other people of European origin who were immigrants from Ireland, Italy, Poland, and other European

FIGURE 8.2 NORTH DAKOTA, UNITED STATES - 2017/02/22: Defiant Dakota Access Pipeline water protectors faced-off with various law enforcement agencies on the day the camp was slated to be raided. Many protesters and independent journalist, who were all threatened with multiple felony charges if they didn't leave were met with militarized police on the road abutting the camp. At least six were arrested, including a journalist who reportedly had sustained a broken hip.

Source: Michael Nigro/Pacific Press/LightRocket/Getty Images

countries, were often labeled "white ethnics" since they did (and some still do) maintain the cultural traditions of the old world, often located in close knit ethnic enclaves. Many white ethnics suffered prejudice, discrimination, and ethnocentrism even though they were "white" because they were viewed as an inferior "other". As they gradually assimilated into the WASP culture, many lost the separate ethnic status.

Jewish Americans constitute an ethnic group whose culture is primarily based on its religious beliefs and practices in Judaism. A group with a long history of global persecution, many Jews immigrated to America to escape the atrocities inflicted upon them. They have endured more stereotyping and prejudice than any other ethnic group and there exists a special name for the prejudice and discrimination of this group—anti-Semitism (Feagin 1989). Anti-Semitism has a long history in America and many Jews have been excluded from common aspects of social life. Presently, groups called Neo-Nazis (also called "skin heads") continue to promote anti-Jewish prejudice, often using the internet to propagate their ethnocentric views.

Another ethnic group based on religion, Muslim Americans, have recently become a major focus of social and political life in America. This Islamic religious group has a long history in the United States, even before its founding as a republic (Curtis 2009), and has adherents spread throughout the world. Many Muslim Americans possess many of the same values, hopes, and aspirations as most other citizens. After the 9/11 terrorist attacks, fear of Muslim Americans has resulted in the rounding up and deportation of Muslims under the USA Patriot Act, calls for surveillance of mosques, intimidation activities by citizens aimed at keeping Muslims out of the area, and alarms sounded

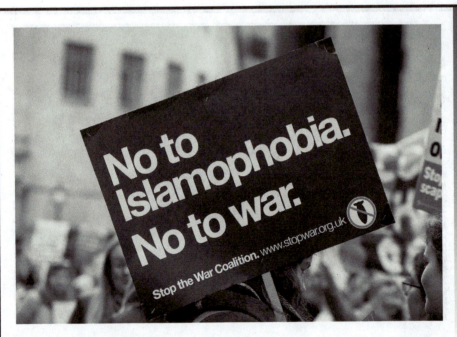

FIGURE 8.3
London, UK. 18th March 2017. March Against Racism - National Demo for UN Anti-Racism Day - Thousands of people turn out for the anti racism - anti Donald Trump rally through central London.

Source: John Gomez/Shutterstock.com

by politicians and others about the potential attempts of Muslims to convert America to Sharia law. Political rhetoric has heated up over the use (and lack of the use) of the term "radical *Islamic* terrorism" (stressing the religion of Islam) which tends to make it seem all followers of Islam are terrorists. As Curtis (2008, 2009) notes, most Muslim Americans are not radical terrorists out to overthrow the country; they are proud of their religious and cultural heritage and wish to be both Muslims and Americans. They also do not desire to not be viewed as dangerous outsiders.

THEORETICAL PERSPECTIVES

Structural Functionalism

One of the components of structural functionalism is the idea that society is ever-evolving and if all institutions are working together appropriately, society will be functional. The evolutionary element is important in understanding the early foundations of the theory as is the belief in the interdependence of the different racial and ethnic groups. Pluralism and multiculturalism, therefore, primarily support the functionalist paradigm.

Herbert Spencer, as mentioned in chapter 2, applied the social evolutionary model to his laissez-faire advocacy for government, but it was also applied to other aspects of society including racial categorization and race relations. Spencer, like Darwin, possessed the general racial prejudices of many people of the era, however, neither theorist believed the human races were different species with distinct evolutionary origins. In addition, despite his social Darwinist ideas, Spencer objected to the colonization efforts by Europeans (Bowler 2015). Leaders of authoritarian governments have often devolved the notion of social evolution into nationalistic and xenophobic policies that led to horrendous actions such as the voluntary sterilization programs of the eugenics movement and acts of genocide such as those found in Nazi Germany and other parts of the world. Unfortunately, some of those policies can be found in American history as well.

Daniel J. Moynihan, sociologist, government bureaucrat, and later a United States senator, published a report on African American families in 1965 called "The Negro Family: The Case for National Action", in which he drew upon the works of black sociologists including E. Franklin Frazier, to describe how African Americans were caught up in a subculture of poverty and that black family life was disintegrating. African American families had become matriarchal, he claimed, and the male and female roles had become reversed, and out of accord with the rest of American society (Katz 2013). Adopting the perspective of the white middle class family, the report was not received positively by black leaders and intellectuals. This widely reported essay basically described working and middle class families as dysfunctional, even though Moynihan was working to improve conditions for these families.

Conflict

Critical theories are those "that are developed and used to understand and investigate oppressive power relations to help advance toward equity in all aspects of life" (Briscoe and Khalifa 2015:10). Critical race theory (CRT) was developed to assess understandings of race and race relations and has very deep roots in sociology. Prominent voices include W.E.B. Du Bois (mentioned in the next section for reasons that shall become known shortly), E. Franklin Frazier, and a host of others too numerous to mention here. It is important to understand racism as an egregious social phenomenon but one that is common in society, Khalifa states that likely the greatest strength of CRT is the "acceptance of racism as normality" (2015:19).

W.E.B. Du Bois' thoughts on race and race relations are primarily based on a critical/conflict perspective, however he is mentioned in the following section as well. He is one of America's greatest race scholars and the first African American to receive a Ph.D. from Harvard University. He was a professor, prolific writer, editor, and one of the founders of the organization that would become the National Association for the Advancement of Colored People (NAACP). Many of his concepts, expressed in metaphorical language (see the next section) are cornerstones in the critical sociology of race. Du Bois felt the sting of racism at an early age and used rejection to excel in his professional career ([1903] 1995). He worked tirelessly to combat racism in its various forms and encouraged the top young black leaders of his era (a group he called the "talented tenth") to carry on the struggle for equal rights.

E. Franklin Frazier was one of the talented young black intellectuals influenced by Du Bois who continued investigations into the sociology of race, especially with his work on the African American family. He received his educational training from the University of Chicago when the institution was well known for using ethnography, the research methodology that observes human behavior in its natural environment (Hall 2002). A person of great boldness, he supported Du Bois when the elder scholar was denounced by colleagues and he taught Marxism during the McCarthy communist witch hunts, despite the potential consequences in a fear-fueled era (Bracey 2002). Frazier was particularly interested in the black middle class that emerged after reconstruction and published the controversial *Black Bourgeoisie* (1957) in which he criticized this group for abandoning the lower class African Americans and attempting to mimic the white upper classes, a group that never considered them as equals. And, as mentioned earlier, he made significant contributions to Myrdal's *An American Dilemma*.

Symbolic Interactionism

It has been posited that race is a social construction and this has been an accepted position in the social science community, though many people refuse to accept this. Even though race is considered by constructionists to be a myth, myths, if widely believed, have real consequences (remember the Thomas theorem); by believing that people are dramatically different based on race, terrible racial actions have occurred throughout history. And one's race and ethnic background can certainly affect the conceptions of self. Racial groups are often used as reference groups, and affiliation with these groups helps form our own personal attitudes and conduct, along with feelings of "we-ness". These issues are central to symbolic interactionist thought.

In his seminal essay, Merton (1946) described how the Thomas theorem can be modified to include how individuals internalize the messages—if a person is often told she is destined to act in a certain way, she is likely to follow that prescribed path and the prediction will come true, and this "truth" will have consequences. This, as mentioned earlier, is called the *self-fulfilling prophecy*. Merton mentioned how specifically after World War II, African Americans, Jews, the Japanese, and other groups have been plagued with prejudice, which becomes institutionalized to the point where behavioral labels become too difficult to escape. He uses as an example a teacher in the deep South in the Jim Crow years who dared to teach against the "natural" superiority of whites and had a short tenure. And he explains how Jews and Japanese Americans, having an excess of in-group identification, will be "securely controlled by the high walls of discrimination" (p. 203).

As mentioned previously, W.E.B. Du Bois' perspectives on race are components of conflict theory, however, some of his ideas are also closely aligned with symbolic interactionism. For example, Du Bois famously describes a "color line" that exists as a barrier between people of different racial groups. He also explains the "veil" as something that keeps people from being able to truly understand the perspectives of other people—in other words, Mead's concept of "taking the role of the other" is impossible when people cannot adequately understand others' perspectives. Another key concept is "double consciousness", the bifurcation of self that occurs when racial minorities follow social norms but still are looked down upon by racial majorities. African Americans experience this double consciousness which in turn affects selfhood, identity, and can lead to the self-fulfilling prophecy that keeps them achieving social equality (Du Bois [1903] 1995).

SEARCHING FOR SOLUTIONS

Civil rights legislation sought to address the inequalities in their earlier treatment of African slaves in America. An early attempt by the federal government to correct some of the inequities of race in the educational system is affirmative action, originally conceived during the administration of President Lyndon Johnson in 1965. The affirmative action policies initially sought to ensure fair hiring practices for black federal employees and employees of firms that had financial transactions with the government and later it evolved to addressing equities in admissions procedures at colleges, graduate, and professional schools, as well as contract work with private businesses, and employment that had traditionally not been available for minorities. In these instances, preferential treatment was given to people of backgrounds that had not had a "fair playing field" in the past, including racial minorities. Affirmative action was expected to be a short-term solution meant to correct unfairness of the past and to bring minority groups entrance into aspects of American society that had been denied to their forebears (Collum 2006). It has proved to be a very controversial subject, especially regarding admission into institutions of higher education.

Is affirmative action an appropriate means of correcting past wrongs and helping minorities gain equality?

Pro: An extensive history of denial of access into positions that allow full participation in American society is long overdue.

Con: Affirmative action means providing preferential treatment to those who might not be capable, denying more qualified people to attain jobs, college admission, etc.

Another issue that seeks to address past inequities is the potential granting of reparations to minorities. During the Civil War, a decree from General William T. Sherman was issued to grant all freed slaves "forty acres and a mule" to compensate victims of slavery. This decree was vetoed but the idea of some form of reparations continued to germinate. In Germany, reparations were given to Jewish Holocaust survivors, and in America, some form of reparations were granted to Japanese Americans who were wrongly incarcerated in World War II internment camps and to Native Americans who had land taken from them. Some local incidents, such as the Rosewood massacre in Florida, have resulted in reparations given to small groups of African Americans but a large-scale reparation program for descents of African slaves has not been instituted in America. This controversial measure to redress wrongs has both advocates and opponents (Collum 2006).

Should reparations be granted to the descendants of African slaves?

Pro: Apologies for something of the magnitude of the enslavement and maltreatment of human beings requires more than a simple apology to a large segment of the population. Reparations send a tangible sign of penitence.

Con: Reparations fail to recognize other groups that have been systematically maltreated and the implementation of such a program would be exceedingly difficult to administer in a fair and just manner.

The Black Lives Matter (BLM) movement was created in response to some high-profile situations in which police officers or civilian vigilantes killed black citizens that many considered unjustified. The movement has brought much attention to the racial strife that occurs in communities of color when the police are viewed as an occupying force rather than people whose function is to serve and protect. BLM was started by three African American women, Alicia Garza, Patrisse Cullors, and Opal Toneli, who sought to engage the public on matters stemming from the acquittal of George Zimmerman for his shooting dead of Trayvon Martin and grew as several other black men and boys were killed at the hands of police. The death of Michael Brown and others caused the movement to grow and expand into many areas, including into higher education to educate and create activism to address their cause (Miller and Schwartz 2016).

Is the Black Lives Matter a progressive movement that can be beneficial in improved race relations and should be actively promoted?

Pro: The BLM movement encourages people to focus on the inequities and power differentials and power relations between minority neighborhoods and the police and therefore is useful.

Con: The BLM encourages people to focus solely on race and distorts the idea that the lives of other racial groups matter as well.

Sanctuary cities refer to cities that offer shelter to people, normally undocumented migrants, who are normally affiliated with religious organizations (McNamee 2017). San Francisco was designated one of these cities in the 1980s in response to what city leaders perceived as a lack of asylum

FIGURE 8.4 NEW YORK CITY - APRIL 5 2015: thousands of New Yorkers filled 5th Avenue marking Easter Sunday with the tradition Easter Bonnet Parade as protesters for Black Lives Matter also took to the streets to protest police killings of black men and boys.

Source: a katz/Shutterstock.com

refugees from El Salvador and Guatemala and later, in the late 1980s and early 1990s, a national law-and-order approach to combat what has been called "crimmigration". Sanctuary activity was revived in recent years over concerns for the rights of immigrants and at the middle of the second decade of the twenty-first century, sanctuary cities, including San Francisco, became a major political issue during the 2016 Presidential election. One incident was cited many times, especially by then-candidate Donald Trump: the 2015 murder of a young woman by an undocumented immigrant with a lengthy criminal and deportation history was used as a justification to promote a national anti-sanctuary law which cleared the U.S. House of Representatives but failed in the Senate. As the national battle played out, state and local policies carried out their own fight. While some saw the sanctuary cities as an impediment from keeping the county safe from crimmigration, others saw them as being simply a "dog whistle" to keep people in fear of immigrants (Lasch 2016). These cities, numbering over 200 by the end of 2016 (McNamee 2017) are still controversial.

Should cities that have sanctuary status lose this status?

Pro: Sanctuary status guarantees that people from different racial and ethnic backgrounds are protected and treated with respect.

Con: Sanctuary status provides people who are in the country illegally and who possibly break the law protections that can harm those who are in the country legally.

CHAPTER SUMMARY

- Race is considered a biological distinction that depends on physical characteristics, but in reality is a social construction based on our stratification system.

- Ethnicity is based on cultural norms and folkways that are passed down within specific groups and consist of customs, traditions, religion, language, and other cultural aspects that separate the group from dominant society.

- Prejudice and discrimination are used to stratify groups based on perceived stereotypes and characteristics. Prejudice is a belief, while discrimination is an actual act that is based on prejudice. And racism refers to the prejudice and discrimination based on a person's perceived race.

- When racism becomes a part of our social system it is considered institutionalized and is integrated into our social stratification system as a way to categorize and marginalize groups based on their physical characteristics.

- Racialism, or the idea that people of color are inferior to white Anglo Saxons, became popular along with the rise of social Darwinism, however, new conceptualizations of race by symbolic interactionist theorists explain race as a social construction used to classify and marginalize groups.

- White privilege has become a recognized term for the invisible power and status that whites have that minority groups such as African Americans and Latin Americans lack. Privilege based on skin color is still a debated topic since many Americans feel that our society is post-racial and discrimination is no longer an issue.

- Structural functionalism perpetuated racism by blaming the African American family for their impoverished communities and adopting the perspective that the white middle class family was the only functional family. While conflict theorists advanced Critical Race Theory to look at how the legacy of slavery and institutionalized racism have made it almost impossible for the African American family to flourish in our society.

- Solutions to institutionalized racism include grassroots movements such as Black Lives Matter, and the emergence of sanctuary cities that provide shelter to undocumented workers. Other solutions are policy oriented, such as affirmative action, and legislation that attempts to protect minorities from discrimination in housing, jobs, and education. Unfortunately, our society has a long way to go before racism and discrimination become part of our past and not an important social problem that we continue to combat.

REFERENCES

Anderson, Elijah. 1990. *Streetwise: Race, Class, and Change in an Urban Community*. Chicago: University of Chicago Press.

Anderson, Elijah. 2012. *The Cosmopolitan Canopy: Race and Civility in Everyday Life*. New York: W.W. Norton and Sons.

Bannister, Robert C. 1979. *Social Darwinism: Science and Myth in Anglo-American Social Thought*. Philadelphia: Temple University Press.

Bowler, Peter J. 2015. "Herbert Spencer and Lamarckism." In Mark Francis and Michael Taylor, *Michael Herbert Spencer: Legacies*. Abingndon, Oxon: Routledge. Pp. 203–221.

Bracey, John H. 2002. "Frazier's Black Bourgeoisie: Talented Tenth or a Parasitic Class?" *E. Franklin Frazier and Black Bourgeoisie*. Columbia: University of Missouri.

Briscoe, Felecia M. and Muhammad A. Khalifa. 2015. "Introduction and Conceptual Framework: Critical Theory, Social Justice, and Autoethnography." In Briscoe, Felecia M. and Khalifa, Muhammad A. *Becoming Critical: The Emergence of Social Justice Scholars*. Albany, NY: State University of New York Press. Pp. 3–15.

Buck, Pam Davidson. 2004. "Constructing Race, Create White Privilege." In Rothenberg, Paula S. *Class, Race, and Gender in the United States*, 6th ed. New York: Worth Publishers.

Collum, Danny D. 2006. *Rising to Common Ground: Overcoming America's Color Lines*. Louisville, KY: Sowers Books and Videos.

Curtis, Edward E. 2008. *The Columbia Sourcebook of Muslims in the United States*. New York: Columbia University Press.

Curtis, Edward E. 2009. *Muslims in America: A Short History*. Oxford: Oxford University Press.

Derezotes, David S. 2014. *Transforming Historical Trauma Through Dialogue*. Thousand Oaks, CA: Sage.

Douglas, Jack D. 1971. *American Social Order: Social Rules in a Pluralistic Society*. New York: Free Press.

Du Bois, W.E.B. [1903] 1995. *The Souls of Black Folk*. New York: Signet.

Essed, Philomena. 1991. *Understanding Everyday Racism*. Newbury Park, CA: Sage Publications.

Feagin, Joe R. 1989. *Racial and Ethnic Relations*, 3rd ed. Englewood Cliffs, NJ: Prentice Hall.

Feagin, Joe R. 2013. *The White Racial Frame: Centuries of Racial Framing and Counter-Framing*, 2nd ed. New York: Routledge.

Frazier, E. Franklin. 1957. *Black Bourgeoisie: The Rise of a New Middle Class*. New York: Free Press.

Guess, Teresa J. 2006. "The Social Construction of Whiteness: Racism by Intent, Racism by Consequence." *Critical Sociology*. 32 (4) : 639–673. Retrieved May 30, 2017 (http://research.flagler.edu:10958/doi/pdf/10.1163/156916306779155199).

Hall, Robert L. 2002. "E. Franklin Frazier and the Chicago School of Sociology: A Study in the Sociology of Knowledge." *E. Franklin Frazier and Black Bourgeoisie*. Columbia: University of Missouri.

Hofstadter, Richard. 1955. *Social Darwinism in American Thought*, revised edition. New York: George Braziller, Inc.

Katz, Michael B. 2013. *The Undeserving Poor: America's Enduring Confrontation with Poverty*. Oxford: Oxford University Press.

Khalifa, Muhammad A. 2015. "Autoethnography and Critical Race Theory." In Briscoe, Felecia M. and Khalifa, Muhammad A. *Becoming Critical: The Emergence of Social Justice Scholars*. Albany, NY: State University of New York Press. Pp. 19–21.

Kivisto, Peter. 2012. "We Really *Are* All Multicultural Now." *Sociological Quarterly*. 53 (1): 1–24.

Lasch, Christopher N. 2016. "Sanctuary Cities and Dog-Whistle Politics." *Northeast Journal on Criminal and Civil Confinement*. 42 (2): 159–190. Retrieved June 22 (http://research.flagler.edu:9839/eds/detail/

detail?sid=13bca1cb-35ff-4a69-abf3-   90b50603a92d%40sessionmgr4009&vid=0&hid=4108&b-data=JnNpdGU9ZWRzLWxpd mUmc2NvcGU9c2l0ZQ%3d%3d#AN=115902672&db=sih).

Machery, Edouard and Luc Faucher. 2005. "Social Construction and the Concept of Race." *Philosophy of Science.* 72 (5) : 1208–1219.

Madge, John. 1967. *The Origins of Scientific Sociology.* New York: Free Press.

McNamee, Gregory. 2017. "Of Sanctuary, Refuge, Migrants, and Refugees." *Virginia Quarterly Review.* 93 (2): 192. Retrieved June 22, 2017 (http://research.flagler.edu:9839/eds/pdfviewer/pdfviewer?sid=4ad2e05d-7197-47f8- b1f7-f75c7335eeaa%40sessionmgr4007&vid=3&hid=4108).

Merton, Robert K. 1946. "The Self-Fulfilling Prophecy." *The Antioch Review.* 8 (2) : 193–210.

Miller, Brian and Joni Schwartz. 2016. "The Intersection of Black Lives Matter and Adult Education: One Community College Initiative." *New Directions for Adult and Continuing Education.* 150 : 13–23. Retrieved June 5, 2017 (http://research.flagler.edu:9839/eds/pdfviewer/pdfviewer?vid=1&sid=9e92b260-0f54-4898-a722–8b42acbadf6d%40sessionmgr4007).

Mukhopadadhyay, Carol C., Rosemary Henze, and Yolanda T. Moses. 2014. *How Real is Race? A Sourcebook on Race, Culture, and Biology,* 2nd ed. Lanham, MD: Altamira Press.

Myrdal, Gunnar. [1944] 1962. *An American Dilemma: The Negro Problem and Modern Democracy,* 20th Anniversary Edition. New York: Harper and Row.

Omi, Michael and Howard Winant. 1986. *Racial Formation in the United States: From the 1960s–1980s.* New York: Routledge.

Omi, Michael and Howard Winant. 1994. *Racial Formation in the United States: From the 1960s–1990s.* New York: Routledge.

Park, Robert E. 1950. *Race and Culture.* Glencoe, IL: Free Press.

Schmidt, Alvin J. 1997. *The Menace of Multiculturalism: Trojan Horse in America.* Westport, CT: Praeger.

Shiao, Tiannbin Lee, Thomas Bode, Amber Beyer, and Daniel Selvig. 2012. "The Genomic Challenge to the Social Construction of Race." *Sociological Theory.* 30 (2): 67–88. Retrieved April 5, 2017 (http://research.flagler.edu:9017/stable/41725504).

Southern, David W. 1987. *Gunnar Myrdal and Black-White Relations: The Use and Abuse of An American Dilemma, 1944–1969.* Baton Rouge: Louisiana State University Press.

Sumner, William Graham. 1940. *Folkways: A Study of the Sociological Importance of Usages, Manners, Customs, Mores, and Morals.* Boston: Ginn and Company.

Trotter, C. James. 2002. *Multiculturalism: Roots and Realities.* Bloomington: Indiana University Press.

Wiltshire, David. 1978. *The Social and Political Thought of Herbert Spencer.* Oxford: Oxford University Press.

Wu, Frank H. 2002. *Yellow: Race in America Beyond Black and White.* New York: Basic Books.

Yudell, Michael. 2014. *Race Unmasked: Biology and Race in the Twentieth Century.* New York: Columbia University Press.

CHAPTER 9

Deviance and Crime

ABOUT THE PROBLEM: DEVIANCE AND CRIME

Defining Deviance

There have been many, many definitions of deviance, far too many to cover in this text; this attests to the fact that the concept is difficult to adequately define. These definitions have different foci and all add some degree of understanding to the phenomenon. We will now turn to some analyses by some of the great sociologists of deviance.

Clinard and Meier (1992) offer four possible ways of defining deviance. The *statistical* definition uses the idea of an "average" or normal set of behaviors that, if violated, constitutes deviance. The *absolutist* perspective assumes commonly agreed upon norms, primarily from a moral set of guidelines. The *reactivist* definition posits that deviant behavior is that which has been labeled such by the system of social control in society. The *normative* approach sees deviance as a violation of a society's norms at a certain place and time that results in a negative sanction from that society. The last definition is more fluid and notices that norms can change as beliefs, attitudes, and values about certain situations change.

There are also *relativistic* views that state that deviance is a result of people failing to follow the norms of the greater society, however Becker (1963:8) makes a keen observation: "a person may break the roles of one group by the very fact of abiding by the rules of another group. Is he then deviant?" Becker argues that the response of others to aberrant behavior is a crucial step in defining deviance and that those who break the rules and obtain the label of deviant are more likely to continue deviant behavior. He also suggests problems with schemas which analogize deviance with pathology (the *pathology* approach), or a disease, using the medical model as a template, as it is more difficult to determine healthy behavior than healthy physical conditions (we will return to this medical analogy in a few moments).

The challenge of defining deviance was also considered by Kai Erikson (1966:5) who stated, "one of the earliest problems the sociologist encounters in his search for a meaningful approach to deviant behavior is that the subject itself does not seem to have any natural boundaries". The lack of "natural boundaries" exposes and amplifies the diffuseness and porosity of the borders that define the lines of demarcation of deviance and non-deviance (the initial consideration was to coin the phrase "squishiness of boundaries" but better sense prevailed).

All these comments about deviance brings us back to the main point—that deviance is hard to define. Perhaps deviance can be better understood in a more simplistic, normative description: **deviance** refers to any type of behavior that deviates from social norms and that elicits some type and degree of social sanction. Every society, in fact every grouping of people, have **norms**—sets of guidelines deemed appropriate for the group—and have a series of responses that happen when people violate these established standards.

> **Deviance** activity that contradicts (deviates from) the norms of society and elicits some type and degree of social sanction.

> **Norms** guidelines of behavior deemed appropriate for the various groups in society.

Other Factors Relating to the Concept of Deviance

Merton (1982) notes that certain acts can be interpreted as either being deviant or non-deviant according to the status of the person performing the activity (remember a status is a position that one occupies within a certain social setting). For example, a child can have a tantrum and this is not considered deviant (it is even expected at certain stages of development) but if some adult in business attire screams out in a restaurant "my tater tots are yucky", the activity would normally be considered deviant. Merton creates a useful distinction between nonconforming vs aberrant behavior: nonconformers are open about their opposition to certain norms, reject previous norms, provide alternatives, are altruistic, and seek to bring about social justice while aberrants try to hide their illicit behavior, try to rationalize their deviance, are egoistic, and seek change for personal interests.

Daniel Patrick Moynihan (1993) a United States Senator and sociologist, coined the famous term "defining deviance down" in which he meant (borrowing from Emile Durkheim and Kai Erikson) that society is willing to accept a certain level of deviance until it begins to relabel certain previously deviant acts as no longer deviance; in other words, what was once deviance is deviance no longer. In describing this catchy alliteration, Moynihan proposed three categories—the *altruistic*, the *opportunistic*, and the *normalizing* types and provided examples: the deinstitutionalization of the mental health field in the twentieth century, the acceptance of (in his words) "alternative family structures" (Moynihan 1993:19), and an increase in the tolerance of violent crime, respectively. Using a dialectical approach, political commentator and media personality Charles Krauthammer (1993) offered an opposing perspective—that of "defining deviance up", in which some acts are redefined as deviance that were formerly not considered deviant; Krauthammer mentioned child abuse, rape, and, what is referred to today as political correctness.

Becker (1963) sees deviance as being an enterprise that is conducted between the "moral entrepreneurs", who produce and maintain the rules (the "rule creators" and "rule enforcers") and those who break the rules ("outsiders"). In his work *Outsiders*, he expresses a concern that most scientific analysis has focused on the outsiders, leaving an examination of the moral entrepreneurs unexplored (Becker 1963). The type of moral entrepreneur known as the rule creators consist of people who consider an activity deviant (even "evil") and work diligently to rid society of that activity. When new rules are created, rule enforcers are required to carry out the new rule—they are, however, in a bind because they are expected to rid society of the deviant act (according to the dictates of the rule creators) but not completely, or they will be out of a job. Conflict exists then between the rule creators who want alternative rules strictly enforced and the enforcers who are required to make sure the alternative rule is carried out (but not totally).

Schur (1980) explains that early sociologists studying deviance often searched for the *causes* of deviant behavior and later they began trying to understand the defining of deviance and the societal reactions to deviance, i.e., how individuals are "deviantized" through a complex labeling process. The concept of deviance should currently be viewed as "a political phenomenon in the broadest sense of the term" (1980:3). Seeing deviance in this light—as a political issue—helps in the analysis of deviant *behavior* as a social problem in need of a social remedy rather than just focusing on *individuals* who are somehow faulty and in need of individual correction.

The Closely Related Concept of Crime

Deviance and crime are different but closely related concepts. Since deviance refers to actions that simply deviate from social norms, not all deviant acts are deemed criminal. A student who breaks out in song during her professor's classroom lecture might be said to commit a deviant act (unless, perhaps it is a music appreciation class), but it would not likely be a criminal act. In fact, just because an act is considered deviant does not necessarily make it wrong; if someone is acting justly in an unjust society, the action might be considered deviant but it is not immoral. **Crime** is activity that is in opposition to the social norms and deemed immoral or otherwise harmful by most people in a society to the point that some action is considered necessary to correct the behavior or at least remove the perpetrator of the act from others. Therefore, whereas deviance is not always a crime, crime is always deviant behavior.

> **Crime** activity that is in opposition to the social norms and deemed immoral or otherwise harmful by most people, is codified into law, and elicits a formal sanction.

According to Gottfredson and Hirschi (1990:15), crime can be viewed as an act involving "force or fraud undertaken in pursuit of self-interest". Another definition sees crime as a set of "rules that prohibit certain forms of conduct to maintain social order" (Albanese 2008:12). A more comprehensive definition reflecting its legal focus describes crime as "conduct in violation of the criminal laws of a state, the federal government, or a local jurisdiction, for which there is no legally acceptable justification or excuse" (Schmalleger 2009:7). Crime is therefore more formal than minor deviance and has a specific institution to deal with it—the criminal justice system comprised of the police, the courts, and corrections. Please note that criminal behavior by juveniles is referred to as delinquency rather than crime, and has a separate system—the juvenile justice system.

Terms Related to Deviance

A related term, which is frequently used incorrectly, is **antisocial behavior**. Antisocial behavior is often used in general parlance to refer to activity considered to be unsociable, or that a person deliberately or unintentionally (for example, due to shyness) avoids other people or social situations. The term antisocial literally means "against society", or against social norms, and refers to behavior that is harmful or offensive to society. The term is often used in clinical situations and the Diagnostic and Statistical Manual of Mental Disorders, now in its fifth edition and lovingly referred to by clinicians as the DSM-5 (APA 2013), describes the mental disorder of Antisocial Personality Disorder

> **Antisocial Behavior** behavior that is harmful or offensive to society due to a conscious lack of regard for social norms.

with certain diagnostic features. These features include nonconformity to social rules, deceitfulness, impulsivity, recklessness, chronic irresponsibility, and a general lack of regard for or empathy toward other people. The informal, non-clinical terms *psychopath* and *sociopath* are often used in referring to people diagnosed with Antisocial Personality Disorder and focus on a person's harmful acts and corresponding lack of empathy for these acts. Examples include aggressive behavior toward others, theft, vandalism, and the use of deceit and manipulation to obtain desired objects or acts. Note that while most of these acts which are listed are criminal in nature (and not all antisocial behaviors are criminal), they are designated as antisocial when the behaviors are intransigent, maladaptive, and consistent (DSM-5:659–663). You should remember we discussed the medical model as an analogy to deviance in Becker's description.

The other extreme of deviance (in this dialectic) is conformity. People either violate the rules or obey them. Many people are familiar with the Milgram obedience study (1974) in which study participants thought they were providing electric shocks to people (actually they were not) when directed to do so by someone in authority. The study followed the same format as the Asch conformity study in which one person in a group was asked a question that others answered incorrectly (there were a part of the study) to see if they would give in to peer pressure (and many did). Society describes some actions as deviant and others as conformist and labels people as deviants or conformists—we will return to this point in our discussion on labeling theory.

Controlling (Regulating) Deviance

All societies deal with deviant behavior by creating institutions to control that behavior. These controls may be informal, such as ostracism, or formal, such as legal actions. Behavior is primarily enforced through negative sanctions to those who deviate through the imposition of a penalty such as incarceration, and positive sanctions, to those who conform to accepted behavior through the provision of praise and status recognition (Clinard 1968).

Social Control
measures taken by social control agents to stop or thwart deviance and crime.

Deviance is often considered something that necessitates some **social control** agent to address the problem—in other words, deviance is "conduct about which something should be done" (Becker 1964:11). However, it should be remembered that the type of deviance mentioned here would be of the more serious type that would warrant official sanctions.

Total Institutions
places that promote resocialization by removing and isolating people from the general population.

Goffman (1961) defined **total institutions** as places where people are removed from the general population and where physical boundaries promote discontinued use of social interaction with those on the outside, at least for a while. Places such as jails, mental hospitals, and others provide this function to people considered deviant (note—Goffman identified other types of total institutions that did not reflect deviance but for this discussion, we will not focus on them). Total institutions that deal with deviance function to "de-socialize" people who commit the acts and, as a goal, to "re-socialize" them, if possible, allowing them to return into the greater society. The status of mental patient or "ex-con" (former jail or prison inmate) will provide a label that contributes to stigma, a concept that Goffman (1963) would develop later. These labels are "sticky" and difficult to remove.

Total institutions are not the only things that function to control deviant behavior. Becker (1964) notes that communities often serve this social control function as a "screener" of deviant conduct. Since no one is deviant in every possible way, the screening process requires some deliberate attention and must take many things into consideration such as past misdeeds, social class,

FIGURE 9.1
Vintage engraving of Titus Oates in the Pillory. Titus Oates (15 September 1649–12/13 July 1705), also called Titus the Liar, was an English perjurer who fabricated the Popish Plot, a supposed Catholic conspiracy to kill King Charles II.

Source: duncan1890 / Getty Images

contrition shown after the offense, in other words, the person's "overall performance" (Becker 1964:11). Since the transgression is only a snapshot of the person-in-society, it is easy for that person to develop a label and its corresponding stigma.

Punishment is, of course, a means of social control, as it is hoped that it will deter not only the offender from future deviant acts (*specific deterrence*) but also others who witness the consequences of the behavior (*general deterrence*). Shaming penalties are a way of enforcing conformity and America has an interesting history that has extended to today. Although shaming penalties have changed since the days of pillories, stocks, dunking stools, and branding, judges today sometimes order offenders to wear signage or place bumper stickers stating the nature of the offense and, most commonly, the names and offenses are published in newspaper or shown on TV or occasionally on billboards. Shaming is controversial but the debates on the effectiveness continue (see Steverson 2011).

In 2012, legal scholar, Michelle Alexander, published a critique of the United States criminal justice system that illustrated how African Americans have been disproportionately targeted and

Are shaming penalties that are currently in use effective in controlling deviance and crime?

Pro: Shaming has proved to be an effective means of deterring deviance and criminal behavior.
Con: Shaming creates labels, stigma, and negative self-images that not only harm the person but society.

FIGURE 9.2 Too many young men of color are incarcerated and branded as criminals early in life.

Source: Skyward Kick Productions/Shutterstock.com

harmed by the war on drugs and subsequent mass incarceration (Alexander 2010). According to Alexander (2012) a new caste system has emerged due to the mass incarceration of poor people of color, particularly black men. In an interview with Frontline, Alexander defines mass incarceration as a "system of racial and social control … a process by which people are swept into the criminal justice system, branded criminals and felons … and then released into a permanent second class citizen status" (Childress 2014:1). By second-class citizen status, Alexander (2012) is referring to being denied the right to vote, serve on juries, and being legally denied or discriminated against in employment, housing, and access to public benefits. Because this system targets minority men at early ages, it serves as a system of not only social, but also racial control.

Criminal Deviance

To narrow our focus on this subject, we will use criminal deviance in our analysis. If you look at the table of contents of all the social problems we discuss in this book, you can see that criminal deviance can be a part of each one (for example, economic crimes such as white-collar activity, governmental crimes that involve corruption, crimes such as domestic violence in families, hate crimes that involve race or ethnicity, the numerous crimes related to substance use and addiction, and crimes involving the environment), in fact, some of these have been addressed in the related chapters. In this chapter, we will use a broad approach in our analysis of criminal deviance.

An indicator of a society's "wellness" often involves its crime rate, particularly if it is increasing. The Federal Bureau of Investigation (FBI) is the national agency tasked with maintaining crime data.

Beginning in 1930, the FBI has produced the Uniform Crime Report (UCR) which tracks and monitors crime in the nation. It currently comprises the efforts of 18,000 city, county, state, federal, tribal, and higher education agencies in this effort and provides sociologists, criminologists, and political leaders data for planning purposes and to the media for dissemination (FBI nd). According to the 2015 data, the latest annual data from the FBI, violent crime rates have increased 3.9% while property crimes have decreased 2.6% from the previous year (FBI nd).

The UCR provides a "crime clock" that illustrates the ratio of crime to fixed intervals of time (FBI nd). According to the most recent annual data collected in 2015, a violent crime occurred every 22.3 seconds; a breakdown of select violent crime is as follows:

- Murder—33.5 seconds

- Rape—4.2 minutes

- Robbery—1.6 minutes

- Aggravated assault—41.3 seconds

In addition, property crimes occurred every 3.9 seconds; select property crimes are broken down in this way:

- Burglary—20.0 seconds

- Larceny/theft—5.5 seconds

- Motor vehicle theft—44.6 seconds

FIGURE 9.3 Violent crime rates remain stable from 2014-2015, as property offenses declined.

Source: Kathryn Seckman Kirsch/Shutterstock.com

Another important document on crime statistics is the National Crime Victimization Survey (NCVS), which reported that there was no significant change in violent crime rates from 2014–2015 and no significant change in violent crimes reported to the police during this period. There was also a decrease in reported property offenses in this period; from 118.1 victims per 1000 households to 110.7 victims per 1000 households. There was also a decrease in violent victimization reported (from 1.11% to 0.98%) during this time (Truman and Morgan 2016).

While all major U.S. cities experience high rates of crime, Chicago has recently experienced particularly high crime rates, especially involving violent crimes. 2016 was the deadliest year regarding murder rates and shooting violence in 20 years, prompting President Donald Trump to announce he was considering sending in federal law enforcement to combat the crime because, he stated, the city was more violent than many areas of the Middle East (Williams-Harris, Crepeau, and Malagon 2017). The President did not elaborate on his suggestion to send in federal forces and, at this point, no actions have been taken.

Should federal forces be used to intervene if cities exceed acceptable crime levels?

Pro: It is sometimes necessary for federal intervention to maintain order as the government is supposed to protect the nation's citizens.

Con: This is an example of federal government overreach; support might be offered but direct intervention sets a bad precedent.

Mass shootings are defined by the Congressional Research Office (CRS) as shootings occurring in public places that result in more than four deaths, not including the perpetrator of the killings, in which the victims are indiscriminately chosen, and without political motivations of the shooter (CRS 2013). Such shootings have defined the American landscape and in 2017, attendees of a country music concert in Las Vegas were victims of the largest mass shooting in the nation's recent history. In October of that year, 58 concert goers were killed and 851 injured as a shooter fired on the crowd from a hotel room overlooking the concert. Prior to the Las Vegas shooting the largest mass shooting occurred in Orlando, Florida at the Pulse nightclub in which a shooter opened fire on the crowd of the primarily LGBTQ Latin American attendees in 2016. Mass shootings have become a common occurrence in the nation and the United States ranks much higher in mass shootings than any other country (Lankford 2016).

Hate crimes refer to traditional crimes that have the additional element of being based on a victim's actual or perceived race, ethnicity, religion, disability, gender, or gender identity (FBI nd). UCR data reveal 6,121 incidents of hate crime (FBI nd) but the number is likely much higher. The Southern Poverty Law Center, a watchdog organization for hate groups, maintains a "hate map" and has identified 917 hate groups currently operating in the United States, including many anti-Muslim groups that have grown 197% since 2015 (SPLC nd). The Pulse night club shooting just mentioned would meet the description of a hate crime.

An incident that happened in August 2017 in Charlottesville, Virginia represents the hate that exists for some racial and ethnic groups. A rally, billed as Unite the Right, that was held by neo-Nazi and neo-confederate groups, had participants marching with torches chanting anti-Semitic statements such as "blood and soil, you will not replace us, Jews will not replace us". When met with counter protesters the next morning, fights broke out, culminating in the death of one of the counter protesters, Heather Heyer. When President Trump claimed there were "good people on both sides" of the protest, further controversy erupted.

THEORETICAL PERSPECTIVES

The earliest assumptions about human behavior that violated social norms were probably based on spiritual or supernatural ideas. People from ancient civilizations to the Middle Ages believed that when citizens were behaving differently to a notable extent, perhaps some type of evil spirit had taken control over their minds or bodies. This idea can easily be found in the various witch tortures and trials that have been carried out throughout history. As time passed, Enlightenment ideas prevailed and moved away from supernatural explanations to those involving rational choice—people commit acts of deviance and crime after weighing the pros and cons of such behavior. As more positivist (scientific) ideas began to appear, scientific notions about deviant behavior offered explanations that would seem laughable today, such as atavism (which states deviants are born criminals with biologically inferior traits) but at least they were trying to advance the field. We will now turn to sociological theories of deviance and crime.

SOCIOLOGICAL THEORIES

Regarding the etiology (or cause) of crime, sociological theories do not focus on spiritual/supernatural events, philosophical questions of human nature, or biological/constitutional predispositions, but instead emphasize assumptions that social factors contribute to, and are affected by, deviant behavior. There is something about the social conditions in a certain place and certain period (as crime is relative) that contribute to abnormal behavior and, in turn, how activity that is deemed as a violation of norms is handled by society.

Structural Functionalism

Emile Durkheim made major contributions to the study of deviance and crime. His insight was that deviance and crime are normal because it is and has been an occurrence in all societies, that it exists in differing forms and degrees in all groups, and that if all actions currently considered deviant were expunged, a new group of designated acts would quickly be assigned the label (1895/1982). Therefore, deviance and crime are an indication of a healthy society (though it still needs to be controlled). The role of the criminal is therefore functional—he helps societies delineate behavior that is acceptable from that which is not. With its emphasis on structure, social order, and the functionality of deviance, Durkheim believed that a form of social disorganization he called *anomie*, in which norms are confused or not stable enough to control society, contributes to deviance and criminality.

Robert K. Merton, himself a gang member in his youth, proposed an often quoted theoretical construct of deviance and conformity, the strain theory of deviance, which is derived from Durkheim's ideas on social disorganization. This theory states that a disjunction exists between a person's desire for socially approved goals (the society's materialistic longings or "the American dream") and the socially approved means to obtain them. When means other than the socially prescribed ones are taken, or when a person doesn't adopt society's goals, a *strain* exists, resulting in deviance (Merton 1938).

Kelling and Coles (1997) can find another by-product of the social disorganization theories in the highly influential broken windows theory of crime and deviance. The authors posit that signs of social disorganization, analogized as "broken windows", can be determined in communities by many different indicators (e.g., dilapidated buildings, abandoned automobiles, bars on store windows, graffiti, and yes, actual broken windows in buildings). To make the community more organized, people need to attend to the small details of community disorganization to make it less appealing to the criminal element. This perspective has been adopted in the field of policing and has been both praised and criticized in recent years.

Have broken windows policing policies been effective in controlling crime?

Pro: By focusing on the small-scale nuisance behaviors, cities have been able to lower serious crime rates.

Con: The focus on nuisance behaviors has created excessive police control, which has had serious consequences.

FIGURE 9.4
According to the broken windows theory of crime and deviance, crime is more likely occur when a neighborhood shows signs of disorganization.

Source: 1000 Words/Shutterstock.com

Conflict theory

The conflict theory approach basically posits that Lady Justice is not actually constrained by a blindfold and is therefore unable to treat people differently based on socioeconomic status, race, gender, etc. Conflict theorists describe how deviance is normally defined by the groups in power to serve their own needs, not the interests and needs of those without such power. Additionally, the theory posits that government often protects those with power, doling out smaller sanctions to them or overlooking their misdeeds all together. By imprisoning the "dangerous classes", the haves can remove the have-nots from society.

Although Marx did not write much about crime directly, he did write at length about how social conditions created by the wealthy and powerful are unfair to those with fewer resources. His ideas about social institutions being created and maintained to reflect powerful bourgeois interests have been applied to the study of crime and deviance by several so-called "socialist criminologists". One theorist who provided a Marxist perspective, Richard Quinney (1977), sees the development of the criminal justice system as being directly tied to the development of capitalism. As he notes "capitalistic justice is by the capitalist class, for the capitalist, and against the working class" (Quinney 1977:50–52). In other words, the activity that is considered deviant is that which has been so designated by those in control of the financial resources. Quinney (1977) describes acts of governmental deviance including crimes of control (e.g., police brutality, due process violations), crimes of government (e.g., crimes committed by Congress, political assassination), crimes of economic domination (e.g., pollution, criminal operations supported by the government), and social injuries (e.g., denial of human rights that result in various forms of discrimination, including race, gender, and class discrimination). Capitalism, in this view, requires a large body of workers and the government must restrain deviant activity to keep the system working.

Is the privatization of correctional institutions and community corrections (probation agencies) more appropriate than government management of these institutions?

Pro: Privatization promotes stronger ideals of capitalism and institutions can be run more effectively and efficiently.
Con: Formal means of social control should be left to the government rather than other private citizens.

Conflict theory can also be found in both feminist theory and critical race theory. From a feminist perspective, deviance and crime are "gendered" as the perspective references and recreates ideas about sex and gender as they relate to deviant behavior. Gender and sexuality also figure prominently in the understanding of deviance and crime. Cesare Lombroso, an early criminologist, believed that women lacked the physical and intellectual development to commit crime at the same levels as men (let that sink in).

Early theories in deviance and crime either recognized no difference in male and female criminality, which would require no investigation into obvious differences in crime rates according to gender, or that women are pathologically different from men; feminist theory changed all that (Smart 1977). In the 1970s, the era of women's liberation, two major works brought gender into the picture, Freda Adler's *Sisters in Crime: The Rise of the New Female Criminal* (1975) and Rita James Simon's *Women and Crime* (1975), which suggested changes in society resulted in increased freedom and opportunity for women to commit crime. Some scholars have rejected these two works as they were seen to neglect the real material and structural forces that affect female criminality (Vold, Bernard, and Snipes 2002). Masculinities theory as proposed by Messerschmidt (1993) also sees the importance of using a "gender lens" in understanding deviance and crime. In his gender-based theory, he puts the spotlight on the sex that has been the primary focus of deviance and criminality—males. Included in this perspective is the concept of "hegemonic masculinity", a cultural script exists in which males are expected to exert power, control, and aggressive competition which can easily be translated into deviant behavior.

Critical race theory has also evolved from conflict theory and focuses on how deviance and crime should be viewed from the lens of race and race relations and the differential treatment of racial and ethnic minorities. This theoretical perspective challenges the Eurocentric view of disorder and crime; it also challenges the white, middle class template of "normal" human activity that ignores life in communities of color (Inderbitzen, Bates, and Gainey 2013). America has a long history of coercive control regarding race and ethnicity and that background "has melded into the history of the treatment of criminal offenders" (Steverson 2014:343). African Americans, Latin Americans, and Native Americans are overrepresented in the American criminal justice system and are often adversely affected by certain policies involving policing ("stop and frisk", "papers please"), the court system (certain drug laws—the powder cocaine vs crack laws), and corrections (mass incarceration in prisons). This overrepresentation does not appear to have much effect on policies within the system, however (Bowman 2014). Regarding incarceration, Dunn (2014) uses Michel Foucault's concept of the carceral—the control mechanisms of the elites in postmodern society to control the behavior of individuals through advanced surveillance techniques that extend beyond the prison such as probation and parole programs—to explain the large numbers of racial minorities in the prison system.

Symbolic Interactionism

Focusing on the social psychological aspects of deviance, symbolic interactionists have made many contributions to the study of deviance. Lemert (1967) was concerned with how a deviant identity contributes to a continuance of the deviant behavior and described two types of deviant behavior—*primarily deviance*, in which someone commits some act deemed unacceptable or undesirable and *secondary deviance*, when the complex process of officially labeling, punishing, and stigmatizing occurs. In secondary deviance, a person accepts the stigmatic label of deviant and the identity of a deviance becomes such that they become a "person whose life and identity are organized around the facts of deviance" (Lemert 1967:41). Merton (1948) devised the commonly used term "self-fulfilling prophecy" to describe the condition in which a person deviates from the norm, is labelled a deviant, and accepts the label to the point where future behavior conforms to the deviant identity.

The subtitle of Erving Goffman's brilliant sociological analysis *Stigma* (1963) is *Notes on the Management of Spoiled Identity*. This terminology is illustrative: when one becomes labeled by some action (though Goffman mentions other "signs" of difference that were not derived through personal choice such as disability and disfigurement) the effect of their personal identity is bound up in how society perceives them. Per Goffman (1963), people manage their appearances to others in a process he terms *impression management*. When one's own identity is "spoiled", as when one is labeled a deviant, people act in a way to persuade others of their true selves. Therefore, one can attempt to avoid any performances that act as a sign to others that they are deviant; alternatively, they might act in a way to prove their deviant status and convince others that they are, in fact, true to their reputation ("street cred"). According to this perspective, when submitting an application which requires information about a criminal history or physical or mental disability, the response can serve as a sign of difference, perhaps a deviant difference.

Braithwaite (1989) sees the very formal process of labeling people as deviant as stigmatizing and damaging not only to the offender but also to the victim and society generally. He advocates what he calls "reintegrative shaming" in which offenders are encouraged to meet with victims face-to-face and provide an apology for the behavior and restitution for any damages. It is hoped that the offenders will assume responsibility and develop some empathy in the future and the victims will receive some degree of comfort and support because of the encounter. Reintegrative shaming is closely related to the philosophy of restorative justice, which occurs after rather than before punishment is meted out, and seeks to restore offenders back to society rather than forcing them to remain "outsiders" (to use Howard Becker's term). In traditional criminal justice policy, offenders are ceremonially punished in what have been called "degradation ceremonies" (Garfinkel 1956) but they are not formally returned to society after their punishment has completed. These two ideas seek to reverse that process and hopefully result in a more just society.

SEARCHING FOR SOLUTIONS

There are many types of behaviors that are considered deviant, therefore there are numerous solutions that have been sought, proposed, and implemented to control mental illness, substance abuse, deviant sexuality, violence, and many others. These solutions are far too abundant for the scope of this text so we will explore the strategies that have been examined to deal with the problem of crime.

The War on Crime

In the 1960s, America experienced an increase in criminal activity and a frightened public called upon the government to act. President Johnson created a commission in 1965 to address the crime problem and the commission produced the famed report entitled *The Challenge of Crime in a Free Society* (President's Commission on Law Enforcement and Administration 1967).

Crime research was conducted to better understand criminality and the responses to it, the fear of crime featuring prominently (Lane et al. 2014). This was the beginning of what President Johnson coined, "The War on Crime" and a whole new era of law enforcement in America. The Law Enforcement Assistance Act, presented by Johnson, and passed by Congress in 1965, was the legislation that gave the federal government a role in local police departments, local and state court systems, and state prisons. The Department of Justice was given a much larger budget to purchase military grade weapons, tanks, helicopters, and other equipment that historically had only been used by the military during war and dispense these to local law enforcement agencies. This was the beginnings of what would become the militarization of law enforcement that finally came to national attention in 2014 when a series of demonstrations in Ferguson, Missouri protesting the police shooting of Michael Brown, a young unarmed African American teenager, ended in local law-enforcement rolling into the town in tanks and full combat gear and dropping tear gas bombs on protesters and civilians alike.

Should local police departments be militarized with full combat gear and deadly military weapons, airplanes, and heavily armored tactical vehicles?

Pro: Local law enforcement needs to be equipped with the proper equipment to deal with serious threats to their safety and the safety of citizens alike.

Con: The needs of a local law enforcement agency are different from an occupying military force. They are not properly trained for this militarization and this results in unnecessary violence against civilians and is a major financial expense.

> **Implicit Bias** refers to preferences or bias toward certain groups of people that is not conscious but affects how we behave around and the stereotypes we associate with a group, usually based on race, ethnicity, gender, and country of origin.

Solving the problem of police shootings of innocent minorities and other civilians will require a major change in how local enforcement agencies function and end the war on crime that has resulted in unnecessary deaths and increasingly large budgets and spending by the Department of Defense for the militarization of local law enforcement agencies. According to The Center for Policing Equity, a non-partisan think tank that works collaboratively with law enforcement and stakeholders in the community, training on racial profiling and **implicit bias** is needed in our local law enforcement agencies. Implicit bias refers to both the preferences or bias toward certain groups of people that is not conscious but affects how we behave towards individuals within these groups, as well as the stereotypes we associate with a group, usually based on race, ethnicity, gender, and/or country of origin. For example, people often associate criminal behavior with black men though they are not conscious that a certain prejudice is influencing their actions. The Center for Policy Equity offers training and conferences on eliminating racial disparities to negate the role implicit bias plays in police arrests and use of force. According to a report released by The Perception Institute (2015), implicit bias is directly related to race related police use of force and stop and frisk.

Black Lives Matter began a "Campaign Zero" plan in 2015 to reduce police violence. This plan calls for clear guidelines on limiting the use of police force and getting rid of police quotas for tickets and arrests. The campaign centers on the effects of systematic oppression and racism in minority neighborhoods by focusing on reducing crime in these low-income communities through greater access to education, jobs, and affordable housing and healthcare—an inside out approach to reducing crime. Those involved in the campaign also seek to end the stop-and-frisk policy as well as advocate for the demilitarization of local police departments. A study conducted by the National Bureau of Economic Research (2016) aligns with the initiatives by Campaign Zero, with findings that police officers are 50% more likely to use force in interactions with black and Hispanic individuals (Fryer 2016).

Mass Incarceration and the War on Drugs

The War on Drugs is intertwined with the War on Crime and thus plays an important role in our search for solutions. In an interview conducted in 2016, legal scholar, Michelle Alexander, who was highly influential in establishing evidence that mass incarceration was a system of social and racial control over minority men, indicated that she did not believe policy changes, such as sentencing reform, would adequately lower incarceration rates, since the majority of people in prisons today would have to be released for justice to be achieved (Mock 2016). Tens of thousands of people who rely on the prison system for employment would then be out of work. In rural areas, many individuals depend on prisons for their economic stability; consequently, they would experience a drastic increase in unemployment. Instead, Alexander suggests downsizing the prison system by dis-incentivizing funding for the war on drugs, and reinvesting that money into communities and schools to build better housing, provide a quality education, and create jobs (Mock 2016). She agrees with activists who call for abolishing our current prison system since these are "sites where we treat people as less than human and put them in literal cages and intentionally inflict harm and suffering on them and then expect that this will somehow improve them" (Mock 2016:1). See chapter 10 on Alcohol and Other Drugs for further ideas for solutions to incarcerating non-violent drug offenders.

Prison Abolition Groups such as The Prison Activity Resource Center, call for a moratorium on any new prison construction, citing institutionalized racism, sexism, able-ism, heterosexism, and classism as problems inherent in our prisons that cannot be solved with our current system. They support hunger strikes by prisoners as well as organized protests that address abuses in the current prison system. They also connect prisoners with prisoners' rights organizations and advocate for better health care in our prison system. Organized community based movements such as these have not made progress in abolishing prisons but they are extremely helpful in working with released prisoners to reduce recidivism. Since 2008, there has been a downward trend in the total correctional population. However, it is primarily driven by a decrease in people on probation (responsible for 68% of total decline), with very little change in the percent who are prisoners or parolees (Kaeble and Glaze 2016:3). It will take some time for reductions in crime to be reflected in the number of people incarcerated, however, new incarceration rates should be declining (Kaeble and Glaze 2016).

Some of the most successful strategies to combat deviance in the criminal justice field have been in the field of crime victimization. Often, these programs provide assistance for victim recovery from violent crime. Examples include, the Battered Women's Justice Project, National Children's Alliance, and the National Organization for Victim Assistance, just to name a few. These groups focus on assisting crime victims with the trauma associated with being a victim of crime, help develop coping skills, as well as provide financial help and support services such as emergency housing, counseling, and support groups.

One of the most successful campaigns to control a specific criminal offense, that of driving while intoxicated, is Mothers Against Drunk Drivers (MADD). One mother, Candace Lightner, founded the program in 1980 after a drunk driver killed her 13-year-old daughter. The goal of MADD is to reduce drunk driving fatalities, support the victims of violent crime, and prevent underage drinking. The group had a great deal of success in the enactment of the National Minimum Drinking Age law that penalized states that did not raise their minimum legal drinking age to 21. MADD was also involved in legislation that worked to reduce the legal limit for blood alcohol content (BAC) to 0.08 which has since been adopted by all states (MADD.org 2017).

Local initiatives that collaborate with police agencies to reduce criminal behavior by making it more difficult for a crime to occur and easier for an offender to be caught have been effective. For example, implementing steering locks on cars in high-risk areas is a physical barrier that results in fewer car thefts. Situational prevention strategies include the use of technology to set up public surveillance systems that monitor and record public areas to reduce property and personal crimes, home security systems, metal detectors in schools, and improved street lighting. Other local initiatives focus on reducing gun violence through gun buy-back programs, gun laws, and law enforcement strategies. These local initiatives have had varying degrees of effectiveness for deterring crime.

Early prevention strategies aimed at high-risk youth are designed to intervene before young people begin to commit criminal acts. Crime by juveniles is higher during the summer months and after school when there is less structure and adult supervision. According to the Afterschool Alliance (2014), an advocacy organization that focuses on community based afterschool programs, these programs for youth have been quite successful at curbing juvenile crime as well as providing a safe and educational environmental during the peak time (3:00 pm–6:00 pm) when children are least likely to have adult supervision. Unfortunately, there is a great deal of unmet need for after school programs in high poverty areas and these are the high-risk communities that would benefit the most from these programs.

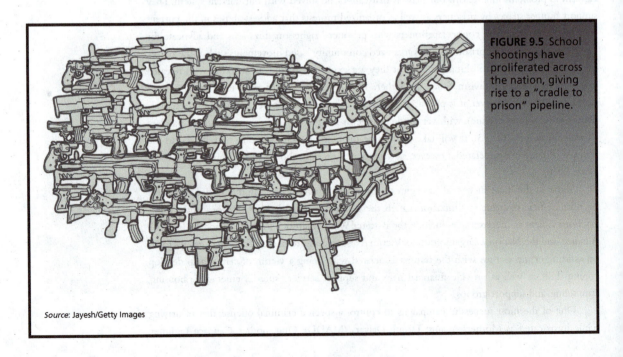

FIGURE 9.5 School shootings have proliferated across the nation, giving rise to a "cradle to prison" pipeline.

Source: Jayesh/Getty Images

School based programs have the potential to be powerful venues for crime prevention and early intervention. Programs that bring together teachers, law enforcement officials, and parents are shown to be effective at targeting high-risk youth and providing intervention strategies for their families. School based crime prevention programs can target students with known risk factors such as hyperactivity, early antisocial behavior, home discord, poverty, and exposure to family violence. Children exposed to multiple risk factors are more likely to become delinquent (U.S. Department of Justice). Teachers play an important role in early intervention and can identify children with high-risk factors for delinquency prevention programs and support the development of the student's assets and resilience, as well as involve the family in prevention strategies. Research shows that early intervention and prevention to stop the "cradle to prison pipeline" is much more effective than remediating long-standing behavioral problems (youth.gov 2017). Some of the programs that schools and community prevention programs employ include: classroom and behavior management programs, mentoring programs, bullying prevention programs, and comprehensive community interventions.

Should juvenile intervention programs remove juveniles living in high-risk homes where there is criminal activity, domestic violence, and other negative behaviors that increase the likelihood of these children becoming criminals?

Pro: Environment is important, and removing children from homes where there is violence and criminal activity will go a long way toward preventing them from engaging in criminal activity as they grow older.

Con: If we remove children from these homes it is not likely to help since they will end up in the foster care system with less guidance and more interactions with juveniles who are at high-risk of becoming criminals.

Solutions for crime and deviance exist on federal, state, and local levels and tend to be most effective when communities organize and mobilize with a variety of prevention strategies that can be implemented in schools, by community leaders and law enforcement, and target high-risk neighborhoods. Community based campaigns and prevention strategies tend to be at least as and possibly more effective at reducing crime than national laws and interventions.

CHAPTER SUMMARY

- Deviance and crime have always existed; however, they are heavily dependent on cultural context and specific intersections of time and place in any given society. There are four ways to define deviance and each is based on social constructions of commonly agreed upon norms, values, and morals. Other factors that must be considered in the concept of deviance are the status of the person in society, the level of deviance a society will tolerate, and the way rules are enacted and enforced by those in power.

- Crime is closely related to deviance. It is an activity that society has created laws around and for which behaviors are enforced by negative sanctions. It involves social control, such as removing people from society and placing them in total institutions (e.g. prisons), and punishment that is designed to deter future deviance, as well as operating as a system of racial and social control for young male minorities who are generally seen as dangerous or a threat to society.

- From a functionalist perspective, crime and deviance are normal and will always exist in various forms and degrees. Laws enforce social order, and the role of the criminal helps society define boundaries and unite in solidarity against criminal acts. Merton's strain theory adds that crime often occurs when there are not legitimate opportunities to acquire socially approved goals or when a person does not adopt society's goals. Another perspective, broken windows theory, suggests crime occurs as a result of social disorganization.

- Conflict theories on crime generally focus on how deviance and crime are defined by the ruling class and tend to target those who are in poverty and racial/ethnic minorities. Feminist theory and critical race theory both evolved from conflict theory and focus on differential treatment by gender, race, and ethnicity.

- Symbolic interactionist theorist, Lemert, described two types of deviance: primary and secondary. Primary deviance is the act of committing a crime and this leads to secondary deviance when labeling, punishment, and assigning of stigma occurs. This can be a self-fulfilling prophecy if the person accepts the label of being a deviant and then conforms to the new identity and continues to commit future deviant acts.

- Solutions for crime and deviance by the federal government include legislation enacted through the war on crime and the war on drugs. Federal policies to combat crime have led to the militarization of local police departments, stop and frisk police activity in communities that are considered high risk for crime and are generally populated by minorities and punitive measures for drug use that have resulted in the mass incarceration of African American and Hispanic men. Strategies to combat the war on crime (solving the solution, so to speak) call for abolishing and/or downsizing the prison system, training law enforcement on implicit bias, and changing laws that criminalize lesser crimes to lower incarceration rates. Crime prevention strategies include targeting at-risk youth, use of technology for more sophisticated surveillance systems, and highly successful crime victimization programs such as Mothers Against Drunk Drivers (MADD).

REFERENCES

Adler, Freda. 1975. *Sisters in Crime: The Rise of the New Female Criminal*. New York: McGraw-Hill.

Afterschool Alliance. 2014. Retrieved July 17, 2017 (www.afterschoolalliance.org).

Albanese, Jay S. 2008. *Criminal Justice*. 4th ed. Boston: Pearson Education.

Alexander, Michelle. 2010. *The New Jim Crow Laws: Mass incarceration in the age of colorblindness.* New York: The New Press.

American Psychiatric Association. 2013. *Diagnostic and Statistical Manual of Mental Disorders.* 5th ed. Washington, DC: Author.

Becker, Howard. 1963. *Outsiders: Studies in the Sociology of Deviance.* New York: Free Press.

Becker, Howard. 1964. *The Other Side: Perspectives on Deviance.* New York: Free Press of Glencoe.

Bowman, Scott. 2014. "What Keeps us Here?: Policies and Practices that Shape Minority Representation." In *Racism in the U.S. Prison System,* edited by Scott Bowman. Santa Barbara, CA: ABC-CLIO.

Braithwaite, John. 1989. *Crime, Shame, and Reintegration.* New York: Cambridge University Press.

Britton, Dana M. 2011. *The Gender of Crime.* Lanham, MD: Rowman and Littlefield.

Campaign Zero. 2015. "We Can End Police Violence in America." Retrieved July 25, 2017 (www.join-campaignzero.org/).

Childress, Sarah. 2014. "Michelle Alexander: A System of Racial and Social Control." Retrieved July 25, 2017 (www.pbs.org/wgbh/frontline/article/michelle-alexander-a-system-of-racial-and-social-control).

Clinard, Marshall. 1968. *Sociology of Deviant Behavior.* 3rd ed. New York: Holt, Rinehard, and Winston, Inc.

Clinard, Marshall and Robert F. Meier. 1992. *Sociology of Deviant Behavior.* 8th ed. Ft. Worth, TX: Harcourt Brace.

Congressional Research Service (CRS). 2013. Public Mass Shootings in the United States: Selected Implications for Federal Public Health and Safety Policy. Retrieved January 28, 2018 (https://fas.org/sgp/crs/misc/R43004.pdf).

Dunn, Ronnie A. 2014. "The Marginalization and Criminalization of the Black Male Image in America." In *Racism in the U.S. Prison System,* edited by Scott Wm. Bowman. Santa Barbara, CA: ABC-CLIO.

Durkheim, Emile. [1895]1982, trans by Steven Lukes. *Rules of the Sociological Method.* New York: Free Press.

Erikson, Kai. 1966. *Wayward Puritans: A Study of the Sociology of Deviance.* New York: John Wiley and Sons.

Federal Bureau of Investigation (FBI). 2015. "Crime Clock Statistics." Crime in the United States 2015. Retrieved July 16, 2017 (https://ucr.fbi.gov/crime-in-the-u.s/2015/crime-in-the-u.s.-2015/resource-pages/crime-clock).

Federal Bureau of Investigation (FBI). 2015. Uniform Crime Report. "Crime in the United States 2015." Retrieved July 16, 2017 (https://ucr.fbi.gov/crime-in-the-u.s/2015/crime-in-the-u.s.-2015/resource-pages/aboutucrmain_final.pdf).

Federal Bureau of Investigation (FBI). nd. What we Investigate: Hate Crimes. Retrieved January 28, 2018 (https://www.fbi.gov/investigate/civil-rights/hate-crimes).

Federal Bureau of Investigation (FBI). nd. Hate Crime by Jurisdiction. Retrieved January 28, 2018 (https://ucr.fbi.gov/hate-crime/2016/topic-pages/jurisdiction).

Fryer, Roland G. 2016. *An Empirical Analysis of Racial Differences in Police use of Force.* Cambridge, MA: National Bureau of Economic Research.

Garfinkel, Harold. 1956. "Conditions of Successful Degradation Ceremonies." *American Journal of Sociology.* Vol. 61(5): 420–424.

Goffman, Erving. 1961. *Asylums: Essays on the Social Situation of Mental Patients and other Inmates.* New York: Random House.

Goffman, Erving. 1963. *Stigma: Notes on the Management of Spoiled Identity*. Englewood Cliffs, NJ: Prentice-Hall.

Gottfredson, Michael R. and Travis Hirschi. 1990. *A General Theory of Crime*. Stanford, CA: Stanford University Press.

Inderbitzin, Michelle, Kristin Bates, and Randy Gainey. 2013. *Deviance and Social Control: A Sociological Perspective*. Los Angeles: Sage.

Kaeble, Danielle, and Lauren Glaze. 2016. *Correctional Populations in the United States, 2015*. U.S. Department of Justice: Bureau of Justice Statistics.

Kelling, George L. and Catherine M. Coles. 1997. *Fixing Broken Windows: Restoring Order and Reducing Crime in Our Communities*. New York: Simon and Schuster.

Krauthammer, Charles. 1993. "Defining Deviancy Up." *The New Republic*. 209 (21).

Lane, Jodi, Nichole E. Rader, Billy Henson, Bonnie S. Fisher, and David C. May. 2014. *Fear of Crime in the United States: Causes, Consequences, and Contradictions*. Durham: Carolina Academic Press.

Lankford, Adam. 2016. "Public Mass Shootings and Firearms: A Cross-National Study of 171 Countries." *Violence and Victims*. 31 (2): 187–199. Retrieved January 28, 2018 (http://docserver.ingentaconnect.com/deliver/connect/springer/08866708/v31n2/s1.pdf?expires=1517169692&id=0000&title-id=75001825&checksum=63BCA37BCAA04ABE19ED9796BB43C1DB).

Lemert, Edwin. 1967. *Human Deviance, Social Problems, and Social Control*. Englewood Cliffs, NJ: Prentice-Hall.

MADD.org. 2017. Retrieved July 25, 2017 (www.mag.org/about-us/history).

Merton, Robert K. 1938. *Social Theory and Social Structure*. Glencoe, IL: Free Press.

Merton, Robert K. 1948. "The Self-fulfilling Prophecy." *The Antioch Review*. 8 (2): 193–210.

Merton, Robert K. 1982. *Social Research and the Practicing Professions*. Cambridge, MA: Abt Books.

Messerschmidt, James W. 1993. *Masculinities and Crime: Critique and Conceptualization of Theory*. Lanham, MD: Rowman and Littlefield.

Milgram, Stanley. 1974. *Obedience to Authority*. New York: Harper Torchbooks.

Mock, Brentin. 2016. *Life after 'The new Jim Crow'*. City Lab. Retrieved July 17 2017 (www.citylab.com/equity/2016/09/life-after-the-new-jim-crow/502472/).

Moynihan, Daniel Patrick. 1993. "Defining Deviancy Down." *The American Scholar*. 62 (1): 17–30.

Perception Institute. 2015. *Implicit bias*. Retrieved July 27, 2017 (https://perception.org/research/implicit-bias/).

President's Commission on Law Enforcement and Administration of Justice. 1967. *Challenge of Crime in a Free Society*. Washington, DC: U.S. Government Printing Office.

Prison Activist Resource Center. nd. Retrieved July 17, 2017 (www.prisonactivist.org/projects).

Quinney, Richard. 1977. *Class, State, and Crime: On the Theory and Practice of Criminal Justice*. New York: Longman.

Schmalleger, Frank. 2009. *Criminal Justice Today*, 10th ed. Upper Saddle River, NJ: Pearson Education.

Schur, Edwin M. 1980. *The Politics of Deviance: Stigma Contests and the Uses of Power*. Englewood Cliffs, NJ: Prentice-Hall, Inc.

Simon, Rita James. 1975. *Women and Crime*. Lexington, MA: Lexington Books.

Smart, Carol. 1977. "Criminological Theory: Its Ideology and Implications Concerning Women." *British Journal of Criminology*. 28 (1): 89–100.

Southern Poverty Law Center (SPLC). nd. Hate Map. Retrieved January 28, 2018 (www.splcenter.org/hate-map).

Steverson, Leonard A. 2011. "Shaming Penalties." In William J. Chambliss, ed. *Corrections*. Los Angeles: Sage.

Steverson, Leonard A. 2014. "Counseling, Treatment, and Culture in Prison: One Size Fits All?" In Scott Wm. Bowman (Ed.), *Racism in the U.S. Prison System*, Santa Barbara, CA: ABC-CLIO.

Truman, Jennifer L. and Rachel E. Morgan. 2016. "Criminal Victimization 2015. Bureau of Justice Statistics." Retrieved July 16, 2017 (www.bjs.gov/index.cfm?ty=pbdetail&iid=5804).

Vold, George B., Thomas J. Bernard, and Jeffery B. Snipes. 2002. *Theoretical Criminology*, 5th ed. New York: Oxford University Press.

Williams-Harris, Deanese, Megan Crepeau, and Elvira Malagon. 2017 "Homicides in Chicago, Outpacing Last Year after Deadliest Day so far in 2017." February 23, 2017. Retrieved July 16, 2017 (www.chicagotribune.com/news/local/breaking/ct-man-61-found-shot-dead-in-garage-in-south-lawndale-20170222-story.html).

Youth.gov. 2017. *Prevention and Early Intervention*. Retrieved July 28, 2017 (http://youth.gov/youth-topics/juvenile-justice/prevention-and-early-intervention).

CHAPTER 10

Alcohol and Other Drugs

ABOUT THE PROBLEM: ALCOHOL AND OTHER DRUGS

This chapter is entitled alcohol *and* other drugs for a reason—alcohol is a drug! This seemingly obviously point must be made as many in our society see alcohol as something else—after all, it is legal (to those of a certain age), liquidy (no, that's not a real word) and its use is often considered a normal, natural part of human socializing. Although alcohol is considered dissimilar from the other drugs, it should be remembered that all drugs have different, but also comparable effects. This chapter will present these effects from both individual, and of course, collective levels.

Problems with the abuse of alcohol and other drugs can be seen from both micro and macro level perspectives. On a micro level of analysis, individuals use certain drugs and experience a series of physiological, behavioral, and social effects the terms tolerance and withdrawal (discussed below) reflect the micro level of analysis. Macro level perspectives move outside the individual and their immediate milieu into a broader scope that includes all social institutions (government, economy, family, religion, and education) and into global concerns of trafficking and massive economic activity that shapes relations between nations.

Defining the Problem

Before we look at the various drugs of abuse, it is fitting to review some terminology. The term **substance abuse** (sometimes referred to as drug abuse) refers to the use of an illicit drug or the use of a prescribed drug in a way other than what it was intended. Drug dependence (or addiction) occurs when the use of the substance causes both tolerance to or withdrawal effects from the drug; tolerance refers to the repeated and increased use of the substance to receive the same intoxicating properties (the "high") and withdrawal means that certain physiological features occur when use of the drug is discontinued. **Substance (or chemical) addiction**, as defined by Kuhn et al. (2008)

Substance Abuse the use of an illegal drug or the use of a prescribed drug in a way other than what it was intended.

Substance Addiction a person's repetitive, compulsive use of a substance despite the negative costs that comes with that use.

is "the repetitive, compulsive use of a substance despite negative consequences to his life and/or health" (Kuhn et al. 2008:275). The above definition refers to a process that occurs when an individual ingests some chemical substance; however, another type of addiction, **behavioral addiction**, has been proposed and suggests a similar psychological process as the chemical variety but with behavioral activity; gambling, sex, and overeating, among others, is being considered by some to fit the addiction concept (Kuhn et al. 2008). It should be noted that of these behavioral addictions listed above, gambling is the only one considered this type of disorder in the Diagnostic and Statistical Manual of Mental Disorders (DSM-5), the official manual for mental health (including substance use) disorders (American Psychiatric Association 2013). This chapter will be concerned, however, with the chemical disorders.

> **Behavioral Addiction**
> behavioral activity that is perceived as resulting in similar repetitive, compulsive outcomes as chemical addiction.

The DSM-5 uses the term *substance use disorder*, disregarding the formerly used terms substance use and substance abuse in earlier editions, and the new title requires the specifiers mild, moderate, and high. Substance abuse disorder requires a specific set of criteria with these features: changes in normal brain functioning that may continue after detoxification; pathological behaviors related to use of the drug; impaired control which includes using more than intended, using longer than intended, having an inability to lessen the use, spending an inordinate amount of time getting, using, and dealing with drug effects; physical and extremely uncomfortable and unpredictable cravings, often involving psychological triggers. It also includes these features related to social impairment: failure to fulfill basic day to day expectations, use that continues regardless of the loss of significant relationships and activities. The category risky use includes use even though it presents potential physical hazards and even with the knowledge of the existence of physical or psychological problems. Pharmacological effects include tolerance and withdrawal symptoms due to attempts to stop use of the drug (American Psychiatric Association 2013).

The Disease Concept of Addiction

The **disease concept** refers to the idea that addictions involve processes that are like those of other medical conditions and can be found across all substances of abuse. In addition, the functioning and structures of the brain are altered, relapse and remission are common, and addiction includes features that are chronic, progressive, and treatable. The idea has become so fixed that it is the model that has guided the Diagnostic and Statistical Manual. The concept, although a consistent theme in addictions treatment for a long time, has recently been under scrutiny.

> **Disease Concept** the idea that addictions involve processes that are like those of other diseases and are uniform across all substances of abuse.

The disease concept of addiction has been around since Aristotle and since the twentieth century in the West, this concept has grown to the point that it is the most accepted view by governments, as well as medical and academic organizations (Lewis 2015). The idea took hold in America when Benjamin Rush, a Philadelphia physician and ardent anti-liquor reformer in the eighteenth century, started to envision alcoholism as a medical problem rather than one that was based on moral failings, an idea that by 1840 was accepted by those temperance groups who sought to outlaw alcohol (Lender and Martin 1987). In addition, many physicians began to accept the idea in the late nineteenth century, and a new medical organization called Society for the Study and Cure of Inebriety, along with the journal *Inebriety* were created (Heyman 2009).

The concept was supported when Alcoholics Anonymous (A.A.) was started in the 1930s by Bill Wilson and Robert Smith. This group changed the way addiction was seen and how relief

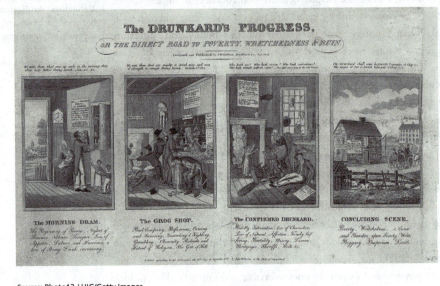

Source: Photo12 / UIG/Getty Images

FIGURE 10.1 The drunkard's progress, or the direct road to poverty, wretchedness & ruin by John Warner Barber, 1798–1885, engraver. Published: New Haven, 1826. Print shows four scenes of the drunkard's progress: the morning dram (father drinking at 8am, ignoring wife and children), the grog shop (bar room brawls, passed out, vomiting, and drinking customers), the confirmed drunkard (father on floor, wife and children afraid, home falling apart), and concluding scene (family evicted, home up for auction).

could be provided by others who had the same affliction, that of alcoholism. The founders perceived alcoholism as a malady rather than a disease, but they favored the idea that addiction was the result of an allergy to some substances (Lewis 2015). The allergy concept certainly was geared toward the medical approach to addiction. The idea certainly became more mainstream with the publication of E.M. Jellinek's *The Disease Concept of Alcoholism* (1960), and when the American Medical Association (A.M.A) affixed their stamp of approval by officially classifying addiction as a disease, it has become a given in the substance abuse literature.

The concept evolved in the 1990s to a position that addiction is specifically a brain disease that has both physiological and social features and in 2007, resulted in a bill called "Recognizing Addiction as a Brain Disease" introduced by Vice President Joe Biden (Lewis 2015). However, not everyone in the substance abuse field sees addiction as a disease and a chorus of voices against it are being heard. Peele and Brodsky (1991) published a book that publicly challenged the idea and was predictably met with a backlash in the chemical dependency treatment community by stating addiction is a habit that can be outgrown. More recently Heyman (2009) dubs addiction a "disorder of choice", explaining that when the costs and rewards of using drugs becomes too high, they can discontinue the use; he also notes that it is possible that the immense literature supporting the notion of disease might actually "make it" a disease since addicts understand they are assumed to have a "chronic, relapsing brain disease" (Heyman 2009:7); in addition, if most of the therapeutic community believes it is a disease, the consequences are a specific diagnosis and course of treatment (think Thomas theorem again here). Similarly, Hart (2013) provides information that supports the idea of choice by claiming that inner-city residents often choose drugs due to the lack of other positively rewarding situations and when offered alternative to drugs, they will take them; again, the issue of choice tends to negate the idea of disease. Lewis (2015) offers many reasons addiction should not be seen as a disease and poses the question: "should Net surfing, hoarding, compulsive shopping, and unrequited love also be classified as diseases or disorders?" (Lewis 2015:23). Lewis' question seems to ask whether substance abuse is a compulsion rather than a disease, and since treatment approaches are different, it would appear an important point to clarify.

There are many **drugs of abuse**, those that are illegal or those that are legal but used illegally, that have the potential for creating problems not only for individuals but also for society. Throughout our country's history, not only have individuals struggled with the effects of drugs, but large groups of people, such as temperance leagues and, more recently, anti-drug trafficking organizations, have formed to create movements to suppress their use. We will now turn our attention to some of these drugs of abuse.

> **Drugs of Abuse** illegal drugs or those that are legal but used illegally, that have the potential for creating problems for both individuals and society.

Various Drugs of Abuse

Alcohol can be found in many types of beverages, including beer, wine, liquor, and others. Alcohol produces feelings of pleasure and often makes people feel at ease in social situations, although a sedative effect normally occurs after the "buzz". Excessive drinking can cause nausea, vomiting, and unconsciousness—when this occurs, medical treatment should be sought. Moderate use of alcohol has some health benefits but long term use has several health risks involving the brain, liver, and digestive system. It is highly addictive and can be quite dangerous if used in certain amounts and over long periods of time; the withdrawal symptoms for alcohol can be life threatening (Kuhn et al. 2008). In America, alcohol use by underage persons has declined since 2002 and the number of people driving under the influence of alcohol has declined slightly (NIDA 2015).

Marijuana, or cannabis, is another heavily used drug that creates feelings of elation and mood elevation in users. Some claim that users can develop a tolerance to and dependence on the drug, however, the effects appear to be psychological rather than physiological; impaired memory and other negative effects on some bodily organs are reported with marijuana use. The drug has some health benefits, however, especially for people who suffer from nausea, glaucoma, and symptoms of illnesses for debilitating diseases such as multiple sclerosis. The issue of marijuana for medical use is a complex one with a number of arguments for and against its legalization (Kuhn et al. 2008). Legalization for recreational purposes is also currently a hot political issue in many states. Use of marijuana has increased in the United States since 2007 while most other drug use has stayed the same or declined. Most new users of illicit drugs started with cannabis (NIDA 2015); supporting the long-held idea that marijuana is a "gateway drug" to harder drugs.

Stimulants include many different drugs including cocaine, amphetamine, methamphetamine, among others. They provide energy, alertness and, when smoked, alertness and feelings of euphoria. All stimulants are highly addictive. When taken in high doses, cocaine can cause seizures, strokes, and death. Amphetamines can cause an increase in heart rate and body temperature that can lead to death (Kuhn et al 2008). While use of cocaine has declined in the last few years, methamphetamine use has increased (NIDA 2015).

Sedatives, sometimes called depressants, have a variety of drugs within this classification. Barbiturates, Secobarbital, methaqualone, benzodiazepines (of which there are many different types), and numerous sleep-producing drugs on the market fall into this category. The effects of the drugs in this class are similar—at moderate doses they provide feelings of relaxation and tranquility but at high doses create classic features of intoxication—lightheadedness, slurred speech, lack of muscle control, and others. Sedatives can be very dangerous, especially if taken with other drugs (Kuhn et al. 2008).

Opiates include opium, heroin, morphine, oxycodone, and hydrocodone, among others. The drugs in this classification produce a rush of euphoria followed by a sense of satisfaction. Withdrawal from opiates produces very unpleasant symptoms and often causes users to continue to abuse their drug of choice to avoid these symptoms, consequently increasing the damaging effects on the body and maintaining the vicious cycle of addiction. The brain is especially affected by opiates, causing users to experience cognitive difficulties. Since the desire to continue use is so strong, opiates are related to many other problems including poor health and hygiene, poor eating habits, risky behaviors, the spread of disease through needle sharing, unprotected sex and prostitution (Kuhn et al. 2008).

Hallucinogens cause users to, well, hallucinate. The drugs in this category include LSD, PCP, mescaline (peyote), psilocybin (hallucination-creating mushrooms), Jimsonweed, ketamine, and Salvia, among others. The hallmark feature of this group of drugs is the alteration in perception that occurs after use in which people experience visual and audible psychedelic hallucinations and "mind-expanding" thoughts of enlightenment. There is no evidence of addiction or physical dependence but users often experience high levels of anxiety with "bad trips" and after use, may have "flashbacks", recollections of using the drug that resembles hallucinations. The belladonna alkaloids in PCP are more likely than the others to create fatal responses and immediate medical attention is required if overdosing occurs (Kuhn et al. 2008).

Entactogens are a group of drugs that often go by the name *ecstasy*—MDMA (known as Molly), MDA, and MDE. Ecstasy causes users to feel a sense of alertness, increased energy, and a sense of empathy toward others; it was due to this last effect that MDMA was initially used in psychotherapy before becoming a recreational use drug, famously used in all night dance parties called raves. The drugs in this category increase body temperature and hypertension and can result in kidney failure and death if overdose occurs (Kuhn et al. 2008). The jitteriness that accompanies ecstasy use resulted in a fashion trend—pacifiers that were used (by adults!) to stop the teeth clenching that occurs with the use of the drug.

The drugs that comprise inhalants are a mixed class but include different substances that are inhaled. They include nitrites, Whippets, solvents, paints, gasoline, glue, and others. Risks of overdose are low but organ damage is high due to the toxicity of the substances. Also, most of the chemicals are flammable, increasing the risk of burns. Inhalants are normally used by young people, especially middle school students, due to the easy access of these chemicals (Kuhn et al. 2008).

Treatment Modalities treatment programs and methods that exist to assist people with drug addiction.

Current Treatment Methods

There are many **treatment modalities** that exist to assist people with drug addiction. There are inpatient programs (long term residential programs) where people are physically housed in programs for six to twelve months, and short term programs in which people are housed for three to six weeks (NIDA 2012); the short term programs are sometimes known as 28 day programs, based on what is known as the Minnesota model, which often uses the Alcoholics Anonymous (A.A.) 12 step model (discussed below) and both types of inpatient programming often have a detoxification unit to ensure patients receive medical treatment for assistance in warding off serious withdrawal effects (often called "detox").

There are also outpatient treatment programs not requiring residential stays that are more suitable for people with jobs or strong support systems. Some are intensive, such as outpatient day treatment programs that meet daily and require much devotion to abstinence while others meet weekly or so with a counselor, either individually or in group sessions. Some of these programs treat patients with both substance abuse and other mental health issues (called dual diagnosis). In addition, many low impact outpatient programs are basically psycho-education programs, which are essentially programs that teach people the effects of drug use (NIDA 2012).

The procedure known as the substance abuse "intervention" refers to a tough love strategy in which family members or other people who have a significant role in an addicted person's life gather and explain directly to the addicted person how the behaviors of that person have negatively affected their lives. This method, named the Johnson Intervention after its creator Vernon Johnson, is often just referred to as an intervention and has been the subject of a recent television reality series. The method is somewhat controversial as it requires an ultimatum in which the addicted person's loved ones must withdraw emotional and financial support if the person does not immediately agree to enter treatment.

Twelve-step programs are certainly among the most common treatment addiction models. They are a major component of programs such as Alcoholics Anonymous (A.A.) and its derivatives (e.g., Narcotics Anonymous, Cocaine Anonymous, Gambling Anonymous, and Sex Addicts Anonymous). These programs are based on a series of steps (twelve, of course) that must be followed specifically for "recovering addicts" to retain "sobriety" (to use some of the terms common in the programs, which also reflect the medical model). These programs use substance abuse groups extensively (rather than individual approaches) and encourage people to disclose their own narratives (using only first names to guarantee anonymity) but unlike most treatment programs they do not normally use a professional therapist, preferring to use other addicted people to guide newer members. The programs normally have no fees and are therefore attractive to many people for this reason. They are often used by court systems but questions arise about the use of mandated treatment, particularly those that espouse and endorse what many consider to be religious ideology.

Should non-violent users of illicit drugs receive treatment based on their addiction type or should they be incarcerated according to current drug laws?

Pro: These are people who experience a medical issue and need medical treatment to overcome it or they will simply end up back in prison.

Con: People should be held accountable for their actions and these are people who broke the law by using illegal drugs and they should not receive special treatment because they may have a drug addiction.

Current Drug Controversies

As many states have moved toward legalizing marijuana—eight have legalized recreational use and 25 have approved medical use of the drug—Attorney General Jeff Sessions has pushed for greater restrictions, sending a memo in 2016 instituting a "rule of law" which seems to abdicate state laws on marijuana prosecution to federal law, a sharp departure from the Trump administration's decentralization and smaller government measures (Wall Street Journal 2018). Prohibitions on marijuana use have a long history in the United States and it is expected to continue.

The "opioid crisis" has sparked a national debate on drug abuse, spurred by a rise in opioid overdoses and amplified by the overdose deaths of popular musicians Prince in 2016 and Tom Petty in 2017. Opioids, derivatives of the drug opium, are drugs that, in their legal usage are meant to control pain. Some opioids such as oxycodone and morphine are legal medications prescribed by physicians but are dangerous because of their addictive properties and their potential for overdose. Fentanyl is a drug used to control pain resulting from surgery. Methadone is another opioid used to relieve pain but is also used to reduce or maintain the effects of other opioids. Perhaps the drug of most concern is heroin, which has no medical usage in America. According to the National Center for Health Statistics, drug overdose deaths have been on the rise, driven in part by heroin (which had triple the number of deaths since 1999), fentanyl and tramadol. Overdose from oxycodone and hydrocodone have decreased in recent years (Hedegaard, Warner, and Minino 2017). The national response to the opioid crisis has been primarily sympathetic and a call for treatment initiatives by

FIGURE 10.2 Protesters rally in support of the legalization of marijuana in front of the White House in Washington D.C. on April 2, 2016.

Source: Rena Schild/Shutterstock.com

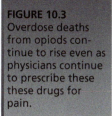

FIGURE 10.3
Overdose deaths from opiods continue to rise even as physicians continue to prescribe these these drugs for pain.

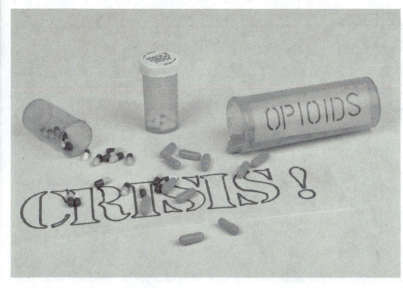

Source: northlight/Shutterstock.com

American legislators has been made. This response is quite different from that of the crack cocaine scare beginning in the 1980s which was primarily seen as an inner city African American problem. The current overdose rate for white Americans was almost 3.5 times higher in 2015 than 1999 and a treatment response to the current crisis compared to the incarceration response to the crack crisis is notable. Another current controversy around opioids involves the use of naloxone, a spray or injection that is used to reverse the effects of opioids—currently people who arrive to the scene of overdoses are often police who administer the drug, however, some concerns have been raised over the liability of non-medical personnel administering a drug to users.

A Macro Level View of Substance Abuse

So far, most of the discussion on drugs has been more at the micro levels of analysis. However, drugs and the abuse of those drugs extends way beyond these levels. Globalization is an inevitable social evolution that has many benefits to the world at large, however there is a dark underside to globalization—the trafficking that is part of the global trade of illicit drugs (Jenner 2011). **Drug trafficking** is defined by the United Nations Office on Drugs and Crime (UNODC) as "a global illicit trade involving the cultivation, manufacture, distribution, and sale of substances which are subject to drug prohibition laws" (UNODC 2016). Whether it is the opium market in Afghanistan, amphetamine market in the Middle East and North Africa, cocaine market in Columbia, or cannabis market in Morocco, governments are trying to intervene into the global trade of drugs, however, corruption often enters the picture due to the large amount of money generated in the trade,

Drug Trafficking a global trade in illicit drugs which involves the cultivation, manufacture, distribution, and sale of these drugs.

FIGURE 10.4 With the rise of globalization, drug trafficking has become a global trade.

Source: Couperfield/Shutterstock.com

contributing to the political instability in the regions, damaging economic structures, and undermining democracy in democratic areas (UNODC 2016).

Although there are many types of trafficking, trafficking in illicit drugs is one of the largest types; it has remained in this category for over 40 years, since U.S. President Richard M. Nixon declared a "war on drugs" in 1971. When illicit drug use became more commonplace in the 1960s counterculture era, the demand for these drugs was met by international entrepreneurs whose practices closely paralleled those of legitimate enterprises in many ways, however the profit margins were extremely high in this business—estimated at 300%—and the dangerousness was much higher than for legitimate enterprises. Monopolies in the field of drug trafficking became commonplace because of the potential consequences of being discovered and the high levels of violence involved. Although Mexico has a high visibility and gets a lion's share of international attention regarding trafficking, other countries also are involved with trafficking in illegal drugs. Associated with this type of criminal activity are trafficking in weapons, trafficking in persons, and terrorism. Each day thousands of kilos of drugs cross international borders and each week hundreds of people are killed due to the violent nature of the business (Jenner 2011).

THEORETICAL PERSPECTIVES

Structural Functionalism

From a structural functionalist perspective, the issue of drugs can be seen as being of three types—functional use of drugs that includes many substances that can help people in their daily lives (e.g., painkillers, antibiotics, analgesics, anti-nausea medications); those that have no medical benefit and are obviously dysfunctional (e.g., tobacco, heroin, PCP); and those that are beneficial when correctly and legitimately used but harmful when used incorrectly, either to individuals, to society, or both.

In chapter 9, we discussed Durkheim's theory of anomie and Merton's *strain theory* that was derived from anomie theory. Anomie is perceived by Durkheim as normlessness and by Merton as strain (Shaw 2002); this concept is an important part of a functionalist position. The use of drugs often takes place when there is a breakdown in the normative structure of a society and people use it as a coping mechanism and to seek solace to the often-challenging conditions of modern society. Drugs also allow users an excuse for their behavior, an escape from external problems, a defense of any unfulfilled potential, and a rescue from ostracism by others (Shaw 2002).

Functionalism focuses on the functions and dysfunctions of any social phenomena (Merton 1968), including, in this case, drug use. For example, an obvious function of licit drugs is the health benefits they provide for users, while an obvious dysfunction is the often-prohibitive costs of pharmaceuticals. Obvious dysfunctions of illicit drugs are the problems associated with addiction as well as criminal activity, while an obvious function is the jobs provided for people in criminal justice and addictions fields. Note that the functions and dysfunctions listed are manifest ones. Latent functions are not listed as they would be great debate points in the classroom.

Conflict

Conflict theorists observe the role of the dominant ideology in understanding drug use and abuse. Regarding illicit drugs, alcohol can certainly be one of the most dangerous substances to society, however since it has been an approved form of interaction in so many social settings (especially among the elite), it has continued to remain legal (except during the "noble experiment" of prohibition and to people of a certain age group). It is easy to notice the role of the long-established use of alcohol in higher circles of society and since the rules are made by the rich, the restrictions against alcohol use are much less than the other drugs, except possibly nicotine. In addition, the alcohol industry is a very large and powerful entity. Making alcohol illegal again would be a major financial loss for shareholders and politicians who accept campaign contributions. Per conflict theory, the promotion of the idea of the "lower, dangerous classes" of people has long helped the well-to-do maintain their status and power. Making the poor out to be dangerous drug users helps keep them "in their place"—in prisons and away from the wealthy.

In a mix of social constructionism and conflict theory, Singer and Page (2014) explain how people, due to their race, ethnicity, or gender, are associated with different types of drug use. For example, black males are more likely to be considered heroin users than other racial groups although white males are in actuality more likely to be users of this drug. Also, women are stereotypically viewed as over-stressed users of anti-anxiety medications, though men use these drugs more than women. The stereotypes create images that result in people being "unworthy beings" (Singer and Page 2014:32). A good example of the differential treatment of drug offenses can be found when years ago, rock cocaine (used more by African Americans) was punished more harshly than powder cocaine (used by upper class whites).

Symbolic Interactionism

A major focus of symbolic interactionism is that behavior is often learned from one's peers. Drug use and abuse results from a socialization process that promotes such activity and the teaching and training of other people in how to behave in regard to alcohol and other drugs, in other words, people normally learn "how" to use these substances prior to use and/or abuse. Becker (1973) rejected psychological explanations for the pleasurable effects of substances and explores the social stages a user goes though in which others create the experience involved in the high. When the novice learns how to use the drug and what to expect, she will only then experience the pleasure derived from smoking.

The interactionist approach, as mentioned before, emphasizes how labeling can create a self-identity and thus reinforces behavior. Think of the terms used to describe drug users, especially frequent users and abusers of drugs, that have been used in the past and the present: addict, dope fiend, junkie, stoner, pot/meth/crack head—and the list goes on. These terms are labels that define the entire person and can create the master status of drug addict or alcoholic. Goffman (1963) describes the effects of stigma as damaging to a person as it creates a "mark" that is visible and carries a host of preconceived notions about that person. And as Merton (1946) mentioned, a self-fulfilling prophecy may develop that continues to provide a blueprint for future drug use.

SEARCHING FOR SOLUTIONS

Alcohol: The Drug of Choice

Because our society's relationship with alcohol is interwoven into both our professional and personal lives and viewed as a positive health behavior when consumed in moderation, we rarely think about alcohol as a deadly and dangerous drug. Scientific articles appear routinely in our news media, touting the benefits of moderate alcohol use. However, the definition of moderate alcohol use is rarely agreed upon. According to the most recent dietary guidelines of the U.S. Department of Alcohol (2005), moderate drinking is no more than one drink per day for women and one to two drinks per day for men. A drink is a 12-ounce beer, 5-ounce glass of wine, or one and a half ounces of spirits. Moderate use is that apex where the health benefits of alcohol outweigh the risks. However, if you look around at a party or even work-related event, people rarely consume one drink. Importantly, drinking patterns in our society are not set-up around this fairly relaxed idea of what actually constitutes moderate drinking. Having four drinks on Friday and three on Saturday is not moderate drinking for women even though it still adds up to seven drinks in a week (in fact that would qualify as binge drinking). And once this moderate amount is exceeded, the health risks far outweigh any possible health advantage. In addition, for people with a genetic pre-disposition for alcohol addiction it is often very difficult to drink moderately, and for those folks, abstinence would be a better choice.

Some of the major problems with alcohol use include binge drinking, underage drinking, alcohol use disorder (alcoholism), the chronic health problems it causes, and alcohol related vehicle fatalities. By far, binge drinking accounts for the majority (75%) of the national costs of alcohol abuse (Sacks et al. 2015). According to a national survey conducted by the National Institute on

Alcohol Abuse and Alcoholism (NIAAA) (2015), almost 60% of college students age 18–22 drank alcohol in the past month and nearly two-thirds of them reported binge drinking in the past month as well. Binge drinking, according to the NIAAA is four drinks for women and five drinks for men—ingested within a couple of hours, on at least one day a month. The NIAAA reported that college drinking is directly linked to academic problems, alcohol use disorder (AUD), as well as sexual assault, unsafe sex, driving under the influence, and physical injuries. Because the first six weeks of freshmen year are considered the most vulnerable time for a student to begin heavy drinking (mostly due to social and peer pressure), it is a critical time for both individual-level interventions (education and awareness program), as well as environmental strategies that target the entire campus and work to change the campus and community environment surrounding alcohol use (NIAAA 2015).

One such program, developed by the NIAAA, is the Alcohol Intervention Matrix– College AIM. This program provides evidence based resources and interventions for college officials to combat underage and excessive drinking by changing the context in which alcohol use occurs on and around campus. According to College AIM, the most effective strategies include restricting happy hours, enforcing the age 21 law with compliance checks, as well as increasing the alcohol tax. To address specific drinking issues on a college campus using individual level strategies it is crucial that college officials teach students how to self-monitor alcohol intake and set goals. One program that targets these challenges is the Alcohol Skills Training Program (ASTP) which provides information on addiction and trains students to identify personal drinking cues, how to refuse alcohol in social settings, and how to manage stress without alcohol.

Since binge drinking is dangerous and is more common among college students than young adults not in college should colleges and universities completely ban all alcohol on campuses?

Pro: Alcohol on college campuses is unmonitored and easy to access and abuse, especially for students under 21 years of age.
Con: Students who are of legal drinking age should be allowed to have alcohol on campus since they are not breaking any laws.

Community based mobilization has a long history of being the main intervention for problems related to alcohol in our society. These interventions work well since they provide a context in which interventions occur and thus change the normative climate for underage drinking. For example, communities have mobilized to reduce outdoor advertising of alcohol, increase age identification checks by restaurants and bars in the community, and to closely monitor retailers for sale of alcohol to minors. Evidence based research and case studies have found that community based coalitions engaging key community resources (e.g. advocacy groups, residents, universities, and government organizations) are effective at addressing underage access to alcohol and high-risk behaviors related to both drug and alcohol use (Bonnie and O'Connell 2004). This is in large part because every community environment is unique, and national "one size fits all" prevention programs do not address the unique needs of the social and environmental context of individual communities.

Solving the Prescription Opioid Crisis

The over-prescribing of opioids is a driving factor in the high rate of mortality from opiate-related overdoses and the increase in the use and subsequent overdoses of illicit opioids such as heroin (Murphy et al. 2016). Reducing use of opioids has proven to be a complex and challenging task made more difficult by the relatively easy access of attaining a prescription for these habit-forming drugs. According to 2015 data from the Centers of Disease Control (CDC), overdose deaths from heroin have tripled over the past four years, a finding almost certainly driven by synthetic opiates since four out of five heroin users report that they began with recreational use of prescribed opioids. Drug overdoses resulting in death from synthetic opioid pain relievers (e.g. oxycodone and hydrocodone), nearly doubled between 2013 and 2014.

Reducing and possibly reversing the opioid epidemic will require a number of strategies that involve public health agencies. Protecting individuals already dependent on opioids from overdose and death is a crucial first step. This requires increasing access to medication assisted treatment and the antidote, naloxone, and providing access to syringe service programs to prevent the spread of hepatitis C and HIV associated with injecting heroin (Volkow et al. 2014). Medication assisted treatment includes the FDA approved drugs, methadone, buprenorphine, and naltrexone. Expanding access includes covering these drugs under Medicaid and state health programs, removing barriers to access such as requiring prior authorization, and ensuring low-income patients can afford treatment.

Prevention is another key component, efforts to encourage medical professionals to reduce opioid prescription and instead prescribe safer prescription pain medication will prevent new cases of addiction and abuse, at least from opioids like oxycodone and hydrocodone that are acquired through pharmacies from legitimate prescriptions (Volkow et al. 2014). Physicians need to empower patients to alleviate their conditions rather than just treat the pain with highly addictive pain medication. For many chronic conditions a mix of physical therapy, weight loss, and exercise is often more effective than taking pain medication.

The National Governor's Association works with states to reduce opioid misuse by combining health care and law enforcement strategies. Statewide efforts include: requiring specialized education courses for all prescribers of opioids that include safe prescribing guidelines, updating opioid prescribing guidelines and dosages, and restricting the number of days for prescription opioids. Enacting policies that increase oversight and regulation of pain management clinics and shutting down "pill mills" is another strategy; this includes unannounced inspections of pain management clinics by state health agencies when they receive complaints. Providing access to opioid prescription data for law enforcement so they know which providers are at high risk of over-prescribing, and can pinpoint the areas in their communities that need more monitoring, is another possible solution. These strategies involve collaboration between public health agencies, pharmacies, law enforcement, and community leaders to enact community based strategies with state level support.

Drug Decriminalization as a Solution

According to the U.S. Department of Justice (2016), half of all federal inmates were serving sentences for drug offenses in 2015. In addition, almost all drug offenders (99.5%) were serving sentences for drug trafficking (which are much longer than for possession) even though 35% had no past criminal history. Nearly 75% of the drug offenders in federal prisons are African American, Hispanic, or Latino. And 99% are male. The Brookings Institute illustrates that the total number of people admitted to prison for drug crimes (almost one-third) exceeds violent crimes (almost one-quarter) from the late 1990s through 2009. The critical question our society needs to address is whether incarcerating individuals for drug use or possession will reduce abuse and use of illicit drugs. Is there a rationale for the high financial expenditures required to incarcerate people who are addicted to illicit drugs? Would this money be better spent on treatment? This distinction between solving the problem or punishing the people who have the problem must be addressed.

Should our society decriminalize drugs, keeping illicit drugs illegal, but changing sanctions from incarceration to treatment programs?

Pro: By decriminalizing drug use, we can apply the medical model and offer the proper treatment modality rather than just incarcerating people for using illicit drugs.
Con: Decriminalizing drugs will increase use and thus increase the number of people addicted to illicit drugs.

Policy shifts toward offering alternatives to incarceration have been successful in a growing number of countries, including Portugal, Spain, and Italy (Hughes and Stevens 2010). In Portugal drugs are illegal and people are arrested, however they very rarely are incarcerated for minor drug charges. Instead, treatment programs are mandated if an individual has repeat drug offenses or is deemed as having a substance abuse problem. Since Portugal decriminalized drug use in 2001, HIV cases have declined drastically as have deaths from drug overdoses. This is a major step forward since Portugal was dealing with a heroin crisis in the 1990s. Harm reduction measures such as medication therapy for opioid users and providing safe needle programs are in large part responsible for a major decline in heroin and opioid use. Heroin is still illegal, however, individuals arrested with less than a ten-day supply are generally referred to treatment, rather than being sent to prison (Domoslawski and Siemaszko 2011).

Globally, there is growing support for drug decriminalization as a solution for minor drug use and possession. Proponents of decriminalization in the United States argue that it will greatly reduce the power of criminal organizations that are responsible for the bulk of drug trafficking, reduce the high cost of incarcerating people for drug crimes, and reduce the number of people in prison for using or possessing small amounts of illegal drugs. Decriminalization does not legalize drugs, it eliminates criminal penalties for drug use or possession. Organizations that support decriminalization include the American Civil Liberties Union (ACLU), the International Red Cross, and the National

Association for the Advancement of Colored People (NAACP). In June 2017, the United Nations Secretary-General, issued a public statement endorsing approaches that focus on prevention and treatment (UN Office of Drugs and Crime 2017). And in 2014, the World Health Organization (WHO) called for drug decriminalization as necessary for global public health, as well as banning compulsory treatment for people who use drugs, promoting clean needle and syringe programs, and reducing incarceration through decriminalizing the use of drugs.

Reducing Tobacco Use

Cigarette smoking continues to be the leading cause of preventable death in the United States (Asvat et al. 2014; CDC 2008). There are many community based and national programs to reduce and prevent tobacco use, specifically, cigarette smoking. However, this problem is complex, as it generally starts at a young age, is embedded in our culture through media depictions, is highly susceptible to peer group influence, and easy for minors to access. These factors, coupled with its legal status, make the success of initiatives and intervention programs especially challenging. To complicate matters further, new technology such as e-cigarettes have surpassed cigarettes in usage among middle and high school students (healthypeople.gov 2017).

According to the Surgeon General's report (2017), prevention efforts must focus on young people since it is very uncommon to start smoking after age 25 and nine out of ten smokers start by age 18. The tobacco industry spends more than a million dollars every hour marketing their products in the United States and although they claim their marketing is only to adults, it encourages under aged people to smoke. More than 80% of young people who smoke choose brands from the three most heavily marketed companies. Through the creative use of packaging, advertising, and product design, tobacco companies create the idea that smoking will make you thin and this is especially appealing to young women. For example, research on the effects of using package design for marketing purposes found that tobacco companies create packaging designed to appeal to young adults and women (Wakefield et al. 2002). This is achieved through colors and words that signify certain cigarettes may be "safer". Laws that regulate packaging could decrease the number of new smokers, especially young women, and young adults more generally.

Community based interventions are associated with higher quit rates, with predictors of successful quitting determined by level of readiness to quit and use of smoking cessation mediation (Asvat et al. 2014). In general, this means that for those who want to quit there are resources to help them quit successfully. Because cigarette smoking is positively correlated with low socioeconomic status and disproportionately effects marginalized populations, these community based programs are an important resource for people who want to quit, but they are not necessarily as effective at reducing the number of new smokers in the community. However, employer based smoking cessation programs that are reward-based are often quite successful *if* the awards are financial and in the form of direct payments (Halpern et al. 2015).

Some of the various federal level attempts to reduce and prevent tobacco use include increasing cigarette excise taxes, providing access to tobacco use cessation treatment through the Affordable Care Act (ACA), and encouraging all states to have smoke-free laws in workplaces, restaurants, and bars, and the first paid national tobacco education campaign, launched by the CDC in 2010 entitled "Tips from Smokers" (CDC 2015). There is empirical evidence that excise taxes (also known as "sin taxes") that create price increases lead to significant reductions in smoking, and are the single most powerful deterrent, especially for young people and for those with low-income (Chaloupka et al. 2002; Thun et al. 2009; Bader, Boisclair, and Ferrence 2011). By implementing policy that combines increases in the price of cigarettes through higher taxes and restricts price-based promotions by tobacco companies, the economic disincentive to smoke is maximized—a very powerful and effective policy tool for reducing the harmful effects of cigarettes. And by combining federal, state, and local cigarette taxes the price of cigarettes would increase substantially. In contrast, it is estimated that to offset the national health costs associated with cancer and other diseases related to smoking the tax would be $19.16 per pack (Bonan 2017).

Since cigarette smoking is the number one cause of preventable deaths, should tobacco companies be banned from marketing their products with advertising packaging that suggests they are less dangerous, etc.?

Pro: Cigarette marketing is essentially the same as marketing toxic poison and should not be allowed. This includes packaging, which should be plain except for the warning label.
Con: Tobacco companies should not be singled out since many other companies produce products that are dangerous and are permitted to market them (e.g. alcohol).

Strategies and interventions to prevent or reduce the abuse of alcohol, and prescription and illicit drugs, as well as reduce cigarette smoking and use of other tobacco products have varying levels of success. It is important to consider the risk factors since socioeconomic status, age, race/ethnicity, and social environment all play a role in determining whether an individual is at high risk of engaging in negative health behaviors. Prevention efforts should be carefully designed to target these high-risk populations before they are adults.

CHAPTER SUMMARY

- Alcohol and other drugs create social problems on both the micro and macro level. These include individual problems such as unemployment and illness, as well as societal problems such as drug trafficking, the high public health costs of cigarette smoking and alcohol use disorder.

- Substance abuse and chemical addiction are principally viewed from a disease concept and treatment modalities range from twelve step programs to long term inpatient rehabilitation programs.

- Structural functionalist perspectives on drugs include the idea that drugs serve an important function in society, by creating jobs for individuals who work in the criminal justice system, addiction fields, and in the medical field. Dysfunctions of drugs include addiction and criminal activity.

- Conflict theorists focus on the powerful role of the tobacco and alcohol companies and how they profit from exploiting marginalized groups. This also serves to create the concept that illicit drug users are dangerous and should be excluded from society.

- From a social constructivist standpoint, society creates our beliefs about which drugs are considered more dangerous and this is closely linked to race, ethnicity, and gender. Differential treatment by the criminal justice system solidifies these stereotypes and more punitive sanctions are given for the use of drugs associated with minorities than those associated with upper class whites.

- Symbolic interactionist perspective views drug use as a behavior and experience that is learned from the socialization process. Labeling and stigma are powerful and can create damaging master statuses and a self-fulfilling prophecy that determines future use and abuse of drugs.

- Solutions to the social problems created by alcohol and drugs are shaped by societal views on the drug. Alcohol abuse by college students receives a great deal of public attention and interventions are both community based and campus wide. The focus is on education and prevention. In contrast, the abuse of opioids is thought of as a national epidemic and considerable public resources are used to combat the trafficking of heroin and proliferation of "pill mills". Funding is spent primarily on punishment rather than treatment and our prisons are teeming with drug offenders with charges that range from marijuana possession to heroin distribution.

- Cigarette smoking is the leading cause of preventable death in our society, however, it is also a very lucrative industry with powerful lobbyists. Thus, the most effective strategies for prevention at young ages, increased taxes on cigarettes, are not leveraged by many states even though they have the potential to save millions of lives. Marketing by tobacco companies continues to target young people and strategies to prevent or reduce cigarette smoking have varying levels of effectiveness.

REFERENCES

American Psychiatric Association. 2013. *Diagnostic and Statistical Manual of Mental Disorders*, 5th ed. Washington, DC: Author.

Asvat, Yasmin, Cao Dingcai, Joel J. Africk, Alicia Matthews, and Andrea King. 2014. "Feasibility and Effectiveness of a Community-Based Smoking Cessation Intervention in a Racially Diverse, Urban Smoker Cohort." *American Journal of Public Health.* 104(Suppl 4): S620–S627. http://doi.org/10.2105/AJPH.2014.302097.

Bader, Pearl, David Boisclair, and Roberta Ferrence. 2011. "Effects of Tobacco Taxation and Pricing on Smoking Behavior in High Risk Populations: A Knowledge Synthesis." *International Journal of Environmental Research and Public Health.* 8(11): 4118–4139. Retrieved July 27, 2017 (http://doi.org/10.3390/ijerph8114118).

Becker, Howard. 1973. *The Outsiders: Studies in the Sociology of Deviance*. New York: Free Press.

Bonnie, Richard J. and Mary Ellen O'Connell. 2004. *Reducing Underage Drinking: A Collective Responsibility*. Committee on Developing a Strategy to Reduce and Prevent Underage Drinking, Board on Children, Youth, and Families, National Research Council. Washington, D.C.: National Academies Press.

CDC. 2008. *Smoking-attributable Mortality, Years of Potential Life Lost, and Productivity losses–United States, 2000–2004*. Centers for Disease Control and Prevention. Nov 14; 57(45): 1226–1228.

CDC. 2015. Wide-ranging online data for epidemiologic research (WONDER). National Center for Health Statistics. Atlanta, GA. Retrieved July 30, 2017 (http://wonder.cdc.gov).

Chaloupka, Frank J., K. Michael Cummings, C. P. Morley, and J. K. Horan. 2002. "Tax, Price and Cigarette Smoking: Evidence from the Tobacco Documents and Implications for Tobacco Company Marketing Strategies." Pp. i62–i72 in *Tobacco Control*. Illinois: Tobacco Control.

Domoslawski, Artur, and Hanna Siemaszko. 2011. *Drug Policy in Portugal: The Benefits of Decriminalizing Drug Use*. New York: Open Society Foundations. Retrieved July 28, 2017 (www.tni.org/en/issues/decriminalization).

Goffman, Irving. 1963. *Stigma: Notes on the Management of Spoiled Identity*. London: Penguin Books.

Halpern, Scott D., Benjamin French, Dylan S. Small, Kathryn Saulsgiver, Michael O. Harhay, Janet Audrain-McGovern, George Loewenstein, Troyen A. Brennan, David A. Asch, and Kevin G. Volpp. 2015. "Randomized Trial of Four Financial-Incentive Programs for Smoking Cessation." *The New England Journal of Medicine*. 2108–2117. Retrieved July 27, 2017 (http://www.nejm.org/doi/pdf/10.1056/NEJMoa1414293).

Hart, Carl. 2013. *High Price: Drugs, Neuroscience, and Discovering Myself*. London: Penguin Books.

Healthypeople 2020. 2017. U.S. Department of Health and Human Services Washington, DC. Retrieved July 25, 2017 (www.healthypeople.gov/2020).

Hedegaard, Holly, Margaret Warner, and Arialdi Minino. 2017. Drug Overdose Deaths in the United States 1999–2015. National Center for Health Statistics. Retrieved January 28, 2018 (www.cdc.gov/nchs/products/databriefs/db273.htm).

Heyman, Gene M. 2009. *Addiction: A Disorder of Choice*. Cambridge: Harvard University Press.

Hughes, Caitlin Elizabeth, and Alex Stevens. 2010. "What Can We Learn from the Portuguese Decriminalization of Illicit Drugs?" *The British Journal of Criminology*. 50(6): 999–1022.

Jellinek, E.M. 1960. *The Disease Concept of Alcoholism*. New Haven, CT: Hillhouse Press.

Jenner, Matthew. 2011. "International Drug Trafficking: A Global Problem with a Domestic Solution." *Indiana Journal of Global Legal Studies*. 18 (2): 899–927. Retrieved July 29, 2017 (www.repository.law.indiana.edu/ijgls/vol18/iss2/10).

Kaeble, Danielle, and Lauren Glaze. 2016. "Correctional Populations in the United States, 2015." *Bureau of Justice Statistics*. U.S. Department of Justice.

Kuhn, Cynthia, Scott Swartzwelder, and Wilkie Wilson. 2008. *Buzzed: The Straight Facts about the Most Used and Abused Drugs from Alcohol to Ecstasy*, fully revised and updated, 3rd ed. New York: W.W. Norton and Company.

Lender, Mark Edward and James Kirby Martin. 1987. *Drinking in America: A History*, revised and expanded. New York: Free Press.

Lewis, Mark. 2015. *The Biology of Desire: Why Addiction is Not a Disease*. New York: Public Affairs.

Merton, Robert K. 1946. "The Self Fulling Prophecy." *Antioch Review*. 8 (2). doi:10.2307/4609267.

Merton, Robert K. 1968. *Social Theory and Social Structure*. New York: Free Press.

Minton, Todd D. and Zhen Zeng. 2016. "Jail Inmates in 2015." Bureau of Justice Statistics. U.S. Department of Justice.

Murphy, Kelly, Melinda Becker, Jeff Locke, Chelsea Kelleher, Jeff McLeod, and Frederick Isasi. 2016. *Finding Solutions to the Prescription Opioid and Heroin Crisis: A Road Map for States*. Washington, DC: National Governors Association Center for Best Practices.

National Research Council and Institute of Medicine. 2004. *Reducing Underage Drinking: A Collective Responsibility*, edited by Richard J. Bonnie and Mary Ellen O'Connell. Washington, DC: The National Academies Press.

NIDA. 2012. "Principles of Drug Addiction Treatment: A Research-Based Guide." 3rd Ed. Retrieved December 17, 2016 (www.drugabuse.gov/publications/principles-drug-addiction-treatment-research-based-guide-third-edition).

NIDA. 2015. Nationwide Trends. Retrieved December 18, 2016 (www.drugabuse.gov/publications/drugfacts/nationwide-trends).

Peele, Stanton and Archie Brodsky. 1991. *The Truth about Addiction and Recovery: Life Process for Outgrowing Destructive Habits*. New York: Simon and Schuster.

Sacks, Jeffery J., Katherine R. Gonzales, Ellen E. Bouchery, Laura E. Tomedi, and Robert D. Brewer. 2015. "National and State Costs of Excessive Alcohol Consumption." *American Journal of Preventive Medicine*. 49(5): e73–e79.

Shaw, Victor L. 2002. *Substance Use and Abuse: Sociological Perspectives*. Westport, CT: Praeger.

Singer, Merrill, and J. Bryan Page. 2014. *The Social Value of Drug Addicts: Uses of the Useless*. Walnut Creek, CA: Left Coast Press.

Thun, Michael J., John Oliver DeLancey, Melissa M. Center, Ahmedin Jemal, and Elizabeth M. Ward. 2009. *The Global Burden of Cancer: Priorities for Prevention*. Carcinogenesis. 31, no. 1 (2009): 100–110.

United Nations Office of Drugs and Crime (UNODC). 2016. "Drug Trafficking." Retrieved June 11, 2017 (www.unodc.org/unodc/en/drug-trafficking/).

United Nations Office of Drugs and Crime (UNODC). 2017. "Secretary-General Message." Retrieved June 11, 2017 (www.unodc.org/unodc/en/frontpage/2017/June/message-of-united-nations-secretary-general).

Volkow, Nora D, Thomas R. Frieden, Pamela S. Hyde, and Stephen S. Cha. 2014. "Medication-Assisted Therapies—Tackling the Opioid-Overdose Epidemic." *New England Journal of Medicine*. 370: 2063–2066. DOI: 10.1056/NEJMp1402780.

Wakefield, Melanie, Christopher Morley, Judith K. Horan, and Michael K. Cummings. 2002. *The Cigarette Pack as Image: New Evidence from Tobacco Industry Documents*. Tobacco control 11, no. suppl 1: i73–i80.

Wall Street Journal. 2018. Jeff Sessions's Marijuana Candor: 2018. "The AG is Forcing Legalizers to Square State and Federal Law." Retrieved January 28, 2018 (www.wsj.com/articles/jeff-sessionss-marijuana-candor-1515197282).

World Health Organization. 2014. *Good Practice Recommendations Concerning Decriminalization*. Consolidated Guidelines on HIV Prevention: Diagnosis, Treatment, and Care for Key Populations. Retrieved July 26, 2017 (http://www.who.int/hiv/pub/guidelines).

CHAPTER 11

Health Care

ABOUT THE PROBLEM: HEALTH CARE

Defining Health Care

Health care refers to the provision of health care services that maintain diagnosis and treat physical and mental health impairments. **Medical sociology** had its genesis in the United States in the later part of the nineteenth century as people began to view health and its connection to social class, gender, race, and larger structural forces. In 1946, the World Health Organization broadened the definition of **health** to "a state of complete physical, mental, and social well-being and not merely the absence of disease or infirmity" (WHO 2017:1). Later, additional principles would be added, however, the original definition from 1946 has not changed. This is when medical sociology really became a sub-discipline and social environment and health along with health disparity research began.

Health Care Policies

Passed into law in 1965, Medicare began accepting clients in 1966; in its early implementation those in high-level health care administration considered the program to be a success and it continues to be the flagship of health care policy in America. Originally designed to assist people who are 65 years old or older, this national program assists in dealing with the health care issues of the elderly. Its roots run deep in American history—its origins are 1935's Social Security Act. Attempts at creating a national health insurance program failed for 30 years until President Lyndon B. Johnson, who spent much time and effort working for its passage, signed it into law.

The creation of Medicaid resulted in an expansion of the national welfare policy to provide health care to low-income children. The disabled, pregnant women and other low-income

> **Health Care** the provision of health care services that treat physical and mental health impairments.
>
> **Medical Sociology** a sub-discipline of sociology that studies the provision of health care services that treat physical and mental health impairments.
>
> **Health** a state of complete physical, mental, and social well-being and not merely the absence of infirmity.

groups were also potential recipients. Although a national plan, the design maintained individual states power over implementation rather than a central administration, and as such, failed to start as smoothly as its sister program, Medicare, which started the same year. In 1972, changes to the law allowed welfare recipients, excluding mothers with children, to become entitled to Medicaid benefits and it continued through the decade with the intent by most Presidents as being a temporary measure in health care, to maintain the current progress until the implementation of a national program could occur. Though President Ronald Reagan sought to reduce the welfare system, it increased during the 1980s. The showdown came in 1995 between President Bill Clinton and congressional Republicans who sought to transform it to a block grant program (originally attempted by Reagan); Medicaid remained intact and even expanded in 1997. President George W. Bush who was unable to get it passed by a Democratic congress again advocated the block grant approach. President Barack Obama continued to promote Medicaid in his administration as a viable part of the welfare and health care system. Medicaid is pervasive in the U.S. health care system and operates in a large complex bureaucracy, prompting legislators to continually contemplate the future of this program (Brasfield 2011).

The nation's largest health care system is the Veteran's Health Administration (VHA), a component of the U.S. Department of Veterans Affairs (VA). Their 1,245 hospitals and medical facilities treat over 9 million veterans every year (U.S. Department of Veterans Affairs 2017). The establishment of the Veterans Administration occurred in 1930 by President Hoover to provide medical care for individuals who have completed military service. Currently the VA offers physical and mental health care for veterans that ranges from general care to specialty care for chronic conditions and mental health issues, including Post Traumatic Stress Disorder (PTSD), which is the most prevalent diagnosis for mental health disorders among veterans who return from active combat (Aakre et al. 2014).

Unfortunately, the VA has a spotty track record of providing quality care to our nation's veterans. For example, scandals have emerged in the media that suggest veterans have died waiting for appointments for surgeries and others had to wait months to see a doctor (Brownstein, Black, and Griffin 2014). CNN spent months investigating and reporting on these delays and obtained documents from the VA indicating the agency was aware of the problems concerning months of delayed care and had not made attempts to solve them (Brownstein, Black, and Griffin 2014). Upon taking office, the Obama Administration established a system of accountability to ensure that the data reports are accurate, and to reduce the long wait times for care. Under the Obama administration veteran's benefits were expanded, more veterans became eligible for health care services through the VA, and legislation was put in place to allow veterans to seek care in private care facilities outside the VA (National Organization of Veterans' Advocates Inc. 2017). However, even after reform, veterans continue to face challenges obtaining quality health care in a reasonable amount of time.

The Affordable Care Act

The Affordable Care Act (ACA), passed by Congress, is composed of the Patient Protection and Affordable Care Act and the Health Care and Education Reconciliation Act of 2010 (Medicaid. gov). Together, these two policies expanded Medicaid coverage to millions of low-income families and improved the Children's Health Insurance Program (CHIP). In addition, it supported prevention and wellness services and added funding for long-term care services, mandated that individuals are not allowed to be denied or charged more for "pre-existing conditions", and allowed young adults to continue coverage on their parent's health care plan until the age of 26. It also created a mandate that everyone must have health insurance coverage, which in theory would make insurance more affordable for everyone since both healthy and less healthy people would pay for health insurance. Unfortunately, even with the ACA, the cost of health care is still extremely high. This is largely because even with Affordable Care Act, our country continues to rely on private health care providers and more importantly, insurance companies, and they still have immense control over the health care system in the United States. Thus, even with marketplace insurance through ACA, high deductibles make the cost of utilizing health care providers prohibitive for many families. This makes health insurance virtually unusable for low-income individuals and families since they cannot afford to spend such a large sum of money before their insurance begins to offset costs. Thus, the Affordable Care Act, though a good start at attempting to provide health care for all Americans, continues the for-profit nature of our health care system and health care continues to be a commodity sold to consumers.

The Social Construction of Illness

Medical sociologists often discuss the social construction of illness from diagnosis to treatment ("naming and framing"), however, many use the term broadly, even though there are different varieties of social construction. As Lorber and Moore (2002) note, far from being simply a physical state of being, illness is also a social phenomenon, one that varies depending on different cultural constructions, since each of these cultures create, and modify the norms and values accordingly. In other words, illness does not exist objectively, but rather because our society has defined and conceptualized it. For example, the bacteria or viruses that cause the flu, are still real. However, how we think about this illness and the words we use to talk about it are constructed and organized in a very specific way. In other cultures, or in a different time period this illness may be conceptualized as some other illness or not as an illness at all. **Illness** is thus a biological, psychological, or social condition that interactions among people in a given culture, have defined as problematic, undesirable, and in need of treatment. It has a social component and exists within a social context—it is not simply biological.

In contrast, Western society generally uses a **bio-model of illness**, in which the concept of disease is as an abnormal condition that exists in the body, equivalent to the same diseases in others, and treated pharmacologically. However, this model fails to account for cultural and demographic variations or how meanings develop through interactions in a social context. The medical model operates under the assumption that disease is not tied to place or time and is a universal condition that exists in nature that is discovered by physicians (Conrad and Barker 2010). In other words, illness is purely biological, has the same shared meaning that is based on scientific and medical 'facts' and exists without historical or social context.

The process of creating illness by defining a condition as a medical problem that requires a medical solution is called **medicalization** (Conrad 2008). Some scholars believe that what are normal or common traits and behaviors are turned into pathologies that need to be treated by medical

Social Construction of Illness illness is a biological, psychological, or social condition that interactions among people in a given culture and social context, have defined as problematic, undesirable, and in need of treatment.

Bio-model of Illness pathology is conceptualized as an abnormal condition that exists in the body, equivalent to the same diseases in others, and treated pharmacologically.

Medicalization the process of creating illness by defining a condition as a medical problem that requires a medical solution.

professionals. According to a study by Fishman and Mamo (2001), impotence, once considered a natural part of the aging process, became erectile dysfunction when it was medicalized and is now considered a treatable medical issue that can be solved by science. In the 1960s, it became re-conceptualized as a psychological condition that could be treated with psychotherapy. Fast forward to the 1980s and the development of penile implants, and then to the late 1990s and the advent of Viagra by Pfizer (which occurred just as the FDA approved marketing prescriptions directly to the public) and it is now considered a biological medical condition that is a health problem and is treatable with pharmaceutical drugs. This is just one example of how medicalization becomes problematic when it creates a medical condition out of a fairly common trait or behavior, and then necessitates expensive treatments and medications. According to several scholars interviewed by Harvard Magazine (2009), a number of societal forces drive this trend toward medicalization. The largest driver is health insurance itself, since costs are only reimbursed when a defined medical condition is diagnosed. Other major drivers are the pharmaceutical companies since they need drug trials for illnesses in order to receive approvals by the FDA; even the individual desire to shift the blame for one's condition to a disease that is treatable and thus distanced from the actions or behaviors of the individual or the result of, in part, one's own lifestyle decisions. For example, obesity, once thought to be largely a result of one's own actions, is now a disease that medical professionals treat. This takes the responsibility for maintaining a healthy diet and cutting back on calories off the individual and places it on health care providers, medications, and interventions such as gastric bypass surgery.

Should obesity be treated as a disease by the health care system?

Pro: Obesity is a serious health condition and as such should be treated by doctors and considered a medical condition and not a lack of personal responsibility.

Con: People need to take personal responsibility for their body weight by making better choices rather than overeating and not exercising and then expecting the health care system to "fix" them.

Social Disparities in Physical and Mental Health

Health Disparities
social factors such as race, ethnicity, gender, and socioeconomic status (including income, occupation, education) that cause chronic and acute health conditions to be unequally distributed across society.

The Western medical system defines illness from the perspective of the white male body. Critical medical sociologists have sought to expose the hegemonic biases in the medical system. For example, as Lorber and Moore (2002) note, "gender, in conjunction with racial and ethnic identification, social class, and sexual orientation, creates different risks and protections for physical illnesses, produces different behavior when ill, elicits different responses in health care personnel, affects the social worth of patients, and influences priorities of treatment research, and financing" (Lorber and Moore 2002:3). In other words, what is considered illness and how illness manifests, and is defined and treated, is highly dependent on gender, race, and socioeconomic class, among other social factors. In addition, the ways that gender, race, and class intersect to produce **health disparities** are complex and the contribution of one factor is often difficult to tease out for researchers (Mullings and Schulz 2006).

Socioeconomic Status (SES)

The link between social class (education, income, and occupation) and health, cannot be overstated. It is often referred to as a "health/wealth gradient" which can be thought of quite literally as a ladder where every rung is a step up or down in social class (gradients) that equates to better or worse health over the life course. Link and Phelan (2010) coined the term "fundamental causes of health and disease" (Link and Phelan 2010:2) to explain the crucial role of social factors in chronic disease. They hypothesize that social factors are not proxies for the true cases of disease, but rather are themselves the fundamental or true cause of illness and disease. This is based on the advantages that higher socioeconomic status confers on those with wealth and advanced education, to avoid the risk factors that lead to disease. For example, education, which is established early in life, is crucial to health. Individuals with more education have more access to health information and technology, as well as the resources to modify their behavior (smoking cessation programs, exercise facilities and personal trainers, healthy foods). Moreover, as new information becomes available they are the first to access and use it to enhance their health. For example, before medical science had determined that cardiovascular disease (CVD) is preventable, the wealthy were more likely to have heart disease (Mirowsky and Ross 2003). However, once medical science found it was preventable, those with resources were the first to adopt new lifestyle behaviors such as quitting smoking, eating less red meat, and exercising regularly. They now have less heart disease than low income Americans. This is in large part because fewer resources and less education not only disseminated this new health information at a slower rate; these folks also had fewer resources available to change their lifestyle behaviors. For *preventable diseases* like CVD, socioeconomic status is more important than genetics or biological risk factors.

Gender

Although women report more health problems overall, use more medical services, and have more chronic diseases, they tend to live longer than men. According to medical sociologists Case and Paxson (2005), men and women rate their health the same when they have the same illnesses, however, women have more non-fatal chronic conditions (chronic pain, migraines/headaches, arthritis, respiratory problems, auto-immune diseases, and depression) while men suffer from more serious life-threatening conditions earlier in life. Women are also more likely to be diagnosed with depression or anxiety; however, that may be in large part because women are more likely to seek help when they experience psychological distress. In addition, women are more likely to sustain injuries from domestic violence and sexual assault, leaving them at risk of long-term chronic pain and increased exposure to sexually transmitted infections. Traditional roles regarding masculinity play a role in why men are less likely to go to the doctor when they are sick or injured, are more likely to engage in risky behaviors, and rarely seek help for mental health disorders.

The health of women, specifically low-income women, is of great concern under the Trump administration. President Trump is working to eliminate Title X family planning grants for health care agencies who provide contraceptives, cancer screenings, and tests for sexually transmitted infections. These are a publicly funded safety net for women who cannot afford to go to the doctor. In the past, Title X funds have never been used for abortion services, however, in many states, agencies that offer abortions have been blocked from receiving any funding. Planned Parenthood is an example of this discrimination against agencies that offer legal abortions. After just three months in office, President Trump successfully blocked Planned Parenthood from receiving Medicaid reimbursements for one year in an attempt to force the agency to stop offering abortions to women. Over four million women use Planned Parenthood and other publicly funded agencies to access birth control, mammograms, wellness screening for ovarian, breast, and cervical cancer, among other services (Berg 2017). Most of the patients are low-income women who would not otherwise have access to contraceptives or reproductive health care. These decisions reflect the political and conflict-oriented nature of the health care system. According to projections from the Congressional Budget Office, barring Planned Parenthood from accepting Medicaid will cost tax payers over a hundred million dollars over the next ten years just for the increase in unintended pregnancies that will result from lack of high quality contraceptive care that the organization provides (Berg 2017).

Since abortion is legal on a federal level, is it unconstitutional for states to pass laws that make it harder for women to get an abortion.

Pro: States have not made abortion illegal so technically they are not violating constitutional rights. They should have the power to create their own guidelines regarding the process of abortion.
Con: States have passed restrictive laws that make it impossible for low-income women to access abortions and this is a violation of their constitutional rights.

Race

The health of African Americans, Hispanic Americans, Native Americans, and many Asian subgroups has always been inferior to that of non-Hispanic white Americans (National Center for Health Statistics 2003). Minority populations, especially African Americans, experience shorter life spans, higher rates of disability, and higher infant mortality rates (Hummer 1996). In chapter 13 on Population, we will discuss excess mortality for African Americans in more detail. What factors are playing a key role in the minority health disadvantage compared to whites? Certainly, the social class differences are significant since there is substantial evidence that income, education, and occupation are all independently associated with health. However, a growing literature suggests that the chronic stress of perceived racism adversely influences the health of minorities. In a highly stratified society like the United States, stress is linked to and determined by the social structure, social status, and social roles individuals occupy (Pearlin et al. 2005; House 2002). In addition, stress is individualized and the daily experience of racial bias and discrimination can have an adverse effect on an individual and cause accelerated aging (Thoits 2010). Studies documenting black/white differences in health conditions such as hypertension, mental health disorders, and general wellbeing have found that even after controlling for socioeconomic status, race-related stress and perceived discrimination, there is a correlation with poorer physical and mental health (Krieger and Sidney 1996; George and Lynch 2003; Williams, Yu, and Jackson 1997).

As discussed in this chapter, many social factors link poor health, chronic conditions, and illness. However, research has also found social factors that have positive effects on health. Social support received from family, friends, and significant others has a host of positive physical benefits including the lowering of blood pressure, an increase in immune system strength, and even the elongation of life to those with terminal illness. Alternatively, social isolation or involvement in negative relationships can result in decreases in health (Newman and Roberts 2013). Therefore, social supports and social networks play an important part in both mental and physical health.

Access to Mental Health Care

According to the National Alliance on Mental Illness (2013) one in four Americans experience **mental illness,** each year and one in 17 live with a serious mental illness. However, at least 60% of these individuals did not receive any **mental health** services in the past year. It is often the individual who is blamed for not seeking help; however, this is a much larger and more systemic problem. The barriers to accessing mental health services include the high cost of mental health care, the relatively few mental health care professionals in rural areas and small towns, and long waiting periods to get an appointment with a mental health professional (Langholz 2014). Mental health care is not easily accessible; an individual must understand how to navigate the system of psychiatrists and psychologists, of which there are often too few. The biggest obstacle to receiving mental health care is the lack of service providers (Mojtabai et al. 2011). It is also driving the trend for people to seek help for mental health disorders from their primary doctors. Other reasons often cited as barriers to mental health care by individuals is a preference for self-reliance or to handle it privately, most likely in part because of the stigma still attached to mental health disorders (Mojtabai et al. 2011). The large number of individuals with untreated mental illness is of concern as these are people who may harm themselves or others and they are often unable to hold down a job. Those with severe disorders and little social support often end up homeless. According to the National Coalition for the Homeless (2009), the third largest cause of homelessness is mental illness. Once an individual is homeless, their chances of receiving mental health care diminishes even further and they often remain untreated for the rest of their lives.

> **Mental Illness** any health disorder that causes psychological and/or emotional distress and originates in the brain.
>
> **Mental Health** emotional, psychological, and social wellbeing.

THEORETICAL PERSPECTIVES

Structural Functionalism

Structural functionalism has been closely aligned with health care—early functionalist theorists likened society to an organism (such as the human body); society is said to be "healthy" if its parts (i.e., the social institutions of government, economy, family, religion, and education) are fulfilling their purposes (or functions), much like the body's parts (e.g., brain, heart, lungs, kidneys, spleen) all individually accomplish their functions. Societies evolve much like bodies do in the temporal process of aging. Both society and human bodies require equilibrium maintenance to keep the interrelated and interdependent parts functioning correctly.

The social institutions, especially of government, economy, and education, are key elements in the health care system. Research, funding, new medications, and technological advancements work in tandem inside these institutions to evolve health care and provide successful treatment to those afflicted with the various health problems encountered in society and help individual and social rewards.

Talcott Parsons (1951) explored the "sick role" of the health care patient. When people enter the health care institution, they must experience a change in role expectations in that they can rest while normal work duties are suspended until they are deemed well. When recovered, the moratorium is lifted and they will return to the normal role responsibilities and stability will return. In the medical field, there are many specializations, this is because such an important field requires a strong division of labor in order to be effective; there are specialist physicians, nurses, administrators, and various other workers and all these are needed to make the medical field functional (like organs in the body).

Conflict

Conflict theories note the inequities in the various social institutions. Engels (1864) early on noted how the working class were more apt to need medical attention than those not exposed to the hazards imposed on the workers. Damp, unventilated factories and homes and exposure to health-related epidemics endangered both the physical and mental health of the lower classes. Engels asked, "how is it possible, under such conditions, for the lower class to be healthy and long lived" (Engels 1864:129)?

A critical/conflict perspective observes how, while advancements in technology, medical procedures, and pharmacology create better life situations for some, they do not increase them for all. Underdeveloped countries often do not have the most basic medical care. Even in America, those in the lower socioeconomic classes have less access to these advancements.

Health care is currently a hotly debated topic in the political realm. In a society that is as capitalistic as America, health care is big business. There is great financial potential in health care delivery, in pharmaceuticals ("big pharma"), and insurance, and while there have been some attempts to nationalize the health care system, this has not happened. Even the Affordable Care Act (ACA, or "Obamacare") is currently under threat of being overturned and a free market system implemented. It is not likely that America will provide universal health care due to the potential for large profits that exist for the health care, pharmaceutical, and insurance industries.

Symbolic Interactionism

The existing medical model requires the use of diagnosis as a beginning stage of treatment. A diagnosis is a label based on a set of pre-established criteria and once that label is affixed to a patient, expectations are made by the patient, medical personnel, and others in the patient's life to follow the dictates of that label. For example, a diabetic, an asthmatic, and a schizophrenic each have a set of expectations that go with their labels the same way those addicted to drugs have expectations with theirs (recall our earlier discussions on these labels). In other words, identities are constructed based on diagnoses, which are created from observed phenomena and categorized. If one believes they are bipolar, then they may act as one with bipolar disorder would be thought to act. After all, hypochondriacs act as if they have a certain disease because they believe it to be true though in fact, they do not.

Goffman (1961) claimed that the behavior of mental patients is more often a response to the situation in which the person finds themselves (the mental institution) than an actual mental illness possessed by the person. His ethnographic study on a mental health hospital (1961) resulted in his claims that people learn how to adopt the expected characteristics of being a mental health patient: "how to be properly mentally ill" (Collins and Makowsky 1998:248). As noted earlier, Goffman called places that re-socialize people "total institutions" and hospitals, particularly mental hospitals, fit this bill. Although intended to provide treatment for a certain condition, the environment instead promotes a continuance of that condition.

Psychiatrist Thomas Szasz (1974) similarly referred to mental problems as a myth, preferring to reframe such conditions as "problems in living". Szasz observes that "powerful institutional forces lend their massive weight to the tradition of keeping psychiatric problems within a conceptual framework of medicine" (Szasz 1974:262) and advocated a redefinition of mental illness and psychotherapy.

SEARCHING FOR SOLUTIONS

The United States spends more on health care than any other developed country, but continues to report worse health outcomes than many Western countries. This is a complex social problem, made more difficult because our population is heterogeneous and thus there are very different needs for every sub-population. There are three approaches for reducing health disparities by offering better and less expensive access to health care services. The first is a community level approach that targets underserved individuals and raises awareness about the importance of positive health behaviors. The second is at the state level, where policies can be changed and put into place to expand Medicaid and provide reproductive and general health care services for low-income women and families. The third approach is to tackle the problem on a national level, which was the approach of past presidential administrations such as President Obama and President Johnson. All three of these approaches should, in theory, work together to provide better access to health care for the millions of individuals who do not either go to the doctor when they are unwell, because they cannot afford it, lack transportation, or experience other obstacles that prevent them from getting the care they need.

Beginning with the community, there are many avenues for reducing health disparities and expanding access to providers, as well as educating and raising awareness about the importance of positive health behaviors. According to Healthy People 2020 (2017), community based health and health education programs can be cost effective ways to improve health, reduce obesity and type two diabetes, treat chronic diseases, and improve health behaviors. Educational and community based programs are designed to target people where they live, study and work: worksites, schools, and community centers as well as outreach into low income areas where there is higher unemployment and less access to community centers. Key strategies focus on engaging local leaders, developing community partnerships, recognizing the influence of culture, and empowering these marginalized sub-populations with the knowledge to engage in better health behaviors and the tools to seek better health services.

Until racial, ethnic and gendered health disparities are reduced, health outcomes will continue to be worse for minorities than for the non-Hispanic white population. According to the

FIGURE 11.1
Community based health education programs continue to be the most inexpensive way to improve health, especially for marginalized groups.

Center for Disease Control (CDC), community based health and health education programs are the most cost-effective ways to improve health, reduce obesity and type 2 diabetes, treat chronic diseases, and improve health behaviors for marginalized groups. To assist in these efforts the CDC implemented the Racial and Ethnic Approaches to Community Health Across the United States (REACH). REACH is the first community based public health program to focus exclusively on health disparities among African Americans, American Indians, Alaska natives, Asian Americans, Hispanics/Latinos, and Pacific Islanders. Though funded nationally, REACH is implemented in communities through local health departments, universities, and community based organizations. Because racial and health gaps are complex and intersect with gender, nationality, and other marginalized group statuses, REACH focuses on the key areas that are linked to premature death, unnecessary illnesses, and disability among minorities. For example, according to the CDC the South Carolina College of Nursing started a health care education program through REACH aimed at improving health care delivery for African Americans with diabetes by increasing knowledge and awareness about self-management of diabetes as well as prevention. This program resulted in a 44% reduction in amputations for African Americans in the two counties in South Carolina (CDC 2013). Other outcomes from REACH community programs focus on chronic disease, diet, exercise, and preventative services reductions in hypertension for Hispanics in communities in the Northeast, decreased rates of smoking among Asian Americans in four communities, and an increase in vaccinations in Native American communities. These programs are implemented largely through family health centers and medical universities, as well as local health education groups. Educating individuals on how poor diet is associated with obesity, diabetes, cancer, and other chronic illnesses as well as how to cook healthy meals appears to be the key to empowering low-income individuals to improve their food choices.

Poor quality of diet is strongly associated with socioeconomic status and by proxy, race, and ethnicity. Many low-income families live in a food desert. According to the United States Department of Agriculture (USDA) (2017), a food desert is an area where the poverty rate is 20% or higher and at least 33% of individuals live more than one mile from a major grocery store. A study by Steven Cummins, Ellen Flint and Stephen Matthews (2014) found that adding a major grocery store to a neighborhood in Philadelphia considered a food desert did not significantly change dietary habits or reduce obesity. It was also not associated with any changes in intake of vegetables and fruit or changes in BMI when compared to a control neighborhood that did not have a major grocery store. In addition, a study by Leung and colleagues (2012), that examined diet trends in low-income individuals from 1999 to 2008, found that users of the Supplemental Nutrition Assistance Program (SNAP) had poorer diet quality and consumed fewer whole grains, and more red meat, potatoes, and sugar sweetened beverages than low-income non-participants. These studies make it clear that access is not the only (or main) factor in diet choices. Evidence from a national study by the U.S. Department of Agriculture (2013), found a strong positive association between nutrition education in schools and healthier food choices by SNAP users. The most successful interventions provided nutrition education for low-income elementary school students *and* take-home materials for parents that addressed how to make healthy food choices on a small food budget. Thus, although access and resources are important, nutrition education appears to be the most crucial ingredient for changing behaviors related to diet.

Should racism and poverty be considered the root causes of poor health outcomes in the United States?

Pro: Racism and poverty adversely influence the health outcomes of vulnerable racial minorities and must be eliminated in order for every person to have the opportunity for comparable health outcomes.
Con: Americans need to take personal responsibility for their health and stop blaming other people and external social forces for their poor health outcomes.

A fairly recent report from the USDA (2016) revealed purchasing habits of SNAP recipients for the first time. According to the report, the top ten food items purchased by SNAP households include soft drinks (number one), bag snacks, ground beef, and cereal. However, compared to non-SNAP households, the purchase of soft drinks is only slightly lower than for those using SNAP benefits. This study received a great amount of media attention, which in turn created public animosity toward SNAP users, and spurred state legislators to request waivers from the USDA to prohibit SNAP recipients from using their benefits to purchase foods that range from candy and soft drinks to seafood and steak (Fifield 2017). As of 2017, the USDA has denied these requests from cities and states. However, many legislators, public health officials, and citizens view these food stamp restrictions as a viable solution to improving the health of low-income families.

In contrast, many public health advocates have pointed out the similarities between spending patterns by SNAP and non-SNAP families that are also documented in the USDA report. Altogether the study found that forty cents of every dollar went to "basic items" such as meat, fruits, vegetables, bread, and milk, while only twenty cents went to salty and sugary snacks and beverages, with 5 cents of each dollar going to soft drinks (USDA 2016). Since SNAP is only part of a household's food budget, it is likely that recipients will still purchase the same products, they will just use their own funds for the purchase of the restricted items. Public health officials argue that restricting food choices will not result in better nutrition. That instead, there are better policy options for improving diet, including rebates for spending on targeted healthy foods, bonus dollars for benefits used at farmer's markets for fresh produce, and nutrition education for SNAP recipients (Fifield 2017).

Can we improve the health of SNAP users by restricting food choices?

Pro: By providing guidelines, SNAP users who must purchase healthy food options will make better choices and this will result in better health for their entire family.

Con: Not only is it discriminatory to legislate what foods individuals should be allowed to buy with SNAP, they will continue to purchase the same foods, they just won't use SNAP benefits for those foods.

Reducing the High Cost of Health Care

The United States spends more on health care per person than any other developed country. Cutting costs is essential to improving our system and reducing the burden on taxpayers. For example, recently it has come to light that drug expiration dates are not necessarily accurate. A 2012 study by Cantrell et al., conducted at the Johns Hopkins University School of Medicine, found that many medications well past their expiration data had not lost potency. In fact, they found that most medications retain their original potency for years after the expiration date. A 2006 study by

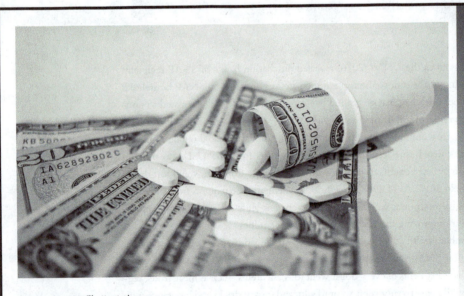

FIGURE 11.2 As health costs continue to rise in the United States, there is little consensus on alternative strategies to reform health care.

Source: mayamaya/Shutterstock.com

Lyon et al., tested 122 medications and found that two-thirds were just as potent and effective long past the manufacturer's expiration date with some retaining original potency for up to four more years. The economic impact of this is astonishing, with experts estimating that hospitals, pharmacies, medical centers, and other health care organizations dispose of billions of dollars in expired medications each year (Allen 2017). The expiration date set by the Food and Drug Administration (FDA) is based on how long the pharmaceutical companies report they can guarantee the medication will be effective. Thus, it is quite financially lucrative to set expiration dates at two to three years since pharmaceutical companies are in the business of selling medications. To extend expiration dates legislation would need to be put in place by the Federal Drug Administration. As far back as 2000, the American Medical Association has tried to push for change in this area by urging officials to re-examine expiration dates. This group has not had any success in eliminating this staggering amount of unnecessary waste that is just one of many ways our country could cut health care costs.

Alternative Health Care Reform Strategies

Strategies to improve health care in the United States are rarely agreed upon. In 2016, presidential candidate and U.S. senator of Vermont, Bernie Sanders, proposed a plan called "Medicare for All", which is similar to a single payer system much like the health care systems in Canada and many European countries. This federally administered single payer system would provide complete health care for everyone and physicians would still remain in private practice. This would separate health insurance from employment and provide care for everyone regardless of employment status. The plan would provide everything from preventative to emergency care, primary care, long term care and palliative care. It would cover prescription medications, medical equipment and supplies, and other treatments. And it would also provide dental care, mental health, and substance abuse services. There would be no out-of-pocket costs for individuals when they need health care. The benefits of moving to an integrated system include: lower administrative costs since there would no longer be thousands of different health insurance plans with different networks and reimbursement rates, as well as the ability to negotiate lower prices on medications from the pharmaceutical companies. In addition, consolidating health care into a single payer system would allow the government to track providers and ensure people in low income and rural communities can access providers. The drawbacks of this plan include higher income tax rates, with the top 1% paying upwards of 50% in taxes. Funding for the plan would also include taxing capital gains and dividends at the same rate as income from work, limiting tax deductions for the wealthy, and taxing the estates of the very wealthy when money is passed down to the next generation.

The Rand Corporation, a nonpartisan, non-profit organization that researches public policy challenges proposed another, less radical, alternative plan for health care reform. The proposal is for a taxpayer-supported basic health plan for all Americans that charges the same price regardless of pre-existing conditions (Eibner 2017). Funding would be attained in part from eliminating the tax benefit employers received when they provide health insurance to employees (even if employees pay the bulk of the premium) that results in $275 billion every year in lost tax revenue. These monies would then be spent on a more equitable approach that is not "insurance" but rather, a basic health plan that ensures equal access to everyone regardless of pre-existing health conditions. Economists Kip Hagopian and Dana Goldman (2012) proposed an approach to paying for a taxpayer-supported plan by using an income-dependent deductible. Deductibles would be based on income, with higher deductibles for those with high incomes, and Medicaid would remain in place for those who could not afford a deductible. With this plan, individuals could still receive private insurance to supplement the basic health plan as well as pay for services not included in the basic plan. This "cost-sharing" plan would benefit individuals who currently have high deductibles and the under-insured, but because it is not all-inclusive, and instead focuses on basic services, people may forgo health care services they need because they are cost-prohibitive (Eibner 2017).

Should those who earn higher incomes subsidize health care costs for the poor?

Pro: The wealthy have a social responsibility to contribute more so that individuals and families in poverty can access basic health care.
Con: This is the equivalent of penalizing people who make good choices, work hard, and are success-ful. It is not their responsibility to take on the heavy burden of high health care costs for those people who have chosen not to provide for themselves or their families.

Not everyone would embrace these alternative health care policy reforms; those who are healthy or have high incomes generally do not want to pay for programs that benefit the sick and the poor. Currently, President Trump is introducing new health care reform that lacks agreement from conservatives and liberals alike. This issue is clearly a hot button for everyone involved and this lack of agreement is in large part why it has taken so many years just to have a system like the Affordable Care Act in place. However, to provide a solution for the high cost of health care, lack of access to providers, and the millions of people who remain underinsured will require substantial changes in the way we think about, organize, and pay for health care in the United States.

CHAPTER SUMMARY

- Creating a high-quality health care system with access for all is a complex and multi-faceted social problem that the United States has struggled with for many decades. Currently, the Affordable Care Act along with Medicaid, Medicare, and the Veterans Administration provide a safety net of sorts for individuals who otherwise would not receive any health care at all. However, access is a challenge for both physical and mental health services for millions of Americans.

- Because health disparities are based on social factors such as race, ethnicity, gender, and social class, the people who need quality health care the most are the ones who are least likely to have access to it.

- Medical sociologists study health care services utilization and delivery and analyze the effectiveness and challenges of our current system. The bio-model of health prevalent in Western countries has influenced medicalization of conditions that were once not thought to be pathology, but are now treated with expensive medications and thus have created even higher costs for patients.

- An area that is especially in need of reform is mental health. Lack of access, shortages in providers, and the high cost of both providers and medications have made a pressing problem since the majority of people with mental health disorders do not utilize mental health services.

- Strategies to solve this problem range from a single payer system to a system that combines a taxpayer supported basic health care system with the option to continue to use employer sponsored plans and private market plans.

- The Affordable Care Act has helped many low-income families, however, it will likely be dismantled during the current presidential administration and replaced by a system that is more restrictive and more expensive since President Trump plans to reinstate a new system that is more conservative in its coverage and approach.

REFERENCES

Aakre, Jennifer M., Seth Himelhoch, and Eric P. Slade. 2014. "Mental Health Service Utilization by Iraq and Afghanistan Veterans After Entry into PTSD Specialty Treatment." *Psychiatric Services*. 65(8): 1066–1069. Retrieved August 8 (https://doi.org/10.1176/appi.ps.201300117).

Allen, Marshall. 2017. *That Drug Expiration Date May be More Myth than Fact*. Retrieved July 20, 2017 (www.npr.org).

Berg, Miriam. 2017. "How Federal Funding Works at Planned Parenthood." Retrieved July 17, 2017 (www.plannedparenthoodaction.org).

Brasfield, James M. 2011. *Health Policy: The Decade Ahead*. Boulder, CO: Lynne Rienner Publications.

Brownstein, Scott, Nelli Black, and Drew Griffin. 2014. "Veterans Dying Because of Health Care Delays." Retrieved April 22, 2018 (www.cnn.com/2014/01/30/health/veterans-dying-health-care-delays/index.html).

Cantrell, Lee, Jeffrey Suchard, Alan Wu, and Roy R. Gerona. 2012. "Stability of Active Ingredients in Long-Expired Prescription Medications." Arch Internal Medicine 172(21): 1685–1687. doi:10.1001/archinternmed.2012.4501.

Case, Anne C. and Christina Paxson. 2005. "Sex Differences in Morbidity and Mortality." *Demography*. 42(2): 189–214. Retrieved August 4, 2017 (www.nber.org/papers/w10653).

Center for Disease Control and Prevention. 2013. "Reach in Action." Retrieved June 12, 2018 (www.cdc.gov/nccdphp/dnpao/state-local-programs/reach).

Collins, Randall and Michael Makowsky. 1998. *The Discovery of Society*, 6th ed. Boston: McGraw-Hill.

Conrad, Peter. 2008. *The Medicalization of Society: On the Transformation of Human Conditions into Treatable Disorders*. Chicago: JHU Press.

Conrad, Peter and Kristin K. Barker. 2010. "The Social Construction of Illness: Key Insights and Policy Implications." *Journal of Health and Social Behavior*, 51(S): S67–S79.

Cummins, Steven, Ellen Flint, and Stephen A. Matthews. 2014. "New Neighborhood Grocery Store Increased Awareness of Food Access but Did Not Alter Dietary Habits or Obesity." *Health Affairs*. 33(2): 283–291. doi:10.1377/hlthaff.2013.0512.

Eibner, Christine. 2017. "Ingredients for Health Care Reform. The Rand Corporation." Santa Monica: CA. Retrieved July 20, 2017 (www.rand.org/blog/2017/07/ingredients-for-health-care-reform.html).

Engels, Friedrich. 1987. *The Conditions of the Working Class in England*. London: Penguin Books (originally published in 1864).

Fifield, Jen. 2017. *Should People Be Barred from Buying Junk Food with Food Stamps?* The Pew Charitable Trusts Research and Analysis. Retrieved July 28, 2017 (www.pewtrusts.org/en/research-and-analysis/blogs/stateline/2017/02/24/should-people-be-barred-from-buying-junk-food-with-food-stamps).

Fishman, Jennifer R. and Laura Mamo. 2001. "What's in a Disorder: A Cultural Analysis of Medical and Pharmaceutical Constructions of Male and Female Sexual Dysfunction." *Body & Society*. 7(2): 181–183.

George, Linda K., and Scott M. Lynch. 2003. "Race Differences in Depressive Symptoms: A Dynamic Perspective on Stress Exposure and Vulnerability." *Journal of Health and Social Behavior*. 44(3): 353–69. Retrieved January 14, 2013 (www.jstor.org/stable/1519784).

Goffman, Erving. 1961. *Asylums: Essays on the Condition of the Social Situation of Mental Patients and Other Inmates*. Garden City, NY: Doubleday.

Hagopian, Kip and Dana Goldman. 2012. "The Health-Insurance Solution." *National Affairs*. 32(2). Retrieved July 20, 2017 (www.nationalaffairs.com/publications/detail/the-health-insurance-solution).

Harvard Magazine. 2009. *On the Medicalization of Our Culture*. Harvard Magazine. Retrieved August 1, 2017 (http://harvardmagazine.com/2009/04/medicalization-of-our-culture).

Healthy People 2020. 2017. U.S. Department of Health and Human Services, Washington, DC. Retrieved July 25, 2017 (https://www.healthypeople.gov/2020).

House, James S. 2002. "Understanding Social Factors and Inequalities in Health: 20th Century Progress and 21st Century Prospects." *Journal of Health and Social Behavior*. 43(2):125–42. Retrieved February 1, 2013 (http://www.jstor.org/stable/3090192).

Hummer, Robert A. 1996. "Black-white differences in health and mortality: A review and conceptual model." *The Sociological Quarterly*. 37(1): 105–125.

Krieger, Nancy, and Stephen Sidney. 1996. "Racial Discrimination and Blood Pressure: the CARDIA Study of Young Black and White Adults." *American Journal of Public Health*. 86(10): 1370–1378.

Langholz, Hannah C. 2014. "Systemic Barriers to Mental Health Care: A Qualitative Study." *Master of Social Work Clinical Research Papers*. Retrieved July 18, 2017 (http://sophia.stkate.edu/msw_papers/352).

Leung Cindy W., Eric L. Ding, Paul J. Catalano, Eduardo Villamor, Eric B. Rimm, and Walter C. Willett. 2012. "Dietary Intake and Dietary Quality of Low-Income Adults in the Supplemental Nutrition Assistance Program." *The American Journal of Clinical Nutrition*. 96(5): 977–88. doi:10.3945/ajcn.112.040014.

Link, Bruce G., and Jo Phelan. 2010. "Social Conditions as Fundamental Causes of Health Inequalities." *Handbook of Medical Sociology*. 6(3): 17.

Lorber, Judith and Lisa Moore. 2002. *Gender and the Social Construction of Illness*, 2nd ed. Walnut Creek, CA: Altamira Press.

Lyon, Robbe C., Jeb S. Taylor, Donna A. Porter, Hullahali R. Prasanna, and Ajaz S. Hussain. 2006. "Stability Profiles of Drug Products Extended Beyond Labeled Expiration Dates." *Journal of Pharmaceutical Sciences*. 95 (7): 1549–1560. doi:10.1002/jps.20636.

Mirowsky, John, and Catherine E. Ross. 2003. *Education, Social Status, and Health*. New York: Transaction Publishers.

Mojtabai, Ramin, Mark Olfson, Nancy A. Sampson, Robert Jin, Benjamin Druss, Phillip A. Wang, Kenneth B. Wells, Harold A. Pincus, and Ronald C. Kessler. 2011. "Barriers to Mental Health Treatment: Results from the National Comorbidity Survey Replication (NCS-R)." *Psychological Medicine*, 41(8): 1751–1761. Retrieved August 1, 2017 (http://doi.org/10.1017/S0033291710002291).

Mullings, Leith and Amy J. Schulz. 2006. *Gender, Race, Class, and Health: Intersectional Approaches*. San Francisco, CA: Wiley, p. 5.

National Alliance on Mental Illness. 2013. "Mental Illness Fact and Numbers." Retrieved April 22, 2018 (http://bhsarkansas.org/pdf/facts_and_stats.pdf).

National Center for Health Statistics. 2003. *Health, United States*. Hyattsville, MD: National Center for Health Statistics.

National Coalition for the Homeless 2009. *Mental Illness and Homelessness*. Washington, DC. Retrieved July 18, 2017 (www.nationalhomeless.org).

National Organization of Veterans' Advocates, Inc. 2017. *Obama Signs VA Reform Bill into Law*. Retrieved July 21, 2017 (https://vetadvocates.org/obama-signs-va-reform-bill-into-law).

Newman, Matthew L. and Nicole A. Roberts. 2013. "Introduction." *Health and Social Relationships: The Good, the Bad, and the Complicated*. Washington, DC: American Psychological Association.

Parsons, Talcott. 1951. *The Social System*. Glencoe, IL: The Free Press.

Pearlin, Leonard I., Scott Schieman, Elena M. Fazio, and Stephen C. Meersman. 2005. "Stress, Health, and the Life Course: Some Conceptual Perspectives." *Journal of Health and Social Behavior* 46(2): 205–19. Retrieved October 8, 2012 (http://hsb.sagepub.com.ezproxy.lib.utexas.edu/content/46/2/205).

Szasz, Thomas S. 1974. *The Myth of Mental Illness: Foundations of a Theory of Personal Conduct*, Rev. Ed. New York: Harper Colophon Books.

Thoits, Peggy A. 2010. "Stress and Health: Major Findings and Policy Implications." *Journal of Health and Social Behavior*. 51(1): S41–S53. Retrieved January 14, 2013 (http://hsb.sagepub.com/content/51/1_suppl/S41).

United States Department of Agriculture. 2016. "Foods Typically Purchased by Supplemental Nutrition Assistance Program (SNAP) Households." *Nutrition Assistance Program Report, Office of Policy Support, Food and Nutrition Service, U.S. Department of Agriculture*. Washington, DC. Retrieved July 18, 2017 (www.fns.usda.gov/snap/foods-typically-purchased-supplemental-nutrition-assistanceprogram-snap-households).

United States Department of Agriculture. (2017). "Food Access Research Atlas." Washington, D.C. Retrieved June 13, 2018 (www.ers.usda.gov/data-products/food-access-research-atlas).

United States Department of Veterans Affairs. 2017. "About Veteran's Health Administration." *Veteran's Health Administration*. Washington, DC: United States Department of Veterans Affairs. Retrieved August 4, 2017 (www.va.gov/health/aboutVHA.asp).

Williams, David R., Yan Yu, and James S. Jackson. 1997. "Racial Differences in Physical and Mental Health." *Journal of Health Psychology*. 2(3): 335–351.

World Health Organization. 2017. Constitution of WHO: Principles. P. 1. Retrieved July 20, 2017 (www.who.int/about/mission/en/).

CHAPTER 12

Terrorism and War

ABOUT THE PROBLEM: TERRORISM AND WAR

Terrorism domestic or international activity by non-state actors through the killing or severe injury to civilian people or public property and which creates negative economic consequences to intimidate or coerce people.

Terrorism is a term (like so many we have addressed in this book) that is difficult to define. Sociologist Neil Smelser painstakingly reviewed definitions that have been proffered and exposed their deficiencies (Smelser 2007). He provides a succinct but encompassing definition which describes terrorism as:

> intended, regular acts of violence or disruption (or the threat of them) carried out in secret with the effect of generating anxiety in a group, and with the further aim, via that effect, of exciting political response or political change.
>
> (Smelser 2007:242)

Another definition describes that terrorism involves activity by non-state actors in the killing or severe injury to civilian people or public property which creates negative economic consequences to intimidate or coerce people—it can be domestic or international in scope (Manning 2015). Currently a major topic, due to the highly-reported actions that have occurred around the globe since the September 11, 2001 attacks in the United States, terrorism is a current issue but has been around since the classical era (Smelser 2007). We will return to the issue of terrorism shortly.

War an organized violent activity waged by groups rather than individuals in which both sides use strategy to defeat the other for the goal of victory or self-preservation.

War is also a very difficult thing to define. Carl von Clausewitz, the famed nineteenth century military theorist whose posthumous work *On War* (1968) is still widely studied by military strategists, states that war is just a duel on a much grander scale; however, he follows that statement with a definition that is almost as concise: "war ... is an act of violence intended to compel our opponent to fulfil our will" (Clausewitz 1968:101). The definition lacks substance to the point where it could be describing a college football game. Clausewitz (1968), however, provided a useful distinction between absolute and real war: absolute war is total war, the essential violent, destructive, and total

212

annihilation of the enemy, while real war is the normal type of limited warfare and national hostilities that are the most common type; the former type is the essence of the innate destruction of warfare.

A more adequate definition of war is reflected in certain characteristics: 1) an organized violent activity waged by groups rather than individuals; 2) a reciprocal arrangement in which both sides use strategy to defeat the other; and 3) a goal which is victory, or at least self-preservation (Creveld 1999). This description provides that the activity must be violent (which makes one question the naming of the Cold War), it takes place between two organizations (usually nation states), and that has an end game of achieving victory or, if defeated, —surviving.

In explorations of war, ethics looms large. The issue of whether a war is "just" has been debated for eons and a very old theory seeks to understand the morality of going to war. **Just war theory**, which has been discussed and debated by war theorists and philosophers for thousands of years, posits these conditions must be present before any military operation could be considered morally justified: "just cause, right authority, right intention, and reasonable hope of success" (Taslaman and Taslaman 2013–2014:2). These conditions are called *jus in bellum* (right to war) and are considered to have greater importance than *jus in bello* (laws of war), the way wars are fought after hostilities begin. The just war thesis was recently used to legitimize the Bush administration's decision to prosecute military operations in Afghanistan and Iraq (Taslaman and Taslaman 2013–2014).

> **Just War Theory** a doctrine that contains a series of conditions that must be met for war to be considered appropriate and just.

We will now look at how sociology has explored the dialectic of opposing forces that constitutes relationships of nations—that of war and peace.

The Sociology of War and Peace

There are a variety of military conflicts considered "war", therefore it is useful to categorize the different types. Chailiand (2014) provides such a classification system. *Ritualized wars* were localized

FIGURE 12.1 War has become linked to larger globalization and as a result warfare has fewer military engagements.

Source: BPTU/Shutterstock.com

skirmishes primarily found in traditional societies and that are not normally fought to the death. *Wars with limited objectives* are military engagements which occur between opponents that have an accepted code of warfare and lack the goal of overthrowing the social structure. The *classical wars of conquest* are those wars that require complete surrender of the defeated by the victors. *Mass wars* require the destruction of the enemy and the annihilation of the civilian population by means including genocide, bombardments, deportations, and executions. *Total wars* are normally civil wars that are fueled by religious differences and are the most merciless and casualty-producing; *ethnic wars* between people who see each other as foreigners are particularly cruel. Chailiand states "the most radical conflict is the conflict between brothers, or where the enemy is considered subhuman" (Chailiand 2014:16).

Malesevic (2014) notes the two dominant views on the changes in global warfare have been primarily analyzed sociologically by two camps: scholars who adhere to the "new wars" approach that posits that warfare is linked to larger globalization processes and that warfare has become more fatal and decentralized, and scholars who see modern military engagements as being less in number, shorter, less fatal, and more localized than in the past. The second camp also believes that war is gradually becoming a relic of the past. What has been missing from the current sociological view of the nexus of war-state-society, according to Malesevic, is how war has been developing in relation to changes in society. War has always evolved in tandem with other aspects of society; in nomadic societies for example, wars were infrequent but as groups became more formalized, they have taken more of a coercive posture to reduce conflict. Limited military engagements ("limited war") evolved into conflicts whose goal is to exterminate the enemy ("total war").

> **New War Thesis** a position that outlines how modern warfare differs from traditional wars by different motivations and due to societal changes.

McSorley (2014) addresses the **new war thesis** that posits that today's wars differ from the wars of the past; traditional military conflicts had regular military troops that fought for a nation that is clearly specified, identifying with a single flag against a similarly distinctly designated group; new wars have a host of non-regular forces and private troops (militias, guerilla groups, and warlords) fighting unconventional campaigns uncommitted to specific nations, motivated by greed rather than nationalistic reasons, and fighting in civil conflicts that often include terrorism as a strategy. And of course, advancements in technology has certainly changed the face of warfare.

Roxborough (1994) believes that despite needing a well-developed sociology of war, many sociologists from the founders on have neglected this area, due in part to the varied agendas that encompass the discipline, resulting in difficulties providing a consistent theoretical formulation of war. McSorley (2014) agrees the subject of war has been disregarded in sociology—there is no developed subfield called the sociology of war, for example, even though wars of various military conflicts have played a major role in shaping society. He states that "war has not been a topic that has regularly captivated the sociological imagination" (McSorley 2014:110). Ironically, the topic of war was mentioned in the very work that produced the idea—*The Sociological Imagination* (1959). In that work, C. Wright Mills mentioned war in his conceptualization of the personal *troubles* of being an individual who is trying to stay alive in it, get promoted in rank in it, die with honor in it, figuring out how to make money from it, or how to end it, vs the structural *issues* that are concerned with the causes of war, understanding the types of people placed in command positions, its effects on the other social institutions in a global perspective. Mills, in the same chapter of the book speaks in blunt terms when he asks the question (posed in 1959): "what dramatic vision of hell can compete with the events of twentieth century war?" (Mills 1959:17). War and the military were major concerns for Mills and we will discuss him again in the theory section.

Sociologists often refer to the concept of power in explaining military conflict because human relationships are the focal point of the discipline. Two types of power in this context can be distinguished: **hard power**, which refers to the power that comes with having the material resources to achieve an objective through coercion, and **soft power**, the power that comes from having an alternative to conflict that is attractive enough to not need coercion to achieve (Smith 2012).

> **Hard Power** the power that comes with having the material resources to achieve an objective through coercion.
>
> **Soft Power** the power that comes from having an alternative to conflict that is attractive enough to reject coercion.

The Utopian Ideal of Peace

Peace can be perceived as the antithesis of war in this dialectic. Pacifism, or nonviolence, has been advocated by many people throughout history. In America during wars in which conscription (also known as the draft) occurred—World Wars I, II, Korea, and Vietnam—allowances were made for people who practiced pacifism based on religious beliefs and a moral conscience that makes it inappropriate to kill others, even in a war situation—this is called conscientious objection. The issue of conscience is also a major component of a closely related concept of civil disobedience (Tollefson 1994).

Boulding (2000) describes a "peace culture" in the following way: "a culture that promotes peaceable diversity. Such a culture includes lifeways, patterns of belief, values, behavior, and accompanying institutional arrangements that includes appreciation of difference, stewardship, and equitable sharing of the earth's resources among its members and with all living beings" (Boulding 2000:1). The idea of a culture—an encompassing ideology—that refrains from violent activity seems like a utopia.

Anthropologist Margaret Mead was a scholar who was very much invested in promoting a more peaceful world. She worked to introduce a peacemaking focus in the social sciences, including advocating an elementary and secondary curriculum which included peace education. She created the "housewives project" in the 1960s (Boulding 2000) and, though the name sounds a bit antifeminist today, its goal was to promote an ideal of women helping prevent some of the world's most pressing social problems, including war (Boulding 2000).

Swedish family sociologist Alva Myrdal also contributed to the advocacy of peace by moving from family relations to international relations. The wife of Gunnar Myrdal (mentioned in chapter 8), she became an ambassador and minister of disarmament and created organizations to promote peace and alleviate the problem of war (Boulding 2000). She won the Nobel Peace Prize in 1982.

Sociologist C. Wright Mills (1958) outlined a series of guidelines that calls for America to "abandon the military metaphysic and the doctrinaire idea of capitalism and, in the reasonableness thus gained, reconsider the terms of the world encounter" (Mills 1958:97). Among his 17 recommendations, he suggested that we change the national idea of the necessity of war, focus our attention on industrialization not for war but to help those in poverty, work with countries such as Russia, and abandon the "idiot race" (Mills 1958:98) for arms superiority, provide a better education for our youth, and focus on scientific advancement for reasons other than warfare. His plan sounds utopian and he acknowledged this perception, but he felt that scientists and intellectuals hold the key to making peace in the world a reality.

Social Change and Warfare

After the Industrial Revolution, advancements in military technology increased tremendously. In the twentieth century, the United States created a military-industrial complex that was far more

FIGURE 12.2 Newer methods of warfare and destruction use computers and technology rather than traditional combat.

Source: Artem Oleshko/Shutterstock.com

sophisticated and powerful than any other country. The term *military-industrial complex* was used during the Eisenhower administration to reflect the ever growing and technically advancing U.S. military and the growing use of contractors which worked hand in hand with creating a strong military and a strong financial sector. Nuclear weaponry has caused global warfare to change exponentially as the prospect of total annihilation of large parts of the planet is now a possibility (Creveld 1999). The damage done to the Japanese cities of Hiroshima and Nagasaki have given a glimpse into the amount of destruction that could be wrought by this new deadly technology. Interestingly many powerful nations since 1945 have been defeated by small guerrilla and terrorist groups, as it appears the more powerful nations, despite their advanced weaponry, have had difficulty figuring out how to effectively combat this more primitive type of warfare. On this issue, Morgenthau (1972) stated that the well-armed American troops trying to fight the sparsely-armed Vietnamese troops during the Vietnam War was like a soldier with a machine gun who is attacked by bees.

Newer forms of technology have created changes in methods of war and terrorism. *Techno-terrorism*, the use of technological advancements in carrying out terroristic acts, finds its most damaging form in the world's vast computer infrastructure. *Cyberattacks*, *cyber exploitations*, and *cyber intrusion*, types of computer-assisted terrorism, have resulted in countless attacks (Wittes and Blum 2015:22–23); most recently the Russian government has been implicated in hacking into the Democratic National Convention computers, causing what some speculate as interference into the 2016 Presidential election results.

Biotechnology in the release of deadly pathogens could soon have the potential to extinguish humankind, or at least set civilization back perhaps 1000 years (Wittes and Blum 2015). For example, immediately following the 9/11 terrorist attacks, a mysterious powder claimed to be the deadly anthrax pathogen was sent to several recipients (Wills et al. 2008). While no deaths were reported, the anthrax scare created an atmosphere of anxiety with many Americans, which is one of the goals of terrorism.

Robotic technology has become increasingly used in military operations. Drones are primarily identified as unoccupied *aerial* military vehicles, though drones are part of robotic, autonomous technology and are now used on the ground or in water. Drone warfare, which was non-existent before the 1980s, became much more prevalent during the Obama administration. Though drones have the capability to reap much damage to military opponents, errant drone strikes also have killed many civilians (Kaag and Kreps 2014). Drones are becoming much smaller and more camouflaged in the natural environment in the form of insect, animal, and reptile replicas, making it easier to be unobtrusive and undetected (Wittes and Blum 2015).

Should the use of drones in military conflicts be increased?

Pro: The use of drones reduces the loss of life of American military personnel and is effective.
Con: The chances of collateral damage, specifically the death of innocent civilians in drone warfare, is too great.

The United States and Russia—a return to the Cold War?

The Cold War began after World War II and reflected the tensions that existed between the U.S. and the Union of Soviet Socialist Republics (U.S.S.R.; now Russia). From 1945 until 1991, the Cold War had five stages: phase one was from 1945–1946 when each side viewed the other as a threat to their separate worldviews. The second phase was from 1947–1962 and was the most dangerous phase as both sides increased the size and power of their arsenals and came close to using them at different points during the period. Phase three, from 1963–1979, is called the period of détente, a pragmatic time when Americans turned their focus to the Vietnam War and Soviets turned their attention to China, with whom they had tense relations. The fourth phase, existed from 1980–1986 under the Reagan administration; Reagan labeled the Soviet Union an "evil empire" and military expansion continued on both sides, however Mikhail Gorbachev became the premier and relations began to thaw. The final phase, which lasted from 1987–1991, saw the Soviet Union collapse as many other Communist regimes disbanded (Karabell 1999).

The Soviet Union's 15-member nations formed their own sovereign states, however there were ethnic conflicts and an instability that reverberated in the West. The unification of Germany had resulted in the tearing down of the Berlin Wall in 1989, which was a major symbol of the Cold War. Gorbachev was dealing with many internal struggles and turned to U.S. President George H.W. Bush who sought to work with the Soviet leader, however Boris Yeltsin took control and moved the country to a free market economy. Conflicts over oil reserves in the Caspian Sea created conflict between Yeltsin and new American President Bill Clinton. The Soviet Union became further threatened by a host of internal problems including mafia crime. In 2000,

FIGURE 12.3 On August 6, 1945 the United States dropped the first nuclear bomb on Hiroshima, Japan.

a little known ex-KGB (Russia's national security agency) official named Vladimir V. Putin became the new Prime Minister. Media outlets and journalists were physically attacked, often viciously, by Putin's henchmen. George W. Bush became the U.S. President and due to his lack of foreign policy experience, he brought in Dick Cheney as Vice President, Donald Rumsfeld as Secretary of Defense, and Colin Powell as Secretary of State, all experienced in foreign affairs (Karabell 1999). Shortly after, foreign affairs made a great shift due to a major event, 9/11, which profoundly affected the world.

In the 2012 United States Presidential election, Republican candidate Mitt Romney claimed that Russia was the biggest geopolitical threat to the country. Relations between the U.S. and Russia were tense but contained during the two terms of the Obama administration. During the 2016 Presidential campaign, Donald J. Trump seemed to signal a potential rewarming of relations with the country Ronald Reagan had called the "evil empire". However, on December 22, 2016, a month before taking office Trump tweeted that he believed there should be a proliferation of nuclear arms; on that same day Putin made the same announcement for his country. These comments seemed to send a marked change in nuclear relations between the countries. However, in subsequent months, President Trump repeatedly stated he wants relations with Russia to be mended. Currently, investigations by U.S. House and Senate committees and a special committee into Russia's involvement in the 2016 elections are ongoing.

The Terrorist Attacks of 9/11 and the Aftermath

On September 11, 2001, a group of terrorist hijackers took control of and guided two passenger jets into the World Trade Center ("twin towers") in New York City, and directed another plane into the Pentagon near Washington, D.C. Another plane was bound for a Washington target but crashed in

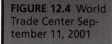

FIGURE 12.4 World Trade Center September 11, 2001

Source: Ken Tannenbaum/Shutterstock.com

southern Pennsylvania due to passengers who thwarted the attack. This tragic event, dubbed "9/11", killed nearly 3000 people, including people from 50 countries other than the United States. This terrorist attack heralded a new fear of terrorism throughout the country and the world. The attacks were carried out by a group led by Osama bin Laden from Saudi Arabia who fostered a hatred for the United States. The U.S. began military operations in Afghanistan and later Iraq on the claim that Saddam Hussein, the country's leader, had weapons of mass destruction (WMD), though the weapons were subsequently never found. America has continued operations in the Middle East to some extent since that time (LaFeber 2008).

Falk (2003), in explaining the harmful effects of the 9/11 attacks, an act which he terms "mega-terrorism", claims that not only did the attacks cause *substantive harm*—the loss of life reflected in the stories of the people in buildings, the emergency responders, the airline passengers, survivors, and observers; but also *symbolic harm*—the institutions attacked were "significant symbols" (Mead 1934) targeted for their symbolism: the World Trade Center, emblematic of America's economic power and the Pentagon, a sign of America's military power. The attacks on these targets revealed the mighty country's vulnerability to attacks of this type.

America's involvement in the Middle East has generated much controversy. Terrorist groups not only include the Taliban, Al-Qaeda, but a new group calling itself ISIS (or ISIL, or Daesh), which took over 30% of Syria and Iraq in 2014, financially supported by confiscated oil money, antiquities, and military equipment and bank takeovers. ISIS became the biggest threat of the Middle East, intimidating people through videotaped beheadings and other gruesome scenes; they continued to grow and take more territory despite an intensive bombing campaign by the United States and allies (Scharf 2016). Currently ISIS is a major global threat, not only in the Middle East but other areas. Many people who acted alone (often referred to as "lone wolves") or in small groups inspired by ISIS ideology attacked many international cities including Paris, Brussels, Nice, Turkey, Yemen, Berlin, and others, and in the American cities of San Bernardino, California; Orlando, Florida; and Columbus, Ohio. Al-Qaeda and ISIS represent a new type of military enemy—non-state actors with large financial resources, effective military training, and a sophisticated organizational structure, which require new strategies to combat them (Scharf 2016).

Effects of War on Returning Veterans

According to a study by Seal et al. (2007), among veterans from Operation Iraqi Freedom (OIF) who sought health care through the U.S. Department of Veterans Affairs (VA), 25% received were consequently diagnosed with a mental health disorder within their first couple of visits, and 56% of those diagnosed had two or more psychological disorders, with the majority of these diagnoses occurring at primary care facilities (Seal et al. 2007:478). The main predictor was age, with the youngest veterans (18–24) at the highest risk of developing Post Traumatic Stress Disorder (PTSD) and other disorders (Seal et al. 2007:480). Policy recommendations include earlier detection, especially for young returning veterans of combat, and evidence-based treatment in both VA and non-VA health care settings. Chronic mental illness in military veterans is an expensive public health burden and takes an immense toll on veterans and their families.

Should the military impose mandatory and immediate screening on all returning veterans deployed or engaged in combat for mental health disorders and provide individual mental health counseling, not just through the VA where there are enormous waits, but also through private health care facilities?

Pro: Immediate screening would provide detection and early interventions for returning veterans and should be mandatory considering the number of veterans who return with mental health disorders and if the VA does not have an immediate appointment, veterans should be able to utilize services at a private mental health facility.

Con: Mental health screening should be voluntary for returning veterans who have served our country since they are in the best position to know if they need help and should not be forced to undergo mental health screening since this could lead to stigma for veterans.

THEORETICAL PERSPECTIVES

Before we begin a description of the sociological explanations of terrorism and war, it might be helpful to look at psychological explanations, to express the micro as well as macro perspectives.

There have been many explorations into the psychological processes that contribute to war and some of the earliest ones give some insight into those of our own sociological examinations. Psychologist Carl Jung saw the "dark side" of individual personalities as contributing to war as they project the dark side images of evil onto others, whom they proclaim the enemy; Jung posited a collective unconscious in which archetypes of warriors and heroes, and these visualizations play into and support war imagery. Alfred Adler believed the inferiority complex of individuals results in them taking out aggressive acts onto others to deflect these feelings. For Harry Stack Sullivan, inhibited communication in individuals causes them to frantically strike out against others considered unlike them ("the other"). Erik Erikson believed the lack of healthy integration by family and society results in **totalism**, a pathologically obedient connection with the state along with a rejection of the selfhood of others, who one perceives as the enemy. Eric Fromm, a member of the Frankfurt School of critical theory, believed that certain leaders who exhibit authoritarian characteristics create conditions leading to war. Sigmund Freud was asked by Albert Einstein to elaborate his ideas on war in 1932 in which the founder of psychoanalysis famously replied in the essay "Why War?" that the apparent inhumanity of people that creates conflict and war is not actually inhumane and is, in fact, the result of the drive known as "Thanatos", the death instinct (Barash 2000).

> **Totalism** a pathologically obedient connection with the government that accompanies a rejection of the selfhood of others, who are perceived as the enemy.

Sociological theories move from the emphasis of individual perspectives of war to social perspectives that move from internal drives to external ones. The Big Three sociological perspectives approach the many facets of war and terrorism in a broad framework.

Structural Functionalism

Structural functionalists look at the ways in which military power can be beneficial in specific instances. Through intranational conflict, international norms are clarified and inculcated, and this is important since functionalists stress the value of cohesion, solidarity, and commonalities. And since most countries are inhabited by citizens from different racial, ethnic, and other backgrounds, conflict with other nations, including the threat of war or terrorism, can create a sense of "we-ness" that might have taken longer without this conflict. In addition, many technological advancements we enjoy today were created for use in the military.

Robert Park, an early American sociologist associated with the Chicago School, offered a functionalist perspective on war in a famous essay called "The Social Function of War" (1941). While not advocating war over diplomatic alternatives, he noted how certain unpopular social phenomena can be functional, in the same way Durkheim commented on the functions of crime. Park stated war aids in the eventual solving of intranational issues relating to boundaries and other national interests. War also creates cohesion and solidarity inside borders and can serve to create internal stability. The historical process of military engagement also hastened the creation of nation-states, forming national boundaries. Using Merton's analysis (mentioned throughout this text), all of these phenomena are arguably manifest or latent functions (you, the reader, can decide which of these are manifest or latent).

Sociologist Pitirim Sorokin sought to find the causes of war and in a content analysis revealed an extensive list of causes, however some were a bit extreme such as sunspots, planet alignment, and overpopulation. Sorokin sought answers by disrupting the multiple causation argument and instead making an exhaustive historical analysis of eighteen hundred years of war and using casualty data to indicate intensity. In analyzing war and peace, he posited that when nations have internally stable and agreed upon values and meanings, peace is the result; while when nations have weak or tenuous value consensus, conflict and war are the outcome (Johnston 1995). This seems unbelievably simplistic, especially since Sorokin's writings are difficult to penetrate, but it well reflects the structural functionalist perspective. The way to reduce war is to formulate a shared system of values. If only it were that easy!

Conflict

Conflict theorists note that military conflicts and terrorism create more than cohesion (contrasting the functionalist argument)—they also create destruction, devastation, and potentially genocide. "Might makes right" is not an acceptable means of dealing with international issues, according to this theoretical perspective. People go to war for a host of reasons and some of these involve such nefarious aims as taking land from other nations, obtaining resources such as oil or precious metals, and enslaving people, among others. Many propaganda campaigns deceive people into believing that war is justified, when in fact, it is not.

C. Wright Mills was very concerned about the consequences of military action and wrote extensively about war in his examinations of power in society. Consider this statement: "When wars happen, an insurance salesman becomes a rocket launcher; a store clerk a radar man; a wife lives alone; a child grows up without a father" (Mills 1959:3). Mills saw power in society as existing between three groups—the government, big business, and the military, a group he called the "power elite" (recall this from chapter 3). Members of this elite group hold power and move about in the higher circles of society—it is easy to see the earlier mentioned idea of the military-industrial complex with this idea. Mills (1958) tried to prepare us for the consequences of a devastating third world war—when "war becomes absurd and total" (Mills 1958:1).

Feminist groups have always been at the forefront of tackling many social ills, in addition to gender inequality. Boulding (2000) states that the skills women developed in dealing with social change, war, plagues, migration crises, and environmental/natural catastrophes have been transferred to improving lives of all people—this "global sisterhood" has extended to international conflicts and war. Regarding war, feminists are concerned with women being able to serve in the armed forces in roles equal to men and for years have pushed for women to receive combat roles and be able to progress in rank. Another concern to feminists (and hopefully many other groups and individuals) is the use of rape during periods of war and military upheaval that occurs around the globe.

Jane Addams exemplifies the ideal of an engaged sociologist and social worker striving to alleviate society's ills including sexism, poverty, racism, homelessness, child abuse, prostitution, and ethnocentrism, among others. Although probably remembered most for her settlement house in Chicago called Hull House, she was involved in several peace groups and conferences. Though her feminist writings are not as progressive as the ideals of second and third wave feminism (see chapter 6), her feminism takes the form of females as nurturers to society, as noted in this passage from *Women at The Hague*:

> women, who have brought men into the world and nurtured them until they reach the age for fighting, must experience a peculiar revulsion when they see them destroyed, irrespective of the country in which these men may have been born.
>
> (Addams, Balch, and Hamilton 1972:128)

This suggests Addams' idea that female strength lies in directing society down an appropriate path. War is not that path. A devoted pacifist, her pacifism was based on pragmatism in that war is an inefficient and wasteful use of resources to resolve conflict, in fact it simply worsens things. Addams turned to the biblical story of the prophet Isiah to explain her ideas on peace—people should focus on building plowshares and pruning hooks instead of swords, putting nature to its proper use (Lasch 1965).

Symbolic Interactionism

War is replete with symbolism such as flags and other national symbols; military uniforms; insignia noting military rank, unit, specialization, etc.; as well as peace signs or slogans such as "Hell no, we won't go" (to war, due to the draft). Interactionism focuses on these as well as emotions associated with the military such as feelings of patriotism and a sense of personal connection to the people in the branch, unit, and specialty area of the military. It also attends to socialization issues such as conformity to group norms, which is imperative to the objectives of the military.

Military institutions are structured around the idea of solidarity, augmented by the symbols mentioned above—if a unit is not cohesive, it is inefficient for use in military engagements. Some people are normally socialized from a very early age to not harm others, it is necessary for the military to re-socialize people to potentially kill other people; this function is normally fulfilled by boot camps that strip new recruits of a personal identity to adopt a collective one, exposes them to degradation ceremonies, encourages patriotism, and prepares them to go to war. Boot camps are what Goffman (1961) called total institutions (we should recall this from earlier discussions).

FIGURE 12.5 Iwo Jima Memorial in Washington, DC on March 20, 2012. The Memorial honors the Marines who have died defending the US since 1775.

Source: EastVillage Images/Shutterstock.com

Labeling also has a place in military operations. People obviously receive labels signifying rank, branch, unit, etc. but the label of "enemy" is equally important, especially during wartime. Labeling the enemy, often supplemented with stereotypes, creates the idea that the opponent is subhuman, defective, and ready to do harm to citizens, country, or way of life. The labeling process makes it easier to perform acts, including torture, denigration, and other acts, including deadly ones, that are counter to how most people are socialized.

SEARCHING FOR SOLUTIONS

This section will focus primarily on possible strategies in controlling terrorist activity. Solutions for the control of war and sustained military activity are much more complex and beyond the scope of this text; indeed, people have debated war for centuries and while peace is normally a goal, some conditions necessitate entering military conflict—one can only speculate on the outcome, for example, if the United States and its allies did not intervene in what would become World War II. We will direct our attention instead to terrorism and its potential solutions.

As a strategy of the federal government, the Department of Homeland Security (DHS) was formed just after the 9/11 attacks and was a significant undertaking by the government to prevent other attacks on the "homeland" (DHS 2016). It was not fully supported by all members of the George W. Bush administration as it entailed the creation of a large governmental bureaucracy but it was legislated in 2002 and officially promulgated the following year. Seeking to prevent many potential effects of terrorism such as cyber-attacks, pandemics created by humans, infrastructure problems, illegal travel, and others (May, Jochim, and Sapotichne 2011), the DHS, according to its website, has at its core a single goal—keeping Americans safe. The website also states the primary focus of the organization is its original concern: terrorism. DHS offers several initiatives that seek to protect the country's borders (such as screening travelers), and some that involve reporting suspicious activity by communities and organizations (such as the "if you see something, say something" campaign) (DHS 2016). Curtailing terrorist activity, especially through enhanced (or even aggressive) surveillance, has resulted in concerns over the loss of civil liberties and racial/ethnic profiling. According to the American Civil Liberties Union (ACLU), the government's efforts to curb terrorism intrude on the private communication of innocent citizens, through both surveillance and collecting sensitive information that is put into "watchlists" that have had severe negative consequences for innocent Americans, such as questioning, harassment and/or detention by authorities and even indefinite bans on travel (ACLU 2017). They contend that this is not a solution, and have called for surveillance reform under the rationale that this level of surveillance runs counter to our constitutional values and includes unwarranted surveillance targeted at religious minorities, critics of the government, and historically marginalized groups.

Enhanced Interrogation aggressive information gathering techniques used on terrorism suspects.

The use of torture as a strategy of information gathering from terrorism suspects has been a controversial one. Euphemistically dubbed **enhanced interrogation,** or aggressive interrogation, this tactic is used by the Central Intelligence Agency (CIA) and has become a prominent strategy particularly since the 9/11 terror attacks. Questions about whether the action was torture, along with questions of its efficacy, became a part of the national discussion on the matter. For substantiation of the controversial nature of the activity, Vice President Dick Cheney, who incidentally

Should the government have the right to surveil and collect international emails and phone calls without a warrant?

Pro: If international communication surveillance will reduce terrorism against Americans the government should gather and use this information to fight terrorism.
Con: The government should not surveil international emails and phone calls since this infringes on the rights of innocent people and discriminates against individuals who have ties to other countries.

supported the techniques, described the interrogation methods as those that work "within the shadows" and "in the dark side". Procedures such as face slaps, water dowsing, physical exertion, psychological humiliation, sleep deprivation, and in some cases serious beatings were reported. Certain controls were included in the facilitation of the interrogations such as having physicians present, monitoring caloric and water intake levels, controlling noise levels, and monitoring water temperatures (Chwastiak 2015)—controls that keep the activity from going "too far". One interrogation technique that drew much attention was waterboarding, in which a suspect is placed on his back, has a cloth placed over his face, and is dowsed with water, creating the sensation of drowning and eliciting profound psychological anxiety.

Are enhanced interrogation techniques an effective means of fighting terrorism?

Pro: Enhanced interrogation deters other possible terrorist activity and the information gathered can help save many American lives.
Con: Enhanced interrogation is torture and makes our country appear extremist and violent.

Theriault, Krause, and Young (2017) suggest that the greatest barriers to implementing programs to counteract terrorism have been the hatred of terrorist groups, which is welcomed by these groups as it seems to invite retaliation through increased terroristic activity. Traditional strategies at prejudice reduction (which primarily used research findings of marginalized groups rather than much more serious extremist groups) aimed at terrorists have not proved successful. An advanced educational program which seeks to better understand the motivations of terrorists, or "knowing our enemies", and understanding the effects of labels on attitudes toward these groups reduces levels of fear and prejudice and could effectively decrease the incidence of terrorist activity.

In response to the "homegrown terrorists", American terrorists who promote terrorism in America and operate independently of large foreign terrorist organizations, the behavior-analysis method utilized by the Federal Bureau of Investigation seeks to prevent terrorist acts from occurring (Tierney 2017). People who have been radicalized into ideologies that support violent extremist activity are observed by the FBI's Behavioral Analysis Unit who seek to deter the pathway to violence through an analytic strategy that examines the process of what is often termed radicalization. According to data from George

Source: nito/Shutterstock.com

FIGURE 12.6
Terrorist organizations continue to cause loss of life and steep financial damage to the economy.

Should prejudice reduction programs about terrorist groups be promoted through education programs?

Pro: These programs will promote a better understanding of terrorist groups and this understanding will decrease terrorism.
Con: These programs simply encourage terrorism by making our nation appear weak and unwilling to actively confront it.

Washington University's Program on Extremism (2017), the majority of individuals charged with terrorist involvement related to the Islamic State (also known as ISIS) were U.S. citizens or permanent residents. Understanding the difficulty in ascertaining information about potential "lone wolves", a partnership of community players such as religious groups, mental health providers, academics, other governments, other security services, and community and family members could receive training in the radicalization process and how to report suspicious activity without employing racial or ethnic profiling. Increased training by line police officers and other law enforcement personnel of the radicalization process and how to interview potential terrorism suspects, could deter homegrown terrorism.

Terrorist organizations are often well-financed from a variety of illegal and legal means to be able to continue their activity; included in these are smuggling, trafficking, money laundering, fraud, corruption, and commodity trading. In addition to loss of life and the effects of fear on populations, financial damage that results from terrorism can be vast. And for that reason, government–business partnerships could assist in terrorism control. Businesses provide services and products such as security services (including surveillance and data security), defense products (such as bullet-proof glass, weapon detection devices, architectural safeguards) and governments, at various levels, can provide jobs, intelligence-sharing, and emergency services to communities (Alexander 2004). While emergency services have been a link between public–private partnerships for some time, these measures offer a reactive approach to terrorism; perhaps more proactive strategies such as those listed above will provide better protection to communities.

CHAPTER SUMMARY

- Terrorism has affected the way America, indeed the world, has functioned, especially since the 9/11 terrorist attacks on the World Trade Center and the Pentagon (major symbols of American power). Connected to the concept of war, which is broad and encompasses many types of military action, is the activity called terrorism, which is more focused and rejects traditional means of warfare. War has changed due to the motivations of the various actors and to technological advancements.

- Sociology has been deficient in developing a sociological analysis of war and other types of military conflict. The discipline's use of the sociological imagination can be beneficial in examining the causes and effects of war and terrorism. Power, in the forms of both hard and soft power, are also important areas of analysis for sociologists. Also, the opposite of war—peace—is an area worthy of sociological examination, despite complaints of it being utopian, thus impossible to achieve.

- Changes in terrorist activity include the use of technology in the forms of cyber activity, biotechnology, and robotic technology. A socio-history of war and terrorism which includes relations with countries such as Russia, as well as post-9/11 relations gives an understanding of America's relationships with other nations today and the potential problems, as well as improved relations we might face ahead.

- While psychology offers internal motivations for military conflict, sociology focuses on larger scale patterns of group relations. Structural functionalists note how military hostilities with outside groups create cohesion inside borders; conflicts also force resolution of differences. Conflict theorists emphasize the destructive nature of military conflict and explore the financial and power-based motivations of war. Symbolic interactionists observe how symbols promote ingroup pride and outgroup hate and provide symbols of status and rank to those actively involved in war related activity.

- Solutions and strategies for acts of terrorism include the formation of the Department of Homeland Security which went into effect in 2003 and seeks to protect the homeland from terroristic activity. The government also implemented techniques of information extraction called enhanced interrogation, a strategy that has been considered by many to be torture. Prejudice reduction strategies aimed specifically at terrorist organizations have been suggested as a means of reducing fear and possible retaliation. The FBI's behavioral analysis unit works to prevent homegrown terrorism by involving communities to spot and report potential terrorists. Also, public–private partnerships between governments and private industry can thwart terrorism by using proactive strategies.

REFERENCES

Addams, Jane, Emily Balch, and Alice Hamilton. 1972. *Women at The Hague: The International Congress of Women and Its Results.* New York and London: Garland Publications, Inc.

Alexander, Dean C. 2004. *Business Confronts Terrorism: Risks and Responses.* Madison, WI: The University of Wisconsin Press.

American Civil Liberties Union. 2017. Privacy and Surveillance. Retrieved July 31, 2017 (www.aclu.org/issues/national-security/privacy-and-surveillance).

Barash, David P. 2000. "Why War: Sigmund Freud." *Approaches to Peace: A Reader in Peace Studies.* New York and Oxford: Oxford University Press. Pp. 9–13.

Boulding, Elise. 2000. *Cultures of Peace: The Hidden Side of History.* Syracuse, NY: Syracuse University Press.

Chailiand, Gerard. 2014. *A Global History of War: From Assyria to the Twenty-First Century.* Translated by Michele Mangin-Woods and David Woods. Berkeley: University of California Press.

Chwastiak, Michele. 2015. "Torture as Norman Work: The Bush Administration, the Central Intelligence Agency and 'Enhanced Interrogation Techniques'." *Organization.* 22(4): 493–511. Retrieved July 26, 2017 (http://research.flagler.edu:10958/doi/pdf/10.1177/135 0508415572506).

Clausewitz, Carl von. 1968. *On War.* Middlesex, England: Penguin Books.

Creveld, Martin van. 1999. "War: Nature of War." In John Whiteclay Chambers II, *The Oxford Companion to American Military History.* Oxford: Oxford University Press.

Department of Homeland Security. 2016. "Preventing Terrorism." Retrieved July 26, 2017 (www.dhs.gov/preventing-terrorism).

Falk, Robert. 2003. *The Great Terror War.* New York: Olive Branch Press.

George Washington University. 2017. "GW Extremism Tracker: ISIS in America." Retrieved July 31, 2017 (https://extremism.gwu.edu/isis-america).

Goffman, Erving. 1961. *Asylums: Essays on the Social Situation of Mental Patients and Other Inmates.* Garden City, NY: Anchor Books.

Johnston, Barry V. 1995. *Pitirim A. Sorokin: An Intellectual Biography.* Lawrence, KS: University Press of Kansas.

Kaag, John and Sarah Kreps. 2014. *Drone Warfare.* Cambridge: Polity Press.

Karabell, Zachary. 1999. "Cold War (1945–91): External Course." In John Whiteclay Chambers II, *The Oxford Companion to American Military History.* Oxford: Oxford University Press.

LaFeber, Walter. 2008. *America, Russia, and the Cold War: 1945–2006.* Boston: McGraw-Hill.

Lasch, Christopher. 1965. "Peace." In Christopher Lasch, *The Social Thought of Jane Addams.* Indianapolis, IN: Bobbs-Merrill CO. Pp. 218–261.

Malesevic, Sinisa. 2014. "Is War Becoming Obsolete? A Sociological Analysis." *The Sociological Review.* 62 (82): 65–86. Retrieved June 11, 2017 (http://research.flagler.edu:9838/eds/pdfviewer/pdfviewer?vid=1&sid=6969d2d1-58fd-404f-8c26-a144dc53addc%40sessionmgr102). doi:10.1111/1467–954X.12192.

Manning, Matthew J. 2015. "Establishing a Comprehensive Definition of Terrorism." *Public Lawyer.* 23 (2): 8–13. Retrieved July 26, 2017 (http://research.flagler.edu:9838/eds/detail/detail?vid=1&sid=0eae6bb7-bed0-4d9b-9e69-c02d1478ca6a%40sessionmgr101&bdata=JnNpd GU9ZWRzLWxpdmUmc2NvcGU9c2l0 ZQ%3d%3d#AN=109454025&db=lgs).

May, Peter J., Ashley E. Jochim, and Joshua Sapotichne. 2011. "Constructing Homeland: An Anemic Policy Regime." *Policy Studies Journal.* 39 (2): 285–307. Retrieved July 26, 2017 (http://research.flagler.edu:9838/eds/detail/detail?vid=0&sid=3f45e3c3-53b2-4c9e-ac0dcf4873643fa2%40sessionmgr103&bdata=JnNpdGU9ZWRzLWxpdmUmc2NvcGU9c2l0ZQ%3d%3d#AN=60313782&db=buh).

McSorley, Kevin. 2014. "Towards an Embodied Sociology of War." *The Sociological Review.* 62 (82): 107–128. Retrieved June 11, 2017 (http://research.flagler.edu:9838/eds/pdfviewer/pdfviewer?vid=1&sid=39a0317b-5e9c-4634-82ee-f56972ea7f4d%40sessionmgr103).doi: 10.1111/1467–954X.12194.

Mead, George Herbert. 1934. *Mind, Self, and Society.* Chicago: University of Chicago Press.

Mills, C. Wright. 1958. *The Causes of World War Three.* New York: Simon Schuster.

Mills, C. Wright. 1959. *The Sociological Imagination.* New York: Oxford University Press.

Morganthau, Hans. 1972. "From Great Powers to Superpowers." In Brian Porter. *International Politics 1919–1969.* London: Oxford University Press.

Park, Robert E. 1941. "The Social Function of War: Observations and Notes." *American Journal of Sociology.* 46 (4): 551–570. Retrieved March 10, 2017 (http://www.jstor.org/stable/2769923).

Roxborough, Ian. 1994. "Clausewitz and the Sociology of War." *The British Journal of Sociology.* 45 (4): 619–636. Retrieved March 9, 2017 (www.jstor.org/stable/591886).

Scharf, Michael. 2016. "How the War Against ISIS Changed International Law." *Case Western Reserve Journal of International Law.* 48 (1/2): 15–67. Retrieved June 11, 2017 (http://research.flagler.edu:9839/eds/pdfviewer/pdfviewer?vid=1&sid=1eca3390-fad7-454a-824d-d0eb3a3de607%-40sessionmgr4008).

Seal, Karen H., Daniel Bertenthal, Christian R. Miner, Saunak Sen, and Charles Marmar. 2007. "Bringing the War Back Home: Mental Health Disorders among 103,788 US Veterans Returning from Iraq and Afghanistan seen at Department of Veterans Affairs Facilities." *Archives of Internal Medicine.* 167 (5): 476–482. doi:10.1001/archinte.167.5.476.

Smelser, Neil J. 2007. *The Faces of Terrorism: Social and Psychological Dimensions.* Princeton, NJ: Princeton University Press.

Smith, Martin A. 2012. *Power in the Changing Global Order: The U.S., Russia, and China.* Cambridge: Polity Press.

Taslaman, Caner, and Feryal Taslaman. 2013–2014. "Contemporary Just War Theory: Paul Ramsey and Michael Walzer." *Journal of Academic Studies.* 15 (59): 1–20. Retrieved June 12, 2017 (http://research.flagler.edu:9838/eds/pdfviewer/pdfviewer?vid=1&sid=711bb8e6-4fe8-421e-8dea-bd4c9fbed5f5%40sessionmgr104).

Theriault, Jordan, Peter Krause, and Liane Young. 2017. "Know Thy Enemy: Education About Terrorism Improves Social Attitudes Toward Terrorists." *Journal of Experimental Psychology: General.* 146 (3): 305–317. Retrieved July 26, 2017 (http://research.flagler.edu:9838/eds/pdfviewer/pdfviewer?vid=1&sid=5f98c0c4-161d-4576-ad06-27553eaed643%40sessionmgr102).

Tierney, Michael. 2017. "Using Behavioral Analysis to Prevent Violent Extremism: Assessing the Cases of Michael Zehaf-Bibeau and Aaron Driver." *Journal of Threat Assessment and Management.* 4 (2): 98–110. Retrieved July 26, 2017 (http://research.flagler.edu:9839/eds/pdfviewer/pdfviewer?vid=1&sid=2fcb13d4-7698-40bb-a699-8fcf0881ed1a%40sessionmgr4007).

Tollefson, James. 1994. "Conscientious Objection to the Vietnam War." *OAH Magazine of History.* 8 (3): 75–82. Retrieved March 20, 2017 (www.jstor.org/stable/25162969).

Wills, Brandon, Jerrold B. Leikin, James Rhee, Chad Tamelingd, and Bijan Saeedie. 2008. "Analysis of Suspicious Powders Following the Post 9/11 Anthrax Scare." *Journal of Medical Toxicology*. 4(2):93–95. Retrieved June 12, 2017 (http://research.flagler.edu:9839/eds/pdfviewer/pdfviewer?vid=1&sid=5b72d8fc-9fab-4b69-b701-9f525a6ab928%40sessionmgr4008).

Wittes, Benjamin and Gabriella Blum. 2015. *The Future of Violence: Robots and Germs, Hackers and Drones; Confronting a New Age of Threat*. New York: Basic Books.

CHAPTER 13

Population

ABOUT THE PROBLEM: POPULATION

Approaches to Understanding Population Studies

Demography, a specialized sub-field within sociology, is the study of human populations. Demographers study changes in **population** over time; specifically they study changes in composition and size of populations. This encompasses several domains: fertility and birth rates, mortality and death rates, migration into and out of countries. In this chapter, we will focus on these three areas, with a special focus on the effect of an increasingly elderly population that has changed the composition of the United States. Let us look at how each of these topics fit into the larger study of social problems.

> **Demography** sub-field within sociology that studies human populations.
>
> **Population** a group of humans that inhabit the same geographic area.

Fertility and Birth Rates

Populations all begin with fertility and births. **General fertility rates** (also referred to as birth rates) are the number of live births for every 1,000 women of childbearing age (generally considered 15–44 years old) in a population during a given year. Another commonly used measure of fertility is **total fertility rates**, the number of children a woman in a given society can expect to give birth to during her lifetime. In the Unites States, both general and total fertility rates have changed a great deal over time. In 1911, women had almost 3.5 births, by 1935 and the Great Depression, the number of births per woman declined to almost two. During the post–World War II Baby Boom, a time of rapid economic growth, rates increased swiftly to the highest of the twentieth century, at almost 3.5 births per woman. It then declined during the 1970s energy crisis, where they leveled off in the

> **General Fertility Rates** number of live births per 1,000 women in a country.
>
> **Total Fertility Rate** the number of children a woman can expect to have over her lifetime.

1980s, then dipped slightly during the Great Recession, but have stayed slightly below two births per woman over the past few decades.

Interestingly, there is a clear decrease in fertility rates for the largest racial and ethnic groups, including Latinas, Black non-Hispanics, and Asian Americans. The biggest drop has been among Latinos and Black non-Hispanics. This is driving the decreasing rates in the United States since over half the of all U.S. births are to racial and ethnic minorities and may be attributed to relatively high unemployment rates, lower incomes, and less education in these two groups (Mather 2012).

Long term trends in fertility are driven by broader societal forces such as economic development, employment rates, cultural norms, women's education, and access to quality birth control. In general, U.S. total fertility rates have declined since 1990 but not to the levels in many areas of Europe where fertility is so low, the population is decreasing. Tracking fertility trends is important since it provides data on future labor shortages, economic growth, and whether there will be enough adults to care for a larger aging population, and long term, whether a country's total population will decrease or increase. **Replacement fertility rates**, the number of births needed to keep a population stable, is 2.1 births per woman, and varies depending on mortality rates (Mather, 2012). The highest fertility rates are in the least developed countries, where **infant mortality rates**, babies who die before they reach one year of age, are highest as well. For example, the highest fertility rates are in Middle and Western Africa, where the following countries average about six live births per woman: Niger, Somalia, Malia, Burundi, and Uganda. The second highest rate, outside Africa, is in Afghanistan (5.2) (CIA 2016). In contrast, in countries such as Spain, Austria, Germany, Italy, Greece, Japan, Poland, Taiwan, and Singapore, fertility are only 1.5 and as low as 0.8 (Singapore), which is considerably lower than replacement fertility rates. This poses population challenges for both high fertility countries and low fertility countries.

A classic example of the consequences of below replacement fertility in Europe is occurring in Germany. According to European 2017 data collected by Eurostat, the German population has declined for over a generation and is predicted to decline another 7.7% by 2050 (this does not take into account the recent migration influx of 2015 and 2016). Data from Eurostat found that Germany currently has the lowest proportion of young people (13.2%), compared to any other country in Europe and one of the highest proportions of people aged 65 and older (21.15). Together, these trends are a serious cause for concern since Germany is already below replacement fertility levels (1.4) and with a growing older population and shrinking younger population the country will continue to get older in terms of age composition (Eurostat 2017). This will likely lead to economic decline in Germany and many European countries that are experiencing the same fertility declines, alongside higher life expectancy. Factors driving economic decline in countries with this type of demographic shift include: a lack of young labor which drives wages higher and often leads to outsourcing, lower rates of innovation since technological change tends to occur when workers are younger, and a rise in the percentage of retirees as compared to the percentage of working age people in the population. In addition, consumer spending will decline since aging populations purchase less than young populations with families. Together, these social and economic factors will constrain the economy and working age adults will shoulder the increasing financial burden to provide social services to a growing aging population.

Replacement Fertility Rates the number of births needed by each woman to keep a population stable.

Infant Mortality the death of children who are less than one year of age; the infant mortality rate is the number of these deaths per 1000 live births.

Mortality

On the other end of the life course is mortality. **Mortality** simply refers to the number of deaths in a given population. Demographers measure mortality using either the **crude death rate**, number of deaths per 1,000 people in a given year, or calculate it by adjusting for the age distribution in a population, which is known as the **age adjusted death rates** for a population given age distribution. For example, countries with a large elderly population are going to have higher mortality than countries with a larger young population, so adjusting for age gives researchers a more accurate picture of mortality rates in a population.

Why do we need an entire sub-field dedicated to studying death? After all, everybody dies, so it is not as if one can prevent it. However, mortality research is how we investigate how and why people die and the unequal distribution of excess mortality by race, gender, and other demographic factors. For example, in the United States, African American men live shorter lives than any other race/ethnic group, and generally die an average of four years younger than white men, while Asian Americans live the longest, with an average life span of 86.5 years as compared to 78.9 years for whites (Kaiser Foundation 2009). These types of racial disparities are indicative of larger societal problems that create disadvantages across the life course which result in premature death for marginalized groups. By better understanding trends in mortality, and how they change over time, we can determine why some sub-groups live longer than others, which diseases are most likely to lead to early death and tease out societal health inequalities by gender, race, ethnicity, and even sexual orientation. With this data, public health policy can target the groups that are most likely to suffer from diseases and pathologies that lead to earlier death, and focus on interventions for improving the health of these marginalized groups.

Mortality the number of deaths in a population.

Crude Death Rate number of deaths per 1,000 people in a population over a year.

Age Adjusted Death Rate number of deaths by age in a population over a year.

FIGURE 13.1 April 25, 2014 Sisters Ella May Factoranan, 13 and Krizna Factoranan, 10 and their friends visit the grave of family members killed during Typhoon Haiyan (Yolanda) at a mass grave in Dulag, Philippines on April 25, 2014. The sisters lost over 30 members of their family to the storm. The official reported number of deceased is 8,000 while the unofficial number reported by relief workers on the ground is closer to 20,000.

Source: Dana Romanoff/Getty Images

Migration Trends

Migration the movement of people into and out of specific countries or regions.

The third major area of study in population research is migration. **Migration** is the movement of people into and out of specific countries or regions. There are two main types of migration: in-migration and out-migration. In-migration rates, also known as immigration, are calculated by the number of people who move into a region per 1,000 people already in the region over a given period. Out-migration rates, also referred to as emigration, are the number of people leaving a country or region per 1,000 people in the region. Calculating migration rates is important since this is the only way to compare whether more people are immigrating to or emigrating from a country, state, or geographic area. Of course, every state, county, and city has people flowing into and out of it every year. Some of this is domestic migration—people relocate to other cities or states for family, employment opportunities, lower cost of living, and other factors. And some of the migration is international—people move into and out of the United States every year as well. The reasons behind international migration are more complex—in-migration is often for family reunification (people joining family already in the United States), for higher education, and for employment opportunities. Tracking net-migration rates over time reveals which states are growing or diminishing in population, the countries of origin for international migrants, as well as where people reside when they move to the United States. This gives policy makers a broader picture of which cities may become over-crowded, which states are likely to suffer economically (from a great deal of out-migration), and other population level trends (Connor 2016).

In 2015 and 2016 Europe experienced the largest mass movement of people since World War II. With an influx of over one million migrants and refugees, mainly Syrians, Afghans, and Iraqis fleeing

FIGURE 13.2
Refugees from Syria make the often deadly voyage to Europe on an overcrowded raft. This photo is purposefully unfocused to protect the anonymity of these individuals fleeing for their lives.

Source: Fishman64 / Shutterstock.com

from violence in their countries, this quickly became a crisis for many countries in Europe. According to data, more than a million migrants and refugees crossed into Europe in 2015 alone (European Commission 2016). The scale of people is especially problematic in countries such as Greece, where their own economic crisis has left them unable to accommodate thousands of migrants who arrive with very few, if any, resources. The European country with the largest number of migrants, over one million in 2015 alone, is Germany. In contrast, Hungary has had the highest surge of migrants seeking asylum in proportion to its smaller population, with Sweden following close behind. Tensions have mounted in Germany for citizens who feel the government has lost control of the refugee crisis. Attacks on refugee shelters have become common, with over 1,000 attacks by German citizens in 2015 (European Commission 2016). The number of refugees has overwhelmed many of Germany's social institutions. Schools, for example, have experienced a shortage of teachers with so many new students, and specifically educators who train to work with refugee children.

The Demographic Transition

Population growth globally, coupled with a large and growing older population is a cause for concern. Population growth and aging populations in developing countries are in large part driven by economic growth and improved standards of living. The population structure in the least developed countries are generally quite young since people do not live as long, in large part because they die of infectious diseases. For example, according to the World Health Organization (WHO) in 2017, the average life expectancy in Sierra Leone is about 50 years. The leading causes of death in Sierra Leone and other least developed countries in Western Africa are from infectious and parasitic diseases such as AIDS-related diseases, respiratory tract infections, diarrhea, and malaria. Infant mortality is high, pneumonia is the leading cause of death for children, and women are more likely to die during childbirth. In contrast, in the United States and Europe people live much longer and they are more likely to die of chronic diseases that generally occur later in life, for example stroke, cardiovascular disease, and cancer.

There are four stages to the **demographic transition** that every country has undergone or is currently undergoing. The first stage is a stable population with births and deaths balanced out since people generally die younger and infant mortality is high. The population is not increasing or decreasing. In the second stage, the population grows very quickly and there are far more births than deaths. During this second stage advances in public health provide clean drinking water, better sanitation, nutrition, and medical care. Basically, innovations in public health makes it possible for individuals to live longer, fewer children and mothers die during childbirth, and infant mortality decreases. However, during the second stage, the birth rate is still very high, and the composition of the population is still young. People are still dying from infectious diseases like AIDS and the Ebola virus. In the third stage shifts in culture and behavior, along with medical innovations, more education, access to birth control, and other technological changes that drive economic growth lead to a decrease in birth rates and the population begins to stabilize again over time. In the fourth phase of the demographic transition, the age composition changes again, since now older people far outnumber new births, and this can lead to a shrinking population. Examples of regions in stage four are the United States, most of Europe, and Canada. In contrast, most of sub-Saharan Africa, Asia, and Latin America are still moving through the transition (Bongaarts 2009).

> **Demographic Transition** the shift in population growth patterns from high fertility and mortality rates to lower fertility and higher life expectancy.

Most of the growth in the world's population occurs in less developed countries. India, China, and much of Africa are experiencing rapid population growth. According to data from the United Nations (UN) 2017 Population Prospectus, China currently has the largest population (1.4 billion), and India has the second largest with 1.3 billion inhabitants. However, this data also predicts that India's population will exceed China's population by 2024 and Nigeria will continue to be the most rapidly growing of the world's ten largest countries, and move from the seventh largest country to the third largest country by 2050. According to Lehmann and Ninkovic (2013), this could lead to food shortages, especially in countries such as India where there is already a food problem driven by insufficient infrastructure (such as road networks and transportation), the use of outdated subsistence level farming, and challenges with water and energy due to industrialization and urbanization. In many areas of Sub-Saharan Africa children suffer disproportionately from malnutrition which leads to stunting in their physical and cognitive growth. Food insecurity, hunger, and death from diarrhea and polluted drinking water are quite common. As the population continues to increase in developing countries this problem will expand in scope and importance.

Trends in Population Aging in the United States

A decline in fertility coupled with an increase in life expectancy causes population aging to occur. According to the Centers for Disease Control (CDC 2014), in 2011 life expectancy at birth in the United States was 76.3 years for males and 81.1 years for females. Longer life expectancy combined with the aging of the U.S. population is one of the most important demographic shifts of the

FIGURE 13.3 Longer life expectancy and declines in fertility have created a demographic shift in the age composition of our society.

Source: Sira Anamwong/Shutterstock.com

twenty-first century. According to 2014 U.S. Census projections, life expectancy will continue to increase and the population of adults aged 65 and older is projected to almost double by 2050—from 43.1 million in 2012 to 83.7 million in 2050, with the aging baby boom cohort and immigration trends driving most of this change. By 2050, 22% of the U.S. population will be composed of adults aged 65 and over (Arias 2010). And within the older population the share of individuals 85 and older, known as the oldest-old, is growing more rapidly than the overall older population itself, with this segment projected to triple from 2012 to 2040 (U.S. Census Bureau 2014). The U.S. Census (2014) projects that the population of the oldest old will grow from 5.9 million in 2012 to 8.9 million in 2030. This group requires considerably more care and public expenditures on health care, disablement, long term care, and other social services. With life expectancies continuing to rise, this is an issue that will be especially challenging since they are the most vulnerable group of older Americans. These individuals need high levels of caretaking; at the same time, they are more likely to live alone, since at this age a large percentage of the elderly are female and widowed. Thus, the demographic profile of the rapidly aging elder population holds diverse concerns regarding the unique needs and/or challenges that arise at different ages.

When examining an age composition in which older people are the weighted majority, very specific challenges arise. Over the next couple of decades nearly a quarter of the U.S. population will be at retirement ages and will most likely rely on pensions, social security, Medicare, and other social programs for older people which will put a considerable economic strain on the economy. At the same time, there will be fewer people in the paid labor market with the mass exodus of older workers and low fertility rates that, together, will quite likely lead to labor shortages in many industries. Spending on health care will increase as will spending on social benefits programs for the elderly. If the government diverts spending on education, infrastructure, and other areas important for economic growth to finance social programs for the elderly, it could also have far reaching consequences on the fiscal and economic stability of U.S. society.

Although women have longer life expectancies than men, they spend more years with disability that makes daily living and mobility challenging. They are more likely to live many years with chronic illnesses, and are more likely to live alone since they live longer than men (Crimmins, Hayward, and Saito 1996). Further compounding this problem, the older population will become increasingly varied with regard to race/ethnicity and nativity (Hummer et al. 2013). For example, the proportion of older Hispanics (65+) is projected to increase from 7% in 2010 to 19.8% in 2050. And the older Asian population will nearly triple from 3.4% to nearly 9% (U.S. Census Bureau 2014). Thus, adults aged 65 and older will compose a more diverse population than any cohort preceding them in terms of both race/ethnicity and nativity. A recent study by Melvin and colleagues (2014), found that severe disability at older ages is significantly higher for Mexican born female immigrants and female African Americans, when compared to white females. These marginalized populations are also more likely to need government assistance for long term care since they have historically had fewer resources and less savings for retirement than their white female counterparts. The burden for subsidizing the high health care and assisted living costs for racial/ethnic minorities will be costly for taxpayers, and will be a burden on the resources of informal support systems, such as adult children who will experience serious challenges saving for retirement when they are caretaking elderly family members and paying for expensive medications and in-home care while they work.

Trends in Global Population Aging

Population aging is not just a challenge in the United States. This is a global phenomenon and it will accelerate in the next few decades. Population aging started in Europe, in large part because this was the first area to enter the demographic transition and thus fertility rates declined while longevity increased in the late nineteenth and early twentieth centuries (United Nations 2016). The result is that the European population is currently the oldest in the world with 24% of the population age 60 or older (United Nations 2016). The United States has the second largest older population globally, followed by Latin America and the Caribbean third, and Asia. Global aging presents serious concerns, especially in highly populated countries in south Asia where 508 million people were over the age of 60 in 2015, which translates to half the global older population residing in Asia, even while its aging population continues to increase (United Nations 2016).

The aging population in Asian countries suffers due to low levels of childbearing, especially in China, Hong Kong, Singapore, South Korea, Taiwan, and Thailand. Many of the elderly have two or fewer children to care for them, and this will quite likely drive increased expenditures on healthcare spending in countries such as Japan and South Korea. In Asian countries that are less developed, aging is occurring much faster than economic growth. This will likely translate to inadequate care for seniors since they lack efficient health care programs, sufficient amount of long-term care facilities and social programs designed to care for their increasingly elderly population. In addition, these countries are still facing higher levels of infectious diseases such as HIV/AIDS, drug resistant tuberculosis, and malaria in their population (East West Center 2017). Global aging will continue to increase over the next few decades, mostly in less developed countries where people have histori-cally relied on informal support systems such as living with family members who will care for them, in addition to their savings and assets. With people living longer there will be an increased need for social programs to care for the elderly in these countries as well as new health care challenges since the needs of an aging population are quite different than those of a younger population. Unfortu-nately, many less developed countries are ill-equipped to deal with the challenges and expenses of a rapidly aging population.

Should the United States step in and control fertility rates in developing countries where women are having an average of six children over their lifetime and there is a high rate of hunger and malnutrition, and babies born with HIV?

Pro: This will prevent thousands of deaths each year and will also increase the health of women and children and thus a healthier population. Ultimately, it will also help these countries go through the demographic transition faster.

Con: Interfering in another country's population problems, even if it saves the lives of thousands of infants, children, and women, could have unintended consequences that are negative. We should let these countries figure out their own solutions.

THEORETICAL PERSPECTIVES

Structural Functionalism

As noted throughout the text, the main concern of functionalist thought is with the effect of social facts, in this case increasing population and demographic changes, on the major social institutions (economy, government, religion, education, and family). As changes occur in populations, economies must adapt to accommodate to the changing needs of citizens, and their governments, and religions must change to address the myriad variations that result from a diversifying population, and the educational system must adapt to preparing a changing workforce and provide intellectual advancement of its citizens. Families are especially important in the sociology of population and demography because the primary role of bringing new people into the world falls to this institution. These institutions must grapple with the problems mentioned earlier—employment/unemployment, mortality issues, food insecurity, access to clean water, and the challenges of an aging population, among others. Structural functionalism is an evolutionary theory and observes how social institutions must change and adapt as needed to population and demographic changes—if the social institutions adequately perform their purposes in conjunction with these changes, the society will be functional for its members.

The seventeenth century population theorist Thomas Malthus believed that as the availability of food increases, there will be a responding increase in population, however, the increase in population will be held in check by war, famine, and other disasters. For generations, Malthusian ideas continued to produce grave concerns for scholars of population. Sociologist E.A. Ross, writing at the turn of the twentieth century, posited there were other events that Malthus did not foresee, such as democracy and women's emancipation that would provide this function of keeping populations under control. Other theorists sought to revive the "Malthusian trap" by suggesting that abundant food supplies or cheap food prices would do the trick; however, when these alternatives are exhausted, overpopulation concerns will reappear (Furedi 1997). In these cases, there is an idea of an evolutionary process operating in conjunction with institutional forces; these are forces that keep social problems from occurring due to population changes.

Conflict Theory

As populations change, they do not necessarily change equally. Some populations have greater access to resources than others. Often migratory changes make the inequality more pronounced, which is of course a major source of concern for conflict theorists. As the Industrial Revolution continued to expand capitalism, Marx and Engels realized the growing influence of factories in the production of goods, a factor that Malthus was less able to observe. The emphasis by conflict theorists is the human labor involved in this process. Mainstream Marxists would state that concerns about overpopulation are unfounded "because every mouth comes into the world with a pair of hands" (Bird 1972:41). Technological advancements in food preparation create less of a concern than the exploitation of workers involved in that preparation, according to conflict theory.

Regarding recent concerns, as an influx of immigrants enter the country (and, as mentioned earlier, refugees as well), often societies change as some governments take a nativist approach, focusing on the needs of long term inhabitants and rejecting immigrant customs (nativism will be discussed in more detail in chapter 15). Fear and concerns over newcomers taking jobs of current residents, draining the welfare system, and committing crimes, fuels the fire of intergroup conflict. In this demographic change, conflict continues between the host community and new arrivals.

> **Should the government create programs that provide incentives for minority populations to successfully assimilate into society?**
>
> **Pro**: It would be advantageous for minorities to assimilate to create financial security for the minority citizens and order and cohesion for society.
> **Con**: The country has a poor history of coercing people to assimilate, which does little more than separate them from their cultural roots.

Symbolic Interactionism

The changes brought about by population fluctuations create new meanings of identity, whether national, ethnic, or personal. As the number of minority populations, for example Latin Americans, continue to grow, the nation, particularly those in the majority, will adapt or resist to the changes brought about. As mentioned earlier, ethnic enclaves often develop in areas to maintain some degree of connection with their native country and to create some degree of community and perhaps provide feelings of security. These changes, based on the macro level issues involved in demographic change, affect personal identity as well.

SEARCHING FOR SOLUTIONS

Demographic Challenges in the Unites States and Europe

Population aging in the United States will require changes in the way we view retirement as a society. Historically, starting in the nineteenth century, employees who lived in large urban areas and worked in the public sector began to receive pensions at older ages. This started with the military, and then firefighters, law enforcement, and teachers also began to receive public pensions. By 1920 private companies started providing workers with some sort of financial support in their later years. In 1943 the federal government introduced the Social Security Act which established 65 as the appropriate age for retirement. However, at this point in history the average life expectancy for men was 60 years of age, so few people even lived to the age of retirement and often died while they were still contributing in the paid labor force. As life expectancies increased over the next five decades, increasingly people were living past retirement age and started retiring in large numbers at age 65. As detailed, retirement is a very recent phenomenon, historically people did not spend decades of their lives out of the workforce and utilizing social security. However, the social norm is to retire at age 65 and most people expect to leave the labor force around this age. With the rapidly aging population, however, this may no longer be financially possible. Any approach to solving the problem of financing the lives of older people must take into consideration the historical context of retirement and the changes that are now necessary since a large cohort of retirees can hurt economic growth and create unsustainable increases in government spending on programs for the elderly.

Would increasing the retirement age to 70 or older be the best way to alleviate the increasing financial burden of the rapidly aging population in the United States?

Pro: Life expectancy is much higher than it was when the retirement age was put into place. It makes logical sense to work longer if you live longer.

Con: Forcing everyone to work longer is unfair to marginalized groups that do not enjoy the same longevity as whites.

One solution that involves retirement is to increase the retirement age at which people can access social programs like social security and Medicare, thus forcing them to continue to work until a later age unless they have adequate assets and resources to fund their own retirement. Another solution that is more inclusive would involve policies that allow for a gradual retirement in phases. For example, people could choose to work fewer hours and remain in the labor force longer. This would allow for older folks to slowly retire rather than just exit the workforce. It would also help the labor force since there will be fewer workers as a result of lower fertility rates. According to research by Milena Nikolova at the Brookings Institute (2016), there are three major benefits to a new 'gradual retirement' system. First, it will reduce expenditures on social programs and pensions and tax revenues would not suddenly decrease drastically. Secondly, older workers can be a valuable source of knowledge and experience for their younger colleagues and for organizations that rely on their experience. Third, according to aging research conducted by Calvo and colleagues (2009), there is a strong positive relationship between working in later life and overall wellbeing. This includes both positive psychological and physical benefits. It provides social support, a social network, and a sense of purpose and meaning in life (Calvo et al. 2009)

There has been a fair amount of support to raise the retirement age to 70. The federal government already has policy in place for the full retirement age to rise to 67 for people born after 1959. Proponents of moving it even further, to age 70, cite the serious funding problems that Social Security faces as the baby boom cohort retires. According to the Social Security Administration's most current forecasts (2017), Social Security's reserve fund will deplete between 2030 and 2034. A solution to this funding gap has proposed cuts to benefits or increases to contributions. Raising the retirement age to 70 would help prevent a sudden decrease in Social Security contributions. However, it is important to consider how life expectancy varies by race, gender, and socioeconomic status. Research shows that African American men have a life expectancy of 72.2 years and low income Americans have an average life expectancy that is ten to fifteen years younger than their middle and upper-class counterparts, and for men it is 72.3 years (Reuell 2016). Raising the retirement age to 70 would put these groups at an even bigger disadvantage. In addition, there is a segment of the older population that cannot work due to chronic health conditions or disability, etc. The composition of this group is disproportionately Latino, African American, and female. Although many of these individuals already receive benefits from social programs, raising the retirement age would also put them at a disadvantage financially. Clearly, there are many factors to consider as our country faces a surge in the aging population that sets a historical precedent.

Population aging is just one part of the demographic problem in Europe. The population in many European countries is decreasing while the members within these populations are becoming increasingly older. This occurrence is due to the aging of the World War II cohort in addition to replacement fertility rates that are below what is necessary to maintain equilibrium. Combatting this demographic challenge will require more than one approach. Increasing immigration from outside Europe would likely increase economic growth since migrants tend to be working age and they also generally have higher fertility rates than native-born women in Europe. According to data from Eurostat, the official statistical office for the European Union (2016), immigrants account for 70% of the increase in the workforce in Europe and they pay more in taxes and social contributions than they receive in benefits. In addition, some countries are developing government policies that provide longer paid parental leave and flexible working hours, in an effort to offer incentives for women so they do not have to choose between a career and a family. For example, Norway provides ten months of paid leave for women during and after their pregnancy or an entire year with 80% of their pay (Eurostat 2016). And in Iceland the government provides equal parental leave for fathers and mothers. Along with providing incentives to increase fertility rates, instituting certain incentives could potentially increase the participation of older workers in the paid labor force by allowing older individuals to work flexible hours, encouraging them to stay in the workforce longer, and providing opportunities to telecommute when possible. Together, strategies to increase migration from outside Europe, create a better work/life balance for women, and provide flexibility so that older people are more likely to remain in the paid labor force longer, will offset the demographic challenges that Europe faces both now and in the near future.

Should the governments in European countries with below replacement fertility rates create monetary incentives such as increased tax breaks, and financial stipends, for adults who have children?

Pro: Financial stipends and major tax incentives would help create a family friendly environment and offset the financial burden of raising a family.
Con: People are likely to have children just for the financial incentives, not because they want a family. This could create an increase in child abuse and neglect, and single parenthood.

Solutions to the Refugee Crisis

The front-line states, Lebanon, Jordan, and Turkey, are the first areas to try to manage the burden of enormous flows of refugees from Syria and other surrounding war-torn countries such as

Afghanistan and Iraq. Providing more financial and humanitarian assistance for both front line states and refugees in these regions is critical. Organizations such as Amnesty International advocate on behalf of protecting refugees worldwide. Among their solutions, they propose creating safe routes to sanctuary; this includes allowing refugees to cross borders along their routes, instead of putting up fences or refusing entry, which forces them to take more dangerous routes to get to safety. They also propose resettlement as a solution for refugees who are the most vulnerable, such as the elderly, those with health problems, and victims of torture. Resettlement involves moving refugees from an asylum country to a country that will allow them to settle permanently. Few countries are part of the United Nations Refugee Agency's resettlement program. However, the United States, Canada, Australia, and Nordic countries have served as resettlement countries. Despite assistance from these countries, the resettlement of refugees in 2015 was less than 1% (United Nations Refugee Agency 2016). This is not a solution until more countries agree to allow resettlement of refugees in asylum countries.

Should the United States offer resettlement opportunities for refugees from Syria, Iraq, and Afghanistan who are temporarily in Europe but need a long term solution?

Pro: The Unites States is a country of immigrants and is built on the principles that welcome political refugees and these should not be treated differently than past refugees.
Con: This group of mainly Muslim refugees poses a threat to the United States and should not be offered the opportunity to resettle here.

European leaders and policy makers have dedicated a great deal of time and resources toward finding solutions for the huge influx of refugees. Local governments are responsible for providing housing, education, and jobs to refugees. This requires some creative strategies since the government needs partnerships with the private sector for financial support and jobs. In Sweden, the government offers a monetary stipend to employers who hire refugees and to connect people with jobs. The multi-national networking company LinkedIn has volunteered to help make those connections. However, until the governments of the wealthiest countries allocate for funding to aid refugees abroad, this crisis will most likely continue indefinitely. Ultimately, the solution is to end the conflicts and persecution that force people to flee from their countries. However, according to Amnesty International, thousands of people are dying while governments spend billions of dollars on controlling their borders rather than welcoming refugees from ravaged countries with nowhere else to go.

Curbing Fertility and Population Growth

Most of the population growth is presently occurring in developing countries and will continue until these countries have moved through the demographic transition. For example, Africa has the highest fertility rates, followed closely by Asia. High fertility populations in the least developed countries can be problematic because they do not have the resources or economic growth to feed and care for a rapidly growing population. This results in malnutrition, high infant mortality, short life expectancy, and serious population health problems. These countries also have very little gender equality, thus women are less valued, have little control over their lives, and are often victims of intimate partner violence.

Providing contraceptives and health services for women has not been successful at reducing fertility in Sub-Saharan Africa. The role of culture and religion play an important part in fertility rates and family size, and in many areas of Sub-Saharan Africa there is still a cultural preference for large families. Rationale for large families include the reliance families place on their children to help with the labor and income necessary to support the family, as well as the informal support they provide for aging parents. In addition, men are more likely to want large family sizes and contraceptives do not align with many of the religious belief systems. According to the 2015 Demographic and Health Survey (DHS) conducted in Africa, in Niger, most women have more than five children and 21% of women reported needing permission from their husbands to seek reproductive health care. Women also reported that they feared disapproval and stigma if they went against cultural norms and used contraceptives.

In addition, more education is needed regarding the different methods available, the advantages of family planning, how much contraceptives cost and where they are available, as well as how to use them properly and the possible side effects. Other solutions include: improved access to comprehensive family planning services, including counseling, information, as well as how to productively and effectively convey the advantages of smaller families in cultures where large families are desired for cultural and religious reasons. Involving men in family planning is also extremely important since they are the decision makers in the family. Community based distribution of information and services on family planning is important, however until cultural, social, and religious norms change, distributing contraceptives and information is unlikely to be effective.

FIGURE 13.4 Large family size is still considered desirable in many developing countries. This is based in part on lack of access to contraceptives and family planning education.

Source: Andrzej Kubik/Shutterstock.com

A key factor in changing these norms is the education of women. There is a positive correlation between years of education for girls and reduced family size. In other words, the more educated the women in a population are, the fewer children they tend to have. For example, fertility trends in Ethiopia, Kenya, and Ghana from 1990–2010 clearly illustrate that women in all three countries with a high school education have much lower fertility rates than women with eight years or less. Women without any education have starkly higher fertility. According to data from the World Bank (Pradhan 2015), in Kenya, initiatives to reduce school fees and the cost of mandatory uniforms and textbooks for girls, resulted in reduced absenteeism, improved test scores and reduced teen pregnancy (Pradhan 2015). Initiatives to empower women and create gender equality, along with providing a high school education for girls, are key factors in solving high fertility rates and subsequent poor health and nutrition in Sub-Saharan Africa. In 2013, the World Bank announced a one-billion-dollar program to support women with health and counseling, legal aid, economic opportunities, and to combat gender based violence. The goal is to strengthen women's roles as leaders and economic stakeholders through promoting education for girls and to provide them with education and economic opportunities.

CHAPTER SUMMARY

- The study of populations, a sub-field of sociology, focus primarily on trends in fertility, mortality, and migration, within and across populations. Social demographers are trained to study global population trends, to address challenges such as over-population, shrinking and aging populations, excess mortality, and how life expectancy and mortality rates are related to demographic and social factors.

- The demographic transition is a process that each country moves through at different times and places, starting with high fertility and mortality and excess death from infectious disease, to lower fertility and mortality and deaths from chronic rather than infectious diseases. This shift occurs over time and the transition consists of four distinct phases.

- Social problems within population studies include the rapidly aging composition of the United States and Europe, below replacement fertility rates in many areas of Europe, rapid population growth in developing countries, and migration and its effects on destination countries.

- Solutions to these challenges are complex and involve population level policy changes, interventions, and strategies. Solutions to demographic problems take time; rarely does change occur quickly, since these problems are generally trends over time that require considerable efforts and large scale macro-level solutions.

REFERENCES

Amnesty International. "Eight Ways to Solve the World Refugee Crisis." Retrieved August 9, 2017 (www.amnesty.org/en/latest/campaigns/2015/10/eight-solutions-world-refugee-crisis/).

Arias, Elizabeth. 2010. "United States Life Tables by Hispanic Origin." *Vital and Health Statistics*. 152(2): 3–30. Maryland: U.S. Department of Health and Human Services.

Bird, Caroline. 1972. *The Crowding Syndrome: Learning to Live with Too Much and Too Many*. New York: David McKay Company, Inc.

Bongaarts, John. 2009. "Human Population Growth and Demographic Transition." *Philosophical Transactions of the Royal Society B: Biological Sciences.* Retrieved August 3, 2017 (http://rstb.royalsocietypublishing.org/content). doi:10.1098/rstb.2009.0137.

Calvo, Esteban, Kelly Haverstick, and Steven A. Sass. 2009. "Gradual Retirement, Sense of Control, and Retirees' Happiness." *Research on Aging.* 31(1): 112–135. Retrieved August 7, 2017 (http://journals.sagepub.com). doi:10.1177/0164027508324704.

Centers for Disease Control and Prevention. 2014. "Life Expectancy at Birth, by Sex and Race/Ethnicity: United States 2011." Retrieved August 8, 2017 (www.cdc.gov/mmwr/preview/mmwrhtml/mm6335a8.htm).

Central Intelligence Agency. 2016. "Country Comparison: Total Fertility Rate." *The World Factbook.* Retrieved August 1, 2017 (www.cia.gov/library/publications/the-world-factbook/rankorder/2127rank.html).

Connor, Phillip. 2016. "International Migration: Key Findings from the U.S., Europe, and the World." *Pew Research Center Fact Tank.* Retrieved August 4, 2017 (www.pewresearch.org/fact-tank/2016/12/15/international-migration-key-findings-from-the-u-s-europe-and-the-world/).

Crimmins, Eileen M., Mark. D. Hayward, and Yasuhiko Saito. 1996. "Differentials in Active Life Expectancy in the Older Population of the United States." *The Journals of Gerontology Series B: Psychological Sciences and Social Sciences.* 51(3): S111–S120.

Demographic and Health Surveys Program. 2015. U.S. Agency for International Development. Retrieved August 8, 2017 (http://dhsprogram.com/topics/Fertility-and-Fertility-Preferences.cfm).

East West Center. 2017. "Asia's Aging Population." Retrieved August 7, 2017 (www.eastwestcenter.org/fileadmin/stored/misc/FuturePop08Aging.pdf).

European Commission. 2017. "The EU and the Refugee Crisis." Retrieved August 9, 2017 (http://publications.europa.eu/webpub/com/factsheets/refugee-crisis/en/),

Eurostat. 2017. "Population Structure and Ageing." Retrieved August 4, 2017 (http://ec.europa.eu/eurostat/statistics-explained/index.php/Population_structure_and_ageing).

Furedi, Frank. 1997. *Population and Development: A Critical Introduction*. New York: St. Martin's Press.

Hummer, Robert A., Jennifer E. Melvin, Connor Sheehan, and Ying T. Wang. 2013. "Race/Ethnicity, Mortality, and Longevity." Pp. 131–152 in *Handbook of Minority Aging*, edited by K.S. Markides and K. Gerst. New York: Springer.

Kaiser Foundation. 2009. "Life Expectancy at Birth (in years) by Race/Ethnicity." Retrieved August 9, 2017 (www.kff.org/state-category/health-status/life-expectancy/).

Lehmann, Jean-Pierre, and Nina Ninkovic. 2013. "India's Food Crises: A Close-Up." *The Globalist.* Retrieved August 22, 2017 (www.theglobalist.com/indias-food-crises-close-up).

Mather, Mark. 2012. "Fact Sheet: The Decline in U.S. Fertility." *Population Reference Bureau.* Retrieved August 1, 2017 (http://www.prb.org/publications/datasheets/2012/world-population-data-sheet/fact-sheet-us-population.aspx).

Melvin, Jennifer E., Robert A. Hummer, Irma Elo, and Neil Mehta. 2014. "Age Patterns of Racial/Ethnic/Nativity Differences in Disability and Physical Functioning in the United States." *Demographic Research.* 31(1): 497–510. doi:10.4054/DemRes.2014.31.17.

Nikolova, Milena. 2016. "Two Solutions to the Challenges of Population Aging." *The Brookings Institute.* Retrieved July 8, 2017 (www.brookings.edu/blog/up-front/2016/05/02/two-solutions-to-the-challenges-of-population-aging/).

Pradhan, Elina. 2015. "Female Education and Childbearing: A Closer Look at the Data." *World Bank: Investing in Health.* Retrieved August 8, 2017 (http://blogs.worldbank.org/health/female-education-and-childbearing-closer-look-data).

Reuell, Peter. 2016. "For Life Expectancy, Money Matters." *Harvard Gazette.* Retrieved August 10, 2017 (http://news.harvard.edu/gazette/story/2016/04/for-life-expectancy-money-matters/).

Social Security Administration. 2017. "Status of the Social Security and Medicare Programs." August 6, 2017 (www.ssa.gov/oact/trsum/).

United Nations Refugee Agency. 2017. Resettlement. Retrieved August 6, 2017 (www.unhcr.org/pages/4a16b1676.htmlz).

United States Census Bureau. 2014. *An Aging Nation: The Older Population in the United States* (Report No. P25–1140). Washington, DC: U.S. Government Printing Office.

World Health Organization. 2017. "Sierra Leone." Retrieved August 14, 2017 (www.who.int/countries/sle/en/).

CHAPTER 14

The Environment and Urbanization

KEY TERMS

Built Environment

Environment

Environmental Justice

Human Ecology

Natural Environment

Risk Society

ABOUT THE PROBLEM: THE ENVIRONMENT

Environment natural surroundings and how human behavior affects and is affected by nature.

The term **environment** refers to different things—it is generally understood as one's surroundings, but these surroundings can be natural (physical) or social. The environment discussed here refers to the natural environment, with the understanding that we perceive the natural environment from the perspective of individuals and groups living in it; in other words, how human behavior affects the natural surroundings and how the natural surroundings in turn affect the lives of humans. *Environmentalism* refers to a concern about the natural world and has an affinity to activism much in the same way as feminism shares such a connection to gender equality. There is much political discussion currently about the environment and perhaps the most discussed issue in this area is climate change. There are many social problems associated with the environment, however, and we will discuss those shortly.

Natural Environment things found in nature such as plants, trees, animals, insects, and other non-human ecological systems.

Built Environment the tangible structures created by humans, such as factories, homes, parking lots, skate parks, and other things created for human use with human (and sometimes animal) labor.

Environmental Sociology

Sociologists distinguish between the **natural environment**—things found in nature such as plants, trees, animals, insects, and other non-human ecological systems, and the **built environment**—the tangible structures created by humans such as factories, homes, parking lots, skate parks, and other things created for human use with human (and sometimes animal) labor. If forests are the ideal representation of a natural environment, buildings are the equivalent for the built environment (Dunlap, Michelson, and Stalker 2002). While the natural environment is the primary area of interest for those in the field of environmental sociology, the built environment is the focus of scholars of urban sociology, which will be discussed soon.

To create a science of the social world, the early pioneers in sociology, Marx, Weber, Durkheim, and Simmel, envisioned a distinction between the social and natural worlds. This separation was a modernist idea resulting from the industrial revolution, because before that the two spheres were not seen as two distinct forms (Carter and Charles 2010). The two visions merged at times by different thinkers, and sometimes nature (as in *human* nature) was used to predetermine a person's status (the dialectic of superior vs. inferior). While the classical sociologists all addressed environmental issues, the sociological subfield known as environmental sociology, which developed later, had several roots (pardon the pun), including human ecology theory, rural sociology, and social movements, connected with the environmental concerns arising in the 1970s, and other ideas based on contributions from ecology and anthropology (Buttel and Humphrey 2002).

The context that created the contemporary environmental movement emerged from events of the turbulent 1960s. The level of social consciousness was heightened in this period due to many concerns such as the Vietnam War, civil rights, gender inequality, etc. This was an increasingly affluent period which ushered in a greater visibility (through television) of social ills, including environmental abuse. The economic prosperity also provided people better access to education, affluence, and increased movement to urban areas, all of which contributed to an emerging focus on the environment. In addition, people visited natural areas such as parks and recreational areas due to the increased leisure time allowed by this emerging prosperity. The original Earth Day was held in 1970 and heralded a new spirit of environmentalism, and the growing social consciousness of this period led to political engagement.

Despite some hampering of enthusiasm as the 1970s progressed, the movement picked up steam in the 1980s, only to diminish then later reestablish itself; these ebbs and flows of the movement accompanied political changes—when it was felt that pro-environment regulations were functioning appropriately, activism decreased but when the government relaxed standards, environmental activists stepped in to protect the Earth (Mertig, Dunlap, and Morrison 2002). Many books of the 1960s and 1970s were instrumental in promoting environmental awareness: in 1962, the book *Silent Spring* by Rachel Carson discussed the grave danger to animal life due to pesticides—the title refers to the death of song birds due to the chemical (DDT) that was intended to kill mosquitos. In 1970, Charles Reich's *The Greening of America* was a call to the 1960s counterculture to heighten consciousness of environmental issues.

Environmental Issues

When we think of environmental problems, we often think of pollution, which comes in many forms. Air pollution comes from both natural factors such as fire, extreme weather, and volcanic activity, and human contributions such as vehicular and factory emissions, poor land management practices, sulfur dioxide emissions, fertilizers, and a lack of green space that could combat some pollutants. From a health standpoint, air pollutants can cause many medical problems including asthma attacks, coughing, lung irritation, and can contribute to or exacerbate chronic health conditions such as cardiovascular disease (United States Environmental Protection Agency nd).

Water pollution also has many sources, including factories, power plants, and other stationary facilities known as *"point source" pollution* and from agricultural property, impervious surfaces such as parking lots, streets, or other materials that prevent water from entering the ground or similar sources, which are known as *"non-point source" pollution*. Human involvement such as dam construction and the introduction of non-native plants into an area can contribute to water pollution. Obviously, unclean water or inadequate supplies of water affects many facets of human life, not only in consumption but also agricultural use, the production of energy, and everyday common use (United States Environmental Protection Agency nd).

Changing water temperatures (called thermal pollution) often are a result of industrial operations and have negative effects on the ecosystem. The fight in 2016 over the Dakota Access Pipeline (DAP) mentioned in chapter 8, was due not only to the intrusion into sacred tribal land but also because the pipeline could endanger the local water supply. Another example of unclean drinking water happened in Flint, Michigan, where in 2014, a change in the city's water source, which occurred due to the projected savings cost, introduced lead into the water, causing medical problems for residents, especially children, in the lower income areas. The situation, called the Flint Water Crisis, is still unresolved currently, and creates larger concerns about infrastructure involving the entire country's water supply (Hanna-Attisha et al. 2016).

Land pollution consists of garbage, such as empty milk cartons, cans, or plastic bags; refuse, such as scrap metal, boards, or containers; sludge from waste and water treatment, or waste control facilities; industrial wastes; and other discarded materials located on or inside the earth's surface (United States Environmental Protection Agency nd). Often these materials end up as municipal solid waste in garbage bins and then sent to landfills, or, if they consist of recyclable material such as certain types of plastic, paper, and glass, they can be placed into specially marked bins to be sent to recycling centers. Recycling, however, only works if people take the time to properly separate the materials.

Does recycling represent an effective way of protecting the environment?

Pro: Items not recycled end up in landfills and contribute to the destruction of the planet.
Con: Recycling is not effective because many people refuse to recycle and recycling costs are prohibitive.

There are other types of activity that are considered pollution, such as noise pollution, when noise levels are too high, harmful, or invasive; visual pollution, when signage or other things obstruct views; and light pollution, when brightness levels are too high, directed inappropriately, or are obtrusive. These types are different from air, land, and water pollution in that the materials considered pollution do not leave an enduring material substance that is difficult to clean up. It also seems that these types would not require major changes in human behavior to correct other than ordinances or other regulations.

Global climate change is another environmental concern. Because of an increase in carbon dioxide levels and the transmissions of other greenhouse gases into the atmosphere from transportation related emissions, factory processes, urbanization, energy production, agricultural practices, and deforestation, the normal changes to the environment have sped up remarkably. Climate change greatly affects ecosystems in many forms such as shifting sea levels which affect coastal areas, threatening drinking water and destroying plant species (United States Environmental Protection Agency nd). Climate change is a particularly divisive political issue between those who believe that climate change is a real event primarily caused by human exploitation of resources and those who feel that the changes that are occurring are primarily the result of natural effects rather than human activity.

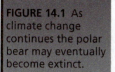

FIGURE 14.1 As climate change continues the polar bear may eventually become extinct.

Source: Floridastock/Shutterstock.com

Environmental justice refers to the equal treatment of people regarding race, ethnicity, and other social characteristics involving ecological concerns. The fact that many racial and ethnic minorities have had greater exposure to environmental contaminants by communities that were built on or near former waste dumpsites, were exposed to dangerous levels of lead, were exposed to various types of water contamination (such as that in Flint, Michigan), are evidence that equal treatment has traditionally not been a salient concern for all groups of people.

> **Environmental Justice** the equal treatment of people regarding race, ethnicity, and other social characteristics regarding ecological concerns.

The problems with the environment are difficult to solve, despite the attention they receive in movies, television, and social media. The potential reasons for this difficulty are: problems related to the environment are multidimensional and complex, many people have environmental interests and organizing them is not an easy task, and the introduction of positive changes would require many people to change their lifestyles—an arduous task for some (Harris 2004).

Should the government regulate human activity to promote environmentalism?

Pro: The issue of protecting the planet for all people is so important that the government must regulate human activity.

Con: Regulating this type of activity represents an infringement on individual liberty and an encroachment into people's lives.

THEORETICAL PERSPECTIVES (THE ENVIRONMENT)

Structural Functionalism

Human Ecology
the ways in which
humans interact in
human environments
which is comparable
to how plants, animals,
and insects interact in
natural environments—
through competition
and cooperation.

As mentioned earlier, the major theorists of the classical era addressed environmental concerns in their work. However, we must remember they lived in an era in which people were trying to understand the changes brought about by the Industrial Revolution, well before the environment became a major social issue in the 1960s and 1970s. They often used sociological terms in relation to ecological ones. For example, Park and Burgess merged the fields of natural ecology with the work of Durkheim and Darwin to create the field of **human ecology**, which posits the ways in which humans interact in human environments is comparable to how plants, animals, and insects interact in natural environments—through competition over resources but also cooperation for survival. The interconnectedness and interdependence of components of both systems reflects a functionalist approach.

Conflict Theory

One contemporary sociologist who specifically addresses the issue of climate change, Sir Anthony Giddens (2009), created what is known as the "Gidden's Paradox", the fact that people litter, or pollute, or do something else destructive to the environment with little or no regard to the long-term consequences. Think about how many times we fail to recycle some object because we have to go to the trouble of cleaning it first. Or, on a larger, scale, when corporations decide to send factories overseas because of less stringent regulations and fewer reservations about dumping sludge into rivers or sending toxic gasses into the air.

Risk Society   the
idea that humans are
creating technological
advances that produce
risk factors for potential
disasters we are unable
to predict or control.

Ulrich Beck (1992) described a **risk society**, a condition that happens when society becomes more complex and people create technological advances that produce risk factors for potential disasters which are unable to be predicted or safeguarded against. The many issues surrounding environmental concerns, once these become known to us and determined to be social problems, require a political response. Traditional risks include natural disasters, natural (but extreme) weather events, and fires; modern risks are related to technological problems such as plane crashes, and nuclear accidents, such as those that occurred at Three Mile Island in the U.S. in 1979, Chernobyl in the former U.S.S.R. in 1986, and Fukushima Daiichi in Japan in 2011. In a study of Beck's risk society as applied in Sweden, the authors note it is probably more appropriate to see technical risks (at whatever stage of social development) as having always existing rather than there being two types—traditional vs modern (Olafsson and Ohman 2007).

Symbolic Interactionism

One effect of the increased focus on the environment is the evolving understanding of ecology and the increasing activism by those who seek to protect the planet. This group has adopted a significant language symbol—that of "green", a term used to denote activities and lifestyles that are friendly to the natural environment. There is even a political party, the Green Party, that has run candidates for many political offices, including the Presidency of the United States, and that advocates environmental policy. Labels abound in environmental activity, for example the slogan "reduce, reuse, recycle" is common, and the triangular symbol placed on recyclable products is familiar to anyone that uses these products. Environmentalists are known by their pejorative label "tree-huggers", a reference to the willingness of activists to tie themselves to trees rather than have the tree removed from green spaces.

SEARCHING FOR SOLUTIONS

The environmental activism movement is quite strong in the United States. These groups often organize and work at a local level to protest and heighten awareness about climate change, air, land, and water pollution in their communities. Their focus is to put pressure on private industry and government to stop new oil, gas and coal projects that affect climate change. Furthermore, they promote social change and rely heavily on social media, and networks of activists around the world. This is a very popular movement currently, with thousands of national and local groups across the nation whose interests range from protecting wildlife, sea life, and the oceans, to groups that work to stop pesticide pollution, fracking, and oil pipelines. Groups dedicated to combatting climate change number in the hundreds in the United States alone and some focus on greenhouse gases while others focus on energy efficiency, but one goal they all have in common is to find a way to mitigate climate change.

FIGURE 14.2 A climate change rally was held in Los Angeles on February 17, 2013 and drew hundreds of people to City Hall steps to hear speakers and organizers and their message for President Obama to take the nation 'Forward on Climate', and say no to the Keystone XL pipeline, Speakers included Ed Begley Jr., U.S. Rep. Henry Waxman and Los Angeles City Councilman Jose Huizar.

Source: Citizens of the Planet/Education Images/UIG/Getty Images

Some of the strategies environmental groups use include social media campaigns, exerting pressure on private industry and government, and organized protests and demonstrations. On April 29, 2017, tens of thousands of demonstrators descended on the White House to protest the administration's denial of climate change (Fandos 2017). The group, the People Climate March, included Hollywood celebrities and other high-profile people, along with thousands of people who traveled from across the country. The effectiveness of demonstrations like this on public policy are unknown, however, the protests are very effective for heightening awareness nationally, capturing media coverage, and bringing these issues to the forefront of a national dialogue.

Actual solutions for climate change involve collaboration between countries since this is a global problem. The Paris Climate Pact, is one such group made up of 195 countries committed to lowering carbon emissions that cause planet-warming and to combat climate change. This landmark climate agreement, achieved in 2015, is the first global plan for slowing the problems caused by climate change. For this deal to work, governments in every country, including developing and poorer countries, must enact public plans for cutting emissions and using alternative sources of fuel. In 2017, the United States withdrew from the Paris Climate Pact, as the Trump administration felt that unfair environmental standards on American corporations would cause losses in profits (Shear 2017).

Members of grassroots environmental activist organizations gathered by the thousands recently to protest a highly publicized plan that would transport oil across four states, including North Dakota, in order to ship it to refineries more efficiently. The Dakota pipeline, as it is known by, passed under a reservoir that provided drinking water to the Standing Rock Sioux and Cheyenne River Sioux Indian reservations as well as their sacred burial sites. The Standing Rock Sioux Tribe protested the project based on possible contamination of their drinking water and violations of religious rights (BBC 2017). Protestors numbered near 10,000 and included U.S. military veterans, high profile political figures and Hollywood actors, along with environmental activists. The campsites in the region where the protests occurred quickly turned violent as police brought in militarized equipment and assaulted the peaceful protesters with tear gas, water cannons, and rubber bullets (Denchak 2017). According to the National Resources Defense Council (nd), the pipeline was rerouted from a higher-income predominantly white community that rejected it which represents systemic injustice and inequality based on race, political power, and historical oppression. Although the protests were not a success in terms of stopping the pipeline, it was successful in building awareness around environmental injustices that disproportionately affect the most marginalized populations, and the enormous financial gains made by banks and investors—the financial institutions that fund these projects.

Environmental Justice Movement

The environmental justice movement grew out of grassroots advocacy focused on building awareness around negative environmental impacts that disproportionately occur in areas that are predominantly low-income and occupied by people of color. For example, as far back as the 1960s, Cesar Chavez led organized Latino farm workers to protest the toxic pesticides they were exposed to while working in agriculture. Currently, the environmental justice movement focuses on issues ranging from health issues such as clean air and water, to climate change and clean energy sources.

Mold in public housing is a major concern as are the toxic levels of lead in drinking water in poor communities such as Flint, Michigan (NRDC nd). National groups such as the Natural Resources Defense Council (NRDC) have made great strides in protecting predominately minority and low-income communities from environmental racism, in large part by working with grassroots groups within these communities.

Environmental justice has gained momentum and popularity through these organized and well attended protests and demonstrations. Coalition building across states between grassroots groups and the proliferation of national environmental groups have brought environmental issues such as land, water, and air pollution, as well as the realities of climate change, to the forefront. Together these groups leverage media coverage and put public and media pressure on corporations to make changes that foster sustainability, encourage social responsibility and transparency, and promote public health. Public pressure, particularly through social media, on retailers to create more sustainable products has led many companies to adopt new practices and create more sustainable practices. For example, Proctor and Gamble have reduced their packaging under public pressure, Puma introduced a line of recyclable jackets, backpacks and biodegradable shoes and shirts, while Nike has utilized modern technology to make their shoes more sustainable by eliminating waste (Winston 2012). Consumer led boycotts and protests are becoming more common and companies are responding to the socially conscious consumers, especially young adults among whom they wish to build brand loyalty.

Should businesses be regulated more strictly by the government for unsustainable practices such as using Styrofoam or excess packaging?

Pro: Businesses are contributing to land pollution and should be held accountable since they are producing products that add to the problem.

Con: Private businesses should not be regulated in this way as it is their choice, and consumers who disagree with their choices are free to purchase products and services from other companies.

These eco-friendly groups promote education and awareness on college campuses and assist students at universities to form sustainability and environmental justice groups focused on issues ranging from encouraging the use of green products and services, discouraging consumption or purchase of products that affect the environment negatively, to lifestyle changes such as buying hybrid or electric cars and smaller homes that have less impact on the environment. Focusing on the younger generation has proven effective, a 2011 survey released by the Pew Research Center reported that young adults were more supportive of environmental laws, were more likely to pay more for products made responsibly, supported green energy development and were more likely to choose public transportation over cars. Millennials reported the highest support for policy proposals such as increasing spending for wind and solar energy sources, and tax incentives for buying hybrid electric vehicles.

In conclusion, solutions to major environmental problems such as climate change are complex and ultimately require the collaboration of all countries. Smaller scale solutions for sustainability

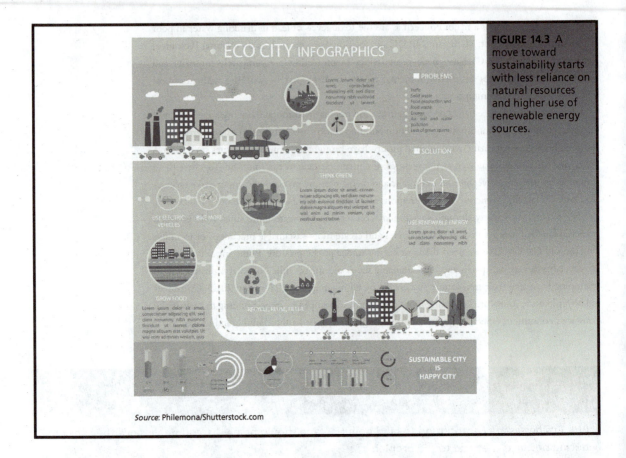

FIGURE 14.3 A move toward sustainability starts with less reliance on natural resources and higher use of renewable energy sources.

Source: Philemona/Shutterstock.com

focus around heightening awareness, education, providing the tools and resources for young adults to organize and make informed choices, and continuing to leverage media coverage of protests and demonstrations to both heighten awareness and pressure companies to use more efficient and sustainable practices. Social media will continue to play a key role in publicizing public boycotts of companies that are contributing to environmental problems and heightening awareness for consumers so they can make more educated choices.

ABOUT THE PROBLEM: URBANIZATION

KEY TERMS	
Gentrification	Urban ecology
Social distance	Urbanism
Urban blight	Urbanization

Urbanization refers to the movement of people from rural communities to cities. *Communities* are a collection of people with special or political commonalities that provide its members with a sense of inclusion and belonging (Schaefer 2014). The city refers to the "web of social activities, economic functions, mobility patterns, and lifestyles, all arrayed in space" (Goldfield and Brownell 1979:9). We conceive of cities as being bigger and more diverse than communities; cities are extremely complex social organizations and they differ from other large multifaceted social establishments, such as military organizations or multinational corporations, in that cities have no central organization. The city's governmental systems have such a structure but cities are complex entities and contain more than just their administrative structures (Flanagan 2010). The city is an economic entity with a variety of income generating systems. It is also an entity that contains systems of belief (which make up a culture). In addition, it has a diversity of people of different races, ethnicities, both sexes, differing sexual orientations, and a host of other variations. Another term related to urbanization is **urbanism**, the human experience as it relates to life in cities, which has been a major interest of sociologists from the classical period to the present.

> **Urbanization** the demographic change of people from rural areas to cities.
>
> **Urbanism** the lived experience of city life.

Urban Sociology

Urban sociology is a subfield that focuses on urban environments and seeks to understand these environments and their consequences on the experiences of people, the patterns of social interaction, and the organizations of social life (Flanagan 2010). Regarding urbanization, sociology's founders were obviously interested in this area as the demographic changes of the period resulted in people moving to cities. **Urban ecology** was a perspective that contributed to the birth of urban sociology; this perspective, originally developed by the scholars of the University of Chicago, likens the city to a biological ecosystem with interrelated components—understanding how a connection develops between these components of human activity and social patterns provides insight into the inner workings of the city (Goldfield and Brownell 1979).

> **Urban Ecology** the analogy of a city life to a biological ecosystem.

Georg Simmel, one of sociology's founders, in his famous essay "The Metropolis and Mental Life" ([1903] 1971) explores the effects that urbanization has on individuals. According to Simmel, urban dwellers experience an amplification of emotionality due to the overload of stimuli that can occur on city streets. A surplus of this type causes them to become dulled or to adopt a blasé attitude toward others, which is an adaptation to the sensory overload. The commercial nature of cities, as contrasted to rural areas, also creates relationships based on materialism, thereby making relationships more superficial and less meaningful (Edles and Applerouth 2015). Simmel's essay is a work in social psychology as it attempts to understand the individual's role in the built environment.

Mirroring Simmel's ideas on the individual in society, Bellah et al. (1985) observe how the complexity of metropolitan life, with the competing demands of work, family, and the community, create a situation "too complex for an individual to comprehend" (Bellah et al. 1985:177). This whirlwind of dizzying activity that characterizes city life can be exciting, but it can also create feelings of loneliness and alienation.

The Chicago School of Sociology scholars, operating from the University of Chicago, developed their sociological perspective primarily in the 1920s and 1930s. Many credit these scholars with introducing the subfield of urban sociology in America. One of the leading sociologists in this group, Robert E. Park, was a former city newspaper reporter whose training taught him how to observe, analyze, and report life on the streets; his journalist's insights led him to derive some major observations about urban sociology. The concentric zone theory, for example, was a product of the Chicago School and posits that urban areas have five zones—the central core (downtown commercial area), the zone of transition (lower status area located just outside the central core), a working class area, a middle class suburb, and a commuter zone. While not all cities geographically extend outward in this clear-cut fashion, the model provides an analysis of social trends as areas urbanize.

Morris (2015) states that W.E.B. Du Bois should receive credit for founding American urban sociology. Du Bois and his colleagues at Atlanta University, whose work is said to have established the idea that race is socially constructed, were doing early fieldwork in inner city areas. His ethnographic study *The Philadelphia Negro* (1899) was the first major sociological analysis of an African American community, offering a quantitative approach that he would later abandon for a more qualitative style, such as found in his most famous work *Souls of Black Folk* ([1903] 1995), which provides a vivid narrative description of race relations. *The Philadelphia Negro* was not only a groundbreaking work on race, but urbanism as well. He and his colleagues did not receive the credit they deserved on urban sociology, presumably due to racial biases.

Urban Problems as Social Problems

Social Distance   a measure of distance between people that is relational rather than geographic, and that separates people on the basis on race, class, gender, etc.

Most of us are aware of the problems associated with city life such as traffic congestion, smog, and a certain level of **social distance**, a relational rather than geographic distance that separates people on the basis on race, class, gender, etc.; issues that are often more pronounced than is normally found in small town life. These are problems inherent in urban areas and most of us normally experience them at the micro level; to truly understand urban life though, it requires a step back to a sociohistorical macro level of analysis.

There have been many changes associated with urbanization as cities have progressed throughout the centuries; this progression has developed through three stages (Schaefer 2014). Pre-industrial cities, beginning about 10,000 B.C., dominated the first stage and were much smaller than major cities today, having only a few thousand residents. The Industrial Revolution of the second stage contributed to cities vastly growing and adopting different organizational characteristics; with a more open class system (as opposed to the early caste types), people had more opportunities to obtain an education and benefit from the economic potentialities created during industrialization. The industrial cities were more secular than their predecessors and greater communication methods led to a more informed populace. The post-industrial cities, occupying the last stage, developed in the latter part of the twentieth century and had as their basis a reliance on information technology, rather than industrial production. The adherence to one or a few religions has been replaced by a growing interest in and acceptance of newer or less observed ones. There is also an increase in corporate power and an emphasis on the scientific and technical fields.

Urban Blight   deplorable housing conditions and dilapidated structures, poor urban planning and unsound investments, and the improper use and functioning of buildings.

The term **urban blight** lacks a precise definition that is useful for analysis, however state statutes commonly cite environments such as deplorable housing conditions and dilapidated structures, poor urban planning and unsound investments, and the improper use and functioning of buildings as characteristics (Hoffman 2012). Related terms that evoke similar mental imagery are "urban decay" and "urban deprivation". All three terms describe life in cities, or at least "pockets of poverty"

(Andersen 2002), that exist in urban areas that need invigoration and renewal. If we remember from chapter 9, this refers to the disorganized areas that produce deviance and crime.

Cities have "hot spots" of criminal activity that, according to some sociologists and criminologists, represent the social disorganization of cities. As we recall from chapter 9, the broken windows theory represents an urban, "place-oriented" view of criminal behavior. If certain areas appear to be run-down, this condition invites criminal behavior. Many elements of city life give off signals of risk and threat and the social reactions to these signals reflect a "harm footprint" that can travel to other areas; the effects of these signals can diminish if proper planning and information dissemination by the police occurs (Innes 2014). Rather than perceiving of police agencies as the organizations required for controlling communities, another perspective sees community groups in inner-city areas as having a role in controlling the behavior of its residents (Sampson and Groves 1989). City planning and organizational strategies, which include provisions which take proactive measures for crime, can be valuable in this area.

Urban housing can be a problematic area as housing shortages are common in urban regions. Furthermore, urban housing is often substandard—some "project" apartments and houses need serious repair. Another housing issue that constitutes a social problem is lack of it—homelessness is a visible reminder of the problem—approximately 555,000 people in the United States are homeless, most of this number occasionally occupy homeless shelters but are otherwise on the streets. On a positive note, however, the number of homeless people has decreased 14% since 2010 (United States Housing and Urban Development 2016).

Cities in America traditionally have had separate residential neighborhoods for different racial or ethnic groups (refer to the enclaves mentioned in chapter 8). Anderson (2015) refers to these regions as "white spaces" and "black spaces"—white spaces are vestiges of a past when certain areas were "white only" areas. There is a certain degree of racial mixing in these areas now, however there are still areas that some view as places where only European Americans belong and those who intrude are interlopers. Black spaces consist primarily of African American residences and establishments; these areas create in many people's minds what Anderson (2015) calls the "iconic ghetto", an image reinforced by media images and that keep people of color associated with stereotypes affiliated with inner cities. As also noted in chapter 8, Anderson (2015) also describes "cosmopolitan canopies" that allow a brief respite from the racial and ethnic segregation of cities. **Gentrification**, another key concept in segregated areas, refers to the process that happens when people of the middle and upper classes move into downtown areas that were originally occupied by lower and working class residents. These areas become "revitalized" through upgrades and renovations and often put the new residents, usually whites, in areas close to important conveniences and moves the former residents, often people of color, to areas away from the city's core. The effect is the segregation of certain areas of the city based on race, ethnicity, and/or class.

> **Gentrification** the movement of the middle and upper classes into downtown areas that were originally occupied by lower and working class residents.

Should the government provide incentives to stop the gentrification of neighborhoods?

Pro: The government should step in because residents are losing not only their homes but their sense of community.

Con: Demographic change is a normal and natural process and should not be subjected to government interference.

THEORETICAL PERSPECTIVES

Structural Functionalism

Ferdinand Tonnies (1957) was a contemporary of Weber and Durkheim who distinguished rural areas (Gemeinschaft or "community") from urban ones (Gesellschaft or "society") and posited how Gemeinschaft areas, with their close-knit ties and similar values, are giving way to Gesellschaft structures, which rely on laws and contracts to main social order. Correspondingly, from Durkheim's perspective, the division of labor in communities creates two distinct levels of social solidarity—homogenous areas, characterized by traditional and shared values, have a "mechanical" type of solidarity while more cosmopolitan areas, characterized by diversity, have an "organic" type of solidarity; urban societies thus, have the latter type. The dialectics illustrated in both conceptualizations (community vs. society and mechanical vs. organic), due to their focus on cohesion, social order, and functionalization, reflect a structural functionalist approach.

Conflict Theory

Marx and Engels believed the problems of urbanization resulted from a world becoming more materialistic, alienated, and stratified. Weber's concern was with the increasing levels of rationalization in the process of urbanization which creates an "iron cage" of human existence. French neo-Marxist Henri Lefebvre, argued that cities are a configuration created by those in power since the owners of the property use the spaces for their own capitalistic needs—if these elites want to create factories, malls, hotels, or exclusive, segregated residential areas, the residents of cities have no voice in the use of the space; therefore, in addition to controlling the economic and occupational life of people (or labor, as Marx would say), they also control the spaces they inhabit (Purcell 2013).

Symbolic Interactionism

Jane Jacobs, an urbanist who, though not trained in sociology, used a sociological framework to create the magnificent work *The Death and Life of Great American Cities* ([1961] 1992). She provided some vivid insights on the atmosphere of city life and the intimate interactions that occur there—she perceived of this interaction as a "ballet" that takes place on the street between diverse people. Her work is reminiscent of the early Chicago School scholars who perceived of the city as a laboratory in which to learn about urbanization and human interaction, and that of Georg Simmel who expressed the vibrancy of human activity found in the urban experience. This type of urban analysis shows up recently in the work of Elijah Anderson (mentioned in chapter 8 and earlier in this chapter), whose observations of street life provide an understanding into how people relate to each other in built environments. These micro-level interactionist approaches have provided rich explorations of city life.

Elijah Anderson has contributed much to the understanding of race and race relations in America. Trained in the ethnographic method, Anderson has immersed himself in the communities he wants to study. He released several popular books, primarily based on observations in inner-city communities on how people navigate the areas and the racial relations that occur on a regular basis.

He classifies individuals in dialectic terms (e.g., "street" vs. "decent" families, "cosmos" vs. "ethnos" citizens, "local old timers" vs. "gentrifiers") and attempts to find meaning in people's surroundings. In a recent work (Anderson 2011), he describes a space in an inner city where two distinct types of people—the culturally relative "cosmos" (short for cosmopolitan) and the ethnocentric "ethnos"—find a place, a refuge from the inner-city which he terms the "cosmopolitan canopy", a space that has cues that give the occupiers meaning about the interactions that are supported there. In a subject that is timely, Anderson (1990) describes the relationship between young black men and the police in which the residents must alter their appearance and behavior to avoid police scrutiny—the "downtown" police are especially to be avoided as they tend to see all young men as potential deviants while the "local" police are more community-oriented and less enforcement driven.

SEARCHING FOR SOLUTIONS

A good example of the connection between the environment and urbanization can be found in the work of famed urban scholar Lewis Mumford. Mumford, ever concerned with the growing encroachment of technology and industrialization in the lives of people, envisioned green cities—urban areas with elements of nature—that he believed would bring some degree of order to the lives of city dwellers. Considered a utopian vision, Mumford called his approach regionalism, which refers to planning cities with regional surveys to ascertain local needs rather than just the commercial needs of the business community. He believed his idea of an "organic community" that balanced citizen work, nature, and civic engagement in a place with aesthetic appeal, would create a sense of pride and identification, making cities more resistant to the effects of the machine-like qualities of most urban areas. By developing the natural beauty of areas using strategically placed green spaces, Mumford's vision has come to fruition, at least in part, to growing cities such as Portland, Oregon (Stephenson 1999).

Rapid urban growth, along with poverty, racial segregation, and shortages in affordable housing, urban decay, and subsequent gentrification all led to the complex social problems created by urbanization. Solutions to these social problems must consider social stratification and the root causes of urban problems—poverty, discrimination, and the lack of jobs in urban areas for low-skilled workers.

Building Coalitions for Affordable Housing, Education, and Employment

The most important driver of social problems in urban areas is poverty. Until local governments promote economic development and job creation in these neglected areas, almost every challenge caused by urbanization will continue to exist. Outsourcing, the 2007 recession, deindustrialization and the subsequent information economy left many of the urban black working class permanently jobless as employment opportunities disappeared from urban areas. Joblessness, combined with a lack of public transportation for commuting to jobs outside these impoverished neighborhoods, created economic disenfranchisement. Creating economic growth and providing more public transportation in low-income, primarily minority neighborhoods is crucial for poor urban areas. This will require local government to provide incentives for companies to establish locations in these areas to provide jobs and building better transportation in low-income neighborhoods. For example, in Pittsburgh, urban workers struggled economically as the large steel plants closed and there was massive out-migration from the urban areas to the suburbs for the middle and upper classes. The loss of taxes and jobs resulted in a steep increase in poverty. However, Pittsburgh's leaders encouraged and incentivized a new economy and attracted employers like Google, and collaborated with local universities and city hospitals to build a new economy. Pittsburgh Medical Center grants a $40,000 college scholarship to every public-school student with a 2.5 GPA and good attendance (Bruner 2012). These innovative solutions that local government initiated in partnership with universities and commerce has created in-migration and an economy that is much stronger, reduced poverty and prepared for future employment and growth by providing educational opportunities for young people.

Affordable housing is a major challenge for low-income urban dwellers. According to a report from the Stanford Center on Poverty and Inequality (2016), citizens in poverty end up in public housing that is in a state of decay, overcrowded, segregated, and as such is a social and economic barrier to employment and inclusion (Lichter, Parisi, and Valk 2016). In San Francisco where affordable housing is in serious shortage, a group of community leaders and Silicon Valley entrepreneurs, along with faculty from UC Berkeley and Stanford formed a partnership to build better affordable housing that is not segregated or plagued by crime, and is near high quality schools and jobs (Mid-Pen Housing nd).

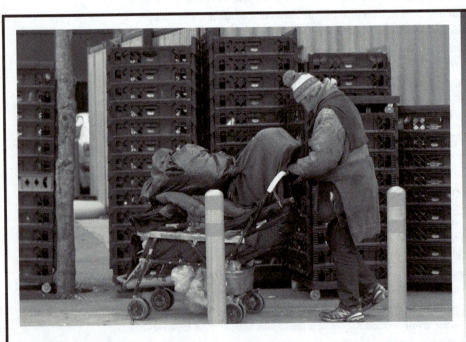

FIGURE 14.4 SAN FRANCISCO – MAY 20 2015: Homeless in San Francisco. The city spent about $1.5 billion on homeless services and has six times more supportive housing units per capita than any major cities in the US.

Source: ChameleonsEye/Shutterstock.com

Their efforts over a forty-year period have provided thousands of people in the San Francisco Bay area, from seniors and low-income families, to the homeless and residents with mental illness or substance abuse, with affordable housing, and services such as computer training, academic tutoring for youth, and English-fluency classes. This solution required a strong network of partners and volunteers, including corporations that provided funding for the initiative. Unfortunately, this is not feasible for all urban areas—but it is an evidence based solution to solving housing shortages, that also combats joblessness, and provides educational opportunities for marginalized populations and community development.

Should housing be a human right rather than a commodity that only those with resources can afford?

Pro: Providing basic shelter for all residents should be treated as a human right and not denied to people who cannot afford rent or do not qualify for a lease based on financial restraints.
Con: Housing is a resource that is rented, bought, and sold on the free market to those who can afford it and should not be treated as a social safety net or basic human right.

Gentrification as a Solution

However, only a handful of cities with severe urban blight, high unemployment, and a crumbling infrastructure have taken this approach to economic growth. Many cities have turned to gentrification as a solution to revitalize impoverished urban areas. City redevelopment offices often try to attract middle and upper income residents to their older urban areas to revitalize the tax base, provide an incentive for new business development in downtown areas, and create more vibrant and aesthetically pleasing neighborhoods. According to a report from the Brookings Institution for Urban and Metropolitan Policy (2001), this tends to occur in cities with housing shortages and historic neighborhoods that are in a state of disrepair. Some of the cities that have undergone the process of gentrification are Boston, Seattle, Chicago, Atlanta, Cleveland, and Detroit (Kennedy and Leonard 2001). The aspects of revitalization that appear as a solution for these cities include renovating the houses and revitalizing the yards, the creation of businesses and services for the new upper-scale community, and reductions in crime. The flow of resources and reinvestment into the physical landscape of these neighborhoods, along with higher tax revenues and increasing property values, has a positive effect on in-migration as well.

Researchers are not in agreement on whether this is a solution for the low-income families living in these neighborhoods. According to research on urban gentrification by Gibson (2015), conducted in New York City, the process of gentrification often displaces racial minorities and other low-income residents. The struggling families are faced with steep rent increases that force them to leave or their older apartment buildings are replaced by new modern condos or mixed-use development and they are displaced and generally must move to even poorer areas. If individuals are fortunate enough to own a home in these areas, their taxes increase steeply as property values increase. Conversely, research conducted by Freeman (2005), found that low-income African Americans are more likely to remain in gentrifying neighborhoods. In addition, low-income individuals who stay can gain from the addition of supermarkets, more retail and service industry, and an increase in jobs in the community. However, rent control is a key factor in whether low-income families experience displacement or can continue to live in these upwardly mobile neighborhoods, since without rent control they can rarely afford the steep increase in rent, and only a few states still have rent control laws (Bodenner 2015). Clearly, the management of the process of gentrification and rent controlled apartments play key roles in whether gentrification is considered a solution for everyone involved: marginalized groups in areas of urban decay and cities, businesses, and new residents.

CHAPTER SUMMARY

- Environmental sociology is the study of the natural and built environment around us. Urban sociology is a subfield that focuses on urban environments and the process and patterns of urban life, including social interaction and the organization of social life in an urban setting.

- Environmental issues that are considered social problems include water, air, and land pollution. These are all types of pollution that cause long term problems on a global scale. Global climate change is currently a major environmental concern that is controversial because it is politically divisive, primarily because some groups, generally conservatives, profit from the companies that are causing climate change, while other groups use a scientific approach to studying evidence based research on climate change. From a scientific standpoint, climate change is very real and is the result of human exploitation of natural resources and will eventually result in the destruction of the planet.

- Solutions to environmental issues rely heavily on the environmental activist movement, which is quite strong in the United States. These groups organize and work in the community and collaborate nationally to heighten awareness about environmental problems and stage protests and demonstrations. Strategies also include use of social media campaigns, leveraging media coverage, and applying pressure to businesses to share in the social responsibility of using more sustainable practices. These groups also promote education and organize student groups on university campuses to focus on environmental activism and justice.

- Urbanization is the result of migration from rural settings to cities. While not problematic as a process, over time, the older parts of cities tend to experience overcrowding, substandard housing, fewer supermarkets and major retailers and thus few employment opportunities. These social factors lead to urban blight, or pockets of poverty that attract crime, racial segregation, and a disproportionate number of homeless people. The school systems suffer, there are few green spaces, and it becomes an unhealthy environment for residents. Gentrification, the process of upper middle and upper class populations moving into these downtown areas and revitalizing them through renovation, new buildings to replace old ones, and upscale retailers that replace smaller family owned businesses, often cause displacement of the low-income residents who can no longer afford to live in their neighborhoods, and are forced to move to even worse areas of the city.

- Solutions to problems caused by urbanization include: building coalitions for affordable housing, employment opportunities and better educational systems. Affordable housing is a major challenge for most cities and requires the efforts of city planning officials, businesses, and non-profit organizations. Increasing incentives for businesses to open in urban areas provides more jobs and raises the tax base, which in turn creates better schools and attracts more experienced teachers. Gentrification has been proposed as a solution, however, scholars disagree on whether it does more harm than good. If the original residents can remain in these neighborhoods as they are revitalized then it tends to provide economic gains, however, if they are forced to move it only increases the burden of poverty on an already marginalized population.

REFERENCES

Andersen, Hans Skifter. 2002. "Excluded Places: The Interaction Between Segregation, Urban Decay and Deprived Neighborhoods." *Housing, Theory, and Society*. 19 (3/4): 153–169. Retrieved June 24, 2017 (http://research.flagler.edu:9838/eds/detail/detail?vid=0&sid=9d4e2fef-fd36–46f7–90b1–6e2632 097b2%40sessionmgr103&bdata=JnNpdGU9ZWRzLWxpdmUmc2NvcGU9c2l0ZQ%3d%3d#AN=9070349&db=buh). doi: 10.1080/140360902321122860.

Anderson, Elijah. 1990. *Streetwise: Race, Class, and Change in an Urban Community*. Chicago: University of Chicago Press.

Anderson, Elijah. 2011. *The Cosmopolitan Canopy: Race and Civility in Everyday Life*. New York: W.W. Norton & Co.

Anderson, Elijah. 2015. "The White Space." *Sociology of Race and Ethnicity*. 1(1): 10–21. doi:101.1177/2332649214561306.

Beck, Ulrich. 1992. *Risk Society: Towards a New Modernity*. London: Sage.

Bellah, Robert N., Richard Madsen, William M Sullivan, Ann Swidler, and Steven M. Tipton. 1985. *Habits of the Heart: Individualism and Commitment in American Life*. New York: Perennial Library.

Bodenner, Chris. 2015. "Why is Gentrification Such a Bad Word? Your Thoughts." *The Atlantic Monthly*. Retrieved August 16, 2017 (www.theatlantic.com/business/archive /2015/06/gentrification-bad-word/396908/).

British Broadcasting Company. 2017. "Dakota Pipeline: What's Behind the Controversy?" Retrieved August 14, 2017 (www.bbc.com/news/world-us-canada-37863955).

Bruner, Jon. 2012. "Ten Comeback Cities." *Forbes Magazine*. Retrieved August 16, 2017 (www.forbes.com/sites/jonbruner/2012/03/05/ten-american-comeback-cities-map/#46dc877a48c2).

Buttel, Fredrick H. and Craig R. Humphrey. 2002. "Sociological Theory and the Natural Environment." Pp. 33–69 in *Handbook of Environmental Sociology*, edited by Riley E. Dunlap, and William. Michelson Westport: CN: Greenwood Press.

Carson, Rachel. 1962. *Silent Spring*. Cambridge, MA: Houghton Mifflin.

Carter, Bo and Nickie Charles. 2010. *Nature, Society, and Environmental Crisis*. Malden, MA: Blackwell Publishing.

Denchak, Melissa. 2017. Natural Resources Defense Council. Retrieved August 14, 2017 (www.nrdc.org/stories/no-environmental-justice-no-peace).

Du Bois, W.E.B. 1899. *The Philadelphia Negro: A Social Study*. Philadelphia: University of Pennsylvania.

Du Bois, W.E.B. [1903] 1995. *The Souls of Black Folk*. New York: Signet.

Dunlap, Riley E., William Michelson, and Glenn Stalker. 2002. "Environmental Sociology: An Introduction." Pp. 1–32 in *Handbook of Environmental Sociology*, edited by Riley E. Dunlap and William Michelson. Westport: CN: Greenwood Press.

Edles, Laura Desfor and Scott Applerouth. 2015. *Sociological Theory in the Classical Era: Text and Readings*, 3rd ed. Thousand Oaks, CA: Sage Publications.

Fandos, Nicholas. 2017. "Climate March Draws Thousands of Protestors Alarmed by Trump's Environmental Agenda." Retrieved August 14, 2017 (www.nytimes.com/2017 /04/29/us/politics/peoples-climate-march-trump.html).

Flanagan, William G. 2010. *Urban Sociology: Images and Structures*, 5th ed. Lanham, MD: Roman and Littlefield.

Freeman, Lance. 2005. "Displacement or Succession? Residential Mobility in Gentrifying Neighborhoods." *Urban Affairs Review*. 40 (4): 463–491. Retrieved November 22, 2017 (http://research.flagler. edu:10958/doi/abs/10.1177/1078087404273341).

Freeman, Lance and Frank Braconi. 2007. "Gentrification and Displacement New York City in the 1990s." *Journal of the American Planning Association*. 70(1): 38–52. doi:10.1080/01944360408976337.

Gibson, D.W. 2015. *The Edge Becomes the Center: An Oral History of Gentrification in the 21st Century*. Overload Press: New York. Pp 34–41.

Giddens, Anthony. 2009. *The Politics of Climate Change*. Cambridge: Polity Press.

Goldfield, David R. and Blaine A. Brownell. 1979. *Urban America: From Downtown to No Town*. Boston: Houghton Mifflin.

Grusky, David and Clifton Parker. 2016. "Stanford Reports Shows that U.S. performs poorly on Measures of Poverty and Inequality Measures," *Stanford News* August 20, 2017 (https://news.stanford.edu/2016/02/ 02/poverty-report-grusky-020216/).

Hanna-Attisha, Mona, Jenny LaChance, Richard Casey Sadler, and Allison Champney Schnepp. 2016. "Elevated Blood Lead Levels in Children Associated with the Flint Drinking Water Crisis: A Spatial Analysis of Risk and Public Health Response." *American Journal of Public Health*. 106 (2): 283–290. Retrieved June 27, 2017 (http://research.flagler.edu: 9839/eds/detail/detail?vid=0&sid=153b-28cb-28e8–429e-aa38-c4a5f4439897%40sessionmgr4008&bdata=JnNpdGU9ZWRzLWxpd-mUmc2NvcGU9c2l0ZQ%3d%3d#db=buh&AN=112413959) doi:10.2105/AJPH.2015.303003.

Harris, Frances. 2004. "Human-Environmental Interactions." Pp. 3–18 in *Global Environmental Issues*, edited by Frances Harris. West Sussex, England: John Wiley and Sons.

Hoffman, Josh. 2012. "Raze the Dead: Urban Blight, Private Universities, and the Path towards Revitalization." *University of Pittsburg Law Review*. 74 (1). Retrieved May 30, 2017 (http://research.flagler.edu:9839/eds/detail/detail?vid=0&sid=667e9bec-b5ac-4551-8a56-8d727d6e0517%40sessionmgr4007&bdata=JnNpdGU9ZWRzLWxpdmUmc2NvcGU9c2 l0ZQ%3d%3d#AN=84380243&db=lgs Pp. 85–105). doi:10.5195/lawreview2012.192.

Innes, Martin. 2014. *Signal Crimes: Social Reactions to Crime, Disorder, and Control*. Oxford: Oxford University Press.

Jacobs, Jane. [1961] 1992. *The Death and Life of Great American Cities*. New York: Vintage Books.

Kennedy, Maureen and Paul Leonard. 2001. "Dealing with Neighborhood Change: A Primer on Gentrification and Policy Choices." *Brookings Institution for Urban and Metropolitan Policy*. Retrieved August 16, 2017 (www.brookings.edu/wpcontent/uploads/2016/06/gentrification.pdf).

Lichter, Daniel T., Domenico Parisi, and Helga de Valk. 2016. "Residential Segregation." *State of the Union: The Stanford Center on Poverty and Inequality.* Retrieved August 20, 2017 (https://inequality.stanford.edu/cpi-research/area/segregation).

Mertig, Angela, Riley E. Dunlap, and Denton E. Morrison. 2002. "The Environmental Movement in the United States." Pp. 448–481 in *Handbook of Environmental Sociology,* edited by Riley E. Dunlap and William Michelson. Westport: CN: Greenwood Press.

MidPen Housing. nd. Retrieved August 24, 2017 (www.midpen-housing.org).

Morris, Aldon D. 2015. *The Scholar Denied: W.E.B. Du Bois and the Birth of Modern Sociology.* Oakland: University of California Press.

National Resources Defense Council (NRDC). (nd) "Environmental Justice." Retrieved January 2, 2018 (www.nrdc.org/about/environmental-justice).

Olafsson, Anna and Susanna Ohman. 2007. "Views of Risk in Sweden: Global Fatalism and Local Control—An Empirical Test of Ulrich Beck's Theory of New Risks." *Journal of Risk Research.* 10 (2): 177–179. Retrieved July 29, 2017 (http://research.flagler.edu:9839/eds/pdfviewer/pdfviewer?vid=1&sid=cf589cb1-a7e3–4d64-ab1b-8cc5eb165fd7%40sessionmgr4008).

Pew Research Center. 2011. "The Generation Gap and the 2012 Election." Retrieved August 14, 2017 (www.people-press.org/2011/11/03/section-8-domestic-and-foreign-policy-views/).

Purcell, Mark. 2013. "Possible Worlds: Henri Lefebvre and the Right to the City." *Journal of Urban Affairs.* 36 (1): 141–154. Retrieved May 30, 2017 (http://research.flagler.edu:9839 /ehost/command/detail?vid=0&sid=cf714528–7fef-4be8–81d4–004c18618ff6%40 sessionmgr4009&bdata=JnNpd-GU9ZWhvc3QtbGl2ZSZzY29wZT1zaXRl#jid=JFA&db =sih). doi:10.1111/juaf.12034.

Reich, Charles A. 1970. *The Greening of America.* New York: Random House.

Sampson, Robert J., and W. Byron Groves. 1989. "Community Structure and Crime: Testing Social-Disorganization Theory." *American Journal of Sociology.* 94 (4): 774–802. Retrieved June 1, 2017 (http://research.flagler.edu:9017/tc/accept?origin=/stable/pdf/278 0858.pdf).

Schaefer, Richard T. 2014. *Sociology Matters,* 6th ed. New York: McGraw-Hill.

Shear, Michael. 2017. "Trump will withdraw U.S. from Paris Climate Agreement." Retrieved August 14, 2017 (www.nytimes.com/2017/06/01/climate/trump-paris-climate-agreement.html).

Simmel, Georg. [1903] 1971. *On Individuality and Social Forms.* Donald Levine, ed. Chicago: University of Chicago Press.

Stephenson, R. Bruce. 1999. "A Vision of Green: Lewis Mumford's Legacy in Portland, Oregon." *Journal of the American Planning Association.* 65 (3): 259–269. Retrieved June 2, 2017 (http://research.flagler.edu:9839/eds/detail/detail?vid=0&sid=2837a759-ee99–4684-93d3-8a2cea3c6fae %40sessionmgr4006&bdata=JnNpdGU9ZWRzLW xpdmUmc2NvcGU9c2l0ZQ%3d%3d#AN= 2202500&db=buh).

Tonnies, Ferdinand. 1957. *Community and Society* (Gemeinschaft and Gesselschaft). Translated by Charles P. Loomis. East Lansing: Michigan State University Press.

United States Department of Justice. 2015. Latest Crime Statistics Released. Retrieved August 14, 2017 (www.fbi.gov/news/pressrel/press-releases/fbi-releases-2015-crime-statistics).

United States Environmental Protection Agency. nd. "EnviroAtlas Benefit Category: Climate Stabilization." Retrieved August 26, 2017 (www.epa.gov/enviroatlas-benefit-category-climate-stabilization).

United States Environmental Protection Agency. nd. "Resource Conservation and Recovery Act (RCRA) Overview." Retrieved August 26, 2017 (www.epa.gov/rcra/resource-conservation-and-recovery-act-rcra-overview).

United States Environmental Protection Agency. nd. "EnviroAtlas Benefit Category: Clean Air." Retrieved August 26, 2017 (www.epa.gov/enviroatlas/ecosystem-services-enviroatlas).

United States Environmental Protection Agency. nd. "EnviroAtlas Benefit Category: Clean and Plentiful Water." Retrieved August 26, 2017 (www.epa.gov/enviroatlas/ enviroatlas-benefit-category-clean-and-plentiful-water).

United States Housing and Urban Development. 2016. Homelessness. Retrieved August 26, 2017 (https://portal.hud.gov/hudportal/HUD).

Winston, Andrew. 2012. "Top 10 Sustainable Business Stories of 2012. Harvard Business Review." Retrieved August 14, 2017 (https://hbr.org/2012/12/top-10-sustainable-business-st.html).

CHAPTER 15

Globalization

ABOUT THE PROBLEM: GLOBALIZATION

Approaches to Understanding Globalization

Globalization is a complex process that involves the integration of the nations of the world, and includes economic, political, and cultural components. Some see globalization as a natural evolutionary process while others see it as a conspiracy by certain groups to promote world domination (Hackmann 2005). The former idea can be understood as "the unfolding resolution of the contradiction between ever expanding capital and its national political and social formations" (Teeple 2000:9). Lechner (2009) states that globalization is the link between human ties over space and, as groups experience each other's cultural differences, they create a "new world society" (Lechner 2009:13). Due to a person's perspective, globalization has different dimensions: governmental, cultural, economic, environmental, ideological, and religious. To assume that globalization is primarily any one of these dimensions ignores the multidimensionality of this social process; globalization incorporates each of these areas.

> **Globalization** the process of the nations of the world engaging in economic, political, and cultural integration.

Globalization is as a dynamic set of processes that are moving the world toward **globality**, a condition in which the world is becoming less separated by borders (Steger 2003); the term assumes that the globalization process will inevitably lead to a world with less reliance on boundaries. And, as Leigh (2001) notes, globality amounts to a choice that nations will make or resist; we will soon discuss some current political climates that are changing in this respect. The term *deglobalization* refers to strategies designed to counter the continued growth of globalism, or, as stated by Robertson, "undo the compression of the world" (1992:10). Deglobalization strategies involve resisting efforts

> **Globality** a condition in which the world is becoming less separated by borders.

269

to integrate nations in terms of trade, migration, communication, idea exchange, and cultural understandings. However, one could argue that we are currently in a period of *reglobalization* as the world since 1970 has seen lower tariffs, increased international trade, lower flight costs, and increased connectivity through the internet (Leigh 2001). Attempts at deglobalization may be currently underway in many countries but it is difficult to imagine a successful resistance to the globalization process. We will likely go through cycles of deglobalization and reglobalization as time passes.

Therefore, globalization in its different forms is contributing to the "flattening" of the world by increasing contact between nations (Freidman 2006). Robertson (1992) describes globalization as an understanding of the world as a "single place". Ritzer (2003) offers a contrasting term to globalization—*glocalization*, which is a resistance to globalization and an appreciation of not only indigenous goods and services, but also ideas and customs because the production is local rather than global.

Global Village a global connection of the vast regions of the world through technology and communication.

Noting the power of technology to transform media to connect the world, McLuhan (1964) announced that "as electrically contracted, the world is no more than a village" (McLuhan 1964:20). The term **global village** caught on and now most people understand it as a reflection of this interdependence of the vast regions of the world through technology and communication. Since that time, our media technology has evolved from television, radio, and other forms to the globalizing potential of the internet. There is little doubt that as technology advances, there will be a greater interconnectivity between people of different nations. However, with the increased use of the internet around the world, there is much greater danger of hacking and other internet crimes.

FIGURE 15.1 An example of how small the world has become figuratively as we become one global village.

Source: Ssokolov/Shutterstock.com

Steger (2003) provides a useful chronology of different waves of globalism throughout history. The prehistoric period occurred from 10,000 BCE–3,500 BCE, as improvements, albeit basic, in agriculture co-occurred with changes in the social structure of various societies and innovations. The premodern period, 3,500 BCE–1,500 CE, saw the invention of the wheel which helped pave the way for more extensive travel and trade, and of writing which helped promote the area's culture; this period also saw the building of various empires across the globe and new advancements in different areas of knowledge. The next period, the early modern period, which occurred between 1500–1750 was a period that included the Enlightenment and the Renaissance and Europe became a global focal point; international trade became more pronounced and the idea of nation-states became more formed. The modern period followed this, 1750–1970 which saw an encroachment of new nations into the European milieu as capitalism and consumerism grew and expanded—it also witnessed colonialism, decolonialization, wars that ultimately changed the face of global politics, population increases and continued scientific and cultural advancements. The last and current stage, from 1970 to the present, continues to provide changes in the economic, political, cultural, and ideological dimensions—ideas we will be discussing in this chapter. The key point being that the process of globalization is not a new occurrence but a complex development that has been a long time in the making (Robertson 1992).

Huntington's **clash of civilizations thesis** (1996) was a controversial one and basically states that conflicts between nations are becoming increasingly based on ideological and religious differences rather than political differences. The idea of a clash between the ideologies of cultural groups can be appealing, particularly in the current global situation in which refugees trying to escape terrorism have generated fear and nationalist sentiments in many countries, along with efforts to stop the flow of immigrants in some nations. The use of the term "civilizations" in this position is interesting as it conjures ideas of history and culture, and creates an ethnocentric perception as cultural groups see others as the enemy and as being inferior.

> **Clash of Civilizations Thesis** the idea that international conflict is becoming increasingly based on ideological and religious differences rather than political ones.

Is it beneficial to adopt a clash of civilizations perspective in the current issues involving international conflict?

Pro: The clash of civilizations approach is evident in the current conflicts the U.S. is experiencing with Russia, North Korea, and terrorist organizations such as ISIS.
Con: The clash of civilization thesis puts too much emphasis on ideology and this runs a risk of "othering" people and creating ethnocentric biases that can lead to isolationism.

A distinction is often made between the *Global North* and the *Global South* (sometimes referred to as the North-South Divide)—the former refers to the wealthier countries ("developed nations") of the United States, Canada, Australia, New Zealand, and the more developed parts of Europe and Asia, while the latter refers to the less industrialized "developing regions" of Africa, Central and South America, and less economically advanced parts of Europe and Asia. Moran (2015) explains that globalization in the Global North is promoted by the "logic of capitalism", particularly in the form of popular culture though clothing, food, and other items produced in various places around the globe; through services such as banking (in which banking institutions are international); through television and movies brought to us via the entertainment industry which is now global; through advanced technology such as the internet; and through travel and relocation to new areas. Globalization in the Global South, however, has distinctive features based not on the logic of capitalism but rather a situation of economic necessity. In the Global South, people often experience the "logic" through involuntary migration, through economic exploitation, and through the propagation of sweat shops.

Approaches to globalization have differed along three lines of political ideology (Kacowicz 2007). One of these approaches—a radical, conflict-based approach—assumes that globalization has increased poverty and social inequities both within and between regions. The liberal perspective, in contrast, sees the potential of globalization for reductions in inequality through trade and the sharing of technological advancements. The third approach, the realist or agnostic perspective, views any connection between globalization and inequality as being too ambiguous due to numerous factors and entertains the possibility that some factors of globalization might alleviate poverty while others might intensify it. This last perspective also acknowledges the effects poverty has on globalization, making the relationship a two-way street.

Nationalism, Cosmopolitanism, and Multiculturalism

Nationalism a strong regard for, pride in, and identity toward one's nationality.

As mentioned in chapter 3, **nationalism** refers to a strong regard for, pride in, and identity toward one's nationality, which has both positive and negative effects. Some consider nationalism as antithetical to globalism; therefore, a discussion of this idea will arise later in this chapter as well. Nationalism requires a certain degree of devotion to one's homeland rather than the world at large. And as noted in chapter 3, when a nation comes to see itself as being more virtuous than other nations, that nation might come to resist any attempts to meld into a singular unit. An extreme version of this resistance to participate in the integrative activity of globalization is present in the concept of *isolationism*, where a nation cuts itself off from the world. The related term *nativism* refers to attempts to resist intercultural intercourse through actions that protect the interests of the long term inhabitants of an area ("natives") and by clinging to traditional cultural values and practices. In 2017, the Trump administration introduced a Senate bill called the RAISE (Reforming American Immigration for

Should nationalism in its most extreme forms be considered a social problem or is it better to conceptualize it as patriotism and social responsibility to one's country?

Pro: Extreme nationalism promotes xenophobia, anti-immigrant sentiment, inequality, and often results in discrimination by race, nationality, and citizen status and is not aligned with the values of a heterogeneous nation of immigrants.

Con: Nationalism should be considered dedicated patriotism, pride in the United States, and a social and civic duty that has a positive effect on the United States.

Strong Employment) act which supported the limitation of *legal* immigration by limiting green card applications; it would also implement a "grading system" by giving preferences to potential immigrants who are able to speak English and that have job skills.

Related to globalism is the term **cosmopolitanism**. Essentially this refers to this idea of a society referred to by the philosopher Kant as "world citizenship" (Kleingeld 2012). Cosmopolitanism is an approach to internationality that runs counter to ideas of nationalism and notes the value of rejecting the nation-state concept in lieu of a global standpoint. To adopt a cosmopolitan perspective, one takes the stand that there exists a universal system of values across the globe. Whereas nationalism emphasizes the value of the nation-state, cosmopolitanism emphasizes the value of the world village. To illustrate the Trump administration's more nationalistic tone from those in recent history, in a 2017 press conference presidential advisor Steven Miller rebuked a reporter for his "cosmopolitan bias", implying the inappropriateness of adopting a cosmopolitan stance.

> **Cosmopolitanism**
> an approach that runs counter to nationalism in which identity is directed toward the world.

Is a cosmopolitan approach to globalization more beneficial to America than a nationalistic one?

Pro: The view of the country as part of one world unit creates a more peaceful, understanding, and culturally relative country.

Con: The cosmopolitan approach limits an understanding of the exceptional characteristics of America and attempts to legitimize dangerous and ineffective nation-states and regions.

The issue of net neutrality reflects the combined consequences of technology and globalization on society. Net neutrality refers to the position that internet providers and governments should allow all internet users the same access to information on the web and not restrict or slow access or apply different fees to different material. Representing another example of culture lag (when technological advancements proceed ahead of cultural values), the amazing amount of information available due to novel technological developments has created new questions about free markets and public access. In 2017, the Federal Communication Commission (FCC) voted to overthrow net neutrality and allow providers more control over access but this decision has come under fire from internet users, advocacy groups, and some members of Congress.

Another concept which bears mention in this discussion is **multiculturalism**. While multiculturalism has some similarities to cosmopolitanism in that both view the convergence of different cultures as positive for society, multiculturalism refers to cultural differences that occur *within* a geographic region or ideological community, rather than between geographic areas. Civil disturbances are therefore thought to be caused due to a lack of understanding of intracultural groups and can be alleviated through a greater commitment toward cultural relativity. The term *contact hypothesis* refers to the greater acceptance of diverse groups due to increased contact with them which can reduce prejudice and discrimination.

> **Multiculturalism**
> cultural differences that occur *within* a geographic region or ideological community, rather than between geographic areas.

FIGURE 15.2 In a country built by immigrants many languages are spoken. Some feel immigration policy should give preference to immigrants who already speak proficient English.

Source: Markus Mainka/Shutterstock.com

Is giving a preference to English speaking and skilled immigrant candidates a sound immigration policy?

Pro: Nations should have a voice in who enters the county; people who can communicate effectively by using the nation's official language and who have job skills will benefit the country more than those without these characteristics.

Con: It was never the intention of the nation's founders to create a system that engages in "demographic engineering"; sometimes those who do not yet speak English and that are not skilled can make great contributions.

Current Problems in a Globalizing World

Globalization has the potential to effect positive changes to the world. However, there are downsides to the rapid changes we are currently experiencing. Recently, the idea of a *risk society* has evolved in social science and outlines some negative effects that globalization has created and will likely continue to create in society. For example, the internet has certainly provided people with access to incredible amounts of information, however, when copious amounts of information (often personal) are available online, this creates a host of problems when people are available to hack into this information. Risk society theories reflect concerns over a future world in which globalization, with its potential for societal benefit, also contains the seeds of unintended disaster.

The problems of genocide and ethnic cleansing are extreme forms of violence and destruction that occur in regions throughout the world. These constitute some of our era's most extreme and barbaric human rights problems as they seek to alter human civilization. **Genocide** refers to a host of acts intended to destroy a group (or part of a group) identified by nationality, race, ethnicity, or religion by means of murder, physical harm, psychological harm, or measures to change life conditions that will bring about destruction. In addition, genocide can include enforcing birth

Genocide   efforts to destroy a group (or part of a group) identified by nationality, race, ethnicity, or religion by various means.

control measures or forcibly removing children from families and transferring them to other groups (Campbell 2001). The twentieth century saw many instances of genocide that occurred in the former Soviet Union, Nazi Germany, Cambodia, the former Yugoslavia, Bosnia, Rwanda, and Kosovo. Stanton (2013) proposes ten stages of genocide formation that provide insight into this activity:

1. classifying people into categories that separates and targets "out-groups" (groups that are excluded);

2. stereotyping the out-group via pejorative names and labels, religious symbols, skin color, among others;

3. discriminating against members of the out-group by not allowing them any political power;

4. dehumanizing the out-group with a variety of strategies;

5. organizing formally to develop strategies against the out-group;

6. further polarizing these "othered" groups through policies or propaganda;

7. promoting identification processes to put the out-group on a targeted list;

8. persecuting people on the basis of their identity;

9. promulgating extermination activity;

10. denying the activity, which is the most prominent indicator of future genocidal activity.

Closely related to genocide is **ethnic cleansing**. Ethnic cleansing is not an actual crime under international law therefore there is no official definition, however, the United Nations states that the term refers to efforts to remove, by a variety of means, an ethnic group from a certain area. These means can include murder, torture, rape, physical assault, forced removal, deportation, confinement to different communities, interference with medical interventions, among many others (UN nd). Ethnic cleansing practices took the lives of over two hundred thousand people in Bosnia between 1992 and 1995. In just ten weeks in 1994, ethnic cleansing practices in Rwanda claimed nearly eight hundred thousand people—to put this in perspective, this occurred ten times faster than Hitler's attempts to exterminate the Jews in Nazi Germany (Campbell 2001).

> **Ethnic Cleansing**
> the physical removal of an ethnic group from a certain area, using a variety of methods.

Global trafficking is possibly the third most prevalent criminal activity in the world (FBI nd). This form of transnational crime involves trade and transport that takes many forms including trafficking in persons, human organs, drugs, and weapons. Trafficking in humans is a social problem that has garnered much interest in the last few decades. It refers to the use of force, fraud, or forms of coercion to transport people from one area to another, often across national boundaries, to exploit certain types of labor and sex work. In many cases, this form of deception promises people a better life but instead they encounter enslavement and forced servitude in domestic labor, farm labor, factory labor, and other types of servitude including prostitution; due to these factors, human trafficking is considered a form of modern day slavery by the U.S. Department of Homeland Security, the national agency that addresses human trafficking (DHS nd). The amount of exploitation that exists with human trafficking is very significant as the people who are trafficked have little or no input into what they must do when they reach their destination and their compensation is often very poor or non-existent (Koser 2007).

FIGURE 15.3
Sydney, Australia, 2017. At Martin place, protesters demand that the UN stop the killing of Muslims in Myanmar.

Source: ArliftAtoz2205 / Shutterstock.com

There are an estimated 21 million human trafficking victims around the world, primarily from central and southeastern Europe, Africa, the Middle East, Asia, and Latin America (UnicefUSA nd).

Migrant smuggling refers to an act in which a person receives payment to illegally transport another person into a region in which they are not a legal resident. Often family members pay for a person's passage. Migrant smuggling is an issue that is in some ways like human trafficking except smuggling is normally a voluntary act in which migrants pay someone to illegally provide transfer. Often this form of illegal activity is less exploitative than human trafficking because after transportation the obligation is fulfilled; however, if a payment is not made and accepted by the smuggler prior to transfer, then the activity is human trafficking if the person who is smuggled owes a debt which must be paid through labor or some other means. In addition, problems in transport can lead to problems for those smuggled, including death.

THEORETICAL PERSPECTIVES

Many of Marx and Engels' ideas involved concerns with global issues—their famous comment in the *Communist Manifesto* called for "workers of the *world*" to unite. These and other early social theorists had globalization and its effects as a key focus in their work. Later Durkheim, Weber, and Simmel experienced a society that had the nation-state as the primary unit of analysis to the extent that Robertson (1992) claims that the nationalism/cosmopolitan polarity created modern sociology. While classical sociologists often view the social world from the perspective of the nation state, a perspective known as methodological nationalism, recent analyses reveal a more global focus (Pendenza 2014). In any event, sociologists have always examined the nature of globalization and its effects on society.

Structural Functionalism

A functionalist approach found its way into investigations of globalization by describing the changes brought about by a rapidly changing world. This perspective took an evolutionary approach to viewing the changes that were occurring post-World War II. During the late 1940s through the 1960s, this approach was very popular and viewed the world as evolving from simple and traditional societies to complex and cosmopolitan. This line of thought, which fit in well with the American structural functionalist sociological perspective, was replaced in the next decade with globalization theory (Robertson 1992).

Modernization theory, the functionalist theory mentioned above, has ideal-typical factors that define it—the perception of societies as well-structured systems with interdependent parts. Two types of social systems developed as societies emerged—the traditional and the modern. This perspective sought to explain the changes to a globalizing world in a rational way and was instructive of how this globalization should take place—in a very Westernized fashion, marked by Western democracy, capitalism, individualism, and science. Challenges arose later as a result of conflict-oriented approaches (Alexander 1994).

> **Modernization Theory** a theory of globalization that posits societies have developed either in a traditional or modern fashion and that all traditional societies will eventually adopt the characteristics of Western society.

Conflict Theory

Marx and Engels envisioned capitalism's effects on a global scale even when they were writing in the nineteenth century. Resulting from a rejection of modernization theory, a new theory emerged in the 1970s termed *dependency theory*, based on the global inequities described by Marx and Engels. Instead of attributing the less developed countries' lack of economic advancement to a failure to appropriately modernize, conflict theorists look to the inequities resulting from historical issues such as colonization and the economic and political exploitation by the wealthier countries. The developing nations, as a result, suffered from internal economic and political destabilization.

Using a primarily Marxist framework, Immanuel Wallerstein (1979) used an investigation of economic and historical activity to create his **world-systems analysis**. Wallerstein (1979) notes that it is better for social scientists to view the world as a "world system" than separate nation-states. This is due to increasing globalization; the key thread between nations is the division of labor that follows a capitalist logic. Capitalism has in effect created three types of hierarchically arranged regions in the world—the core, the periphery, and the semiperiphery; the core is comprised of the areas with the strongest economies and most skilled workforces (currently the United States, Europe, Japan, and China), the periphery contains regions with weaker economies and lower skilled, exploited labors (currently Africa, the Caribbean, and Central America, among others), and the

> **World-systems Analysis** a view of globalization which focuses on a "world system" rather than individual nation states and, in contrast with modernization theory, posits there is not one eventual form (a Western model) resulting from globalization.

semiperiphery is made up of regions that are economically somewhere in between (presently Eastern Europe, Mexico, and certain areas in South America). Wallerstein (1979), deviating from strictly Marxist thought, notes the importance of race in this global inequality rather than just economics and class (Applerouth and Edles 2016).

Symbolic Interactionism

Micro-level conceptions of globalization explore how the effects of this macro-level social phenomenon affect individual lives. For example, globalization involves different forms of crossing of various national boundaries, which is the essence of the concept. Boundaries are important in symbolic interaction and have four primary features. The first feature is they help classify groups into categories, which makes the world easier to understand. The second feature is that boundaries emphasize the statuses of race, ethnicity, religion, gender, and social class, which can have profound effects on our social experiences and way of perceiving the world. The third feature is that boundaries provide self-identification with a certain group (our reference groups). The fourth feature is that boundaries help to maintain the group's norms through sanctioned activity (Hewitt and Schulman 2011). Therefore, identifying with a certain nationality involves a classification system which creates and maintains an ingroup/outgroup viewpoint and effects how one thinks and acts. Symbols such as national flags, national anthems, international athletic symbols, etc., all aid in reinforcing this identity. The creation of strong national identity makes a globalist approach more difficult.

As noted above, the issue of identity is important in symbolic interactionism; however, identity does not have to be limited to localized areas. The idea of *global citizenship* refers to "awareness, caring and embracing, cultural diversity while promoting social justice and sustainability, coupled with a sense of responsibility to act" (Reysen and Katzarska-Miller 2013:858). In this case, and in opposition to the more nationalistic models, identity is understood within the frame of a borderless world. Global citizenship is currently being incorporated in school curricula in some areas.

Moran (2015) maintains that global capitalism has contributed to our ideas of personal and social identity. Personal identity, a salient concept of interactionism, has changed over time, based on social changes that were a byproduct of capitalism and globalization. According to Moran (2015), the concept of identity, as revealed in changes since the 1960s, particularly in regard to identity politics, has abandoned the element of "sameness" from previous periods. The newer version of the identity concept has three forms—legal (verified through documents such as a driver's license or other identifying information), personal (uniqueness and a differentiation of other people), and social (the affiliation to a group based on several characteristics, including race, ethnicity, religion, and others). Therefore, in this analysis, globalization on a macro-level contributes to identity and selfhood at the micro level.

SEARCHING FOR SOLUTIONS

The world, and developing countries, has benefitted from rapid globalization and technological innovation. The opening of trade and markets to goods and services as well as investments and technology has reduced poverty and provided jobs and longer life expectancies in many less developed countries. Globalization leads to a positive and productive flow of information and ideas, as well as the collaboration of experts across nations. However, there are always negative effects or unintended consequences to rapid technological progress and innovations. Tackling problems caused or contributed to by globalization and technology requires individual efforts, national level government involvement, as well as new policy and the inclusion of all global leaders. The solutions are complex and generally on a macro level since it involves national security and interventions.

Interconnection and integration are fundamentally important to globalization. Interconnection of computer systems worldwide, integration of societies that transcend borders, and integrated financial systems, are all key components of globalization. However, with integration comes risk. This includes the risk of information being used by extremist groups, of financial markets collapsing when nations face an economic crisis, and of the exploitation of people in developing countries working in deplorable conditions to produce products for wealthy countries. There is also the risk of Western banks and governments lending money to less developed countries that will be unlikely to repay those loans.

Human Trafficking

Global immigration often results in the smuggling of people into a country by other people who exploit migrants financially, endanger the lives of migrants, and provide illegal access to the destination countries. For example, in July of 2017, a semi-trailer of undocumented immigrants in San

Antonio was found in a Wal-Mart parking lot. Emergency workers reported eight people were found dead at the scene from heat exposure and asphyxiation, two more died in the aftermath, while over a dozen more, including children, were in various states of medical distress from extreme heat and lack of water (Moravec, Frankel and Selk 2017). This type of mass human smuggling across borders not only exploits vulnerable populations living in poverty and deplorable conditions in their country of origin, it also contributes to international trafficking of adults and youth, essentially a form of modern-day slavery. Organizations that combat this problem include the Polaris Project, which advocates for stronger federal and state laws, provides services and support for victims, and works to develop long term strategies for solutions. Their three-pronged approach includes responding to victims effectively, equipping stakeholders and communities to spot and prevent human trafficking and to pursuing systematic changes such as policy reform and collaborating with the governments of countries that have the highest prevalence of human trafficking networks. Since 2004, Polaris has led advocacy efforts and was involved in drafting more than 127 anti-trafficking bills at both state and federal levels (Polaris 2017). They provide training for law enforcement, educators, and the Department of Health and Human Services.

The U.S. federal government has also developed strategies and initiatives to prevent and target human trafficking into and across the country. However, global poverty is directly linked to human trafficking and factors that are driving the human trafficking chain internationally for both sexual exploitation and forced labor are rooted in poverty, lack of economic opportunity, political instability, corruption, and gender inequality (since the majority of victims are women and children). It is unlikely that a solution to these human rights violations, that have become a global problem, will arise until the poverty in the countries of origin, and the demand for cheap labor in the destination countries are addressed and safe and legal migration opportunities and pathways are provided by countries like the United States.

Reducing Extreme Nationalism

Groups with a nationalist ideology generally resist globalization and place nationality, patriotism and the perceived improvements and needs of one's country over the needs of the rest of the world. This creates an ethnocentric view that one nation is superior to others and should not take on new values or innovations from other nations. It fosters xenophobia and prejudice toward outsiders. Solving or reducing the impact of this problem is important since it rejects immigration, multiculturalism and often promotes (through a subtle agenda), racism, xenophobia, and traditional values that contribute to gender inequality. According to the Southern Poverty Law Center, as of 2016, there were many active "White Nationalist" groups; the Council of Conservative Citizens is the largest active white nationalist group, and was formed in the 1950s to resist desegregation (Southern Poverty Law Center 2017). The Council of Conservative Citizens opposes mixing races, abolishing affirmative action and immigration, and recommends promoting Western European culture in the United States (Wines and Alvarez 2015).

This example reveals the racism and distrust of immigrants inherent in extreme nationalist groups. The first step toward reducing nationalism starts at the individual level. Organizing a grassroots organization that promotes a heightened awareness of what nationalism is and why it is problematic is necessary since so many people are not aware of the rise in nationalism or why it is a social problem. Forming community groups and student groups on college campuses can be effective. These groups can then bring this issue to the forefront for existing community groups that focus on equality, global solutions, and immigration discrimination. For an anti-nationalist movement to gain momentum, community level groups must collaborate with other like-minded groups. Currently, the community groups that are anti-nationalist generally focus on building solidarity for resisting the Trump administration's agenda.

Technological Solutions

Another social problem created in part by globalization relates to the advancing technology that links almost every country together in an online capacity. New types of technologies have had a profound effect on the way countries and people communicate with each other and have also created an interdependence between nations. Countries and people around the globe are more connected socially, politically, and economically than ever before. The implications of sharing and improving access to information has many advantages, since the flow of information to less developed countries can be used to improve infrastructure, public heath, and advance economic growth. However, the dark side of such rapid technology includes the use of the internet for exploitive and criminal purposes, such as economic losses and extremist groups using the internet as a platform for extremist ideologies that recruit new members from around the world.

FIGURE 15.5 As globalization links creates interdependence on technology, criminals use the internet as a plaform for extremist ideologies and cybercrime.

Source: Elnur/Shutterstock.com

More common technological challenges include, internet fraud, phishing scams, and identity theft. These often use malware to hack into accounts or link accounts that appear to be legitimate. A study by McAfee and the Center for Strategic and International Studies reported economic losses of over $100 billion annually from cybercrime, and this does not take into account the cost of cybercrime to national security (Baker and Lewis 2013:3). Strategies promoted for individuals by the Department of Homeland Security (DHS) to protect individuals from cyber threats such as phishing attacks and viruses that access your computer, as well as other nefarious activity include: never clicking on links in emails (go to the site directly), never opening attachments from retailers or unknown senders, keeping your operating system, browser, and security software up to date, creating strong and unique passwords, avoiding revealing too much data about yourself on social media and networking sites. For example, if you are going on vacation it is risky to post this on a social media site if your address and other demographic information is available online. In addition, various campaigns have been launched to provide cyber security awareness. For example, the DHS launched a national campaign called *Stop. Think. Connect,* that strives to empower the American public to exercise safety online and encourages collaboration from non-profit organizations, universities, and community groups to become involved.

Cyber-crime or computer related crime can be a dangerous threat not only for individuals, but also for countries. For example, in 2013, the Associated Press' Twitter account was hacked and fake messages concerning white house attacks and stating that President Obama was injured by the attacks caused major decreases in the stock market and public panic. The Syrian Electronic Army took credit for this incident and it was later discovered that this extremist group had already hijacked many media sites in the United States in an attempt to denounce the United States (Fisher 2013). Where do we draw the line between vandalism and terrorism? And how do we defend our country and our citizens against the constantly changing and innovate forms of cybercrime?

Should cyber-crime that involves militant groups targeting the government, such as the example involving the Associated Press, be classified as vandalism or as terrorism?

Pro: Extremist groups that target the President and government agencies with allegations that result in public panic and billions of dollars lost, should be prosecuted as terrorist attacks since their intention is to harm the United States.

Con: This would set a precedent that harshly punishes anyone who is using cyber-crime to express free speech and should be treated as vandalism if there is not a physical terrorist attack.

The Department of Homeland Security (DHS) has created special divisions dedicated to combating cyber-crime. Their efforts include recruiting and training the best technical experts and developing standardized methods for investigating and responding to cyber-crime. Proposed solutions by DHS require cooperation and collaboration among countries. Strategies include establishing global norms on communicating regularly regarding issues of economic cybercrime and national security. In addition, there needs to be a global agreement regarding policy on how to investigate and prosecute cyber-criminals and groups that conduct malicious hacking. In 2008, the

International Multilateral Partnership against Cyber-Terrorism (IMPACT) was created to prevent and counter cyber threats. This group partnered with a United Nations agency, the International Telecommunications Union (ITU) and became the first collaborate attempt to work to prevent cyber threats that is a public–private partnership and is politically neutral (IMPACT 2015). Currently, 152 countries have joined that include regions in Europe and areas in the Middle East and Africa. Their strategy is to help governments organize and collaborate to defend against this type of crime. They offer resources and tools to combat cyber threats, training, and skills development for governments to build more secure infrastructure and respond more effectively to immediate threats. Their main goal is to solve a problem caused by globalization with globalization—one country cannot solve this global social problem. Further solutions to problems created in part by globalization will require the cooperation and agreement of all countries. This is a challenge that will continue to evolve and solutions will need to become more innovative as well.

CHAPTER SUMMARY

- Globalization is a process that interconnects nations economically, politically, and culturally. It is characterized by the ideology of the world as a global village, rather than being made up of different countries that are independent of one another.

- Technology has contributed to a rapid increase in globalization and has both advantages and disadvantages. With technological advances great connectivity between nations are formed, however, there is also an increase in interest and cyber-related crime that is an unintended consequence of innovations in technology.

- There have been several waves of globalism throughout history and the most recent stage started in the 1970s and was driven by technological innovations. Sinologists that study globalization have very different approaches depending on the theoretical perspectives that frame their research and views. Modernization theory, for example, is a proponent of globalization taking on Western values of democracy, capitalism, and individualism. Other theorists focus on issues of identity and the importance of being a global citizen.

- Some of the problems associated with globalization are the backlash of extreme nationalism that values the United States and eschews the idea of a global connectedness. Human trafficking has emerged as a problem that is harder to prevent in a seemingly borderless world.

- Technological challenge such as cyber-crime that attacks both individuals and nations is a serious concern that requires a collaboration among countries as well as heightening awareness about cyber-crime for individuals so they can protect themselves from hackers accessing their computers. The Department of Homeland Security and other organizations have launched campaigns to identify, respond to, and reduce cyber-crime. However, a global problem necessitates global solutions. Nations must unite and collaborate on the best way to effectively reduce technological crimes that attack national security and the major economic loss from cyber-crimes each year.

REFERENCES

Alexander, Jeremy C. 1994. "Modern, Anti, Post, and Neo: How Social Theories Have Tried to Understand the 'New World' of 'Our Time.'" *Zeitschrift fur Soziologie*. 23 (3):165–197.

Applerouth, Scott and Laura Desfor Edles. 2016. *Classical and Contemporary Sociological Theory*, Text and Readings. Thousand Oaks, CA: Sage.

Baker, Stewart A. and James A. Lewis. 2013. "Estimating the Cost of Cybercrime and Cyber espionage." *Center for Strategic and International Studies*. Retrieved August 11, 2017 (www.csis.org/events/estimating-cost-cyber-crime-and-cyber-espionage).

Campbell, Kenneth J. 2001. *Genocide and the Global Village*. New York: Palgrave.

Department of Homeland Security. nd. "Combatting Cyber Crime." Retrieved August 12, 2017 (www.dhs.gov/topic/combating-cyber-crime).

Department of Homeland Security. nd. "Stop. Think. Connect." Retrieved August 12, 2017 (www.dhs.gov/stopthinkconnect).

Federal Bureau of Investigation. nd. "Human Trafficking/Involuntary Servitude." Retrieved August 7, 2017 (www.fbi.gov/investigate/civil-rights/human-trafficking).

Fisher, Max. 2013. "Syrian Hackers Claim AP Hack that Tipped Stock Market by $136 billion." The Washington Post. Retrieved August 12, 2017 (www.washingtonpost.com/ news/worldviews/wp/2013/04/23/syrian-hackers-claim-ap-hack-that-tipped-stock-market-by-136-billion).

Freidman, Thomas L. 2006. *The World is Flat: A Brief History of the Twenty-first Century*, Updated and Expanded. New York: Farrar, Straus, and Giroux.

Hackmann, Rolf. 2005. *Globalization: Myth, Miracle, Mirage*. Lanham, MD: University Press of America.

Hewitt, John P. and David Shulman. 2011. *Self and Society: A Symbolic Interactionist Social Psychology*, 11th ed. Boston: Allyn & Bacon.

Homeland Security. nd. "Protect Myself from Cyber Attacks." Retrieved August 11, 2017 (www.dhs.gov/how-do-i/protect-myself-cyber-attacks).

Huntington, Samuel P. 1996. *The Clash of Civilizations and the Remaking of the World Order*. New York: Simon and Schuster.

IMPACT. 2015. "Centre for Policy & International Cooperation." Retrieved August 11, 2017 (www.impact-alliance.org/services/centre-for-policy-overview.html).

Kacowicz, Arie M. 2007. "Globalization, Poverty, and the North-South Divide." *International Studies Review*. 9 (4): 565–580.

Kleingeld, Pauline. 2012. *Kant and Cosmopolitanism: The Philosophical Ideal of World Citizenship*. Cambridge: Cambridge University Press.

Koser, Khalid. 2007. *International Migration: A Very Short Introduction*. London: Oxford University Press.

Lechner, Frank J. 2009. *Globalization: The Making of a World Society*. New York: Wiley-Blackwell.

Leigh, Andrew. 2001. "Globalization and Deglobalization." *Australian Quarterly*. 73 (1): 6–8. Retrieved August 4, 2017 (http://research.flagler.edu:9839/eds/detail/detail?vid=0&sid=d09ad2dd-651a-4a8c-8b3a96a0df20d498%40sessionmgr4010&bdata=JnNpdGU9Z WRzLWxpdmUmc2NvcGU9c2l0ZQ%3d%3d#AN=edsjsr.20637966&db=edsjsr).

McLuhan, Marshall. 1964. *Understanding Media*. New York: McGraw-Hill.

Moran, Marie. 2015. *Identity and Capitalism*. Los Angeles: Sage.

Moravec, Eva R., Todd C. Frankel and Avi Selk. 2017. "9 people dead after at least 39 were found packed in a sweltering tractor-trailer in San Antonio." Washington Post. Retrieved August 11, 2017 (www. washingtonpost.com/national/at-least-39-people-found-packed-into-sweltering-tractor-trailer-in-san-antonio/2017/07/23/c160b680–3b41–43ab-9e9c-cf133a3ca683_story.html?utm_term= .01399bf8581f).

Pendenza, Massimo. 2014. *Classical Sociology Beyond Methodological Nationalism*. Leiden and London: Brill.

Polaris Project. 2017. "127 Anti-Human Trafficking Laws Passed." Retrieved August 10, 2017 (https:// polarisproject.org/successes/127-anti-human-trafficking-laws-passed).

Reysen, Stephen and Iva Katzarska-Miller. 2013. "A Model of Global Citizenship: Antecedents and Outcomes." *International Journal of Psychology*. 48 (5): 858–870. Retrieved December 12 (http:// eds.b.ebscohost.com/eds/pdfviewer/pdfviewer?vid=1&sid=ab23e5b8-66a3-4ee9-b343-691338 e2d015%40sessionmgr104).

Ritzer, George. 2003. "Rethinking Globalization: Glocalization/Grobalization and Something/Nothing." *Sociological Theory*. 21 (3): 193–201.

Robertson, Roland. 1992. *Globalization: Social Theory and Global Culture*. London: Sage Publications.

Southern Poverty Law Center. 2017. "White Nationalist." Retrieved August 11, 2017 (www.splcenter. org/fighting-hate/extremist-files/ideology/white-nationalist).

Stanton, Gregory H. 2013. "Genocide watch: Alliance against genocide." Retrieved August 11, 2017 (http:// genocidewatch.net/wp-content/uploads/2012/06/The-Ten-Stages-of-Genocide-handout.pdf).

Steger, Manfred B. 2003. *Globalization: A Very Short Introduction*. Oxford: Oxford University Press.

Teeple, Gary. 2000. "What is Globalization?" Pp. 9–23 in *Globalization and its Discontents,* edited by Stephen McBride and John Wiseman. Houndmills, Basingstoke, Hampshire, UK: Macmillan Press.

Unicef USA. nd. "Infographic: A Global Look at Human Trafficking." Retrieved August 7, 2017 (www. unicefusa.org/stories/infographic-global-human-trafficking-statistics).

United Nations. nd. "Office on Genocide Prevention and the Responsibility to Protect." Retrieved March 29, 2017 (www.un.org/en/genocideprevention/ethnic-cleansing.html).

U.S. Department of Homeland Security. nd. "Human Trafficking." Retrieved March 29, 2017 (www.dhs. gov/topic/human-trafficking).

Wallerstein, Immanuel. 1979. *The Capitalist World-Economy*. Cambridge: Cambridge University Press.

Wines, Michael and Lizette Alvarez. 2015. "Council of Conservative Citizens Promotes White Primacy, and G.O.P. Ties." *The New York Times.* Retrieved August 11, 2017 (www.nytimes.com/2015/06/23/ us/politics/views-on-race-and-gop-ties-define-group-council-of-conservative-citizens.html?_ r=0).

INDEX